Culturally Speaking

2nd Edition

Culturally Speaking

Culture, Communication and Politeness Theory

Edited by
Helen Spencer-Oatey

Continuum International Publishing Group

The Tower Building
11 York Road
London SE1 7NX

80 Maiden Lane, Suite 704
New York
NY 10038

First published by Continuum, 2000

British Library Cataloguing-in-Publication Data
A catalogue record for this book is available from the British Library.

ISBN :978-08264-9309-5 (hardback)
978-08264-9310-1 (paperback)

Library of Congress Cataloguing-in-Publication Data
The Publisher has applied for CIP data.

Typeset by Newgen Imaging Systems Pvt Ltd, Chennai, India
Printed in Great Britain by MPG Books Ltd, Bodmin, Cornwall

Contents

List of Figures and Tables viii
Contributors ix
Acknowledgements x
Transcription Conventions xi

1 Introduction 1
Helen Spencer-Oatey

Part 1 BASIC CONCEPTS

Editor's Introduction 9

2 Face, (Im)Politeness and Rapport 11
Helen Spencer-Oatey

3 Culture and Communication 48
Vladimir Žegarac

Part 2 CROSS-CULTURAL PRAGMATICS: EMPIRICAL STUDIES

Editor's Introduction 71

4 Apologies in Japanese and English 73
Noriko Tanaka, Helen Spencer-Oatey and Ellen Cray

5 British and Chinese Reactions to Compliment Responses 95
Helen Spencer-Oatey, Patrick Ng and Li Dong

6 Interactional Work in Greek and German Telephone Conversations 118
Theodossia-Soula Pavlidou

Suggestions for Further Reading for Part 2 136

Part 3 PROCESSES IN INTERCULTURAL INTERACTION

Editor's Introduction 139

7 Pragmatic Transfer 141
Vladimir Žegarac and Martha C. Pennington

8 Communication Accommodation Theory 164
Virpi Ylänne

9 Adaptation and Identity 187
Martin Fougère

Part 4 INTERCULTURAL PRAGMATICS: EMPIRICAL STUDIES

Editor's Introduction 205

10 Negotiating Rapport in German–Chinese Conversation 207
Susanne Günthner

11 Negative Assessments in Japanese–American Workplace Interaction 227
Laura Miller

12 Impression Management in 'Intercultural' German Job Interviews 241
Karin Birkner and Friederike Kern

13 Issues of Face in a Chinese Business Visit to Britain 258
Helen Spencer-Oatey and Jianyu Xing

Suggestions for Further Reading for Part 4 274

Part 5 METHODOLOGY

Editor's Introduction 277

14 Data Collection in Pragmatics Research 279
Gabriele Kasper

15 Recording and Analysing Talk Across Cultures 304
Meredith Marra

16 Projects 322
Helen Spencer-Oatey

Glossary 326
References 338
Index 363

List of Figures and Tables

Figures

2.1 The bases of rapport 14
8.1 A generalized model of CAT processes 170
8.2 An extended model of sociolinguistic processes in CAT 172
13.1 Seating arrangements at the meeting 261

Tables

1.1 Frameworks of cultural variation in basic values/orientations to life 5
2.1 Bases of perceived sociality rights and obligations 15
2.2 Semantic components of five common speech acts 24
2.3 Strategy types for making requests, on a scale of directness–indirectness 25
2.4 Types of downgraders/upgraders commonly associated with requests and apologies 27
2.5 Linguistic strategies of expressiveness–restraint 29
4.1 Design of the questionnaire scenarios 79
4.2 Mean ratings (and standard deviations) of contextual assessment factors in the scenarios 80
4.3 Percentages of production responses containing different types of semantic components 84
5.1 Taxonomies of compliment response types in English and Mandarin Chinese 97
5.2 Frequencies of selected types of compliment responses in English 99
5.3 Frequencies of selected types of compliment responses in Chinese 99
5.4 Mean evaluations (and standard deviations) of acceptance compliment responses 102
5.5 Analysis of variance results showing the effect of nationality on the ratings of the acceptance responses 102
5.6 Mean evaluations (and standard deviations) of rejection compliment responses 104
5.7 Analysis of variance results showing the effect of nationality on the ratings of the rejection responses 104
6.1 Frequency of use of phatic talk in Greek and German telephone openings 123
6.2 Distribution of reason for calling in Greek and German telephone calls 124
6.3 Use of phatic utterances according to reason for calling 124
6.4a Use of phatic talk in Greek telephone openings according to the relationship of the participants (transactional calls only) 125
6.4b Use of phatic talk in German telephone openings according to the relationship of the participants (transactional calls only) 125
7.1 Likely pragmatic perspectives of the interlocutors in Tyler's (1995) tutoring session 156
13.1 The Chinese visitors' 'expertise' and 'position' titles 267

Contributors

Karin Birkner is Professor of German Linguistics at the University of Bayreuth, Germany.

Ellen Cray is Associate Professor in the School of Linguistics and Applied Language Studies at Carleton University, Canada.

Li Dong is Associate Professor in the Translation Institute of Beijing Foreign Studies University, China.

Martin Fougère is Assistant Professor in the Department of Management and Organisation at the Swedish School of Economics and Business Administration, Helsinki, Finland.

Susanne Günthner is Professor of German Linguistics at the Westfälische Wilhelms-University in Münster, Germany.

Gabriele Kasper is Professor of Second Language Studies at the University of Hawai'i at Manoa, USA.

Friederike Kern is a Lecturer in Communication Studies and Linguistics at the University of Potsdam, Germany.

Meredith Marra is a Lecturer in the School of Linguistics and Applied Language Studies at Victoria University of Wellington, New Zealand, and Research Fellow for Victoria's Language in the Workplace Project.

Laura Miller is Professor of Anthropology at Loyola University Chicago, USA.

Patrick Ng is a Lecturer in the Department of Chinese and Bilingual Studies at the Hong Kong Polytechnic University, Hong Kong SAR, China.

Theodossia-Soula Pavlidou is Professor of Linguistics at the Aristotle University of Thessaloniki, Greece.

Martha C. Pennington is Professor and Chair of Writing and Linguistics at Georgia Southern University, near Savannah, USA.

Helen Spencer-Oatey is a professorial fellow and Director of the Centre for English Language Teacher Education at the University of Warwick. She is also manager of the eChina-UK e-Learning Programme.

Noriko Tanaka is Professor of Pragmatics in the Faculty of Arts and in the Graduate School of Humanities, Seisen University, Japan.

Jianyu Xing is Associate Professor in the School of International Studies at the University of International Business and Economics, Beijing, China.

Virpi Ylänne is Lecturer at the Centre for Language and Communication, Cardiff University, UK.

Vladimir Žegarac is Reader of Language and Communication at the University of Bedfordshire, UK.

Acknowledgements

I would like to thank the many people who have played a part in both the first and second editions of this book. My interest in the relationship between language and culture was stimulated by students, friends and even strangers in China who brought to my attention many differences between British and Chinese ways of speaking. Without them I would not have started down this road.

When I started teaching the subject at the University of Bedfordshire, my students stimulated me to explore and re-think issues through their scepticism of existing 'politeness' frameworks and through their comments and questions. They were a tremendous help in developing and refining my ideas. When the first draft of the first edition had been completed, members of the Intercultural Communication Research Discussion Group at the University of Bedfordshire read and discussed each chapter carefully and made very useful suggestions for improvements. They provided me with professional and personal support which was a great encouragement to me, and I would particularly like to thank John Twitchin and Vladimir Žegarac in this respect.

I am grateful to all the authors for writing and updating their chapters and for being so helpful and cooperative. I would also like to thank the reviewers of the new chapters of the book for their willingness to help in this way.

Finally, I would like to express a big 'thank you' to my husband, Andrew Spencer, for his tremendous support and encouragement throughout the project. He not only provided me with wonderful emotional support, but willingly spent extra time looking after our children and helped me with many tedious parts of the editing process. 'Thank you' to you all.

The publishers and authors wish to thank the following for permission to use copyright material: ABC News for an extract from World News Tonight, broadcast by NHK in Tokyo, 20 February 1992; Cambridge University Press for Figures 8.1 and 8.2 which were originally published in N. Coupland, J. Coupland, H. Giles and K. Henwood (1988) Accommodating the elderly: invoking and extending a theory. *Language in Society*, 17: 1–41; and Elsevier Science for Tables 6.1, 6.4a and 6.4b which were originally published in T. Pavlidou (1994) Contrasting German–Greek politeness and the consequences. *Journal of Pragmatics*, 21: 487–511.

Transcription Conventions

Meaning	Symbol	Example
The Words Themselves		
Unintelligible text	(???)	(???) I mean natural
Guess at unclear text	(word?)	(leaves?) nothing to the imagination
False start	wo-word	idea is cl-very clear to me now
Omitted segment	word segment'word	es kommt nicht an d'Öffentlichkeit
Links between words or utterances		
Overlapping text	word [word] word [word] word	Doris: all men think this is [just great] Andrea: [of course]
Latching, i.e. two utterances run together with no pause	=	A: D'yuh like it= D: =(hhh) Yes I DO like it
Pausing		
Micropause	(.)	well (.) enjoy (.) hm (.) what do I enjoy
Brief pause	(-)	it (-) eh you can look at other
Pause of indicated length	(0.5)	when (0.2) when in a country
Words spoken differently from surrounding text	word <<symbol> word word >	
Words spoken loudly	<<f> >	oh I see <<f> then from school>
Words spoken softly/very softly	<<p> > / <<pp> >	<<pp> not as bad as here>
Words whispered	<<wh> >	leaves nothing <<wh> to the imagination>
Words spoken faster	<<all> >	and then <<all> they also asked me if I> could imagine that
Words getting faster	<<acc> >	because of the files <<acc> indeed I thought it's an interesting job>
Vocalizations		
Laugh particles	(hihi)	too (hihi) much?
Outbreaths	(hhh)	(hhh) yes I do like it
Inbreaths	(.hhh)	(.hhh) maybe
Inbreathed fricative	(.hss)	(.hss) is that so?
Prominence		
Lengthened/very lengthened segment	wo:rd / wo::rd	it is re:ally cosy
Emphasized syllable/word	NEver / NEVER	Yang: this is natural Andrea: this is not NATURAL

(*Continued*)

Transcription Conventions—cont'd

Meaning	Symbol	Example
Intonation		
Strongly rising tone	word?	this is from the traditional? or political?
Slight rising tone	word,	however, if you say, eh they are not equal
Low rising tone	word´	I mean natural´
Slightly falling tone	word;	and come back again in the evening;
Slightly falling, final tone	word.	yes yes right.
Continuing tone	word_	did you ever, have (0.5) well any_
Relevant additional information	{descriptive comment}	{coughs}/ {smacks lips}
English translation/gloss	$English English$	A: *Gut?* $Good?$

Based on the GAT system, Selting *et al.* (1998)

1 Introduction

Helen Spencer-Oatey

> One afternoon after work, a British teacher of EFL, who had recently started teaching at a college in Hong Kong, decided to visit some friends who lived in a different part of the city. She went to the appropriate bus stop, and as she walked up, a group of her students who were waiting there asked, 'Where are you going?' Immediately she felt irritated, and thought to herself, 'What business is it of theirs where I'm going? Why should I tell them about my personal life?' However, she tried to hide her irritation, and simply answered, 'I'm going to visit some friends'.
>
> Several months later this British teacher discovered that 'Where are you going?' is simply a greeting in Chinese. There is no expectation that it should be answered explicitly: a vague response such as, 'Over there' or 'Into town' is perfectly adequate. Moreover, according to Chinese conventions, the students were being friendly and polite in giving such a greeting, not intrusive and disrespectful as the British teacher interpreted them to be.

This incident, which I personally experienced during my first overseas teaching post, highlights three features that are important foci of this book:

- people's use of language can influence interpersonal rapport (the students' question irritated the teacher and she started to form a negative impression of them);
- people may try to 'manage' their relationships with others (the teacher did not want the students to know that she was irritated, and so she tried to hide her annoyance);
- different cultures may have different conventions as to what is appropriate behaviour in what contexts ('where are you going?' is a polite greeting among acquaintances in Chinese, but is an inappropriate explicit question in this context in English).

The title of this book is *Culturally Speaking*, but as the subtitle *Culture, Communication and Politeness Theory*, hints at, the 'culture and speaking' component focuses on the management of interpersonal rapport. People sometimes think of communication as 'the transmission of information' but, as many authors have pointed out, communication also involves 'the management of social relations'. Watzlawick et al. (1967), for example, propose that all language has a *content* component and a *relationship* component. If two people have a disagreement, for instance, there will be a *content* aspect to their disagreement, which concerns the '*what*' of the disagreement, such as disagreement over the accuracy of a piece of information, or the suitability of a course of action. However, there will also be a *relationship* aspect to their disagreement; for example, whether the expression of disagreement conveys lack of respect for the other person, whether it is interpreted as a bid for one-upmanship or whether it leads to feelings of resentment or dislike.

Similarly, Brown and Yule (1983) identify two main functions of language: the *transactional* (or information-transferring) function, and the interactional (or maintenance of social relationships) function. They suggest that discourse is either primarily transactional in focus, or primarily interactional in focus, and that the goals of these two main types of discourse are different. The goal of transactional language is to convey information coherently and accurately, whereas the goal of interactional speech is to communicate friendliness and goodwill, and to make the participants feel comfortable and unthreatened. Weather forecasts and academic lectures are typical examples of primarily transactional language, while greetings and small talk are typical examples of primarily interactional language. In this book, however, I maintain that the two functions are very closely interconnected, and that the relational aspect of language use is of central importance in all communication.

One of the main areas of linguistic theory that is relevant to 'relational communication' is politeness theory, and that is why the term 'politeness' has been included in the subtitle. However, I have avoided using the term 'politeness' as much as possible in this book, except when discussing well-known theories of politeness, because the term is so confusing. 'Politeness' is often interpreted in everyday life as referring to the use of relatively formal and deferential language, such as formal terms of address like *Sir* or *Madam*, request patterns such as *would you be so kind as to . . .*, and formal expressions of gratitude and apology. From such a perspective, sentences such as '*Would you mind passing the salt*' would be classified as 'more polite' than '*Pass the salt, will you*'. However, there are many occasions when it is more appropriate to use '*Pass the salt, will you*' than '*Would you mind passing the salt*' (at home, to a family member, for example). And as Fraser and Nolan (1981: 96) point out, politeness is actually a contextual judgement: 'No sentence is inherently polite or impolite. We often take certain expressions to be impolite, but it is not the expressions themselves but the conditions under which they are used that determine the judgement of politeness'. In other words, sentences or linguistic constructions are not *ipso facto* polite or rude; rather, politeness is a social judgement, and speakers are judged to be polite or rude, depending on what they say in what context. Politeness, in this sense, is a question of appropriateness.

A further limitation of the term 'politeness' is that it emphasizes the harmonious aspect of social relations, and in fact politeness theory has traditionally focused on this aspect. However, people sometimes attack rather than support their interlocutors and, as Turner (1996) and Culpeper (1996, 2005) both argue, 'politeness' theory needs to incorporate this component. Tracy (1990) and Penman (1990) maintain that politeness should be studied within the broader framework of facework. Tracy (1990), for example, suggests that people may want to make a variety of identity claims, apart from the claim to be pleasant and likeable (the one she maintains is most closely associated with politeness); for instance, they may want to be seen as competent, trustworthy, intimidating, strong or reasonable. Tracy proposes, therefore, that politeness theory should be extended to incorporate these notions. However, this would take us into the fields of impression management and self-presentation, and would obviously include far more than the scope of traditional politeness theory: the maintenance and/or promotion of harmonious interpersonal relations. Although such issues certainly need addressing, they are not the focus of this book. This book concentrates on the management of interpersonal relations: the use of language to promote, maintain or threaten harmonious social relations. I suggest the term *rapport management* to refer to this area.

The second component of the title refers to 'culture'. Culture is notoriously difficult to define. In 1952, the American anthropologists, Kroeber and Kluckhohn, critically reviewed concepts and definitions of culture, and compiled a list of 164 different definitions. Apte (1994: 2001), writing in the ten-volume Encyclopedia of Language and Linguistics, summarizes the problem as follows: 'Despite a century of efforts to define culture adequately, there was in the early 1990s no agreement among anthropologists regarding its nature'. This is a view that is still widely shared. Despite these problems, I propose the following definition for the purposes of this book:

> Culture is a fuzzy set of basic assumptions and values, orientations to life, beliefs, policies, procedures and behavioural conventions that are shared by a group of people, and that influence (but do not determine) each member's behaviour and his/her interpretations of the 'meaning' of other people's behaviour.

This definition draws attention to a number of key issues. First, culture is associated with social groups. All people are simultaneously members of a number of different groups and categories; for example, gender groups, ethnic groups, generational groups, national groups, professional groups and so on. So in many respects, all these different groupings can be seen as different cultural groups. However, in this book, 'culture' is operationalized primarily in terms of ethnolinguistic and/or national or regional political identity; for example, authors analyse and compare the language and behaviour of Greeks, East and West Germans, Canadian English speakers, British English speakers, Hong Kong Chinese, Mainland Chinese and so on. This is not to deny the cultural element in other types of groupings, nor is it meant in any way to imply that members of these groups are a homogeneous set of people (see Chapter 8 for discussion of such issues). However, it would obviously be impossible to deal adequately in a single volume with all variables that are associated with different social groups, and so the book is deliberately limited in scope.

Secondly, culture is manifested through co-occurring regularities within the social group. These regularities can be found in a wide range of elements, including basic assumptions, fundamental values, deep-seated orientations to life, attitudes, beliefs, policies, procedures and behavioural conventions. Much cross-cultural research in psychology and anthropology has focused on the elements that people are less consciously aware of (basic assumptions, values and orientations to life) and has attempted to identify a limited number of universal dimensions on which all cultural groups can be mapped. Two of the most well known of these frameworks are shown in Table 1.1. In linguistics, on the other hand, most culture-related research has focused on people's use of language, either comparing the similarities and differences in patterns of use between different cultural/linguistic groups, or else analysing the discourse of intercultural interaction (i.e. the interaction that occurs when people from different cultural groups converse with each other). Some linguistics (e.g. Higgins 2007) have restricted their interpretation of interculturality to the ways in which people make their ethnic and national group membership relevant in interaction and orient towards it. In this book, I take a broader perspective than this; I believe culture can affect a variety of aspects of language use and is by no means limited to (direct or indirect) verbalized references to group membership. Moreover, as I mention in Chapter 2, I believe that there can be interconnections between language use and individually held cultural values, even though these interconnections are complex and dynamic (see Spencer-Oatey and Franklin, forthcoming, for a broader exploration of culture, communication and intercultural interaction).

Thirdly, cultural regularities are not manifested in all members of a given cultural group or to the same degree of strength in all members; some members may display certain regularities but not other regularities, and for any given member, some regularities may be firmly and more extensively displayed than others. In other words, members display 'family resemblances' in the various elements they have in common. In this sense, the notion of culture is fuzzy. As Žegarac (2007 and Chapter 3 in this book) explains, epidemics provide a useful analogy for understanding this. When an epidemic occurs, not everyone gets ill; however, the fact that a number of individuals remain healthy, does not disprove the occurrence of an epidemic. Furthermore, not all people catch an identical version of the disease; the virus may be stronger in some people than others and there may be slight mutant variations. In analogous ways, members of cultural groups rarely share identical sets of values, beliefs etc., and there is thus no absolute set of features that can provide a definitive basis for distinguishing one cultural group from another. Nevertheless, this does not disprove the existence of regularities across the group members as a whole.

Table 1.1 Frameworks of cultural variation in basic values/orientations to life

Hofstede's (1991, 2001) Five Dimensions of Country Variation

Individualism	⟷	***Collectivism***
(loose ties between individuals who give priority to their own needs)		(strong ties within cohesive in-groups who give priority to the goals and needs of the group)
High power distance	⟷	***Low power distance***
(the extent to which less powerful members of a cultural group expect and accept that power is distributed unequally)		
Masculinity	⟷	***Femininity***
(clearly differentiated social gender roles)		(overlapping social gender roles)
High uncertainty avoidance	⟷	***Low uncertainty avoidance***
(the extent to which members of a cultural group feel threatened by uncertain or unknown circumstances)		
Long-term orientation	⟷	***Short-term orientation***
(whether the focus of people's efforts is on the future or the present)		

Kluckhohn and Strodtbeck's (1961) Cultural Orientation Framework

Orientations	Cultural Responses
Relationship to the Environment	***Subjugation to Nature – Harmony with Nature – Mastery over Nature***
Relationships among People	***Lineality*** (preference for hierarchical relations) – ***Collectivism*** (preference for group identification) – ***Individualism*** (preference of individual autonomy)
Mode of Human Activity	***Being*** (acceptance of the status quo) – ***Becoming*** (preference for transformation) – ***Doing*** (preference for direction intervention)
Belief about Basic Human Nature	***Evil – Mixture of Good and Evil – Good***
Orientation to Time	***Past – Present – Future***

Fourthly, cultural regularities can influence people's behaviour and the meanings they attribute to other people's behaviour. However, this does not mean that cultural patternings determine people's behaviour, nor that they are the only factors influencing people's behaviour. Rather, it is vital to consider carefully the role that cultural regularities may (or may not) have on communicative interaction. First, it is essential to remember that there are conceptual problems in applying group-level measures (as, for example, Hofstede's, 2001, country level scores) to individual behaviour, because these group scores simply represent the central tendencies of the group as a whole and thus do not apply directly to individuals. Hofstede (1991: 253) himself warned against applying group-level scores to the behaviour of individuals (an error known as 'the ecological fallacy'), because any single individual may well be significantly different from the group average. Gudykunst (1998) argues that group-level (such as country-level) values can have an indirect effect on individual behaviour because they can influence the socialization processes that individuals may experience and in this way they may have an indirect effect (to a greater or lesser extent) on people's use of language. This is undoubtedly correct; nevertheless, this does not mean that group level scores should be applied to individuals. One way of reducing the problem of moving from group-level measures to individual behaviour is to assess people's values and beliefs at the individual level (e.g. the psychologist Shalom Schwartz has developed instruments for doing this – see Schwartz et al. 2001). However, even if this is done, it is important to remember that these are just decontextualized measures. When people interact with each other, they do not passively reproduce their decontextualized preferences (no matter whether those preferences are similar to those of other groups members, or are personal or idiosyncratic preferences). Rather, they dynamically co-construct their discourse with their co-participants. So a second key point to remember when studying the ways in which cultural regularities may influence communicative behaviour is that the analytic frameworks should not be limited to concepts of cultural differences (e.g. like those shown in Table 1.1). Instead, they should be interactional frameworks that are broad enough to allow for the impact of cultural regularities but not be limited only to the study of this. Chapters 2 and 3 present some conceptual frameworks that are suitable in this way. Moreover, it is important to remember that cultural factors do not necessarily lead to communicative problems; on the contrary, they can be a major source of comity and enrichment. Nevertheless, people working in international/intercultural contexts often do experience problems and may request advice for dealing with them; I believe linguists should be able to help address such practical concerns.

Throughout the book, the term 'cross-cultural' is used to refer to comparative data – in other words, to data obtained independently from two different cultural groups; the term 'intercultural' is used to refer to interactional data – in other words, data obtained when members of two different cultural groups interact with each other.

This is in line with the usage proposed by a number of theorists (e.g. Gudykunst and Kim 1997: 19). All the chapters of the book revolve round the two main themes discussed above, rapport management and culture, and explore the interrelationship between the two.

The book is divided into five parts:

Part 1: Basic Concepts
Part 2: Cross-Cultural Pragmatics: Empirical Studies
Part 3: Processes in Intercultural Interaction
Part 4: Intercultural Pragmatics: Empirical Studies
Part 5: Methodology

As this list indicates, there are three types of chapters in the book: theoretical chapters which explore conceptual issues, empirical chapters which describe research studies, and methodological chapters which discuss research procedures. Some readers may find such a combination strange, and feel that empirical studies belong more naturally in a different kind of book. I believe it is very important, however, to include them here. As Hall (1976: 46) points out, 'Most cross-cultural exploration begins with the annoyance of being lost', and so for readers who have little experience of living or working with people from different cultural backgrounds, theoretical discussion of cross-cultural and intercultural issues can be little more than a dry academic exercise. In-depth studies of cross-cultural differences and intercultural encounters can help reduce this problem. They also illustrate different ways of investigating cross-cultural and intercultural questions, and so I hope that, along with the methodological chapters, they will stimulate readers to start (or continue) exploring this fascinating area for themselves.

Some readers may feel it would be more 'logical' to start the book with the methodology section. Thompson and Tenenbaum (2002: 187), for example, in a review of the first edition of this book, comment that if the methodology section had been placed at the beginning of the book, it 'would give student readers greater confidence in understanding the constraints faced by researchers and the ability to critically evaluate the contributors' studies'. Such a placement could well have that advantage. On the other hand, before planning and evaluating research, it is important to have a good grasp of the types of topics and issues that need analysing, and of the theoretical frameworks that can be used for conducting such analyses. The chapters in Parts 1–4 of the book help provide this. In my view, if the methodology chapters were placed before them, it could be more difficult for readers to contextualize and apply the procedures and arguments. Nevertheless, for readers who are particularly interested in research processes, or who are planning to carry out research in this area for themselves, it could be helpful to read the methodology chapters in conjunction with the empirical chapters.

Part 1 of the book thus deals with 'basic concepts' and provides a framework for understanding and interpreting the theories and studies discussed in most of the rest of the book. It deals with key conceptual issues relating to rapport management, culture, and communication, and has two chapters. Part 2 of the book reports three empirical cross-cultural studies and illustrates the kinds of differences in language use/interpretation that can occur between different cultural groups. Parts 3 and 4 turn to intercultural interaction. The chapters in Part 3 explore different conceptual issues, and those in Part 4 report empirical studies of intercultural interaction. The book concludes with Part 5 on methodology. More detailed information on the chapters in Parts 2–5 is provided in the introduction to each of the parts.

Each of the chapters in the book (except this introductory chapter) ends with three things:

- a list of key points that readers can use for study purposes;
- a list of discussion questions/tasks for exploring the concepts and issues in greater depth;
- a list of follow-up references for further reading.

The book as a whole attempts to draw together and interrelate as many concepts as possible, especially through cross-referencing and the discussion questions. However, the field of intercultural communication is very large, and draws on several different disciplines (e.g. psychology, anthropology, linguistics). This book does not take such a broad approach; it does not address (let alone explain) all aspects of the complex interrelationship between culture and communication. It focuses on the rapport management issues, and approaches this from just one main angle – an applied linguistic/politeness theory perspective. However, the rich mix of conceptual, empirical and methodology chapters will, I hope, offer in-depth insights into the strengths, potentials and limitations of research in this field. It does not pretend to 'have all the answers', but I hope it will stimulate further interest and research.

Part 1
Basic Concepts

Editor's Introduction

Part 1 is a theoretical section and introduces key concepts and theories relevant to the study of culture, communication and politeness. It provides the conceptual foundations for all the other chapters.

Chapter 2, 'Face, (Im)Politeness and Rapport', draws primarily on social pragmatics, politeness theory and face theory, and presents a framework for exploring how language is used to manage relationships. The framework can incorporate the impact of cultural regularities, but is relevant to all communicative interaction. Chapter 3, 'Culture and Communication', tackles the thorny issue of culture and its interconnection with language use. It draws mainly on cognitive pragmatics (especially relevance theory), and explains how pragmatic knowledge, which can include culturally specific knowledge, impacts on language interpretation.

The two chapters have different pragmatic foci and thus complement each other. Chapter 2 takes a social pragmatic perspective and gives greater weight to the speaker and language production than to the hearer. Chapter 3, on the other hand, takes a cognitive pragmatic perspective and gives greater weight to the hearer's interpretive processes. Both perspectives are needed for a comprehensive understanding of the interrelationship between culture, communication and politeness.

Face, (Im)Politeness and Rapport 2

Helen Spencer-Oatey

Chapter Outline

2.1 Introduction 11
2.2 'Face' and rapport management 12
2.3 Rapport-threatening behaviour: managing face, sociality rights/obligations and interactional goals 17
2.4 Rapport management strategies 21
2.5 Factors influencing strategy use: (1) Rapport orientation 31
2.6 Factors influencing strategy use: (2) Contextual variables 33
2.7 Factors influencing strategy use: (3) Pragmatic principles and conventions 40
2.8 Rapport management outcomes 42
2.9 Rapport management across cultures 43
Key points 44
Discussion questions 44
Notes 46
Suggestions for further reading 46

2.1 Introduction

One morning, a British teacher of EFL and TEFL trainer was observing a reading class at a university in China. The teacher of the reading class was an experienced Chinese member of staff, and the students were all in-service teachers of English who had previously been taught by the British teacher. It was the Chinese teacher's first lesson with the class. During the course of the lesson, she asked the students in turn to read part of the passage aloud, and to answer the questions she posed. If students tried to query her feedback to their answers, she avoided any discussion and simply moved on to the next student. The class became increasingly uncomfortable with this style of teaching, and eventually one student challenged the teacher, asking 'Why do we have to read the passage aloud? And why don't you discuss our queries? What you're doing is not at all useful for us!' Both the teacher and the students were shocked by the remarks, and the atmosphere was extremely strained for the rest of the lesson. During the following weeks and months, both the students and the British teacher failed to develop a harmonious relationship with this teacher, despite repeated efforts.

This incident illustrates the crucial importance of *face* in our interactions with people. The Chinese teacher felt she had lost face, not only in front of her students, but also in front of the 'foreigner' who was observing her. Her authority and teaching expertise had been challenged, in a society where such incidents are extremely rare in that context. The British teacher was 'blamed' for allowing such an incident to occur, and neither the British teacher nor the students were ever able to fully repair the relational damage that had been done.

Needless to say, words can have a dramatic effect, both positive and negative, on our relationships with people. As explained in the introduction, all language has a dual function: the transfer of information, and the management of social relations. This book focuses on the management of social relations, an aspect of language use that I call *rapport management*. In this chapter, basic concepts and issues in the field of rapport management are explained, in order to provide a framework for the analysis of language use from this perspective. From a theoretical point of view, the material is based primarily on politeness theory and draws particular attention to the notion of face. However, I use the term *rapport management* rather than *face management* because its scope is broader: like face management, it examines the way that language is used to construct, maintain and/or threaten social relationships but, as explained below, it also includes the management of sociality rights and interactional goals. In addition, the term 'face' seems to focus on concerns for self, whereas *rapport management* suggests a greater balance between self and other.

This chapter deals with the following issues:

- face, politeness and rapport management;
- strategies for managing rapport;
- factors influencing strategy use (rapport orientation, contextual variables, pragmatic conventions);
- rapport management outcomes;
- rapport management across cultures.

2.2 'Face' and rapport management

Brown and Levinson (1987), in their seminal work on politeness, propose that *face* is the key motivating force for 'politeness', and they maintain that it consists of two related aspects, negative face and positive face. In their model, negative face is a person's want to be unimpeded by others, the desire to be free to act as s/he chooses and not be imposed upon; positive face is a person's want to be appreciated and approved of by selected others, in terms of personality, desires, behaviour, values and so on. In other words, negative face represents a desire for autonomy, and positive face represents a desire for approval.

Other linguists have challenged Brown and Levinson's (1987) conceptualization of face. For example, Matsumoto (1988), Ide (1989) and Mao (1994) all refer to the importance of 'social identity' as a concept in Japanese and Chinese society. Matsumoto (1988: 405), for instance, argues as follows:

> What is of paramount concern to a Japanese is not his/her own territory, but the position in relation to the others in the group and his/her acceptance by those others. Loss of face is associated with the perception by others that one has not comprehended and acknowledged the structure and hierarchy of the group. . . . A Japanese generally must understand where s/he stands in relation to other members of the group or society, and must acknowledge his/her dependence on the others. Acknowledgement and maintenance of the relative position of others, rather than preservation of an individual's proper territory, governs all social interaction.

In other words, Matsumoto's (1988) criticisms of Brown and Levinson (1987) are twofold: that they have ignored the interpersonal or social perspective on face, and that they have overemphasized the notion of individual freedom and autonomy. As Gu (1998) points out, it is not that concerns about autonomy, imposition and so on do not exist in Eastern cultures, but rather that they are not regarded as face concerns.

Taking these arguments into consideration, I propose a modified framework for conceptualizing face and rapport. I maintain that Brown and Levinson's (1987) conceptualization of positive face has been underspecified, and that the concerns they identify as negative face issues are not necessarily face concerns at all. I propose instead that rapport management (the management of harmony–disharmony among people) entails three main interconnected components: the management of face, the management of sociality rights and obligations, and the management of interactional goals (see Figure 2.1)

Face management, as the term indicates, involves the management of face sensitivities and, following Goffman (1967: 5), I define face as 'the positive social *value* a person effectively claims for himself [*sic*] by the line others assume he has taken during a particular contact' [my emphasis]. The management of sociality rights and obligations, on the other hand, involves the management of social expectancies, which I define as 'fundamental social *entitlements* that a person effectively claims for him/herself in his/her interactions with others'. In other words, face is associated with personal/relational/social value, and is concerned with people's sense of worth, dignity, honour, reputation, competence and so on. Sociality rights and obligations, on the other hand, are concerned with social expectancies, and reflect people's concerns over fairness, consideration and

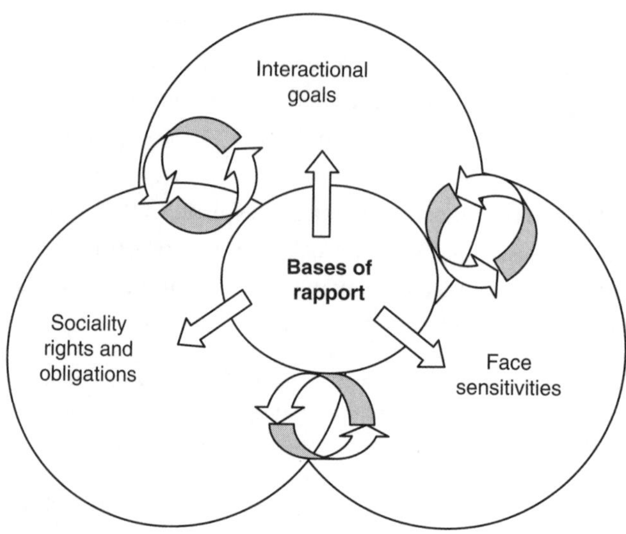

Figure 2.1 The bases of rapport.

behavioural appropriateness. Interactional goals refer to the specific task and/or relational goals that people may have when they interact with each other.

2.2.1 Face

Face is a concept that is intuitively meaningful to people, but one that is difficult to define precisely. It is concerned with people's sense of worth, dignity and identity, and is associated with issues such as respect, honour, status, reputation and competence (cf. Ting-Toomey and Kurogi 1998). As Lim (1994: 210) points out, the claim for face relates to positive social values: 'people do not claim face for what they think are negative [values]'. Along with many other theorists (e.g. Brown and Levinson 1987; Leech 1983; Ting-Toomey and Kurogi 1998), I believe face to be a universal phenomenon, in the sense that everyone has concerns about face.

Face is closely related to a person's sense of identity or self-concept: self as an individual (individual identity), self as a group member (group or collective identity) and self in relationship with others (relational identity). In all three respects, people often regard themselves as having certain attributes or characteristics, such as personality traits, physical features, beliefs, language affiliations and so on. They usually perceive some of their attributes positively (e.g. clever, musical), some of them negatively (e.g. overweight, inartistic) and others neutrally. People have a fundamental desire for others to evaluate them positively, and so they typically want others to acknowledge (explicitly or implicitly) their positive qualities, and *not* to acknowledge their negative qualities. Face is associated with these affectively sensitive attributes; however, exactly which attributes are face sensitive can vary from person to person and from context to context. (See Spencer-Oatey (2007) for a more detailed discussion of the interconnection between face and identity.)

The attributes that people are face-sensitive about can apply to the person as an individual and also to the group or community that the person belongs to and/or identifies with. For example, let us consider the attribute 'talented'. A person could regard him/herself as a talented individual (e.g. a talented artist), and s/he could regard the small group or community that s/he belongs to as being talented (e.g. a talented family or a talented work team or sports team). Sometimes there can also be a relational application; for example, being a talented leader and/or a kind-hearted teacher entails a relational component that is intrinsic to the evaluation.

2.2.2 Sociality rights and obligations

The second factor that can influence interpersonal rapport is perceived sociality rights and obligations. People regard themselves as having a range of sociality rights and obligations in relation to other people, and they typically base these on one or more of the factors shown in Table 2.1. People develop behavioural expectations in relation to their perceived sociality rights and obligations, and if these are not fulfilled, interpersonal rapport can be affected. This can be particularly common if the participants of an interaction hold differing views as to the nature of their sociality rights and obligations – a situation that is relatively common in intercultural interaction.

As Table 2.1 indicates, people's perceived sociality rights and obligations can sometimes be based on legal/contractual requirements; more frequently, however, they are

Table 2.1 Bases of perceived sociality rights and obligations

Basis of perceived sociality rights and obligations	Types of behavioural expectations for self and other
Contractual/legal agreements and requirements	Behavioural expectations based on business or other types of contract, as well as societal requirements such as equal opportunities of employment and avoidance of discriminatory behaviour
Explicit and implicit conceptualizations of roles and positions	Behavioural expectations associated with roles and social positions. Although they can be contractually based (e.g. the duties specified in a job contract), very often they are far more implicit. They include three key elements: equality–inequality, distance–closeness and the rights and obligations of the role relationship.
Behavioural conventions, styles and protocols	Behavioural expectations associated with the conventions, styles and protocols that people are used to encountering. For example, work groups usually develop conventions for handling team meetings, such as whether there is an agenda and if so, how strictly it is adhered to, or whether they can sit where they like or whether they should sit according to status or role.

derived from normative behaviour. People develop conceptions as to what frequently or typically happens in a given context and come to expect that. They may then develop a sense that others should or should not perform that behaviour, and prescriptive or proscriptive overtones become associated with that behaviour. As a result, people start perceiving rights and obligations in relation to them, with the result that if the expected behaviour is not forthcoming, those people may then feel annoyed.

Sometimes behavioural norms and conventions are not arbitrary. They may reflect efficient strategies for handling practical demands, and they may also be manifestations of more deeply held values. For example, conventions in relation to turn-taking and rights to talk at business meetings are partly a reflection of the need to deal effectively with the matters at hand, but they are also likely to reflect more deeply held beliefs about hierarchy and what is socially appropriate behaviour for given role relationships. In other words, people typically hold value-laden beliefs about the principles that should underpin interaction. I label these beliefs as sociopragmatic interactional principles (SIPs) (Spencer-Oatey and Jiang 2003), and suggest that two fundamental ones are equity and association:

Equity: We have a fundamental belief that we are entitled to personal consideration from others, so that we are treated fairly: that we are not unduly imposed upon, that we are not unfairly ordered about and that we are not taken advantage of or exploited. There seem to be two components to this equity entitlement: the notion of *cost–benefit* (the extent to which we are exploited or disadvantaged, and the belief that costs and benefits should be kept roughly in balance through the principle of reciprocity), and the related issue of *autonomy–imposition* (the extent to which people control us or impose on us).

Association: We have a fundamental belief that we are entitled to social involvement with others, in keeping with the type of relationship that we have with them. These association rights relate partly to *interactional involvement – detachment* (the extent to which we associate with people, or dissociate ourselves from them), so that we feel, for example, that we are entitled to an appropriate amount of conversational interaction and social chit-chat with others (e.g. not ignored on the one hand, but not overwhelmed on the other). They also relate to *affective involvement – detachment* (the extent to which we share concerns, feelings and interests). Naturally, what counts as 'an appropriate amount' varies according to the nature of the relationship, as well as sociocultural norms and personal preferences.

On different occasions, and for contextual and goal-related reasons, people may give greater weight to equity than association, or vice versa. However, this may also be influenced by their personal values (which in turn may be influenced by the communities that they are members of). Equity can be linked with (but of course is not identical to) individualism and to an independent construal of self, and Association can be linked with collectivism and to an interdependent construal of self (see Table 1.1 in

Chapter 1, and Chapter 13). I discuss the notion of SIPs again in Section 2.7.1, where I link it with Leech's Politeness Principle and politeness maxims.

2.2.3 Interactional goals

The third factor that can influence interpersonal rapport is interactional goals. People often (although not always) have specific goals when they interact with others. These can be relational as well as transactional (i.e. task-focused) in nature. These 'wants' can significantly affect their perceptions of rapport because any failure to achieve them can cause frustration and annoyance.

As I discuss below, there can be contextual, individual and cultural differences in the emphases that people give to these various components of rapport management. For example, some interactions are more goal-driven than others, and some people may be more face-sensitive over certain issues than other people are. In addition, there can be significant differences in the ways in which people conceptualize the components. For example, Spencer-Oatey (1997) reports differences in British and Chinese conceptualizations of the tutor-student role relationship, and hence of the sociality rights associated with the role relationship. I discuss these potential differences again towards the end of this chapter.

2.3 Rapport-threatening behaviour: managing face, sociality rights/obligations and interactional goals

As the popular phrase 'lose face' conveys, we do not always receive the respect from others that we would like. People may criticize us or boss us around, insult us and call us names; and when they do, we typically feel embarrassed or uncomfortable. Brown and Levinson (1987), in their politeness model, propose the notion of *face-threatening acts* to explain this phenomenon. They claim that certain communicative acts inherently threaten the face needs of the interlocutors, and that these illocutionary acts can be called *face-threatening acts (FTAs)*. How then does this concept of face-threatening acts apply to the framework outlined above?

I suggest that positive rapport (harmony) between people can be threatened in three main ways: through face-threatening behaviour, through rights-threatening/obligation-omission behaviour and through goal-threatening behaviour. When people threaten our goals, they hamper in some way what we want to achieve; for example, if we need a letter of support from our supervisor in order to apply for a job or course of study, and s/he fails to provide it before the submission deadline, the supervisor has threatened our goal and we are likely to feel annoyed with him/her. This same behaviour might also threaten our sociality rights, if we believe our supervisor has a (contractual) obligation to write such a letter. When people threaten our rights, they infringe our sense of social entitlements, and as a result we feel offended, uncomfortable, annoyed or angry. For instance, if someone tries to force us to do something, and we feel s/he has no right to expect us to do this, s/he threatens our perceived rights to equitable treatment. Similarly, if someone speaks to us in a way that is too personal for our liking, we may feel s/he has threatened our rights to (non-)association. In all these cases, we are likely to feel annoyed or irritated, but we do not necessarily feel a loss of face. On other occasions, however, people's treatment of us may not simply irritate or annoy us; it may go a step further and make us feel as though we have lost credibility or have been personally devalued in some way. When this happens, our face has been threatened, and we talk of 'losing face'. This can happen when people criticize us or oppose us, or make us 'look small' in some way.

To clarify some of these concepts, let us think back to the incident cited at the beginning of this chapter. When the student said to the teacher, in front of all the other students, 'Why do we have to read the passage aloud? And why don't you discuss our queries? What you are doing is not at all useful for us!', she was focusing on her own interactional goals (and maybe those of her classmates). The whole class had been unhappy about having this new teacher, and were concerned that the quality of their in-service training would be affected. So in speaking her mind, this trainee was foregrounding her task-related goals. However, her comments were very threatening to the teacher's face. They challenged the teacher's sense of competence as a teacher, making her doubt her ability to teach well, and thus making her lose face in relation to the attribute of competence. At the same time, the fact that the student challenged her at all, and especially in public, can also be seen (at least in this context) as a threat both to her sociality rights and to her face. In terms of sociality rights, the behaviour infringed on the teacher's perceived role rights (e.g. the right for a teacher to be treated with deference) and behavioural conventions (e.g. in traditional Chinese classrooms, students do not usually challenge teachers in this way). Such infringements were likely to annoy the teacher. In terms of face, there was a mismatch between the identity qualities that the teacher was implicitly claiming ('superior status' and 'worthy of deference') and those that the trainee was attributing to her. The comments did not give her the deference and authority, especially in a public context, that she perceived herself to be worthy of, and in this sense the incident also threatened her face.

A more minor incident, on the other hand, might not have threatened the teacher's face, but rather just have infringed her sociality rights. For example, if a student had asked the teacher to check a complicated piece of work within a very short period of time, or to write an important letter of support with virtually no notice, the teacher would probably have felt imposed upon and that her sociality rights had been infringed.

However, she would probably not have found the request face-threatening; she would most likely just have felt irritated rather than degraded.

Brown and Levinson (1987) discuss FTAs primarily in relation to speech acts, such as requests, offers, compliments, criticism and so on, which they designate as inherently face-threatening. So let us first consider how a selection of common speech acts can be viewed from a rapport management perspective.

1. *Orders and Requests:* As indicated in the examples above, orders and requests can easily threaten rapport, because they can affect our autonomy, freedom of choice and freedom from imposition, and thus can threaten our sense of equity rights (our entitlement to considerate treatment). They need to be worded, therefore, in such a way that we feel our rights to fair treatment have been adequately addressed, otherwise they may make us feel irritated or annoyed. However, not all orders and requests threaten our sense of equity rights. If we perceive a directive as being within the scope of our obligations, we are less likely to regard it as an infringement of our rights. Moreover, contrary to Brown and Levinson's (1987) designation of orders and requests as inherently face-threatening, they are not necessarily so from a rapport management perspective: they *may* be face-threatening, but need not always be. For example, if we are ordered to do something menial that we feel is 'below us', and we feel devalued in some way, then we may perceive the order to be face-threatening. On the other hand, on a different occasion, we may feel pleased or even honoured if someone asks us for help, feeling that it shows trust in our abilities and/or acceptance as a close friend. In this case, the request can 'give' us face. At other times, though, when people ask us to do something, we simply feel inconvenienced or imposed upon, but do not feel we have lost credibility or been devalued. In this case, the request has simply infringed our sense of sociality rights. In other words, orders and requests are rapport sensitive speech acts, and thus need to be managed appropriately. However, whether they are perceived to be threatening/enhancing of face or infringing/supporting of sociality rights (or a combination of these), depends on a range of circumstantial and personal factors.
2. *Apologies:* Apologies are typically post-event speech acts, in the sense that some kind of offence or violation of social norms has taken place. In other words, people's sociality rights have been infringed in some way; for example, if they have been kept waiting for an hour, their equity rights have been infringed through the 'cost' of wasting their time; or if they have been excluded from a conversation because of others using a language they do not know or because of their choice of an unfamiliar topic, their association rights have been infringed. In these circumstances, there is a need to restore the 'balance' by the other person giving an apology. Brown and Levinson (1987) categorize apologies as inherently face-threatening to the speaker. In fact, there are two elements involved: the impact on the offender's face of other people's awareness of the offence, and the impact on the offender's face of the act of apologizing. Both are likely to be affected by the seriousness of the offence. If the offence is a minor, neither is likely to be face-threatening to the offender. However, if the offence is more substantial, both can be very face threatening to the offender: it can threaten his/her face in terms of personal competence, and if many people know about it and/or the apology is very public, it can also threaten his/her face in terms of general reputation or standing among others. Yet if no apology is forthcoming, perhaps for strategic reasons, this can be rapport threatening to the offended person. It can aggravate his/her sense of sociality

rights, because no (verbal) repair has been made for the infringement that occurred through the offence. And if the offended person feels that s/he has been treated with too much contempt, this can also result in a sense of face loss.

3. *Compliments*: According to Brown and Levinson (1987), compliments are inherently face-threatening acts, yet they can also be regarded as face-enhancing speech acts, in that they are usually intended to have a positive effect on interpersonal relations. Personal compliments typically enhance people's face by conveying support for, or approval of, some of their positive attributes. On the other hand, if the receiver feels that a compliment is too personal, and reflects a more intimate relationship with the complimenter than s/he feels comfortable with, the compliment can have a different effect: it can threaten the receiver's sense of sociality rights. In this case, the overall effect of the compliment could be rapport threatening, because the person being complimented might be annoyed at the unwarranted level of assumed intimacy, and hence feel that his/her association rights (sociality entitlements regarding appropriate degree of affective involvement–detachment) have been infringed.

These examples illustrate (but not exhaustively) how complex it is to manage rapport effectively. Rapport threat and rapport enhancement are subjective evaluations, which depend not simply on the content of the message, but on people's interpretations and reactions to who says what under what circumstances.

To complicate matters further, rapport management is not only a matter of handling selected speech acts appropriately. Brown and Levinson's (1987) conceptualization of FTAs could be interpreted as implying that certain communicative acts intrinsically threaten face whereas others do not. So Matsumoto (1989: 219) argues in relation to Japanese that *all* use of language is potentially face-threatening:

> Since any Japanese utterance conveys information about the social context, there is always the possibility that the speaker may, by the choice of an inappropriate form, offend the audience and thus embarrass him/herself. In this sense, any utterance, even a simple declarative, could be face-threatening.

Perhaps a more balanced way of considering this is to say that all use of language (in other words, not only the performance of certain speech acts, but other aspects too) can affect people's interpretations of how appropriately face, sociality rights and interactional goals are managed, and can therefore affect rapport. Tsuruta (1998) takes Matsumoto's argument a step further by suggesting that Brown and Levinson (1987) and Matsumoto (1989) are each discussing different 'domains' of politeness. She argues that Brown and Levinson's model deals primarily with 'illocutionary politeness', whereas Matsumoto's discussion of Japanese honorifics deals primarily with 'stylistic politeness'. Research by Spencer-Oatey and Xing (1998, 2004 and Chapter 13 in this book) supports this contention that politeness is managed through multiple aspects of language use. Analysis of authentic interactions between British and Chinese business people suggests that the following interrelated 'domains' all play important roles in the management of rapport.

1. *Illocutionary Domain*: This is the domain that Brown and Levinson (1987) deal primarily with. It concerns the rapport-threatening/rapport-enhancing implications of performing speech acts, such as apologies, requests, compliments and so on. Speech acts such as these need to be handled appropriately if harmonious relations are to be created and/or maintained.
2. *Discourse Domain*: This domain concerns the discourse content and discourse structure of an interchange. It includes issues such as topic choice and topic management (for example, the inclusion/exclusion of personal topics), and the organization and sequencing of information. These issues need to be handled appropriately if harmonious relations are to be created and/or maintained, because the raising of sensitive topics, for example, can be rapport-threatening, as can frequent, sudden changes of topic.
3. *Participation Domain*: This domain (which usually is regarded as a component of discourse but can usefully be analysed as a domain in its own right) concerns the procedural aspects of an interchange, such as turn-taking (overlaps and inter-turn pauses, turn- taking rights and obligations), the inclusion/exclusion of people present, and the use/ non-use of listener responses (verbal and non-verbal). These procedural aspects need to be handled appropriately if harmonious relations are to be created and/or maintained.
4. *Stylistic Domain*: This domain concerns the stylistic aspects of an interchange, such as choice of tone (for example, serious or joking), choice of genre-appropriate lexis and syntax and choice of genre-appropriate terms of address or use of honorifics. These stylistic aspects need to be handled appropriately if harmonious relations are to be created and/or maintained.
5. *Non-verbal Domain*: This domain concerns the non-verbal aspects of an interchange, such as gestures and other body movements, eye contact and proxemics. These non-verbal aspects also need to be handled appropriately if harmonious relations are to be created and/or maintained.

Clearly, as Brown and Levinson (1987) point out, speech acts need to be handled carefully because the import of many of them (e.g. criticisms, complaints) can easily threaten rapport. However, as Spencer-Oatey and Xing (1998, 2004 and Chapter 13 in this book) illustrate, the appropriate management of other domains also plays a vital role.

2.4 Rapport management strategies

As explained in Section 2.3, losing face is a painful experience and for this reason Brown and Levinson (1987) suggest that it is generally in every participant's best interest to maintain each other's face. Every language, therefore, provides a very wide range of linguistic options that can be used for managing face and sociality rights, and hence for managing rapport. Naturally, the exact range of options, and their social significance, varies from language to language. However, in all languages, every level of language can play a role in each of the rapport management domains. For example, within the illocutionary domain, the following (to name just a few) can each have highly significant effects on interpersonal relations: choice of intonation and tone of voice, choice of lexis, choice of morphology and syntax, choice of terms of address and honorifics. And within the participation and stylistic domains, choice of code and/or dialect, speed of speech, choice of lexis, choice of syntax and so on, can also each have major effects on interpersonal relations. This section describes some of the main strategies that have been identified so far.

2.4.1 Illocutionary domain: speech act strategies

Up to now, a very large proportion of work on politeness, and hence rapport management, has focused on the illocutionary domain. As a result, considerable attention has been paid to the wording of speech acts, and three important types of features have been analysed in a wide range of studies: the selection of speech act components, the degree of directness–indirectness and the type and amount of upgraders/downgraders. Let us consider the following examples:

a. *Do you mind if I ask you a big favour? I know you don't like lending your car, but I was wondering if I could possibly borrow it just for an hour or so on Tuesday afternoon, if you're not using it then. I need to take my mother to the hospital and it's difficult getting there by bus.*
b. *Thanks ever so much for lending me your car. It was really extremely kind of you, and I very much appreciate it. If I can ever help you out like that, be sure and let me know.*

One way of analysing speech act utterances like these is to examine their main semantic components. Speech acts typically have a range of semantic formulae or components associated with them (often known as 'speech act sets' (Olshtain and Cohen 1983)). Naturally, exactly what these components are varies from one speech act to another. Normally, there is a head act, which conveys the main illocutionary force of the set of utterances; before or after the head act (or both) there may be additional components (these additional components are often not essential, though). Analysing the above examples in this way provides us with the following descriptions:

Request

Do you mind if I ask you a big favour?	Mitigating supportive move (preparator)
I know you don't like lending your car,	Mitigating supportive move (disarmer)
but I was wondering if I could possibly borrow it just for an hour or so on Tuesday afternoon,	Head act
if you're not using it then.	Mitigating supportive move (imposition downgrader)
I need to take my mother to the hospital and it's difficult getting there by bus.	Mitigating supportive move (grounder)

Expression of Gratitude

Thanks ever so much for lending me your car.	Head act
It was really extremely kind of you,	Complimenting of other person

and I very much appreciate it.	Expression of appreciation
If I can ever help you out like that, be sure and let me know	Promise of repayment/reciprocation

Table 2.2 lists the main semantic components of five common speech acts. Speakers normally select one or more of these speech act formulae in order to reflect their rapport orientation (see Section 2.5) in a given situation. However, cultures may differ in both the frequency of use of a given formula in a given situation, and also in the face-management value associated with the use or omission of a given formula in a given situation. So in cross-cultural speech act studies, it is common to compare different groups for the use of the different semantic components. Chapters 4 and 5 illustrate this approach.

Another way of analysing speech acts, especially ones such as requests and disagreements, is in terms of linguistic directness/indirectness. If we want someone to do the washing up, for example, we can choose from a range of options such as the following:

- Wash the dishes!
- I want you to wash the dishes.
- How about washing the dishes?
- Can you wash the dishes?
- What a lot of dishes there are!

All of these utterances differ in the degree of directness with which the illocutionary force of requesting is conveyed, and choosing one form rather than another can have a major impact on social relations. For reference purposes, Table 2.3 shows the range of direct and indirect strategies identified by Blum-Kulka, House and Kasper (1989) for conveying requests.

Needless to say, as with speech act components, cultures may differ in both the frequency of use of given levels of directness in given situations, and also in the rapport-management value associated with the level of directness chosen for a given situation. In Greek (Sifianou 1992a) and Chinese, for example, direct strategies (mood derivable utterances) are used more frequently than in English, and are often used in situations where a conventionally indirect form would be likely in English. However, such utterances are not usually interpreted as 'rude' in Greek and Chinese, because they are normally softened with particles, affixes and/or tone of voice.

A third way of analysing speech acts is in terms of upgraders/downgraders or, as they are also called, boosters/hedges, intensifiers/downtoners or maximizers/minimizers. Upgraders increase the force of the speech act, whereas downgraders reduce or weaken the force. For speech acts such as requests and disagreements, downgraders have a mitigating effect; in other words, they function to reduce any negative impact associated with the speech act. Upgraders have the opposite effect, and usually function to strengthen the negative impact of the speech act. On the other hand, for speech acts

Table 2.2 Semantic components of five common speech acts

Requests (based on Blum-Kulka et al., 1989; list is non-exhaustive)

1. Head act, which can be modified
2. Alerter. e.g. *Excuse me . . .; Mary . . .*
3. Mitigating supportive move
   3.1. Preparator, e.g. *I'd like to ask you something, . . .*
   3.2. Getting a precommitment, e.g. *Could you do me a favour?*
   3.3. Grounder, e.g. *Judith, I missed class yesterday. Could I borrow your notes?*
   3.4. Disarmer, e.g. *I know you don't like to lend out your notes, but could . . .*
   3.5. Promise of reward, e.g. *Could you give me a lift home? I'll give you something for the petrol.*
   3.6. Imposition downgrader, e.g. *Could you lend me that book, if you're not using it at present?*
4. Aggravating supportive move
   4.1. Insult, e.g. *You've always been a dirty pig, so clear up!*
   4.2. Threat, e.g. *Move that car if you don't want a ticket!*
   4.3. Moralizing, e.g. *If one shares a flat one should be prepared to pull one's weight in cleaning it, so get on with the washing up!*

Refusals of Invitations (based on Kinjo, 1987)

1. Explicit refusal, e.g. *I can't make it.*
2. Expression of appreciation, e.g. *Thanks for the invitation.*
3. Excuse or explanation, e.g. *I'm busy.*
4. Expression of regret, e.g. *I'm sorry.*
5. Expression of positive feelings or wishes, e.g. *It sounds like fun/I wish I could make it.*
6. A conditional, e.g. *If you had told me earlier, I could have gone with you.*
7. Offer of an alternative, e.g. *How about Sunday?*
8. Request for further information, e.g. *Who'll be there?*
9. Repetition, e.g. *Dinner on Sunday. Well, thanks very much, but . . .*

Apologies (based on Blum-Kulka et al. 1989)

1. Illocutionary Force Indicating Device (IFID),* e.g. *I'm sorry.*
2. Taking on responsibility, e.g. *I'm sorry, my mistake!*
3. Explanation or account, e.g. *I'm sorry I missed the meeting. I was off sick.*
4. Offer of repair, e.g. *I'm very sorry. I'll buy you another one.*
5. Promise of forbearance, e.g. *I'm so sorry. I promise you it won't happen again.*

Gratitude (based on Eisenstein and Bodman 1986)

1. IFID,* e.g. *Thank you.*
2. Complimenting of other person, action or object, e.g. *Thanks a lot. That was great.*
3. Expression of surprise or delight, e.g. *Oh wow. Thank you so much.*
4. Expression of appreciation, e.g. *Thanks, I really appreciate it.*
5. Promise of repayment or reciprocation, e.g. *Thanks, I'll give it back to you on Monday.*
6. Expression of lack of necessity or obligation, e.g. *It's lovely, but you didn't have to get me anything.*
7. Reassurance, e.g. *Just what I wanted.*

Disagreement (based on Beebe and Takahashi 1989a)

1. Explicit disagreement, e.g. *I'm afraid I don't agree.*
2. Criticism or negative evaluation, e.g. *That's not practical.*
3. Question, e.g. *Do you think that would work smoothly?*

Table 2.2—cont'd

4. Alternative suggestion, e.g. *How about trying . . .?*
5. Gratitude, e.g. *Thanks very much for your suggestion*, . . .
6. Positive remark, e.g. *You've obviously put a lot of work into this*, . . .
7. Token agreement, e.g. *I agree with you, but* . . .

* 'IFIDs are formulaic, routinized expressions in which the speaker's apology [gratitude] is made explicit.' Blum-Kulka, House and Kasper 1989: 290, word in brackets added. See also the Glossary.

Table 2.3 Strategy types for making requests, on a scale of directness–indirectness (based on Blum-Kulka, House and Kasper 1989: 18)

Direct Strategies

1. *Mood derivable:* utterances in which the grammatical mood of the verb signals illocutionary force, e.g. *Stop talking/ Re-write that paragraph.*
2. *Performatives:* utterances in which the illocutionary force is explicitly named, e.g. *I'm asking you to re-write that paragraph.*
3. *Hedged performatives:* utterances in which the naming of the illocutionary force is modified by hedging expressions, e.g. *I would like to ask you to give your talk a week earlier than scheduled.*
4. *Obligation statements:* utterances which state the obligation of the hearer to carry out the act, e.g. *You'll have to re-write that paragraph.*
5. *Want statements:* utterances which state the speaker's desire that the hearer carries out the act, e.g. *I really wish you'd stop chattering.*

Conventionally Indirect Strategies

6. *Suggestory formulae:* utterances which contain a suggestion to do something, e.g. *How about re-writing that paragraph?*
7. *Query preparatory:* utterances containing reference to preparatory conditions (e.g. ability, willingness) as conventionalized in any specific language, e.g. *Could you stop talking, please? / Would you mind re-writing that paragraph?*

Non-conventionally Indirect Strategies

8. *Strong hints:* utterances containing partial reference to object or elements needed for the implementation of the act, e.g. *You've made a lot of mistakes in that paragraph.*
9. *Mild hints:* utterances that make no reference to the request proper (or any of its elements) but are interpretable as requests by context, e.g. *I'm getting a headache* when other people are talking loudly.

such as apologies, expressions of gratitude and compliments the reverse is the case. Upgraders strengthen the positive impact associated with the speech act, and downgraders weaken it. In other words, whether the use of upgraders improves or worsens social relations depends on the speech act concerned. For reference purposes, Table 2.4 lists some common upgraders and downgraders associated with requests and apologies.

Table 2.4 Types of downgraders/upgraders commonly associated with requests and apologies (based on Blum-Kulka, House and Kasper 1989: Appendix)

Downgraders/upgraders for requests	**Downgraders/upgraders for apologies**
(Selected Examples)	*(Selected Examples)*
Can you tidy up your desk?	*I'm sorry.*
Syntactic downgraders	**Downgraders**
Negation of preparatory condition, e.g. *You couldn't tidy up your desk, could you?*	Query precondition, e.g. *Are you sure we were supposed to meet at 10*?
Aspect, e.g. *I'm wondering if you can tidy up your desk*?	Act innocent, e.g. *Am I late*?
Tense, e.g. *I was wondering if you could tidy up your desk?*	Future/task-oriented remark, e.g. *Let's get to work then*.
	Appeaser, e.g. *Let me get you a cup of tea*.
Lexical and phrasal downgraders	**Upgraders**
Politeness marker, e.g. *Can you tidy up your desk, please*?	Intensifying adverbial, e.g. *I'm terribly sorry*!
Understater, e.g. *Can you tidy up your desk a bit*?	Emotional expression, e.g. *Oh no*.
Hedge, e.g. *Can you sort of tidy up your desk?*	Expressions marked for register, e.g. *I do apologize* . . .
Subjectivizer, e.g. *I wonder if you could tidy up your desk/I'm afraid you're going to have to tidy up* . . .	Double intensifier or repetition, e.g. *I'm really dreadfully* sorry/I'm *very very* sorry/I'm *sorry, please forgive me*.
Downtoner, e.g. *Could you possibly tidy up your desk*?	Concern for hearer, e.g. *I hope you weren't worried about me*.
Cajoler, e.g. *You know, you really need to tidy up* . . .	
Appealer, e.g. *Tidy up your desk, will you?*	
Upgraders	
Intensifier, e.g. *Your desk is in a terrible mess.*	
Expletive, e.g. *Tidy up your bloody desk*!	
Time intensifier, e.g. *Tidy up your desk right now*!	

If we return to the request and apology examples given near the beginning of this section, the role of the upgraders and downgraders can be seen more clearly. The request in the example is a major one, so the head act contains four different types of downgraders in an attempt to reduce the negative impact of the request on the other person. Similarly, the expression of gratitude relates to a major act of helping, and the utterances contain three different upgraders. Analysing them in terms of downgraders/upgraders gives the following descriptions:

Request	
I was wondering	Syntactic Downgrader (tense and aspect)
if I could possibly borrow it	Lexical and Phrasal Downgrader (downtoner)
just for an hour or so on Tuesday afternoon.	Lexical and Phrasal Downgrader (understater)
Expression of Gratitude	
Thanks ever so much for lending me your car.	Upgrader (intensifying adverbial)
It was really extremely kind of you,	Upgrader (double intensifier)
and I very much appreciate it.	Upgrader (intensifying adverbial)

Needless to say, the range and precise forms of upgraders/downgraders available in one language differ from those available in another language. And as with the other choices of wording, cultures probably vary in both the frequency of use of upgraders/downgraders in given situations, and also in the rapport-management value associated with their use in these contexts. Furthermore, there may be differences in the ways in which the three types of wording choices[1] (selection of semantic components, degree of directness/indirectness and use of upgraders/downgraders) interact with each other, and in the rapport-management value of these combined choices. More research is needed on these combinations of choices.

2.4.2 Other rapport management domains

Comparative research into the strategies used in other rapport management domains has been less systematic, although individual researchers have explored certain components. For example, within the discourse domain, Pavlidou (1994; and Chapter 6 in this book) has investigated phatic talk in the opening and closing sections of telephone conversations. She reports that Greek speakers use a greater amount of phatic talk than Germans do, and that in German–Greek telephone conversations, this can lead to negative evaluations of the other speaker. Within the participation domain, Wieland (1991), for example, has examined turn-taking in French and American dinner conversations. She focused particularly on overlaps, and counted the frequencies with which each interlocutor attempted to take a turn without waiting for the other speaker to finish. She found that French speakers overlapped much more frequently than American speakers did, and that this had a significant effect on participants' evaluations of each other.

Spencer-Oatey and Xing (1998; and Chapter 13 in this book) investigated all five rapport management domains in their analysis of Chinese–British business discourse and, within each domain, they have been seeking to identify strategies that are used to manage rapport.

2.4.3 Communication style and interactional ethos

All of the linguistic strategies discussed so far are relatively specific, and yet a number of theorists (e.g. Brown and Levinson 1987; Clyne 1994; Scollon and Scollon 1995; Fitzgerald 2003; House 2003; Spencer-Oatey and Franklin 2009) maintain that there are patterns of choices that convey a more generalized style of interaction, known as a communication style.

A communication style is a manner of language use that exhibits clusters of co-occurring features. All aspects of language use and interactional behaviour can be reflected in the style, including choice of vocabulary and syntax, prosody and paralinguistic behaviour (e.g. intonation, stress, tone of voice, pitch, pacing, pausing and loudness) as well as non-verbal behaviour (e.g. gestures, spatial relations and touch). At present, there is no consensus as to how clusters of these features are best grouped and labelled, but they are typically presented as dichotomous options (although there is no doubt a continuum of variation from one extreme to the other).

One communication style dichotomy that is widely referred to in both linguistics and communication studies is variously labelled as positive politeness–negative politeness (Brown and Levinson 1987), involvement–independence (Scollon and Scollon 1995) and immediacy: expressiveness–distance (Andersen et al. 2002). Table 2.5 illustrates some linguistic strategies that are associated with these dichotomous options, which are similar but not identical, and which I label here as associative expressiveness–restraint.

Brown and Levinson (1987: 243) point out that people's choices of communication style influence interactional ethos, and that there can be significant differences between sociocultural groups in this respect:

> Every observer in a foreign land knows that societies, or sub-cultures within societies, differ in terms of what might be called 'ethos', the affective quality of interaction characteristic of members of a society. . . . In some [positive- politeness] societies interactional ethos is generally warm, easy-going, friendly; in others [negative-politeness societies] it is stiff, formal, deferential.

Another distinction in communication style that linguists (e.g. House 2003: 49) often refer to is directness–indirectness. This distinction can be viewed from three perspectives: linguistic, pragmatic inferential and interpersonal.[2] So far in this chapter we have only considered directness–indirectness from a linguistic point of view.

Table 2.5 Linguistic strategies of associative expressiveness–restraint (adapted from Scollon and Scollon 1995: 40–1)

Linguistic strategies of associative expressiveness: some examples	Linguistic strategies of associative restraint: some examples
1. Notice or attend to hearer: *I really like your new shoes.* *Are you feeling better today?*	1. Make minimal assumptions about hearer's wants: *I don't know how you'll feel about this, …*
2. Exaggerate (interest, approval, sympathy with hearer): *Please take a rest; you're looking very tired.* *You always do so well in school.*	2. Give hearer the option not to do the act: *It would be lovely if you could help me with this, but don't worry if you're too busy.*
3. Claim in-group membership with hearer: *All of us linguists …*	3. Minimize threat: *I just need to borrow a little piece of paper, any scrap will do.*
4. Claim common point of view, opinions, attitudes, knowledge, empathy: *I know just what you mean. I too was very disappointed about that.*	4. Apologize: *I'm sorry to trouble you, could you tell me where the nearest post office is?*
5. Be optimistic: *I'm sure we'll be able to increase our sales within the next 6 months.*	5. Be pessimistic: *I don't suppose you know where the nearest post office is, do you?*
6. Indicate speaker knows hearer's wants and is taking them into account: *I know you'd like to try that again, so I'll give you another chance.*	6. Dissociate speaker, hearer from the discourse: *This is to inform our employees that …*
7. Assume or assert reciprocity: *I know you want your report to be as well received by the senior management as I do.*	7. State a general rule: *University regulations require every employee to…*
8. Use given names and nicknames: *Andy, can you get that report to me by tomorrow?*	8. Use family name and titles: *Dr Taylor, there's a Professor Zhang in reception for you.*
9. Be voluble.	9. Be taciturn.
10. Use hearer's language or dialect.	10. Use own language or dialect.

From this perspective, directness–indirectness is related to explicitness–implicitness. Explicitness is the extent to which a message is coded unambiguously in the words that are chosen; for example, *I can't come* is a more explicit refusal than *I need to work on my essay tonight*, and *Thanks very much* is a more explicit expression of gratitude than *That's really kind of you*. An explicit message is more direct than an implicit message. Table 2.3 illustrates linguistic directness–indirectness in relation to requests.

From a pragmatic inferential perspective, directness–indirectness is not only related to explicit encoding but also to communicative strength in a specific interaction. Communicative strength refers to the extent to which a message is clear or ambiguous *in the particular context* in which it is uttered. For example, suppose a shop customer selects two products and takes them to the cashier; if the cashier says *That's £10*, the meaning is very clearly *Pay me £10*. However, those same words in a different context could mean something different; if two friends were browsing in a shop, and one pointed at an object and said *That's £10*, s/he would not be asking for payment, but simply commenting on the cheapness (or costliness) of the product. The notion of conventionality has a major impact on judgements of communicative strength. For example, *Can you open the window* is technically an implicit request, because literally the words ask whether the person is able to open the window; however, the *can you . . .* pattern is used so frequently for requests in English that few people would perceive it as implicit. This is a very important point for intercultural communication, because conventionalized patterns may be different across languages and cultures. For example, a rhetorical question may be conventionalized as a normal way of expressing disagreement in one language/culture (and hence be perceived as a clear and unambiguous expression of disagreement) but not in another (and hence be perceived as an indirect expression of disagreement).

From an interpersonal perspective, directness–indirectness is also related to bluntness. Bluntness is the extent to which the message is softened or mitigated. It can be managed in various ways:

- Through the use of downgraders/upgraders; for example, *I'm sorry I can't come* is less blunt than *I can't come*; and *tidy up, will you?* is less blunt than *tidy up*.
- Through the number of elements that are used to convey a message; for example, *I'm sorry I'm late* is more blunt an apology than *I'm sorry I'm late. The traffic was terrible. I hope you aren't too cross with me.*
- Through discourse structure and timing; building up to a major request is less blunt than asking it immediately, and asking sensitive questions shortly after meeting someone is more blunt than waiting until you know the person well.

A blunt or 'bald' (Brown and Levinson 1987) message is more direct than a cushioned message.

Much of the intercultural communication literature (e.g. Gudykunst 1998; Ting-Toomey 1999) and some of the applied linguistic literature (e.g. House 2003) refer to differences across cultural groups in communicative directness–indirectness. For example, House reports that in her data, German speakers display greater directness than Anglophones. Chapter 11 in this book illustrates how differences in directness–indirectness affect Japanese–American communication in the workplace. However, three notes of caution need to be sounded. Firstly, context can have a very major influence on people's use of directness–indirectness and this can interact with cultural differences. For example, in my experience, Chinese speakers can be very direct in comments about personal appearance with persons they know well and they are often much more direct than British people in this respect; however, in the workplace, and especially with people they are unfamiliar with or who are their superiors, they are often much more indirect than British people. Secondly, from a rapport perspective, people's assessment of the other person's directness–indirectness is usually relative to their expectations. So, for example, British people may be regarded as indirect by German speakers and Polish speakers (Wierzbicka 2003: 64) but as direct by Chinese or Japanese speakers. Thirdly, research needs to take greater account of the threefold perspective in directness–indirectness, especially the pragmatic inferential one, and not treat this stylistic issue primarily in terms of explicitness–implicitness, with or without mitigation.

A third communication style that is frequently referred to in the intercultural communication literature is self-enhancement–self-effacement. Ting-Toomey (1999: 107–8) explains it as follows:

> The self-enhancement verbal style emphasizes the importance of boasting about one's accomplishments and abilities. The self-effacement verbal style, on the other hand, emphasizes the importance of humbling oneself via verbal restrains, hesitations, modest talk, and the use of self-deprecation concerning one's effort or performance. . . . In the U.S. culture, we encourage individuals to 'sell and boast about themselves'. For example, . . . an American ad [in a personal column of a magazine] might begin, *a handsome, athletic male with a good sense of humor seeks a fun-loving partner . . .*; the comparable Japanese ad might read, *Although I am not very good looking, I'm willing to try my best to work hard.*

I take up this issue of degrees of modesty or 'boasting' again in Section 2.7.1, in the discussion of Leech's politeness maxims.

2.5 Factors influencing strategy use: (1) Rapport orientation

One key factor that influences people's strategy use is their rapport orientation. It is useful first to distinguish between two fundamental orientations: support of one's own face needs, sociality rights and interactional goals, and support of the other person's. Brown and Levinson maintain that it is generally 'in every participant's best interest to maintain each others' face' (1987: 61), because of the mutual vulnerability of face: if person A attacks person B's face, then person B is likely to attack person A's face in return, and the result will be an uncomfortable loss of face for both. So as Ting-Toomey and Cocroft (1994: 323) suggest, a third orientation may be usefully added: mutual support.

Although people may often try to take a 'mutual support' orientation, there are nevertheless occasions when people do attack other people's face. So as Turner (1996) and Culpeper (1996, 2005) both argue, 'politeness' theory needs to incorporate this notion.

I suggest, therefore, that speakers can hold any of the following four types of rapport orientation:[3]

1. Rapport enhancement orientation: a desire to strengthen or enhance harmonious relations between the interlocutors;
2. Rapport maintenance orientation: a desire to maintain or protect harmonious relations between the interlocutors;
3. Rapport neglect orientation: a lack of concern or interest in the quality of relations between the interlocutors (perhaps because of a focus on self);
4. Rapport challenge orientation: a desire to challenge or impair harmonious relations between the interlocutors.

When people hold a rapport enhancement orientation, they want to enhance the harmony of the relationship. Their motives for holding such an orientation could be various; for example, to start an incipient romantic relationship; to win a lucrative business contract; to show genuine friendliness to someone who is lonely; and so on. But whatever people's motives, their desire is for positive change: to improve the rapport between them. The appropriate 'giving of face' is an important way of doing this.

When people hold a rapport-maintenance orientation, on the other hand, their desire is not so much for change as for preservation. In other words, people simply want to maintain the current quality of relationship and level of rapport. This orientation is often reflected in the choice of appropriate terms of address, honorifics, social indexing markers, and other relevant aspects of register. However, this orientation also relates to the appropriate handling of rapport-threatening behaviour. As discussed in Section 2.3, rapport can be threatened by overlooking other people's face sensitivities, by infringing their perceived sociality rights, and by hampering their interactional goals. When people hold a rapport-maintenance orientation, their aim is to minimize such threats by selecting appropriate rapport-management strategies.

When people hold a rapport-neglect orientation, they have little concern for the quality of the relationship between the other speaker(s) and themselves. This may be because their attention is fully focused on task matters (for example, when dealing with an emergency or when trying to convey accurate information); it may be because they genuinely do not care about the relationship for some reason; or it may be because they are more concerned about their own face sensitivities, sociality rights and interactional goals than about maintaining interpersonal rapport. For example, when a speech act is more face-threatening to the speaker than to the hearer (e.g. an apology), and when the speaker is more concerned about maintaining his/her own face than maintaining or restoring rapport, the speaker's orientation will count as rapport-neglect. (What the effect will be on the hearer is another matter, as we consider in Section 2.8.)

When people hold a rapport-challenge orientation, they want to challenge or impair the harmony of the relationship. Once again, people's motives for holding such an orientation could be various; for example, to assert personal independence; to rebuff a romantic advance; to repay a previous offence; and so on. But whatever people's motives, their desire is for negative change: to worsen the rapport between them. Deliberately causing people to lose face is one way of doing this.

Needless to say, people's rapport orientations are not available for open inspection. Unless people talk about them explicitly, they can only be inferred from their choice of rapport-management strategies. Even so, it may still be difficult to distinguish clearly one orientation from another. Nevertheless, the notion of interpersonal intent is an important issue in real-life interaction, and for that reason, I believe it needs to be included in any description of relational management.

Another perspective on rapport orientation is provided by Communication Accommodation Theory (CAT) (see Chapter 8 in this book). CAT proposes that speakers adopt different socio-psychological orientations vis-à-vis their interlocutors, depending on a range of background factors. The theory suggests two main types of orientation:

1. Convergent Orientation versus Divergent Orientation: Speakers with a convergent orientation aim to adapt their communicative behaviours to those of the other speaker(s), whereas speakers with a divergent orientation aim to accentuate the differences between their communicative behaviours and those of the other speaker(s). (See Chapter 8 in this book.)
2. Intergroup Orientation versus Interpersonal Orientation: Speakers with an intergroup orientation tend to perceive an encounter primarily in intergroup terms, whereas speakers with an interpersonal orientation tend to perceive an encounter primarily in interpersonal terms. (See Gallois et al. 1995; Gallois et al. 2005.)

CAT also suggests some of the motives that may underlie both of these types of orientations.

2.6 Factors influencing strategy use: (2) Contextual variables

A second set of factors that have a crucial influence on people's choice of rapport management strategies are contextual variables. In this section I discuss four important ones: participant relations, message content, social/interactional roles and activity type.

2.6.1 Participants and their relations

Participant relations are a very important group of factors that influence use of rapport management strategies. Several classic studies have helped establish *power* and *distance* as key variables relating to participant relations. For example, Brown and Gilman (1960) in their study of the use of pronouns in French, German and Italian, argue that choice of pronoun is affected by two fundamental dimensions of participant relations: *power* and *solidarity*. Similarly, Brown and Levinson (1987) maintain that interlocutors consider the *power* and *distance* of their relationship when choosing among different options for conveying a given speech act.

Moreover, a large number of empirical studies have provided considerable evidence for an association between language use and the variables *power* and *distance*. For example, many linguists have explored the wording of speech acts, such as requests (e.g. Blum-Kulka et al. 1985; Holtgraves and Yang 1990; Lim and Bowers 1991), apologies (e.g. Holmes 1990; Olshtain 1989), directives (e.g. Holtgraves et al. 1989) and disagreement (e.g. Beebe and Takahashi 1989a), and a very large number of them have found *power* and *distance* to be significant variables.

2.6.1.1 Power

This variable has several different labels; for example, *power, social power, status, dominance, authority*. Brown and Gilman (1960/1972: 225) define this variable as follows:

> One person may be said to have power over another in the degree that he is able to control the behavior of the other. Power is a relationship between at least two persons, and it is nonreciprocal in the sense that both cannot have power in the same area of behavior.

In sociolinguistic and pragmatic research, power is typically operationalized in terms of unequal role relations, such as teacher–student, employer–employee. Very often there is no problem with this, but sometimes it can lead to confusion. For example, Blum-Kulka et al. (1985) refer to 'driver and passenger' as an unequal relationship, whereas Wood and Kroger (1991) classify 'taxi driver and passenger' as an equal relationship. Similarly, Olshtain (1989) treats 'waiter/customer' as an unequal relationship, whereas Wood and Kroger (1991) classify it as an equal one. It is useful, therefore, to think a little more deeply about the meaning of 'power', and French and Raven's (1959) classic characterization of the five main bases of power is a useful starting point. They argue that there are five main bases of power:

1. reward power: if a person, A, has control over positive outcomes (such as bonus payments, improved job conditions) that another person, B, desires, A can be said to have reward power over B;

2. coercive power: if a person, A, has control over negative outcomes (such as demotion, allocation of undesirable tasks) that another person, B, wants to avoid, A can be said to have coercive power over B;
3. expert power: if a person, A, has some special knowledge or expertise that another person, B, wants or needs, A can be said to have expert power over B;
4. legitimate power: if a person, A, has the right (because of his/her role, status, or situational circumstances) to prescribe or expect certain things of another person, B, A can be said to have legitimate power over B;
5. referent power: if a person, B, admires another person, A, and wants to be like him/her in some respect, A can be said to have referent power over B.

Teachers typically have the first four of these types of power (and may have referent power too) in relation to their students, as do employers in relation to their employees. However, the role relations of waiters/customers and taxi drivers/passengers are more complex than this. From one perspective, customers and passengers have power (reward power and coercive power) over waiters/taxi drivers, in that they can choose whether or not to use the restaurant/taxi company again in future, and this may motivate the waiter/taxi driver to provide good service. On the other hand, from another perspective, waiters and taxi drivers have power (legitimate power and coercive power) over customers/passengers, in that they have the right to make certain demands, such as whether people should wait to be seated, or how many people can sit in the taxi, where the luggage should be placed, and so on. In fact, under special circumstance, they can even refuse to accept people's custom if they wish.

2.6.1.2 Distance

This variable also has a number of different labels: *distance, social distance, solidarity, closeness, familiarity, relational intimacy*. Brown and Gilman (1960/1972: 258) describe it as follows:

> Now we are concerned with a . . . set of relations which are symmetrical . . . Not every personal attribute counts in determining whether two people are solidary enough to use the mutual T.[4] Eye color does not ordinarily matter nor does shoe size. The similarities that matter seem to be those that make for like-mindedness or similar behavior dispositions. . . . The T of solidarity can be produced by frequency of contact as well as by objective similarities. However, frequent contact does not necessarily lead to the mutual T. It depends on whether contact results in the discovery or creation of the like-mindedness that seems to be the core of the solidarity semantic.

Most people have an intuitive understanding of what it means to have a 'close' or 'distant' relationship, but many different strands can be involved. For example, sometimes length of acquaintance seems important; we may classify a stranger, for instance, as distant from us, and a childhood friend as close. On the other hand, we may work with someone for many years, yet dislike them, and so regard them as distant from us.

Spencer-Oatey (1996: 7) lists the following possible components (which are often overlapping), based on a review of a range of pragmatic studies:

1. Social similarity/difference (e.g. Brown and Gilman 1960/1972)
2. Frequency of contact (e.g. Slugoski and Turnbull 1988)
3. Length of acquaintance (e.g. Slugoski and Turnbull 1988)
4. Familiarity, or how well people know each other (e.g. Holmes 1990)
5. Sense of like-mindedness (e.g. Brown and Gilman 1960/1972)
6. Positive/negative affect (e.g. Baxter 1984)

It has been suggested (Slugoski and Turnbull 1988; Brown and Gilman 1989) that *distance* and *affect* should be treated as separate parameters, since some research has indicated that *affect* has a separate and differential effect on language use from the influence of *distance*. Social psychological research (see Spencer-Oatey 1996 for a review) also indicates that *distance* may not be a unitary variable, but as yet there is no clear consensus in either field as to how, or whether, the variable should be split.

2.6.1.3 Interrelationship between power and distance

Thomas (1995) points out that it is sometimes difficult to distinguish between *power* and *distance*, and that in the Cross Cultural Speech Act Realization Project (CCSARP, reported in Blum-Kulka et al. 1989), the researchers did not maintain the distinction in practice. This is because in many cultures the two variables co-occur. However, this is not necessarily the case in all cultures. For example, Spencer-Oatey (1997), in research into British and Chinese conceptions of the tutor–postgraduate student relations, found that the variables *power* and *closeness* were significantly negatively correlated for the British respondents, but unrelated for the Chinese respondents. In other words, for the British respondents, the greater the degree of power difference perceived between tutors and postgraduate students, the greater the degree of distance perceived, and vice versa. For the Chinese respondents, on the other hand, there was no link between the two: the degree of power difference perceived between tutors and postgraduate students was not associated with the degree of distance perceived.

2.6.1.4 Number of participants

Another important feature relating to participants is the number of people taking part, either as addressors/addressees or as audience. Face-management norms seem to be 'number-sensitive', in that what we say and how we say it is often influenced by the number of people present, and whether they are all listening to what we say. For example, in many cultures, it is much more embarrassing and face-threatening to be criticized in front of one or more other people (for example, in front of a class of students) than to be criticized privately, on a one-to-one basis (for example, in the teacher's office, with no one else present). And similarly, it can be much more embarrassing to be praised in front of other people than to be praised privately, on a one-to-one basis.

2.6.2 Message content: cost–benefit considerations

Message content also has a major influence on the choice of rapport management strategies. Messages can have 'costs' associated with them. These costs are not necessarily financial (although they may be); they can be costs of time, effort, imposition, inconvenience, risk and so on. For example, asking a friend to drive you to the airport can be costly for the friend in terms of time, inconvenience, financial costs, effort and so on. And offering to help someone move house can be costly for the offerer in terms of time and effort. Needless to say, some messages are more 'costly' than others. For example, asking a next door neighbour for a lift home from a party you are both attending is less costly (in terms of imposition, effort and inconvenience) than asking him/her to make a special trip somewhere else. So normally this difference in the 'costs' associated with the request would result in different wording.

Conversely, messages can have 'benefits' associated with them. For example, offering to drive a friend to the airport can be beneficial to the friend in terms of time, convenience, financial costs and so on. And as Sifianou (1992b: 160) points out, customers' requests to shop assistants can be beneficial to both parties. Sometimes it may be difficult for a speaker to anticipate whether an addressee will interpret a message as 'costly' or 'beneficial'. For example, a guest may interpret the offer 'Have another sandwich!' as beneficial if s/he is hungry and likes the sandwiches, but as costly if s/he has indigestion and/or dislikes the sandwiches.

In the commercial world, costs lead to debts if the bills are not paid. In the world of social interaction, there is also a sense of indebtedness and a need for book balancing. For example, if someone does a favour for a friend, a slight disequilibrium results, with a greater favour leading to a greater imbalance. Similarly, if someone commits an offence, a disequilibrium results, with a greater offence leading to a greater imbalance. In both cases, balance needs to be restored, and apologies and expressions of gratitude are typical verbal ways respectively of restoring the equilibrium. Cost–benefit considerations in relationships (whether immediate or in the longer term) are so fundamental that, as explained in Section 2.2.2, they form a key component of the equity SIP.

2.6.3 Social/interactional roles

Social/interactional roles are a third set of factors that can influence the use of rapport management strategies. When people interact with each other, they often take up clearly defined social roles, such as teacher–student, employer–employee, friend–friend, sales assistant–customer, chairperson–committee member. These role relationships not only partially influence the power and distance of the relationship, but also help specify the rights and obligations of each role member. People have the right to expect certain things of the other member and an obligation to carry out certain other things. For example, a teacher has an obligation to handle classroom management issues, and a right to expect the students to comply with classroom management directives.

However, there are limits to the scope of teachers' and students' rights and obligations. Whereas it is acceptable for teachers to give directives such as 'Get into groups of four and work on this problem', it is less acceptable (at least in Western societies) to give more personally oriented directives such as 'Get me a cup of coffee'. The legitimacy of the directive, therefore, depends partly on the nature of the role relationship and partly on the specific content of the message.

2.6.4 Activity type

A fourth major factor that can influence the use of rapport management strategies is the type of communicative activity that is taking place; for example, a lecture, a job interview or a court trial.

Levinson (1979: 368) proposed the notion of an activity type, and defined it as follows:

> A fuzzy category whose focal members are goal-defined, socially constituted, bounded, events with *constraints* on participants, setting, and so on, but above all on the kinds of allowable contributions. Paradigm examples would be teaching, a job interview, a jural interrogation, a football game, a task in a workshop, a dinner party and so on.

Thomas (1995: 190–1) describes the key elements of activity types as follows:

Goals of the Participants: i.e. the goals of the individuals, rather than the goals of the event. The goals of one participant may be different from those of another.

Allowable Contributions: social or legal constraints on what can be communicated within a given type of activity.

Degree to which Gricean maxims (see Section 3.3.1 in this book) are adhered to or are suspended within a given type of activity, and expectations in relation to this.

Degree to which interpersonal maxims (see Section 2.7.1) are adhered to or are suspended within a given type of activity, and expectations in relation to this.

Turn-taking and topic control: the degree to which an individual can exploit turn-taking norms in order to control an interaction, establish his or her own agenda, etc.

Manipulation of pragmatic parameters: the degree to which an interactant can use language in order to increase/decrease social distance, power, rights and obligations and size of imposition, and the degree to which an individual can increase or decrease the formality of the situation.

Communicative activities often have *communicative genres* associated with them: 'historically and culturally specific conventions and ideals according to which speakers compose talk or texts and recipients interpret it'. (Günthner 2007: 129) These communicative genres may exhibit characteristic patterns in each of the five domains of rapport management (see Section 2.3), and their culturally specific conventions and ideals influence how participants compose and interpret talk. For instance, obtaining an appropriate balance between modesty and boasting is a recurrent communicative problem, but what counts as appropriate can vary from one activity type to another.

For example, in job interviews in Britain, candidates are typically expected to 'sell' themselves, but not to appear 'too' proud; yet at an awards ceremony, the person receiving the award (e.g. the actor, writer, etc.) is supposed to minimize his/her achievements and to give credit to others (e.g. the director, fellow actors, supportive wife, etc.).

Similarly, speaking rights and turn-taking can vary from one activity type to another. For example, in an interview in Britain, it is normally only the panel members who can ask questions, until they pass that right to the interviewee; on the other hand, at a dinner party there is much greater freedom over who can speak when, yet there are still conventions over the fine-tuning of turn-taking (e.g. the acceptability of overlaps).

2.6.5 Overall assessments of context

The contextual features discussed above can play both a 'standing' and a 'dynamic' role in influencing language use. In any interaction, we typically have pre-existing conceptions of these various contextual components, based on our relevant previous experience. For example, we have conceptions of the degree of power and distance of given role relationships and of specific personal relationships; we have conceptions of the scope of the rights and obligations of the people we are interacting with; and we have an understanding of the costs and benefits, face considerations and so on associated with certain speech acts. However, in the course of an interaction, assessment of these variables often change dynamically; for example, a person may be more distant and offhand than expected, or s/he may have differing conceptions of the role related rights and obligations. This will affect how the interaction proceeds. If the interaction is to be 'successful' in terms of rapport management, we need to incorporate effectively these 'dynamic' assessments of context in making our linguistic strategy choices and in co-constructing the interaction. However, at present we do not fully understand how this is done.

Brown and Levinson (1987) propose an additive model of these contextual variables, suggesting that speakers make an overall assessment of the amount of facework required by adding up the following: the amount of power difference between hearer and speaker, the amount of distance between speaker and hearer and the degree of imposition of the message. Holtgraves and Yang (1992: 252), on the other hand, suggest the following:

> When any of the three interpersonal variables reaches a particularly high level, the effects of the remaining variables lessen or drop out completely. For example, if an interactant has committed an extremely offensive act or intends to ask for an extremely large favour, he or she will be polite regardless of the closeness of the relationship with the other person.

Considerable further research is needed in this area to clarify such issues. Nevertheless, it is clear that in the course of an interaction people's initial conceptions interact with the dynamics of the interchange, both influencing and being influenced by the emerging discourse. If the interaction is to be 'successful' in terms of rapport management, participants need to be very sensitive to these complex processes.

2.7 Factors influencing strategy use: (3) Pragmatic principles and conventions

A fifth set of factors that play a key role in people's use of rapport management strategies are pragmatic principles and conventions. Leech (1983) and Thomas (1983) draw a distinction between sociopragmatics (the sociological interface of pragmatics) and pragmalinguistics (the more linguistic end of pragmatics). Both aspects can affect the ways in which people manage rapport.

2.7.1 Sociopragmatic principles

It seems that all societies have developed social principles or 'rules' which help to minimize the conflict that might arise from the self-centred pursuit and gratification of face needs and sociality rights. Leech (1983: 132) focuses on this component in his conceptualization of politeness, and specifies the following maxims:

1. TACT MAXIM (in impositives and commissives)
   a. Minimize cost to *other*
   b. Maximize benefit to *other*
2. GENEROSITY MAXIM (in impositives and commissives)
   a. Minimize benefit to *self*
   b. Maximize cost to *self*
3. APPROBATION MAXIM (in expressives and assertives)
   a. Minimize dispraise of *other*
   b. Maximize praise of *other*
4. MODESTY MAXIM (in expressives and assertives)
   a. Minimize praise of *self*
   b. Maximize dispraise of *self*
5. AGREEMENT MAXIM (in assertives)
   a. Minimize disagreement between *self* and *other*
   b. Maximize agreement between *self* and *other*
6. SYMPATHY MAXIM (in assertives)
   a. Minimize antipathy between *self* and *other*
   b. Maximize sympathy between *self* and *other*

A number of authors (e.g. Fraser 1990; Thomas 1995) have criticized Leech's formulation for not providing any motivated way of restricting the number of maxims. However, in a more recent version of his model, Leech (2005: 13) argues that 'these are not a set of distinct constraints or maxims, but rather variant manifestations of the same super-constraint, the GSP [Grand Strategy of Politeness]'. His GSP specifies that 'In order to be polite, S expresses or implies meanings which place a high value on what pertains to O or place a low value on what pertains to S' [S = self or speaker; O = other person(s), mainly the addressee] (2005: 12).

Ruhi (2006), however, criticizes Leech's approach for another reason – for grounding 'politeness' in consideration of the other and for downgrading the importance of self-politeness. She defines self-politeness as the display of self-confidence and/or individuality and, with the help of examples from her corpus of compliment responses, she demonstrates the complex interaction of consideration for both self and other in authentic interaction. Studies by Spencer-Oatey et al. (Chapter 5 in this book; Spencer-Oatey forthcoming) provide further empirical support for this. For effective rapport management, therefore, the concerns of both the self and other need to be taken into account by all parties.

In his updated model, Leech (2005, 2007) explains that he wishes to avoid the term 'maxim' because people could easily misconstrue this as implying some kind of moral obligation. He replaces it with the term 'constraint', to help clarify that in his view, it is a descriptive concept which refers to a regularity or a norm that speakers can be observed to follow in communicative interaction. However, in my rapport management model, I maintain that such norms frequently have prescriptive and proscriptive overtones for the participants, and may link with their beliefs and values. For example, the tact and generosity maxims/constraints are concerned with cost–benefit, and people frequently hold strong views as to how impositions and reciprocity 'should' or 'should not' be handled. Similarly, the modesty maxim/constraint is concerned with self-enhancement–self-effacement (cf. Section 2.4.3 on self-enhancement–self-effacement communication style), and people frequently develop strong views as to whether people 'should' or 'should not' boast or be very self-effacing in given contexts. When someone fails to uphold a given principle, others are likely to make evaluative judgements and this can sometimes have serious interactional consequences. (See Chapters 12 and 13 in this book for some authentic examples.) I believe it is important to incorporate this evaluative element into the model, because it is this element that makes the management of the 'norms' rapport-sensitive. I therefore label them value-laden norms sociopragmatic interactional *principles* (SIPs), in order to draw attention to their non-neutral quality.

In Section 2.2.1, I identified two high-level SIPs which feed into people's perceived sociality rights and obligations: equity (including principles associated with cost–benefit and autonomy–imposition) and association–dissociation (including principles associated with interactional involvement–detachment and affective involvement–detachment). In addition, people seem to hold lower-level principles regarding styles of interaction; for example, how warm, assertive or modest it is appropriate to be in a given context. These are reflected in people's choices of communication style (see Section 2.4.3). As Ruhi (2006: 96) rightly points out, people are likely to show individual variation in the principles that guide their (non-)linguistic behaviour and their style of relational work, and there may well be cultural variation in addition. More research is needed to explore these issues, including how and to what extent SIPs impact on interaction in different contexts.

2.7.2 Pragmalinguistic conventions

In addition to sociopragmatic principles, societies also have pragmalinguistic conventions which affect the management of rapport. These are the conventions of strategy use which affect how a given pragmatic meaning is conveyed in a given context. For instance, White (1997) reports the following example. When he was staying in a hotel in Korea, he went to the reception desk to report a fault with the telephone in his room and to ask for someone to come to collect his laundry. The clerk contacted the people responsible and then said to him, 'I think you had better wait in your room'. White comments that this choice of wording would, in a comparable British context, be used by someone with some authority or power to make a recommendation to someone in a subordinate position. Such a relationship does not apply to the hotel clerk–hotel guest role relationship, and so White felt it to be inappropriate. He suggests that more tentative wordings such as 'If you'd like to wait in your room, someone will be along shortly' or 'Perhaps you could wait in your room until someone comes from housekeeping' would sound more solicitous.

White points out that this is a question of pragmalinguistic competence. Pragmalinguistic failure (Thomas 1983) occurs when there is a mismatch between the linguistic form chosen by the speaker and the pragmatic meaning that they intend to convey. Further examples of pragmalinguistic conventions and failures (as well as sociopragmatic conventions and failures) are discussed in Chapter 7 in this book and illustrated in Table 7.1.

Each of the rapport management domains has pragmalinguistic conventions for conveying given pragmatic meanings in given contexts. For example, there are conventions regarding topic choice, the use of listener responses and amount of speaker overlap, the physical proximity of the interlocutors, to name just a few. All the conventions are context specific; in other words, for a given pragmatic message the conventions of strategy use are affected by the contextual factors discussed in Section 2.6. Much cross-cultural pragmatic research (e.g. the CCSARP project; see Blum-Kulka et al. 1989) has focused on identifying the pragmalinguistic norms associated with the performance of different speech acts in different languages/cultural groups.

2.8 Rapport management outcomes

Rapport management outcomes are similar in type to rapport management orientations. In other words, the degree of rapport between interlocutors can be enhanced, it can be maintained or it can be reduced. Goffman's (1963: 7) concept of 'negatively eventful' behaviour is useful here. Some types of behaviour (e.g. routine expression of thanks) may pass unperceived as an event when they are performed, but give rise to negative relational outcomes when they are not. Conversely, other types of behaviour (e.g. appropriate degree of unsolicited help given to a stranger) may pass unperceived as an event when they are *not* performed, but give rise to positive relational outcomes when they are.

Needless to say, the perceived relational outcomes of encounters do not always correspond to the initial orientations. Moreover, the perceived outcomes may be different for different interlocutors. There can be various reasons for this, one of which could be cultural differences in ways of managing rapport. (See Chapter 8 for an explanation in terms of Communication Accommodation Theory.)

2.9 Rapport management across cultures

Cultural differences in language use can have a major impact on people's assessments of appropriate language use, and hence rapport management outcomes. Variation can occur in at least the following aspects:

1. *Contextual assessment norms*: people from different cultural groups may assess contextual factors somewhat differently. For example, when assessing a role relationship such as teacher–student or employer–employee, people from different cultural groups may have differing expectations regarding the typical degree of power and distance, and/or rights and obligations associated with the role relationships. For example, as reported in Chapter 11, Japanese and American work colleagues were found sometimes to interpret the purpose of a meeting differently, because they held differing assumptions about their respective roles.
2. *Sociopragmatic principles*: people from different cultural groups may hold differing principles for managing rapport in given contexts. For example, some societies may value overt expressions of modesty in interactions with acquaintances and strangers, while others might prefer more 'honest' evaluations. Similarly, some societies may value explicit expression of opinions and accept more open disagreement among new acquaintances than other societies do. Chapter 10 reports differences between Chinese and German students in this respect.
3. *Pragmalinguistic conventions*: people from different cultural groups may have differing conventions for selecting strategies and interpreting their use in given contexts. For example, two cultural groups may agree that an apology is necessary in a given context (and that the offence is equally severe), but have different conventions for conveying it. For instance, people from one group may typically include an explanation, whereas people from another group may typically use acknowledgement of fault as a key component. Similarly, as pointed out in Chapter 11, 'let's think about it' (*kangaete okimashô*) functions as a formulaic preface to a negative assessment in Japanese, but has a more literal meaning in English.
4. *Fundamental cultural values*: research in cross-cultural psychology has identified a small number of universal dimensions of cultural values (see Chapter 1), and found that both ethnolinguistic groups and individuals differ from each other in terms of their mean location on each of these dimensions. More research is needed to explore how these dimensions relate to contextual assessment norms and sociopragmatic principles.

5. *Inventory of rapport management strategies*: every language has a very large inventory of rapport management strategies. Some of these occur in many languages (e.g. the T/V distinction – the distinction between a formal form of 'you' Vous and an informal, solidary form of 'you' Tu); others occur in certain languages but are virtually absent in the rest (e.g. honorific forms in Japanese which are virtually absent in European languages).

Part 2 of this book comprises empirical studies which investigate cultural similarities and differences in one or more of the above areas of differences. However, we cannot simply assume that any differences will necessarily affect the way language is used in intercultural encounters, and so Part 3 of the book provides some theoretical perspectives on this. Part 4 then reports empirical studies of intercultural interactions.

Much more research is still needed, though, on the various potential sources of variation and their interrelationships. Up to now, empirical cross-cultural pragmatic research has focused on investigating pragmalinguistic conventions, and more recently, contextual assessment norms; research in cross-cultural psychology and intercultural communication, on the other hand, has focused more on fundamental cultural values. What is now needed is a synthesis of the different perspectives.

KEY POINTS

1. Interactional rapport is affected by the management of three main factors: face sensitivities, sociality rights and obligations and interactional goals. When one or more of these factors is not handled effectively, rapport can be threatened.
2. Rapport management entails the effective handling of speech acts; however, it is not limited to that. Other 'domains', such as discourse, participation, stylistic and non-verbal, also play a crucial role.
3. A very large proportion of cross-cultural pragmatic research has focused on speech act strategies, and three elements have been found to be particularly important: the selection of speech act components, the degree of linguistic directness–indirectness and the type and amount of upgraders/downgraders.
4. People's choices of linguistic strategies sometimes cluster to portray different communication styles. Three dichotomous styles that are widely mentioned in the literature are associative expressiveness–restraint, directness–indirectness and self-enhancement–self-effacement.
5. Three main factors influence people's use of rapport management strategies: their rapport orientation, contextual variables (including the participants and their relations, message content, social/interactional roles, activity type) and pragmatic principles and conventions.
6. Both cultural and individual differences can occur in all aspects of rapport management, and so great mindfulness and sensitivity is needed.

DISCUSSION QUESTIONS

1. For each of the situations given below, consider the following issues:
   - Is the situation likely to affect interpersonal rapport – why/why not?

- Is the situation likely to be face-threatening to any of the participants, and if so, why?
- What type of face, sociality right and/or goal is primarily threatened or infringed?

  1.1. You are a secretary, and have recently started working for a new boss. One morning he storms into the office and shouts at you saying, 'Can't you take better minutes than this?'

  1.2. Three friends, Paul, Daniel and Matthew, go out for a meal together one evening. During the meal, Paul and Daniel spend nearly the whole time talking about a film that Matthew hasn't seen. Matthew is unable to join in the conversation, and any attempts to steer the conversation to a different topic are ignored.

  1.3. You are extremely busy with your work/studies at present, and need to work in the evenings and at the weekends to meet your deadlines. However, a good friend needs to decorate his/her new home, and asks you to help for two weekends.

2. During the next week, pay attention to every occasion when someone annoys or upsets you, and you feel offended or hurt in some way. Try to note down what they said or did, how you felt and why. Then try to relate your experiences and feelings to the concepts of face and sociality rights presented in this chapter.
3. Using the information given in Tables 2.2, 2.3 and 2.4, label the semantic components, the level of directness and the upgraders/downgraders used in the following requests.

   3.1. (Asking to borrow lecture notes) *Judith, could I please borrow your notes from the lecture yesterday because I missed it.*

   3.2. (Asking to borrow a car) *Hello Paul. Could I possibly borrow your car if you don't need it? My car has broken down. I promise I'll take good care of it.*

   3.3. (Asking a student to give his/her presentation a week earlier than scheduled) *I'm sorry to have to ask you this, but could you please do your presentation a week earlier than planned? I'm afraid I have to give all the marks in earlier than I expected.*

   3.4. (Asking a younger brother, who is watching TV, to go to the shop) *Phil, do me a favour and get these from the shops for me, will you?*

   3.5. (Asking a flatmate to hurry up and get out of the shower) Come on, get out of the bathroom. You've been in there too long. Don't be selfish.

4. Suppose you want to thank someone for doing something for you. Choose one variable from each list and work out what you would say or do in each situation and why.

Interlocutor	*Favour done for you*
1. close friend	(a) picked up your pen
2. mother	(b) cooked a special dinner for you

3. new neighbour (c) paid for your bus ticket
4. teacher/line manager (d) gave you a lift home

5. Look at the following true scenario, and discuss the questions that follow.
   A Puerto Rican woman, who had been living for many years in the United States, was visited by her father. During his stay, he helped her take care of her son (his grandson). When she thanked him for his help, he became angry and felt hurt. Her mother called her and said: 'How could you have been so thoughtless? You thanked your father. He was happy to take care of Johnnie. Have you forgotten how to behave? He's your father and he loves you. How could you be so cold – to thank him?' (From Eisenstein and Bodman 1993: 74)
   5.1. Why did the woman thank her father?
   5.2. Why were her father and mother offended?
   5.3. What would they have preferred her to say/not say?
   5.4. Try to describe the misunderstanding using the concepts given in Section 2.9.

Notes

1. And also other types of wording choices not dealt with here, such as the person orientation of requests (Can I borrow your car versus Can you lend me your car) and stress and intonation.
2. I am grateful to Vladimir Žegarac for his insights on this, and especially for his explanation and examples of pragmatic inferential directness–indirectness.
3. Compare Shimanoff's (1987, cited by Ting-Toomey and Cocroft 1994: 317) categories: face-honouring, face-compensating, face-neutral and face-threatening.
4. 'Mutual T' refers to an 'intimate' form of address. Many languages, such as French and German, require speakers to choose between two types of personal pronoun, according to the relationship between the participants.

Suggestions for further reading

Fraser, B. (1990) Perspectives on politeness. *Journal of Pragmatics*, 14: 219–36.

This article provides a useful summary of four key perspectives on politeness: the lay person's social norm view, the conversational-maxim view, the face-saving view and the conversational-contract view.

Holmes, Janet. (1995) *Women, Men and Politeness*. London: Longman.

This clearly written book discusses many different politeness strategies, particularly in relation to men's and women's use of them.

Kasper, G. (1990) Linguistic politeness: Current research issues. *Journal of Pragmatics*, 14: 193–218.

Kasper, G. (1996) Linguistic etiquette. In F. Coulmas (ed.) (1996) *Handbook of Sociolinguistics*. Oxford: Blackwell, 374–85.

These two papers discuss current issues and controversies within politeness theory, and are useful for those who want to start exploring the area in greater depth.

Scollon, R. and Scollon, S. W. (1995) *Intercultural Communication*. Oxford: Blackwell.

Chapters 2 and 3 provide a lively discussion of many of the issues discussed in this chapter.

Spencer-Oatey, H. and Franklin, P. (2009) *Intercultural Interaction. A Multidisciplinary Approach to Intercultural Communication*. Basingstoke: Palgrave Macmillan.

Chapter 5 uses rapport management theory to analyse in depth authentic examples of intercultural interaction.

Thomas, J. (1995) *Meaning in Interaction: An Introduction to Pragmatics*. London: Longman.

Chapters 5, 6 and 7 of this book provide an excellent account of many of the issues discussed in this chapter.

Watts, R. J. (2003) *Politeness*. Cambridge: Cambridge University Press.

This book presents a discursive analysis of politeness and face, and is useful for those who want to start exploring the area in greater depth.

3 Culture and Communication

Vladimir Žegarac

Chapter Outline

3.1 Introduction 48
3.2 Culture 49
3.3 Communication 52
3.4 Culture and communication 64
3.5 Conclusion 67
Key points 68
Discussion questions 69
Suggestions for further reading 70

3.1 Introduction

This chapter introduces some basic features of culture and communication and provides a brief outline of the interplay of cognitive and environmental factors in explaining cultural variation. I consider the implications of an analogy between cultures and epidemics for culture research and describe and illustrate the importance of two features of human cognition for explaining culture and communication: our capacity to form representations of representations, and, therefore, to think about our own or other people's thoughts (technically, the capacity to form metarepresentations) and our tendency to seek novel information which seems worth having (technically, the orientation of human cognition and communication towards relevant information). I try to show how these features provide the basis for a psychologically plausible account of the relation between communication and culture and a framework for analysing communicative interaction.

3.2 Culture

The concept 'culture' is rather intuitive. People generally have clear judgements about whether particular objects, behaviours, relationships and beliefs are cultural. At the same time, the word 'culture' is thought of as referring to something abstract that defies definition. As Kroeber and Kluckhohn (1952: 181) observe:

> Culture consists of patterns, explicit and implicit, of and for behavior acquired and transmitted by symbols, constituting the distinctive achievements of human groups, including their embodiments in artifacts; the essential core of culture consists of traditional (i.e. historically derived and selected) ideas and especially their attached values; culture systems may, on the one hand, be considered as products of action, and on the other as conditioning elements of further action.

This definition points to several important features of culture:

1. Culture does not consist only of physical objects.
2. Culture involves symbolic mental and physical (i.e. public) representations of the world.
3. Only those representations which are relatively stable and which form systems shared by the members of a social group are cultural. Therefore, culture distinguishes one social group from another.

To be sure, these are not the only important characteristics of culture, but they provide a good starting point for introducing this term and for explaining the importance of culture in communication.

Perhaps the clearest way to illustrate the observation that culture crucially involves the way we mentally represent and think about the world is to consider a simple example. Imagine that you are walking on a pebbly beach. Are the pebbles under and around your feet part of culture? Are they cultural things? Let us assume that a particular pebble catches your eye, say because of its shape and colour, and that you pick it up. You have formed a mental representation of this pebble and you may also have some affective representations relating to it (i.e. you like it, you would be sorry to lose it, etc.). This makes the pebble a prized possession, but I hope you will agree that the pebble is not really a cultural thing. It means something to you, but this meaning is not shared by the social-cultural group you consider yourself a member of, because the pebble does not have (even roughly) the same meaning for the group that it does for you. Now imagine that you put the pebble in your pocket, you take it home and spend some time thinking about what you could do with it. You might display it as a decorative object on the mantelpiece, you could use it as a paperweight or perhaps as a doorstop. Let us say that, having given this matter some thought, you have come to the conclusion that your pebble is best used as a paperweight (it seems too light to be an effective doorstop, and if used as a paperweight, it can be decorative and practical at the same time). Is your pebble-as-paperweight now a cultural thing? In a way, it is, because a paperweight is certainly an artefact, and artefacts are generally assumed to be cultural things. However, in another respect your pebble is not a cultural thing, because only you think of it as a paperweight. Now, let us assume that your flatmates also come to think of your pebble as a paperweight: they go to the beach, they collect similar pebbles and they start using them in the same way as you. One of them has the bright idea of setting up a stall at the market in his native town, which is much further inland, and to start selling pebbles-as-paperweights. Let us further assume that he is successful, that the idea has caught on: a relatively large number of people have come to think of pebbles of this shape and size as paperweights. In this event, both your pebble and other similar pebbles will have become cultural things. In sum, for pebble paperweights to become cultural things, several conditions needed to be met:

1. Certain things needed to be represented mentally, i.e. thought of, as pebbles (e.g. OOO are pebbles).
2. Some people needed to form some beliefs about these representations of those things (e.g. pebbles like OOO make good paperweights) and
3. These beliefs about pebbles like OOO as paperweights needed to be shared and presumed to be shared by a considerable number of people over a period of time.

This simple example shows how culture comes to include both the tangible, physical, things and why it also always has an intangible component. Culture can be characterized as a system of cultural representations. A cultural representation is a particular type of metarepresentation (i.e. representation of a representation). It is a belief (e.g. these pebbles are paperweights) about another mental representation (e.g. OOO are pebbles) which has become widespread across a human population over a significant time span (for detailed discussions on metarepresentations, see articles in Sperber 2000). It is important to note that both elements of a cultural representation may be intangible. For example, social relationships such as friendship or marriage involve beliefs about mutual rights and duties that those who enter into the relationship accept, and these differ significantly across cultures. From this perspective culture is a comparative, rather than a classificatory concept, because particular (types of) things can be more or less cultural. For example, the category 'pebble-paperweight' is more cultural if more people think of (particular types of) pebbles as paperweights and it is also more cultural if this belief persists over a longer time span (e.g. if it is passed on from generation to generation rather than being a short-lived fashion). Another important aspect of cultural categories is that they are not equally important. For example, practical artefacts, such as paperweights, do not interact with vital spheres of social life in the ways that systems of moral, religious or political beliefs do. The latter are intuitively more central parts of culture, because they inform many important decisions and plans people make, including those about what sorts of things are considered appropriate for use as decorative paperweights (e.g. in most cultures, a pebble or a small stone would be deemed more appropriate for this use than a human skull).

If this sketchy account of what makes a thing part of culture is along the right lines, then the study of culture appears to be similar to the study of epidemics. For instance, it is often observed that culture is both an individual and a social construct (see Matsumoto 1996: 18). There is no epidemic without diseased individuals, but the study of epidemics cannot be reduced to the study of individual pathology (see Sperber 1996: 56–76). By the same token, a culture cannot exist without some cultural representations being in the brains/minds of individuals, but it does not follow that the study of culture can be reduced to the study of individual psychology. Just as infections are in individual peoples' bodies, mental representations are in their minds/brains. And, just as the spreading of diseases is explained by investigating the interaction between strains of microorganisms with the environment that they live in, the distribution of cultural representations is explained in terms of communicative, as well as other types of, interaction between people and their environment. From this perspective, the boundaries of a given culture are not any sharper than those of a given epidemic. An epidemic involves a population with many individuals being afflicted to varying degrees by a particular strain of microorganisms over a continuous time span on a territory with fuzzy and unstable boundaries. And a culture involves a social group (such as a nation, ethnic group, profession, generation, etc.) whose members share (and presume that they share) similar cultural representations held by a significant proportion of the group's members. In other words, people are said to belong in the same culture to the extent that the set of their shared cultural representations is large. This characterization of a culture naturally accommodates the existence of multicultural nations, professions and so on. It also suggests a straightforward characterization of subculture in terms of a set of cultural representations within a given culture which are shared (mainly) by a subset of its members (e.g. an age group, members of particular professions and different social classes within a national or ethnic cultural group). Although the term 'a culture' is more often used to describe an ethnic group or a nation, there is no reason in principle why it should not equally be used to describe a professional or an age group.

The analogy between cultures and epidemics also provides an intuitive account for the observation that all members of a culture do not share all, and exactly the same, cultural representations. Just as an epidemic does not affect all individuals in an area to the same extent (typically, some people are more seriously afflicted by the disease than others), we should not expect all members of a culture to share all cultural representations. The 'epidemiological' perspective on culture suggests that it is cultural regularity, rather than cultural diversity, that should be surprising. Cultural variation occurs within the range of possibilities allowed by human cognition. For example, it seems that people in all cultures distinguish between right and wrong, so it is reasonable to assume that the moral faculty is biologically specified. Moreover, it seems that there are moral values which are universal. Thus, there is no culture in which it is considered morally acceptable to take the life of another human being. This may not seem true, as in most cultures humans often take human life. However, this is considered acceptable only in specific circumstances, and these need to be socially ratified (e.g. killing another person in self-defence where the person who has been attacked has used only justifiable force to protect their own life). Given that human populations live in different environments and have different histories, it is surprising that their cultures should share as many regularities as they do (for a detailed account of the epidemiological approach to culture, see Sperber 1996). From a cognitive perspective, research in the field of culture should focus on the causal links between biologically determined aspects of culture and culture-specific phenomena which are due to the interplay between the human cognitive make-up and various environmental factors. Social approaches to culture tend to focus more on describing cross-cultural differences and identifying their implications for intercultural interaction (e.g. rapport management in situations of intercultural communication, or adaptation to life in a foreign culture). The culture of a given group can be seen as a complex web of cultural representations relating to different types of regularities, or themes, such as the following (cf. Spencer-Oatey 2005 and Chapter 1 in this book):

- orientations to life and beliefs;
- values and principles;
- perceptions of role relationships, including rights and obligations associated with them;
- behavioural rituals, conventions and routines, which may involve the use of language;
- various norms and conventions of communication;
- institutions, which may be formal, such as the legal, political and educational system, or informal, such as a poetry reading group, a cocktail party or a knitting club.

Members of some cultural groups share more cultural representations relating to some regularities than to others. This observation has some interesting implications. To give but one example, it leads to predictions about the relative ease with which new or non-members are likely to be able to integrate into a group: other things being equal, the more similarities there are in the relevant types of regularity between the person's home culture and their host culture, the easier it will be for them to integrate into the host culture. For instance, if the home culture and the host culture share the same language and, possibly, also various culture-specific norms and conventions of communication, cultural adjustment should be easier.

3.3 Communication

A particularly important aspect of culture which has both universal and culture-specific characteristics is our communication system. This section looks at some universal characteristics of human communication and tries to show how they can be systematically related to cultural differences in the way the general mechanisms of communication are used. The following are the main features of human communication introduced in this section:

- Communication is a form of social interaction which involves the production and the interpretation of the evidence of the communicator's intentions.
- The interpretation of a communicative act is a reasoning process which takes as input the signal produced by the communicator and the context (assumptions drawn from the addressee's background general knowledge and immediate perceptual environment).
- The addressee's search for the right context is best explained on the view that communication is driven by a general principle and some culture specific, more or less standardized, strategies.
- Communication is made easier by the organization of the pool of general world knowledge from which the context is drawn into mental structures known as schemata, frames and scripts.
- These assumptions also provide the basis for a natural account of communicative (in)directness.

Our cognition tends to be oriented towards improving our general world knowledge (i.e. our belief system). This does not mean merely that people value novel information. Rather, we tend to value novel information independently of any other practical goals. This is a major difference between humans and other species, which tend to seek new information in response to immediate practical needs, such as finding food or shelter. Virtually everything that impinges on our senses is potentially informative, but we have limited cognitive resources (e.g. memory capacity and attention span), so we are constantly under pressure to decide what to pay attention to, and how much time and mental processing effort to invest into figuring out new information on the basis of the available evidence. In other words, our quest for novel information that is worth having is constrained by the need for cognitive efficiency. The efficiency measure which guides our quest for novel non-trivial information is technically called relevance. Relevance is defined as a positive function of novel information (technically, cognitive effects) and as a negative function of mental processing effort required for figuring out novel information on the basis of the available evidence. It should be clear that communication is a very powerful means of improving the world knowledge of those we communicate with as well as our own. In other words, communication boosts the chances of success of our cognitive system's quest for novel relevant information. Although we generally tend to pay attention to phenomena which seem relevant to us, there is no guarantee that what we have decided to pay attention to (by representing it mentally and integrating this representation with the context) will actually turn out to be relevant. In other words, there is no guarantee that the mental processing effort expended will turn out to have been well spent. (These are the main assumptions of the approach to human communication known as Relevance Theory. For a detailed account of this approach to communication, see Sperber and Wilson 1986/1995).

The difference between the general orientation of human cognition towards relevance and the role of relevance in human communication is clearly illustrated by ordinary real life situations such as the following:

(1) It is Sunday morning and you are in a part of town you do not know well. You are trying to find your way to the local market, which you know takes place on Sundays. You are not sure where the market is, but you know that it is not far from where you are. What sorts of things are likely to seem relevant to you in this situation? Answer: those which provide evidence about the market's location. For instance, you see some people in the street carrying the sorts of goods normally purchased on the market. You assume that they were purchased at the market and you pay attention to the direction from which most of the people carrying what looks like market shopping are coming from. You conclude that the market is that way and you walk in that direction.

The chances are that your guess was correct and that you will find your way to the market, but it is also possible that you were mistaken (say, the shopping the passers-by were carrying came from the local shopping centre). Let us now consider a slightly different scenario:

Upon seeing people carrying what looks like goods purchased at the local market you approach one of them and say: 'Excuse me, is this the way to the market?' while pointing in a particular direction. The passer-by replies: 'Yes, it's just round the corner after the traffic lights.'

You are now in possession of far more reliable information about the way to the market, than when you were basing your conclusions on the evidence which happened to be available in the environment (i.e. the sight of people coming from a particular direction with particular types of goods). It is more reliable because you do not have any reason to doubt the sincerity and the competence of the passer-by. Of course, the quality of their directions depends on their own knowledge of the local geography and their ability to communicate it clearly, as well as on their good intentions. However, if they deliberately mislead you, you will, intuitively, be justified in assuming that they were not communicating genuinely. Thus, if you follow the passer-by's instructions accurately and discover that they were not correct, you will assume either that the passer-by was sincere but not competent, or that he was competent but insincere for some reason (e.g. they might not want to be seen not to be unable to help, or they might, somewhat perversely, enjoy their power to deceive others). The important point here is that we intuitively feel entitled to assume that a person who engages in communication commits himself/herself to observing certain standards of social behaviour. This is an important difference between novel information obtained by communication and by relying on our general cognitive ability to seek relevant information. Communication is a social activity in which novel information comes from a helpful source, helpful in the sense that, by engaging in communication, communicators commit themselves to observing certain norms, for example that they are sincere and that they are giving only information which is worth having in the best way they can or that they consider appropriate. This commonsensical intuitive insight was the basis of the explanation of communication put forward in the mid-1960s by the Oxford philosopher Paul Herbert Grice (see Grice 1989: 22–40).

3.3.1 Grice's Co-operative Principle

Grice argued that human communication should be explained as a form of social interaction whose success depends on the interactants' presumption that communicative behaviour is driven by certain norms and rules. On his view, the most important of these norms is the generalization that communicators are co-operative in that they aim to make their communicative acts appropriate to the situation of communication in content and form:

The Co-operative Principle

Make your conversational contribution such as is required, at the stage at which it occurs, by the accepted purpose or direction of the talk exchange in which you are engaged.

On Grice's approach, the Co-operative Principle is generally observed by meeting specific criteria which he called the Maxims of Conversation:

Maxim of Quantity (informativeness)

1. Make your contribution as informative as is required (for the current purposes of the exchange).
2. Do not make your contribution more informative than is required.

Maxim of Quality (truthfulness)

Supermaxim: Try to make your contribution one that is true.
Submaxims:

1. Do not say what you believe to be false.
2. Do not say that for which you lack adequate evidence.

Maxim of Relation (relevance)

Be relevant

Maxim of Manner (style)

Supermaxim: Be perspicuous.
Submaxims:

1. Avoid obscurity of expression.
2. Avoid ambiguity.
3. Be brief (avoid unnecessary prolixity).
4. Be orderly.

The Co-operative Principle and the Maxims of Conversation purport to explain how it is possible to communicate more than 'what is said' (i.e. more than the thought directly expressed by the utterance). In other words, this approach explains the systematic dependence of meaning on context (where the context is the set of assumptions used in interpreting a communicative act). The basic idea is that if people who engage in communication presume that the Co-operative Principle and the Maxims of Conversation are observed, then it is possible to give an explicit, step-by-step account of the way the reasoning process involved in utterance comprehension takes the linguistic meaning of an utterance and the context as inputs and yields the interpretation as output.

3.3.2 Relevance Theory and the Communicative Principle of Relevance

Relevance Theory, which is the most important theoretical development of Grice's approach to communication, calls into question two general theoretical (and a number of more specific) assumptions of Grice's approach. First, the view that co-operation, understood in Grice's sense, is central to explaining how communication works seems implausible. According to Grice, co-operation presupposes a pre-established task on which the participants are working together. However, many, perhaps most, instances of communication do not fit this description. Communication often begins by introducing a topic, and topics often change in the course of (most interesting) conversations. Interesting conversations often do not have a specific goal or stable direction. Of course, a social disposition to be generally co-operative may well explain why we decide to engage in communication in some situations, say, when the information is purely in the interests of the addressee, rather than the communicator. For example, when a passer-by stops you saying: 'Excuse me, have you got the time?' the information requested is relevant to the passer-by, rather than to you. The only reason why you might decide to answer the question is some degree of a general human disposition to be co-operative. This general disposition to co-operate is very different from what Grice had in mind, and, though important in explaining social interaction, it is not specific enough to explain how people actually succeed in interpreting communicative acts and responding to them.

Second, Grice did not spell out the standards or measures which people who engage in communication use in order to decide whether and to what extent the communicator has observed the Maxims of Conversation. For example, it is not clear on what basis we make judgements about whether a particular utterance is optimally informative, relevant and brief. Relevance Theory (Sperber and Wilson 1986/95) characterizes explicitly Grice's Maxim of Relevance (Relation) as a design feature of human cognition and communication, rather than a norm. In Sperber and Wilson's framework, relevance is a property of inputs to cognitive processing. It is a cognitive efficiency measure defined as a positive function of novel information and a negative function of processing effort required for deriving this information. On this approach, human cognition tends to be oriented towards relevance, and this generalization is known as the Cognitive Principle of Relevance. The Cognitive Principle of Relevance is important in human communication for the following reason: a communicative act (such as an utterance or pointing gesture) makes it evident that the communicator intends to draw the audience's (hearers' or readers') attention to this act. An important consequence of the Cognitive Principle of Relevance for communication is that the communicator can be justified in evidently claiming the audience's attention only provided the effort involved in mentally representing the communicative act and mentally processing this representation will lead to enough novel information (technically, to enough cognitive effects) to warrant the mental processing effort expended in deriving this information. In other words, every act of (overt) communication makes evident a guarantee (technically, a presumption) that it is worth paying attention to. This generalization is known as the Communicative Principle of Relevance.

The Communicative Principle of Relevance

> Every act of overt communication communicates (i.e. makes evident) the presumption that it is optimally relevant.
> [Note: a communicative act is optimally relevant if processing it leads to some relevant cognitive effects without putting the audience to the expenditure of greater mental processing effort than is necessary for deriving those effects.]
>
> (Adapted from Sperber and Wilson 1995: 260–70)

Like Grice's approach, Relevance Theory views human communicative behaviour as co-operative. The Communicative Principle of Relevance can be seen as the criterion of co-operativeness. It follows from this principle that the communicator could be said to be co-operative to the extent that he is sincere in aiming at optimal relevance. This contrasts with Grice's Co-operative principle, according to which co-operation in communication involves contributing to the established topic or purpose of the communication event. In terms of Relevance Theory, violations of Grice's maxims of conversation can be described as different ways in which the utterance or other signal falls short of being optimally relevant. Consider again the asking-for-directions-to-the-market scenario:

> Upon seeing people carrying what looks like goods purchased at the local market you approach one of them and say: 'Excuse me, is this the way to the market?' while pointing in a particular direction. The passer-by replies:
>
> (a) 'Yes, it's just round the corner after the traffic lights'.
> (b) 'Yes, it's just round the corner after the traffic lights, and the National Gallery is at the other end of London'.

Both (a) and (b) give accurate directions but (b) is more complex and requires more processing effort without leading to any novel information which is relevant in the context of your question. Therefore, in this situation, answer (b) is less relevant than answer (a), although it is more informative. In Grice's terms, (b) violates the Maxim of Quantity (informativeness), because it gives more information than is required. This example shows that the Communicative Principle of Relevance makes it possible to characterize overinformativeness explicitly without positing a special Maxim of Informativeness (Quantity). The same type of explanation carries over to the Maxim of Quality (truthfulness). Accepting false assumptions as true will most likely lead you to make plans and carry out actions which will not fulfil your goals. Thus, if the passer-by has advised you to turn left at the traffic lights, whereas, the market is in fact on the right, his instructions will have been be less than optimally relevant to you, because they will have led you to form an assumption which is likely to interact with your other beliefs in a counterproductive way (by guiding you to go the wrong way). In other words, misinformation is not relevant because it does not make a positive contribution to our existing beliefs. Therefore, we do not need to posit a Maxim of Quality (truthfulness) to account for the observation that people generally expect communicators to be truthful.

Three further observations are important here. First, from the Relevance-theoretic perspective, the quality of an utterance is (partly) determined by the truth of the message which is communicated by that utterance, rather than by the truth of the utterance itself. Thus, metaphorical utterances (e.g. 'You are the sunshine of my life') do not violate the Communicative Principle of Relevance because, though false, they communicate something true (e.g. 'You are very dear to me', 'When I see you, I am happy', 'You make me feel optimistic about life', 'I could not live without you' and so on). Second, misinformation does not necessarily lead only to the formation of false beliefs which are detrimental to the addressee's general world knowledge. The expression 'white lie' denotes a deliberately communicated untruth whose integration with other beliefs leads to some cognitive effects worth having. For example, when encouraging somebody to complete a task the communicator may well deliberately convey something false (e.g. 'You can finish it in three days if you work hard.') while also genuinely communicating something true (e.g. 'The communicator believes that the hearer should not give up trying to complete the task', 'The hearer will complete the task successfully if they try hard,' 'Completing the task is more feasible than the hearer assumes'). Third, communicators often fall short of being optimally relevant for many different reasons, such as lack of concentration, poor awareness of the addressee's background knowledge and abilities, poor communication skills and many others. This does not go against the Communicative Principle of Relevance. What follows from this principle is that the addressee is entitled to expect that the communicator is aiming to be optimally relevant. That is why accidental failures to be optimally relevant are generally found more acceptable than deliberate ones (such as the manipulative withholding of relevant information).

3.3.3 The role of contextual knowledge in communication

Recent work in the theory of human communication has emphasized the role that general world (contextual) knowledge plays in determining the thought expressed by the utterance (see Carston 2002). The thought (or proposition) expressed by the utterance is a mental representation capable of being true or false, and thus specific enough for it to be possible to integrate it with other beliefs and to figure out the consequences for the belief system as a whole (i.e. to figure out the cognitive effects). The evidence from everyday conversation and other forms of communication strongly favours the view that contextual knowledge contributes to the thought expressed by the utterance (technically called the 'explicature'), and not just to the assumptions which follow from the thought expressed by the utterance and the context (technically called 'implicatures'). Consider (2):

Vlad: Can you play the twelve-string guitar?
Nic: It's the same.

By saying, 'Can you play the twelve-string guitar?', Vlad indicates that he expects Nic to give him some information relating to this question, and Vlad's ability to interpret Nic's answer correctly depends on his assumption that Nic is aiming to say something relevant in the context of his question. As the speaker, Nic bases his choice of words on his estimate of Vlad's background knowledge about him as an individual and about musical instruments. As the hearer, Vlad needs to figure out the best explanation about what Nic intends to convey by saying: 'It's the same'. Since he has the required contextual knowledge (that Nic can play the six-string guitar) and is aware of having requested information about Nic's ability to play the twelve-string guitar, Vlad is in a position to interpret Nic's utterance correctly, as expressing the thought: 'Playing the twelve-string guitar is (roughly) identical to playing the six-string guitar'. In the context of the assumption: 'Nic can play the six-string guitar', the thought expressed by his answer leads to further conclusions: 'Nic can play the twelve-string guitar', 'Nic did not need special training to learn how to play the twelve-string guitar', 'Nic probably does not play the twelve-string guitar as well as the six-string guitar' and probably others. So, in this situation, the less direct answer that Nic actually gave was more relevant than a more direct answer such as 'Yes' would have been, because it is more informative while not putting the hearer to the expenditure of significantly greater processing effort.

This example illustrates clearly two ways in which what is communicated by an utterance depends on the context and goes well beyond the meanings of the words used. A plausible explanation of context selection in communication also needs to address successfully the problem of 'mutual knowledge', which is well known in the philosophy of language (see Smith 1982). In a nutshell, the problem of mutual knowledge for explaining communication is that if communication depends on the participants' mutual knowledge (informally, 'presumed shared knowledge'), then it appears that communication could never take off the ground because establishing mutual knowledge involves infinite regress of inferences of the following type: the communicator knows that the addressee knows that the communicator knows that the addressee knows that the communicator knows, and so on, ad infinitum. Within the Relevance-theoretic approach to communication and cognition (Sperber and Wilson 1986, 1995), this problem is solved by assuming that the notion of knowledge, which involves actual mental representation, should be weakened and replaced by the notion of manifestness (of belief assumptions), which refers to the psychological disposition for mental representation. Sperber and Wilson argue that once we assume that people who engage in interaction are disposed to treat particular beliefs (including cultural beliefs) as mutual (i.e. presumed shared), the problem of infinite regress disappears. For a detailed discussion of their solution to the problem of mutual knowledge, see Sperber and Wilson (1986/95).

An interesting consequence of this approach is that communication – especially where it depends on culture-specific beliefs – is generally likely to be at risk of failure: if beliefs are presumed shared without being actually mentally represented, then incorrect estimates of what can and what cannot reliably be presumed shared are likely to occur. Consider (3):

(3) A British family had lived in an African country for several years. They had become familiar with the local language and culture. After the breakout of civil war in the region, they were forced to leave the country. Before leaving, they accepted the local peoples' offer of help and asked them to try and 'rescue' some of their 'special things'. Quite some time later, they were somewhat surprised to find that their TV set and video recorder were the main rescued items.

(Example contributed by Joy Caley)

The British participants incorrectly assessed the extent to which their cultural assumptions about objects considered special to their owners were salient (i.e. manifest and easily accessible) to their interlocutors. Of course, the participants in a communication event cannot establish with certainty which relevant contextual assumptions they share, but the chances of success in communication across cultural boundaries can be improved with appropriate attention to checking, establishing and maintaining the set of presumed shared (technically, mutually manifest) beliefs which are culture specific and are likely to be critical for communicative success.

3.3.4 Schema, frame and script

Selecting the context for the interpretation of an utterance from a mental knowledge database in the form of a random list of unrelated belief-assumptions would take a great deal of time and mental processing effort. However, communication (even when it involves reading texts at leisure) takes place over a fairly limited time span and people have finite cognitive resources which they need to (and tend to) use sparingly. Imagine the difficulty the hearer would face trying to make sense of an ordinary word such as 'university' in an utterance like (4) if various beliefs that we have about individuals, institutions and so on were scattered, as it were, in our minds:

(4) James: I am going to university in September.

Even if we know very little about the speaker (say, the speaker is 18 and has just passed his entrance examinations), we would most likely conclude with confidence that he is going to university in order to study, because the expression 'go to university' has been used often enough and long enough to acquire the conventional meaning: 'go to study at university'. Many other assumptions will also become very salient to us. These might include the following: 'James will, or at least, he intends to, spend several years as a university student', 'James will need to attend classes, do coursework and take examinations as part of his programme of university studies', 'James will obtain a degree qualification when/if he completes his programme of studies at university', 'James may be moving away from home' and so on. These and other assumptions are made almost instantly available to us on the basis of what we know about the meaning of the word 'university', the standardized meaning of the phrase 'go to university' and about young people of James' age and education (A levels [in the UK]).

It should also be noted that a slight change in our background knowledge may make a big difference to the way we interpret a communicative act. For example, if we know that James is 18 years old, but that he has failed all his entrance examinations, we may be puzzled by his utterance in (4). We might think that he is joking, or that he has applied for a non-degree course at university. If James intends to communicate that he will go to university without committing himself to all of these assumptions he should indicate this clearly (e.g. by saying: 'I am going to university to do an access course'), otherwise he will fail to be optimally relevant as his utterance will be unnecessarily difficult to interpret in the context available to the hearer who is left wondering what exactly James intends to do at university, given that he does not qualify for enrolling on a BA degree. This example illustrates the generally accepted view that knowledge is organized into mental structures called schemata (see Augustinos and Walker 1995; Ringland and Duce 1988). These structures may have fixed, stable contents, in which case they are called 'frames'. For example, the frame associated with the word 'car' includes the information that it has a steering wheel, an engine and so on. The knowledge associated with types of events is stored in mental structures called 'scripts'. For example, the scripts for 'going to a party' and 'taking part in a business meeting' include assumptions about the typical parts of these events and things involved in them.

Frames and scripts can be thought of as types of schemata. Since mental schemata are knowledge structures which provide the basis for forming expectations about new situations, they can be said to be theories that people have, systems of hypotheses which we expect are true. For example, our mental schema for the word 'university' includes our knowledge about who goes to university, why people go there, what student life at university is like and so on. When we hear the word 'university', our university schema is activated and all the assumptions which are stored in this format simultaneously become more salient to us, so we can readily represent them mentally and process them together with other assumptions which have also been drawn to our attention by the communicative act. In the context of our knowledge about specific circumstances relating to the speaker, for example James in (4) (say, he is 18 and has just passed his entrance examinations), the script associated with the expression 'going to university' will be activated. This script might include the following assumptions among others: 'university studies take several years to complete; they involve taking examinations, written assignments and, probably, other forms of assessment; studying at university involves living close to the university as well as attending lectures and other classes regularly'. In the context of these assumptions, James' utterance directly communicates the thought, roughly: 'James is going to the university to study for a degree'. When integrated with various assumptions made available by the 'going to university' script and, possibly, other sources, this thought will lead to further conclusions, such as: 'James will spend several years as a university student; after completing his programme of studies at university successfully, James will be awarded a university degree; James will need to move away from his hometown for the duration of his university studies; …'. These assumptions which follow from the thought expressed by the communicator's utterance and the context are said to be communicated indirectly (i.e. implicitly) and are called 'implicatures', while the thought expressed by the communicator's utterance is said to be communicated directly (i.e. explicitly) and is called the 'explicature'. The distinction between direct and indirect communication is important because most communicative acts of linguistic communication convey more than the thought expressed by the utterance.

3.3.5 Directness–indirectness in communication

Imagine that you are in a large room with a few friends. One of them gets up (without explanation) and starts walking. You readily assume that your friend is walking with some intention in mind: to open the door and go out of the room, or perhaps to open the window or in order to pick up something that he has spotted on the floor. It is only as your friend approaches the door or the window or whatever it is that happens to be lying on the floor, that you are in a position to assume confidently that he intends to open the door, or the window or to pick up the object. And when your friend lifts his or her hand towards, say, the door handle, you will be more or less certain that he intends to open the door. There are two points to be made here. First, the assumptions we make about other people's behaviour depend on the available evidence. If the door, the window and the object lying on the floor are to the same side of the room, and if your friend is still at a fair distance from them, you may well not have enough evidence to conclude what it is that your friend is trying to do. Your ability to draw conclusions about your friend's behaviour improves as his actions begin to provide more and more conclusive evidence about his intentions. Second, people generally tend to conceptualize other people's behaviour in terms of intentions. In the situation described here, we do not think of our friend's arms or his legs as having moved, we think of him intentionally moving them with some purpose in mind. Likewise, when we see two people facing each other and taking turns at making sounds, we will assume that they are engaged in an intentional form of behaviour: verbal communication, and we will make this assumption even if we do not understand a word of what we take to be the language in which they are presumably conversing.

These observations about the interpretation of behaviour in general carry over to the way acts of communication are understood. The more conclusively a communicative act supports a particular interpretation, the more strongly communicated the information in question is; and conversely: the poorer the evidence for a particular interpretation, the more weakly it is communicated. So, communicative strength can be defined as a positive function of the evidence for particular interpretations. When particular linguistic items are frequently used to perform a particular communicative strategy, they become conventionally associated with that strategy. For example, requests such as 'Can you…', 'Could you…' and a number of others are *conventional* indicators of polite behaviour. The speaker who uses one of these will be not be taken to have communicated anything very relevant about his or her politeness, but rather to have simply fulfilled a social convention (except, of course, when the speaker is well known for lacking good conversational manners, in which case even the observance of a social convention is sufficiently unusual to seem fairly relevant). Hence, conventionalization has a direct consequence for the study of indirectness: the more an expression is conventionalized as a marker of indirectness, the less weakly communicated the message will be. The reason for this should be quite clear: if an expression has become a conventional way for communicating, say, disagreement, then it will provide conclusive evidence that the speaker is in fact expressing disagreement with the hearer, and that he or she is observing a social norm of appropriate (polite) linguistic behaviour.

Although the distinction between (relatively) strongly and (relatively) weakly communicated assumptions is closely related to that between direct and indirect communication, the two should not be conflated. An assumption is said to be communicated directly if it is a part of the thought expressed by the meanings of the words used (technically called the 'explicature' of the utterance). For example the passer-by's reply in (1) communicates directly that the passer-by knows where the market is and that it is further from the place of communication than a particular set of traffic lights. The same utterance communicates indirectly that the market is open, that going to the market is likely to be worth the hearer's while and a few other assumptions (technically called 'implicatures'). The distinction between direct and indirect communication is also known as the distinction between explicit and implicit communication. Both the degree of indirectness and the degree of strength with which particular types of communicative acts (such as refusal, disagreements, criticisms and others) are expressed, depend on the extent to which the expression of the communicative act is conventionalized. As a general rule, the more the expression of a communicative act is conventionalized, the more directly the act is performed and the more strongly its meaning is communicated. However, while the degree of indirectness is determined by the number of contextual assumptions which must be supplied in deriving a particular implicature and the complexity of the reasoning process which leads to their derivation, the strength with which an implicature is communicated depends on how sure we can be about which premises it follows from and how reliable those premises are. Thus, a polite request beginning with 'Can you/Could you . . .' does not communicate 'request for action' very indirectly, because the only contextual assumption we may need for this interpretation is that 'Can/Could . . .' is used to make 'polite requests'. As this is a well-established social convention, there can be no doubt that a 'polite request' is also communicated strongly by utterances beginning 'Can/Could you ...'. But, in principle, the two distinctions are independent. This is important for analysing rapport management, because the strength with which an assumption is communicated may be more important than the degree of indirectness. Consider the following exchange (5):

(5) James: Do you want to watch the FA Cup Final with us in the pub?
Peter: I don't like pubs much, and I hate football.

In (5) Peter very strongly communicates that he does not want to watch the FA Cup Final in the pub, because his utterance provides conclusive evidence for this interpretation. Nevertheless, he communicates this rather indirectly, because the intended interpretation depends on a number of contextual assumptions (such as 'people don't choose to go to places they do not like', 'people do not watch on television events which they dislike intensely,' etc.).

3.4 Culture and communication

The degree of indirectness and strength is determined by the relation between the utterance and the context, and contextual knowledge is largely culture specific. This is an important way in which context provides the link between communication and other aspects of culture, which is illustrated in this section.

3.4.1 Culture and contextual knowledge

In many ordinary communicative exchanges, culture-specific knowledge plays a very important role. Consider the following exchange (6):

(6) Mary: Did you have a good trip to London?
Peter: Yes, but I forgot to pay the congestion charge.

Peter's ability to interpret Mary's answer depends on his knowledge about the 'congestion charge' which is rather culture specific: *it is a kind of tax that motorists driving cars have to pay when driving in the central area of London; anyone who has been driving within the congestion charge zone and fails to pay this charge by a particular time will be fined* and so on. Example (6) shows that the availability of the contextual assumptions required for the interpretation of a communicative act is largely culture specific. The more familiar communicators are with particular culture-specific belief-assumptions, the more they are at risk of failing to realize that these belief-assumptions may not be available to their interlocutors, which may lead to misinterpretation, as the situation described in (3), repeated as (7), illustrates:

(7) A British family had lived in an African country for several years. They had become familiar with the local language and culture. After the breakout of civil war in the region, they were forced to leave the country. Before leaving, they accepted the local peoples' offer of help and asked them to try and 'rescue' some of their 'special things'. Quite some time later, they were somewhat surprised to find that their TV set and video recorder were the main rescued items.

In this situation, the misunderstanding was not due to different assumptions about the linguistic meaning of the phrase 'our special things'. For both sets of participants, this phrase had the meaning, roughly: 'personal belongings which are particularly important to their owners'. The misunderstanding was caused by different cultural assumptions about the kinds of items likely to be considered prized personal possessions.

3.4.2 Culture and schemata

The concepts of 'mental schema/frame/script' are very important in analysing cross-cultural and intercultural communication issues. When a schema (frame or script) is presumed shared, its content need not be mentioned explicitly in communication. In situations of intercultural communication, this may be a problem, because it may be unclear whether and to what extent the relevant schemata (frames and scripts) are actually shared. Just as the members of many (though by no means all) different cultures have different languages, they may also have different schemata for the same or similar types of things or events. As the assumptions in mental schemata are typically very intuitive, they are not always easily available to consciousness. For example, if you want to find out what the content of the schema for 'university' or 'restaurant' is, you cannot simply ask people to tell you. Of course, they will be aware of many assumptions which are in their 'restaurant' or 'university' schema, but they may not be aware of some of these assumptions, typically those which are so central to the meaning of the word or phrase that the members of the culture take them for granted and treat them as inherent parts of the meaning of that word or phrase. To give but one example, Beekman and Callow (1974: 47) (cited in Gutt 1989: 80 and adapted below) describe how a biblical passage (in the Gospel of Mark) was mistranslated due to different cultural schemata associated with 'house' and 'roof':

(8) The biblical passage reports how four people lowered a paralysed man through an opening in the roof of a house in order to get him to Jesus. The translation into a local language was produced with the assistance of a local person who relied on his cultural schema for 'roof', which included the following assumptions, among others: roofs are thatched; roofs are very steep; it is not possible to walk on the roof of a house. In the context of these (and a few other) assumptions the local translator first misinterpreted, and then mistranslated, the lowering of the man through the roof as implying a miracle.

(Adapted from Gutt 1989: 80)

Because implicit beliefs are intuitive and not easily amenable to consciousness, they are hard to change, and may be radically different from consciously held beliefs, without those who hold them being aware of this. For example, if an intuitive belief is socially unacceptable (say, 'blonde women are dumb'), people who hold this belief may replace it consciously by a more socially acceptable and better evidenced assumption (say, 'there is no correlation between hair colour and intelligence'), while continuing to behave according to their old, intuitive stereotype ('blonde women are dumb'). Research into culture-specific knowledge often has to rely on observation and indirect evidence, precisely because direct self-reports of the members of a given social-cultural group generally reveal their explicit beliefs rather than their implicit beliefs. Yet is it their implicit beliefs that reflect their internalized values, inform their views and influence their actions.

Example (7) also shows that the regularities in the differences between cultures are largely differences between particular (types of) schemata. It is a clear illustration of miscommunication due to different cultural schemata associated with the concept of *valuables* (denoted by the phrase 'special things'). The speakers incorrectly presumed that their schema for the concept *valuables* was shared by their interlocutors. The exchange in (9) is another example which illustrates this point:

(9) Situation: A French person is at a restaurant. An Indian colleague arrives late. The French person does not know his Indian colleague well. He has tried to make a best guess about the type of drink the Indian person likes and has placed the order. The Indian colleague has arrived in the restaurant.

French person: I ordered wine for the table and ordered you a soft drink.
Indian person: Okay, I'll drink both.
French person: [surprised] Oh, good.

(Example contributed by Kate Berardo)

The French person's decision to order a soft drink for his Indian colleague is based on his schema for 'Indian person' which includes the assumption: 'Indian people do not drink alcohol because their religion prohibits it'. In the context of the assumption: 'My colleague is Indian', this schema, associated with 'Indian person', makes highly salient the hypothesis: 'My colleague does not drink alcohol', and this hypothesis is the basis for the French person's decision to order a soft drink for his Indian colleague. In light of the Indian participant's reply, the French participant will most likely revise his schema for 'Indian person'. He can do this in a superficial way, by forming the assumption like: 'Some Indian people drink alcohol'. However, this revision of his 'Indian person' schema would not be very useful, because it would include incompatible assumptions: 'The religion of Indian people prohibits drinking alcohol' and 'Some Indian people drink alcohol.' If a schema includes contradictory assumptions, then it is very likely that it will give rise to conflicting predictions in a given situation. For this reason, the French person will be better off if he revises his 'Indian person' schema by finding out more about the reasons why some Indian people drink alcohol, as this may be useful on similar future situations.

We could say that the French person in (9) made the mistake of acting on a stereotype of 'Indian person', which raises the question of the relation between schemata and stereotypes (see Hinton 2000 for a detailed account of stereotypes in the context of human cognition and culture). Essentially, stereotypes are schemata which, though very general, are held with great conviction, so they provide the basis for unwarranted predictions about members of the stereotyped category (which may be defined in terms of culture, race, profession, age, sex, religion, etc.). One important aspect of cross-cultural research is to describe and explain the similarities and the differences between cultures without stereotyping. Another goal is to uncover the differences between culture-specific schemata which are likely to have a significant impact on intercultural communication. Both of these endeavours are difficult. All research into culture involves generalizations about groups of people or sets of objects or activities. So, the important thing is to uncover generalizations which are warranted. As generalizations can often be based on small samples of category members, ensuring that these samples are representative, avoiding overgeneralizations and unwarranted generalizations, in general, are major challenges for such research.

3.5 Conclusion

In this chapter I have tried to show that, being part of culture, communication can be explained largely in terms of the same cognitive mechanisms as other cultural categories.

What distinguishes it from other cultural things is that it involves evidently informative behaviour which is presumed to be aimed at providing enough information worth having, without requiring more mental processing effort than is necessary for figuring out this information. On this view, the comprehension of a communicative act, such as an utterance or a gesture, is an inferential (i.e. reasoning) process which takes the communicative act and the context as inputs and yields the interpretation as output. Therefore, communicative success largely depends on the communicator's ability to assess which contextual assumptions are readily available to the addressee, and the addressee's ability to process the communicative act in the context intended by the communicator. Such assessments are not possible unless the participants can presume with some confidence that they share certain beliefs about each other, the situation of communication and the world. Clearly, the more confident the participants can be that they share many cultural beliefs, the more reliably and the more economically they can assess which contexts are available to them. In situations of intercultural communication the set of cultural beliefs which can be presumed shared by the participants is limited and it may be difficult to establish which beliefs are shared. As cultural beliefs are stored in the form of mental structures called schemata, rather than random lists of items, it is important that work in the field of intercultural communication should focus on cultural schemata.

KEY POINTS

1. Culture is a system of cultural representations. A cultural representation is a belief (e.g. these pebbles are paperweights) about another mental representation (e.g. OOO are pebbles) which has become widespread across a human population over a significant time span.
2. Communication is a form of social interaction which involves the production and the interpretation of the evidence of the communicator's intentions. The interpretation of a communicative act is a reasoning process which takes as input the signal produced by the communicator and the context (assumptions drawn from the addressee's background general knowledge and immediate perceptual environment).
3. Successful context selection in communication is explained by three factors:
   a. Communicative behaviour is guided by one general principle and various culture-specific norms and rules.
   b. The context is drawn from the presumed shared knowledge of the participants.
   c. The general world knowledge from which the context is drawn is organized into mental structures called schemata.
4. The smaller the shared knowledge of the participants is, the more difficulty they will have in communication. Communication between participants from different cultures is particularly at risk of failure because the shared knowledge of the participants is likely to be relatively small and because the participants cannot be sure what their shared knowledge is.
5. Research in the field of intercultural communication should focus on culture-specific schemata: what they have in common, how they differ, how they are learnt and how they can change.

DISCUSSION QUESTIONS

1. Taboo topics are generally avoided and talked about indirectly (usually, euphemistically). The choice of euphemisms is largely culture specific. For example, northern India is one of many cultures in which married women do not talk about sexual intercourse openly and directly, but it is one of the few cultures in which sexual intercourse is described by the use of words meaning 'converse' (*batchit*) and 'speak' (*bat karna*).

   Question: How can we explain this culture-specific association between the concepts of conversing/speaking and sexual intercourse?

   You may find the following additional information useful: in this culture there is a prohibition against women being seen by or talking to men to whom they are related in a particular way.

   Task: Try to find more examples of euphemisms which can be explained in terms of the local culture in which they are used (Lambert 2001).
2. Consider the following claim about communication:

   > 'All behaviour is communication, with message value, whether intended or conscious or not.'
   >
   > (Wilden 1987: 69)

   2.1. How plausible do you find this claim?

   2.2. Is this claim compatible with the view of communication outlined in this chapter?

   Answer these questions giving detailed reasons for your opinions.
3. The act of offering food to guests has different (indirect) meanings in various cultures. Describe how food is offered and accepted in different ways in two or more cultures explaining what you think are the indirect meanings of the offer of food in these cultures.
4. It is generally assumed that communication involves conveying assumptions which the communicator believes to be true. However, it is equally true that in many situations lying (telling so-called white lies) is considered preferable to telling the truth. The well-known anthropologist Clifford Geertz even argued that in Javanese culture, lying was the norm:

   > When we tell white lies, we have to justify them to ourselves ... we usually have to find some sort of reason for telling a lie. For the Javanese (especially the prijaji), it seems, in part anyway, to work the other way around: the burden of proof seems to be in the direction of justifying the truth. ... In general, polite Javanese avoid gratuitous truths.
   >
   > (Geertz 1960: 246)

4.1. Can you think of situations in your culture in which there is a conflict between politeness and truthfulness?
4.2. Describe these situations and explain how they are appropriately dealt with.
4.3. Compare your answers with those of people from other cultural backgrounds and identify the cultural differences and similarities that you have observed.

Suggestions for further reading

Duranti, A. (ed.) (2001) *Key Terms in Language and Culture*. Malden, MA: Blackwell Press.

Foley, W. A. (1997) *Anthropological Linguistics*. Oxford: Blackwell.

Hendry, J. and Watson, C. W. (2001) *An Anthropology of Indirect Communication*. London: Routledge.

Kramsch, C. (2001) *Language and Culture*. Oxford: Oxford University Press.

Part 2
Cross-Cultural Pragmatics: Empirical Studies

Editor's Introduction

In Chapters 1, 2 and 3, it was mentioned quite frequently that there are often differences between cultural groups in their normative pragmatic use of language. This section presents three empirical studies that report research findings in relation to this.

It will be useful to read these empirical chapters in conjunction with the theoretical frameworks presented in Chapters 1–3, as they provide concrete illustrations of many of the issues presented in a theoretical manner in these chapters. In addition, it will be useful to compare the data collection procedures used in these studies with the insights and research findings presented in Chapter 14, and to consider their data analysis procedures in the light of recommendations in Chapter 15. This means some 'skipping to and fro' in the book, but this is likely to be more helpful than simply reading the book sequentially.

Chapter 4, 'Apologies in Japanese and English', compares the apologizing behaviour of native speakers of Japanese, British English and Canadian English, both in terms of the strategies used and the situations requiring an apology. It questions the widely held stereotype that 'Japanese are always apologizing'. Chapter 5, 'British and Chinese Reactions to Compliment Responses', explores how British, Mainland Chinese and Hong Kong Chinese evaluate different types of compliment responses. It discusses how people's reactions relate to concerns about modesty, agreement, face and self-presentation, and whether there are cultural differences in the relative weighting of such concerns. Chapter 6, 'Interactional Work in Greek and German Telephone Conversations', moves beyond speech act analysis and examines the opening and closing sections of authentic Greek and German telephone conversations, comparing the preferences of the two groups for attending to the relationship aspect of communication.

Obviously these three studies can only touch on a very small proportion of different features and variables that affect rapport management, and they can only include a limited number of different languages and cultural groups. So Part 2 also contains a reading list, suggesting other comparative empirical studies that could be of interest to readers.

By the end of Part 2, readers should have a clear understanding of key concepts and issues associated with rapport management, and should be aware of various types of normative differences between cultural groups in how they handle relationship issues. However, cross-cultural (i.e. comparative) studies do not tell us how people will necessarily behave or react when they take part in intercultural interactions. Such studies provide useful 'baseline' data but, in analysing intercultural encounters, we need theoretical clarification of the factors that influence people's performance. Part 3, therefore, returns to theoretical issues.

4

Apologies in Japanese and English

Noriko Tanaka, Helen Spencer-Oatey and Ellen Cray

Chapter Outline

4.1 Introduction 73
4.2 Cross-cultural perspectives on apologies 74
4.3 Research procedure 77
4.4 Results 80
4.5 Discussion 85
4.6 Concluding comments 87
Key points 87
Discussion questions 88
Notes 88
Suggestions for further reading 89
Appendix 89

4.1 Introduction

It was 1986, and I (Tanaka) was in Canberra, experiencing my first long stay abroad. I had bought a desk lamp but, when I got back to my apartment, I found that it was broken. I returned to the store to exchange it, and the person at the desk simply said, 'I see. Do you want to exchange it?' I was shocked and felt insulted, because in Japan the person at the store would apologize profusely in such a situation. Later, an Australian told me that Australian people tend to regard it as the customer's fault, because the customer did not notice it was broken. I felt that this idea of 'customer responsibility' contrasted sharply with the Japanese belief that 'customers are gods'. Although I could understand that shop assistants cannot be held responsible for manufacturing defects, I felt that Japanese people would

> not *feel* this way, because their apologies are not only linked to a sense of personal responsibility, but also to a desire for a harmonious atmosphere.
>
> On another occasion, an Australian student drove into the car of one of my Japanese friends, causing some minor damage. The next day, my friend went to the Australian's house to discuss compensation, but she was not in. Although her parents were there, they did not express any apology for what their daughter had done. My Japanese friend was shocked and offended at their behaviour, feeling that Japanese parents would have apologized in that situation, and that the Australian parents were impolite and even insulting. However, discussing the incident with some Australian friends, I was told that the Australian parents' attitude was acceptable, because their daughter was an adult.

Incidents such as these point to possible cultural differences in so-called polite behaviour, and at the same time highlight the tendency for people to react emotionally to unexpected behaviour. If such incidents occur in an intercultural encounter, people may attribute them to 'cultural differences', especially if they offer support for previously held stereotypes. This chapter explores such issues with respect to apologizing behaviour in Japanese and English.

4.2 Cross-cultural perspectives on apologies

People in most cultures would probably agree that an apology is needed when an offence or violation of social norms has taken place. However, there may be differing opinions as to when we should apologize (what situations call for an apology), and how we should apologize (what semantic components are necessary for an adequate apology in a given context).

4.2.1 Apologies in Japanese and English: stereotypical conceptions

It seems that both Japanese and westerners hold similar stereotypical conceptions of apologizing behaviour in each other's cultures; namely, that Japanese apologize more frequently than native speakers of English, and that an apology in Japanese does not necessarily mean that the person is acknowledging a fault. Consider, for example, the following reports in the English-speaking media:

> (ABC News broadcaster reporting on a Japanese ice-skater, Midori Ito, who fell at the Olympics) 'I am sorry, I made a mistake', she said. No one questioned her sincerity, but apologies are almost automatic in Japan; every day, everywhere, everyone here says they are sorry. Apologizing is so much a part of Japanese culture that foreign executives who want to do business here now go to school to learn the techniques. But the instructor Eiichi Shiraishi

> admits 'saying you are sorry does not mean you have done something wrong. <*shazai no imi de, tsukau baai mo ari-masu keredomo*> [video-taped clip of Shiraishi speaking; interrupted before the utterance was completed; $there are some occasions we use it as an apology but we also$, Tanaka's translation]. [Broadcaster continues] I believe that in most cases the phrase "I'm sorry" or "sumimasen" is often used to be diplomatic. People here don't always mean that they are truly sorry, which brings up the question of the sincerity of Japan's recent apologies. Was Prime Minister Miyazawa really sorry when he apologized for questioning Americans' work ethic? A month ago, Japanese Prime Minister Miyazawa visited South Korea and said he was sorry that Korean women had been forced to provide sex for Japanese soldiers during World War II, but today the Japanese Foreign Ministry said there would be no compensation at all for those women.
>
> (ABC News, shown on *World News Tonight*, broadcast by NHK Tokyo, 20 February 1992)

Edward Pilkington, writing in the *Guardian* newspaper (Don't mention the war, 15 August 1995), comments how strange it is that Japan's war crimes cannot be laid to rest and he argues that this is fuelled by the country's seeming inability to issue an unambivalent apology (e.g. controversy over Japan's war crimes, and apologies for them, surfaced again in August 2006 and in March 2007). Pilkington points out that this is peculiar for a country that thrives on saying sorry, and he quotes Richard Bowring, Professor of Japanese at Cambridge University, on Japanese apologizing behaviour: 'In daily life the Japanese apologise every other sentence. They do it 50 times a minute – it's the way they oil society.'

An article in *The Times* newspaper (16 August 1995) on the fiftieth anniversary of the end of the Second World War states that the Japanese language has 'many forms of apology which present a bewildering pattern of complexity to anyone unfamiliar with Japan's culture.' Ten years later, a headline in the same newspaper (16 August 2005) reads 'Leader's apology about war gets lost in translation'. The journalist claims that the Japanese Prime Minister issued two statements to mark the sixtieth anniversary – one that said sorry and one that did not.

Japanese writers also seem to acknowledge such complexities and differences. Naotsuka (1980), for example, describes American apologizing behaviour (in comparison with Japanese) as follows:

> 'I am sorry' – guilty – take responsibility – compensation. Such a system prevents American people from saying 'sorry' as Japanese do. One attacks the other furiously. If not, the other takes advantage of his/her weakness. Being attacked, counterattack. That's their way.
>
> (Naotsuka 1980: 57, translated by Tanaka)

Sugimoto (1998: 254) compared the norms of apology as depicted in American and Japanese etiquette books and manuals and argues as follows:

> Etiquette books suggest that Japanese are expected to apologize for actions of a far greater number of people than are U.S. Americans. In U.S. American conduct manuals,

> people apologize only for their own mistakes, with the exception of women's apologizing for the mishaps of their spouses, young children or pets (. . .). By contrast, in Japanese conduct manuals, the readers are told to apologize for offenses committed by a greater range of people beyond themselves. In addition to examples of women's apologizing for the mishaps of their husbands (. . .), children (. . .), and pets (. . .), Japanese conduct manuals contain numerous examples of people apologizing for others' misconduct such as: (a) parents' apology for offenses committed by their adult children, in situations such as a car accident (. . .) or not keeping in touch with a former school teacher (. . .); (b) matchmakers' apology to one party for the delay in reply by the other party or for their rejection of the match (. . .) and (c) apology for recommendees' misconduct by those who recommended them for employment, when the recommendees quit the job or embezzled the company money.

Takahashi (2005) investigated American and Japanese students' opinions about apologies in criminal cases, and found that more Japanese students than American students believed the case would not be fully resolved without an apology from the offender. She concludes that Japan would be well suited to a restorative criminal justice system in which one-to-one apologies are used to help achieve a sense of justice.

However, there is often a disparity between people's beliefs and their behaviour. For example, as Sugimoto (1998: 251) points out in relation to her study, it cannot be inferred that people actually apologize according to the norms depicted in etiquette literature; rather, they are better seen as behavioural ideals for a dominant segment of the population. To find out how people actually apologize, we need to turn to linguistic studies.

4.2.2 Linguistic studies of Japanese and English apologies

A number of linguistic studies have explored cultural differences in apologizing behaviour; for example, Cohen and Olshtain (1981), Olshtain (1989), Vollmer and Olshtain (1989). A range of semantic components for performing apologies have been identified (see Table 2.2), and some differences in frequency of use of the various components have also been found. Several studies have focused on Japanese and English apologies (Barnlund and Yoshioka 1990; Tanaka 1991; Kotani 1997) and have found a number of differences between Japanese and English apologies.

Barnlund and Yoshioka (1990) devised a questionnaire containing 12 scenarios describing offences of varying degrees of severity (e.g. having an accident in a borrowed car and causing minor damage; having an accident in a borrowed car and seriously injuring someone). For each scenario, respondents were asked to select their preferred way of handling the situation from the following 12 options: not say or do anything, explain the situation, apologize ambiguously, apologize non-verbally, casually say 'sorry', act helpless, say directly 'I am very sorry', write a letter of apology, apologize directly in several ways and several times, offer to do something for the person, leave or resign a position and commit suicide. 120 Japanese university students and 120 American university students completed the questionnaire, and the researchers found both similarities and differences in the responses. For both groups, the most frequent overall choice was 'say directly "I am very sorry"' (28.7 per cent for the Japanese and 23.3 per cent for the Americans). For the Americans, though, the second-most frequent overall choice was 'explain the situation' (21.5 per cent for the Americans, 12.2 per cent for the Japanese), whereas for the Japanese it was 'do something for the other person' (21.1 per cent for the Japanese, 15.3 per cent for the Americans). On the basis of these questionnaire results and accompanying interview data, the authors claim 'the results indicate that Americans seem less comfortable in giving and receiving apologies and tend to prefer less direct and extreme forms of apologizing. The tendency to explain failure rather than admit to it may strike more deeply into the American psyche than it appears to do' (Barnlund and Yoshioka 1990: 204).

Tanaka (1991) used a discourse completion questionnaire (see Chapter 14) to explore apologies in Japanese and Australian English (ten university students for each). She found that participant relations (social distance and relative power) had a greater effect on Japanese apologizing behaviour than on English; and she also found that the Japanese respondents had a greater tendency to apologize for offences caused by other family members than Australian respondents did.

Kotani (1997) used in-depth interviews to explore Japanese university students' experiences of apologizing behaviour in the United States. She interviewed 15 Japanese students, and found that they did not consider it appropriate to offer lengthy explanations in apologies, irrespective of whether the person was at fault or not. They also tended to expect their apologies to be reciprocated or denied by others, rather than be accepted as an admission of responsibility. It would be interesting to carry out a similar study with American students.

All of these studies have identified some differences in apologizing behaviour in Japanese and English. However, some of them have research procedure weaknesses (e.g. Barnlund and Yoshioka (1990) only allowed respondents to choose one option when in reality people might use more than one, and Tanaka (1991) only used a very small number of respondents). So there is clearly a need for much more empirical research in this area. This study is an attempt to add to our understanding of apologizing behaviour in Japanese, British English and Canadian English, focusing on the effect of 'personal fault'. We decided to focus on this factor since little linguistic research has been done on this to date, and since the stereotype of Japanese and Western apologizing behaviour suggests that Japanese are more willing to apologize when they are not at fault than westerners are.

4.3 Research procedure

A production questionnaire with accompanying rating scales (see the appendix) was used to explore the issue. This enabled us to obtain comparable data in Japan, Britain and Canada. Naturally we cannot be sure that people's responses in authentic situations would necessarily be the same as those given in the questionnaire. Nevertheless, a questionnaire of this kind can act as a useful starting point for further more authentic research, and, as Beebe and Cummings (1996) found, can model the 'canonical shape' of authentic responses.

4.3.1 Design of the questionnaire

The questionnaire comprised eight scenarios, all of which contained a similar complaint against the respondent. Since we were interested in finding out whether people apologize in situations where 'guilt' and 'responsibility' are in doubt, we decided to omit scenarios in which the accused person is clearly responsible for the offence. So for half of the scenarios, responsibility for the offence lay mainly with the person who was making the complaint (henceforth, CP scenarios); for the other half, responsibility for the offence lay mainly with a third party or with external circumstances (henceforth, EC scenarios). This resulted in four pairs of scenarios, in which the offence was kept constant (a late arrival of 30 minutes), but the participant relations were varied across the pairs. The order in which the scenarios were presented was randomized. The research design is shown in Table 4.1. (See the appendix for the exact scenarios used.)

For the first two pairs, the complaint was against the respondent personally (the student and the friend respectively); for the second two pairs, the complaint was against a 'relevant party' to the respondent (the respondent's employing company and the respondent's father respectively). We hoped in this way to probe people's sense of corporate (non-)responsibility, as well as personal (non-)responsibility.

Respondents were asked to respond to a first-pair prompt by writing the exact words they thought they would use in reply. In addition, they were asked to provide some contextual assessments of the scenarios: how annoying they thought the problem was for the person complaining; how far they felt responsible for the problem occurring; and how important they felt it was to placate the person complaining. These were included so that we could check whether the different groups of respondents perceived the scenarios in similar ways. Three 5-point Likert-type rating scales were thus listed under each scenario, and respondents were asked to circle the numbers on these scales that corresponded to their evaluations.

Japanese and English versions of the questionnaire were produced using backtranslation and the decentring process suggested by Brislin (1976; see also the glossary entries in this book). This was to ensure that the scenarios and the rating scales were not only equivalent in meaning for speakers of Japanese, British English and Canadian English, but also culturally appropriate for them all.

Table 4.1 Design of the questionnaire scenarios

	Complaining person mainly responsible for the problem (CP scenarios)	Third party/external circumstances mainly responsible for the problem (EC scenarios)
[Complaining] Lecturer – [Responding] Student **(Scenario 5)**	✓	
[Complaining] Lecturer – [Responding] Student **(Scenario 3)**		✓
[Complaining] Friend – [Responding] Friend **(Scenario 2)**	✓	
[Complaining] Friend – [Responding] Friend **(Scenario 8)**		✓
[Complaining] Customer – [Responding] Company Employee **(Scenario 4)**	✓	
[Complaining] Customer – [Responding] Company Employee **(Scenario 7)**		✓
[Complaining] Father's boss – [Responding] Son/Daughter **(Scenario 1)**	✓	
[Complaining] Father's boss – [Responding] Son/Daughter **(Scenario 6)**		✓

4.3.2 The respondents

The questionnaires were completed by undergraduate university students in Japan, Britain and Canada.[1] They were distributed in class, and filled in immediately. In Britain and Canada, only students who identified their main home language as English as well as their nationality as British or Canadian respectively were included in the sample. The numbers of students who completed the questionnaires were as follows: 131 Japanese, 165 British and 96 Canadian. There were slightly more male than female respondents in Japan and Britain (65 per cent and 54 per cent males respectively), and almost equal proportions in Canada (48 per cent males). In all three countries, 89 per cent or more of the respondents were aged between 17 and 24.

4.4 Results

4.4.1 Contextual assessments

The three groups of respondents' mean ratings (and standard deviations) of the CP and EC scenarios (averaged across the four situations) are shown in Table 4.2.

As can be seen in Table 4.2, all three groups of respondents rated both the CP and EC scenarios as 'annoying' to the person complaining. There was a tendency for the Japanese respondents to rate them as slightly less annoying than the British and Canadian respondents did, and for both CP and EC scenarios, ANOVA tests showed this difference to be statistically significant (Annoying, CP: $F = 5.19$, $df = 2$, $p = 0.001$; Annoying, EC: $F = 7.21$, $df = 2$, $p = 0.006$). However, β^2 figures show that only 2.6 per cent and 3.8 per cent respectively of the variance is attributable to nationality, which indicates that the statistical differences are not meaningful, and that all three nationality groups perceived the scenarios to be similarly annoying to the person complaining.

In terms of responsibility, all three groups of respondents rated themselves as 'not very responsible' for the problems described in the scenarios, although the mean ratings for EC scenarios were slightly higher than for CP scenarios (see Table 4.2). ANOVA tests showed that nationality had no statistically significant effect on the ratings of CP scenarios (Responsibility, CP: $F = 0.79$, $df = 2$, $p = 0.46$), but had a slight but non-meaningful effect on the ratings of EC scenarios (Responsibility, EC: $F = 3.36$,

Table 4.2 Mean ratings (and standard deviations) of contextual assessment factors in the scenarios

	Japanese	British	Canadian
'Annoying': CP	3.94 (.88)	4.09 (.57)	4.23 (.47)
'Annoying': EC	4.07 (1.00)	4.35 (.63)	4.41 (.47)
'Responsible': CP	1.99 (.61)	1.96 (.65)	1.89 (.58)
'Responsible': EC	2.42 (.66)	2.25 (.64)	2.44 (.65)
'Make less annoyed': CP	3.11 (.80)	3.84 (.74)	3.69 (.68)
'Make less annoyed': EC	3.71 (.80)	3.85 (.83)	4.02 (.68)

Note: Ratings are based on a 5-point Likert-type scale from 1 (*not at all annoying/responsible/important*) to 5 (*very annoying, responsible/important*).

df = 2, $p = 0.04$, $\beta^2 = 0.018$). These findings thus confirm that all three groups of respondents regarded themselves as not being responsible for the problems that occurred, and that their perceptions were similar.

In terms of the importance of 'making the person less annoyed', all three groups of respondents rated this as 'important' for EC scenarios, with the Canadian respondents giving the highest ratings. An ANOVA test showed that there was a slightly significant difference in ratings across the nationality groups (Make less annoyed, EC: F = 4.34, df = 2, $p = 0.014$, $\beta^2 = 0.023$), but since only 2.3 per cent of the variance was attributable to nationality, this is not a meaningful difference. For the CP scenarios, British and Canadian respondents rated these as more important to 'make the person less annoyed' than the Japanese respondents did. An ANOVA test showed that nationality had a very statistically significant effect on these ratings (Make less annoyed, CP: F = 35.29, df = 2, $p < 0.001$, $\beta^2 = 0.157$), and that 15.7 per cent of the variance is attributable to nationality, indicating that this is a fairly meaningful difference. Comparing the EC and CP scenario ratings for the importance of 'making the person less annoyed', there was a bigger drop in the ratings for the Japanese and Canadian respondents than for the British respondents. Paired-sample *t*-tests showed that 'source of responsibility' had a significant effect on both Japanese ($t = -9.15$, df = 122, $p < 0.0001$) and Canadian ($t = -5.27$, df = 95, $p < 0.001$) ratings of the importance of 'making the person less annoyed', but not for the British respondents ($t = -1.01$, df = 139, $p = 0.31$). This indicates that to the Japanese, and to a lesser extent the Canadians, the importance of placating the complainant depended on who was responsible for the offence. For the British the source of responsibility had no significant effect on the felt need to placate.

In this study, therefore, all three groups of respondents had basically similar perceptions of the CP and EC scenarios in terms of 'annoyance' and 'personal responsibility'. They were also fairly similar for the EC scenarios in terms of 'importance of making the person less annoyed'. However, for the CP scenarios, the effect of nationality was greater, with Japanese respondents judging it to be significantly less important to placate the person than the British and Canadian respondents did.

4.4.2 Production responses

The production responses given by the three groups of respondents were analysed for the semantic components that they contained. The CCSARP coding scheme (Blum-Kulka et al. 1989) was used as the starting point for the analysis; however, we found that we needed to make some minor modifications to it, particularly in respect to the strategies *Taking on Responsibility* and *Explanation or Account*. It seemed that 'Responsibility' formed a continuum from 'clear acceptance of responsibility' at one end, through 'indeterminate responsibility' in the middle, to 'clear rejection of responsibility' at the other end. Sometimes, an explanation or account seemed to be neutral in terms of responsibility (e.g. Scenario 1, *He's gone for a health check*); but at other times it seemed to be a strategy for minimizing responsibility (e.g. Scenario 3, *I met another lecturer and I couldn't get away from him.*) So we decided not to use *Explanation or Account* as a separate category. Instead, we used 'Responsibility' as a main category, with three principal subcategories: admission of responsibility, indeterminate responsibility and rejection of responsibility.[2] Many respondents used a number of strategies in relation to responsibility; however, for the purpose of this analysis, we looked at the overall thrust of the responsibility comment(s) and gave just one coding. If the respondent clearly admitted responsibility, we classified it as 'admission of responsibility'; if the respondent clearly rejected responsibility, such as by denying fault or referring to an agreement, we classified it as 'rejection of responsibility'; and if s/he gave a more ambiguous response in terms of responsibility, such as by simply giving an explanation, by referring to some kind of misunderstanding, or by stating what s/he thought had been agreed, we classified it as 'indeterminate responsibility'. Sometimes it was difficult to categorize the responses in this way, but in most cases there was no problem.

For *Offer of Repair*, we broadened this category to include not only offers of repair or help, but all comments that functioned to 'manage the problem or offence' in some way; for example, comments of reassurance, task-oriented remarks and so on.

The following categories were thus used in this analysis:[3]

1. IFID (Illocutionary Force Indicating Device) examples
   - *I'm sorry for the misunderstanding.*
   - *I apologize for being late.*
   - *Mooshiwake gozaimasen*. [$I apologize.]
   - *Okurete sumimasen*. [$I'm sorry for being late.]
2. Responsibility
   2.1. Admission of Responsibility examples
   - *I thought we agreed to meet at half two. I must have misunderstood.*
   - *I got caught up in a discussion with another prof. My fault completely.*
   - *Kochira no techigai desu*. [$That's our fault.]
   - *Watashi no kikichigai deshita*. [$I misunderstood.]

   2.2. Indeterminate Responsibility examples
   - *I heard him mention that he has his annual health check up today, so I think he's still there.*
   - *That's strange sir. It says here that it was to be delivered tomorrow morning. There must have been some sort of misunderstanding.*
   - *Chichi wa kenkoo-shindan ni dekakete iru to omoimasu*. [$I think my father went for the health check.]
   - *Ekimaette yuu yakusoku ja nakattakke*? [$Didn't we agree to meet in front of the station?]

   2.3. Rejection of Responsibility examples
   - *Last week I overheard him telling you that he had a doctor's appointment today.*
   - *Actually sir, you signed for the goods to be delivered tomorrow.*

- *Yakusoku shita toori ekimae de matteta yo*. [$I was waiting in front of the station as we had agreed.]
- *Okurete masen yo. Niji-han ni au yakusoku desukara*. [$I'm not late. We agreed to meet at 2:30.]

2.4. Other Responsibility-related comment examples

- *I'll explain on the way.*
- *I'm afraid I don't know.*
- *Dokoe ittaka wakarimasen*. [$I don't know where he is.]

3. Manage Problem examples

- *I'll take a message so that I can pass it on to him*. (Offer of help/repair)
- *Nanika wakarimashitara renraku itashimasu*. [$I'll let you know if I get some information.] (Offer of help/repair)
- *I'll see if I can get them to deliver it this afternoon*. (Offer of help/repair)
- *Hirugohan ogoru kara yurushite*. [$I'll buy you lunch, so forgive me.] (Offer of help/repair)
- *We'll not be able to deliver the goods now until tomorrow*. (Refuse repair)
- *I'm sure he'll be there soon*! (Reassure)
- *Mamonaku tsuku to omoimasu*. [$It will get there soon.] (Reassure)
- *You can try and call him on his mobile*. (Make a suggestion)
- *Let's get going or we'll miss the concert*. (Task-oriented comment)
- *Tonikaku isogoo*. [$Let's hurry anyway.] (Task-oriented comment)

Table 4.3 shows the percentage of production responses that contained each of these strategies. For the main categories, *IFID*, *Responsibility* and *Manage Problem*, the figures show the percentage of responses that contained one or more phrases with these codings (i.e. in contrast with the percentage of responses that did not include any phrases with these codings).[4] The subcategories of *Responsibility* and *Manage Problem* were analysed as mutually exclusive categories, as explained above.

As can be seen in Table 4.3, the responses produced by all three groups of respondents contained a very high percentage of 'Responsibility' comments; and for the CP scenarios, the proportion of responses that explicitly rejected responsibility (typically, by pointing out how the person who was complaining was to blame) was also very similar across the three nationality groups.

In terms of use of IFIDs, the percentages of responses containing at least one IFID were very similar across the three nationality groups for the EC scenarios, but showed a significant difference for the CP scenarios. Chi square tests confirmed that nationality had no significant effect for EC scenarios ($\chi^2 = 5.03$, df = 2, $p > 0.05$), but did have a significant effect for CP scenarios ($\chi^2 = 49.41$, df = 2, $p < 0.001$). Looking at the use of IFIDs in CP scenarios compared with EC scenarios, it can be seen that for all three nationality groups the percentage of responses containing at least one IFID was lower for the CP scenarios than for the EC scenarios. However, the size of the drop varied across the three nationalities: it was smallest for the British respondents (16.26 per cent)

Table 4.3 Percentages of production responses containing different types of semantic components

	Complaining person mainly responsible for the problem (CP scenarios)			Third party/external circumstances mainly responsible for the problem (EC scenarios)		
	Japanese	British	Canadian	Japanese	British	Canadian
Total number of responses	521	642	384	514	584	384
Percentage of responses with IFID coding	**21.88**	**41.28**	**34.64**	**64.01**	**57.54**	**59.12**
Responsibility						
Admit (%)	4.22	2.49	3.13	1.95	1.37	1.30
Indeterminate (%)	51.25	47.51	57.29	90.08	88.01	91.15
Reject (%)	33.78	37.85	32.55	0.78	4.80	3.91
Other (%)	4.42	5.76	3.38	—	1.71	1.56
Percentage of responses with responsibility coding	**93.67**	**93.61**	**96.35**	**92.81**	**95.89**	**97.92**
Manage problem						
Refuse repair (%)	0.77	0.93	0.52	—	—	0.78
Offer help/repair (%)	4.41	13.24	19.01	2.53	5.48	10.68
Reassure (%)	0.96	6.39	5.21	7.98	13.36	19.79
Suggest (%)	4.22	1.56	0.52	8.17	0.86	0.52
Task-oriented (%)	0.77	4.67	3.91	—	5.31	9.64
Percentage of responses with manage problem coding	**11.13**	**26.79**	**29.17**	**18.68**	**25.00**	**41.41**

and highest for the Japanese (42.13 per cent). This is broadly in line with the differences in the EC and CP 'make less annoyed' ratings shown in Table 4.2.

With regard to 'Manage Problem', there were also some clear nationality differences. For the EC scenarios, they were much more frequent in the Canadian responses than in either the British or the Japanese responses, with the Japanese showing the lowest percentage frequency of use. For the CP scenarios, a similar pattern was found, although the gap between the British and Canadian percentage frequency of use was smaller than for the EC scenarios. Once again, chi square tests showed nationality to have a significant effect (EC scenarios: $\chi^2 = 59.60$, df = 2, $p < 0.001$; CP scenarios: $\chi^2 = 55.73$, df = 2, $p < 0.001$).

4.5 Discussion

These results do not fit in with either Western or Japanese conceptions of Japanese versus English apologizing behaviour. Overall, the Japanese did not apologize (in terms of use of IFIDs) significantly more frequently than the British or Canadian respondents, and when the person who was complaining was at fault, the Japanese respondents actually apologized very much *less* frequently than either the British or Canadian respondents. Subsequent research has offered some support for Japanese reluctance to apologize when the other person is at fault. For example, Abe and Ohama (2006) explored Chinese and Japanese apologizing behaviour, and report that their Japanese informants tended not to apologize when the complaining person was at fault. Oka (2006) used a modified version of our questionnaire to compare the apologizing behaviour of Japanese sign language users and hearing Japanese. Her results showed that sign language users assessed the CP scenarios as slightly less annoying and as needing less repair than the hearing Japanese, and they apologized less frequently in CP scenarios, clearly rejecting their responsibility. Both these more recent studies add further evidence for the inaccuracy of the traditional stereotype that Japanese apologize very frequently, even when they are not responsible for the fault. What, then, might explain such findings?

4.5.1 'Sumimasen' versus 'I'm sorry'

One possibility is that people's stereotypical conceptions of the apologizing behaviour of Japanese compared with that of English speakers are inaccurate. English speakers might think that Japanese apologize more frequently than they really do because '*sumimasen*' is used so frequently. *Sumimasen* can be translated as 'I'm sorry' and be used for an apology; however, it can also be used for various others purposes. Ide (1998), for example, identifies seven different functions of *sumimasen*, after observing how it was used authentically in a clinic in Tokyo. She found that in addition to it being used to convey sincere apologies, *sumimasen* was also used to express thanks, to convey a mixture of thanks and apologies, as a preliminary to a request, as an attention-getter, as a leave-taking device and more ritualistically (i.e. with little semantic content) as a device to confirm what someone has said or simply to acknowledge it. Ide (1998: 510) argues that *sumimasen* thus 'functions in both a "remedial" and a "supportive" manner in discourse, carrying pragmatic and ritualistic functions that extend beyond conveying the semantic meaning of regret or gratitude in actual discourse.' One possibility, therefore, is that people with only a superficial knowledge of Japanese and English think that *sumimasen* and 'I'm sorry' are equivalent. So when they hear the Japanese use *sumimasen* much more frequently than they hear English speakers use 'I'm sorry', they interpret this as indicating that Japanese apologize more frequently than English speakers do.

4.5.2 The effect of situation

Another possible explanation for the findings is that people's conceptions of Japanese and English apologizing behaviour are accurate for certain types of situations, but not for others. For example, it could be that IFIDs are used more routinely in Japan than in Britain and Canada, and/or are used more frequently in situations where the person apologizing is personally at fault and the offence is more substantive. Such types of contexts were not included in this study, so it is possible that a different set of results would have emerged with scenarios that manipulated a different set of contextual features. Even in this study, there was a certain amount of variation from scenario to scenario. For instance, the Japanese respondents used IFIDs more frequently than the British and Canadian respondents did (86.72 per cent compared with 68.84 per cent and 65.63 per cent respectively) when responding to Scenario 7, where the customer complains and external circumstances are to blame. And they used them much less frequently than the British and Canadian respondents did (12.31 per cent compared with 59.84 per cent and 61.46 per cent respectively) when responding to Scenario 5, here the lecturer complains but is in fact responsible for the misunderstanding. So it is clearly possible that a different set of scenarios might have yielded a different set of results. Nevertheless, this cannot explain why the variable 'source of responsibility' should have had a consistently much greater effect on the Japanese responses than on the British and Canadian responses, when according to the stereotype (that Japanese apologize more frequently than English-speakers do even when they are not personally at fault), the opposite should have emerged.

4.5.3 Representativeness of the respondents

A third possible explanation of the unexpected findings could be that the respondents were not truly representative of their respective national cultures. For example, Gudykunst and Nishida (1999) argue that Japanese college students demonstrate high levels of individualism, and may in fact be more individualistic than American students. If this is the case, then they may not be representative of Japanese people in general, on which the stereotype is based. In keeping with this, Tanaka (1999) argues that Japanese traditional norms may be changing. She gathered production questionnaire data, using the same discourse completion scenarios, from Japanese students in 1986 and in 1997. Comparing the two sets of data, she found that the use of IFIDs was less frequent in 1997 than in 1986, especially for scenarios where the person complaining was at fault.

So it is possible that the stereotype of Japanese versus Western apologizing behaviour is derived from traditional Japanese norms, which university students do not necessarily subscribe to (and may decreasingly be subscribing to), but which many ordinary adult Japanese people still uphold.

4.5.4 The research procedure

A final possible explanation of the findings is that it is an artefact of the research procedure; in other words, that the responses given by the respondents do not reflect what they would really say in authentic situations. This is obviously a genuine concern, and as Chapter 14 explains, research has shown that production questionnaire data and authentic data differ in various respects. Although there is often substantial overlap in the speech act strategies and linguistic resources used to implement a given speech act, at a detailed level there can be some noticeable differences. Nevertheless, DCTs (discourse completion tasks) and other questionnaire formats (see Chapter 14, Section 14.3) can be useful for eliciting people's intuitions about what they would say in given contexts as well as insights into the contextual factors that influence their choices. So this suggests that even if the frequency of use of the various semantic components is different in real life from the percentage frequencies found in the questionnaire responses in this study, the effect of the variable 'source of responsibility' is likely to be similar.

4.6 Concluding comments

More research is clearly needed into Japanese and English apologizing behaviour. It would be interesting to collect data from a different sample of respondents (e.g. business people, or university staff) and, using a similar production questionnaire to the one in this study, to compare the results with the findings from this study. If feasible, it would also be particularly helpful to gather authentic data, paying particular attention to the variable 'source of responsibility'. Only then can we be clearer about the relative accuracy of Japanese and Western conceptions of apologizing behaviour in Japanese and English.

KEY POINTS

1. This study illustrates how there can be cross-cultural similarities and differences in people's assessments of 'apology situations', such as in terms of how annoying the offence is, how responsible people feel for the offence and how important they feel it is to placate the other person. It is important, therefore, to explore such contextual assessments in any cross-cultural study of language use.
2. Perceptions of 'responsibility for the offence' can have a significant impact on people's apologizing behaviour, and were found to vary cross-culturally in this study.
3. This study illustrates how there can be cross-cultural similarities and differences in the ways in which people perform speech acts such as apologies.
4. This study illustrates, in relation to apologies, how people's stereotypical conceptions of the behaviour of members of other nationality groups are not necessarily accurate, and need to be checked through empirical research.

5. In conducting cross-cultural studies, it is essential to consider the representativeness of the sample and to be aware that there may be generational differences in people's normative behaviour. Such factors inevitably limit the generalizability of any findings.

DISCUSSION QUESTIONS

1. Look again at the two incidents in Australia that Tanaka describes. How would you have felt in those circumstances? Would you have been offended as she and her friend were? Why/why not?
2. Look again at the news broadcast about the Japanese ice-skater, Midori Ito, who apologized for her sports performance.
   2.1. Why were the Americans surprised that Midori Ito apologized to the Japanese nation? Do you find it surprising? Why/why not?
   2.2. Why does the broadcaster question the sincerity of Japanese apologies?
   2.3. How might a Japanese person explain such language use?
3. Look again at the possible explanations given in Section 4.5 for the findings of this study. Which of them do you find more convincing? Give reasons for your choice(s).
4. Why do people from other countries sometimes feel that English speakers are insincere in their use of 'sorry' and/or 'thank you', and are such feelings justified? To what extent are these phrases used ritualistically in English, that is, with little semantic content?
5. A Chinese student studying in Britain was invited to a British home for dinner. As she got up to leave, the following conversation took place:

Chinese student:	Sorry. I've caused you a lot of bother this evening.
British host:	Bother? It's been no bother. What do you mean? I hope you've enjoyed yourself.
Chinese student:	Yes, of course. But I've really given you trouble. I've taken up so much of your time.
British host:	But we invited you to come . . . we wanted you to come.
Chinese student:	Next time you must come to my home and I'll cook you a Chinese meal.

   5.1. How usual/unusual do you find this conversation and why?
   5.2. Considering the notion of 'cost/benefit', in what ways are apologies and expressions of gratitude similar, and in what ways are they different?

Notes

1. We would like to thank the students at Meikai University, University of Bedfordshire and Carleton University for their co-operation in completing the questionnaire.

2. A few other responsibility-related comments occurred, such as *I'll tell you later*. These are classified as 'Other' in this analysis.
3. In addition, we coded the responses for use of address terms, and for expressions of concern. However, only a very small percentage of the responses contained such strategies, so the results of these additional codings are not reported here.
4. If a response had two or more phrases with the same semantic coding (for example, if someone used two IFIDs in their response), this was only counted once in this analysis.

Suggestions for further reading

Grainger, K. and Harris, S. (2007) Apologies. Special issue of *Journal of Politeness Research: Language, Behaviour, Culture*, 3(1).

This special issue includes an introduction by the editors, and five studies: apologies in young Israeli peer discourse, institutional apologies in UK higher education, apologies in English and Setswana, apologies in Greek reality TV and historical perspectives on Chinese apologies.

Holmes, J. (1995) *Women, Men and Politeness*. London: Longman.

Chapter 5 of this book provides an excellent overview of apologies and responses to apologies.

Meier, A. J. (1998) Apologies: what do we know? *International Journal of Applied Linguistics*, 8(2): 215–31.

This article reviews research on apologies and argues that research needs to progress beyond a descriptive goal to an explanatory goal in terms of the underlying cultural assumptions that indirectly inform apology behaviour.

Appendix

The scenarios and rating scales used in the production questionnaire were as follows:

English Version

1. This morning your father went to a clinic for his annual medical health check (which his company provides for their employees). About a week ago, you overheard your father telling his boss about the date and time of the health check on the phone. However, mid-morning today, the telephone rings and it is your father's boss. He says in an annoyed tone:

   Father's boss: *I'm phoning to ask where your father is. He's supposed to be here for our team meeting, and we've all been waiting for him for about 30 minutes. What's happened to him?* [Please write the EXACT words you think you would say in response.]

   You: ....

2. You arrange to go to a concert with a friend. As you clearly agreed, you wait for him in front of the train station, but after 30 minutes he still does not appear. You give up on him, and go into the station. You then find him at the ticket gate. It is still just possible to get to the concert in time. Your friend is cross with you and says in an annoyed tone:

   Your friend: *You're 30 minutes late! What happened?*

   You: ....

3. You have a meeting with your lecturer at 2.00 p.m. As you are on your way, another lecturer stops you to talk about a serious problem with one of your assignments. Because of your discussion, you arrive 30 minutes late for your meeting. Your lecturer is cross with you and says in an annoyed tone:

   Your lecturer: *You're 30 minutes late! We agreed to meet at 2 o'clock. What happened?*

   You: ....

4. You are working in the Customer Service section of a department store. The telephone rings, and a customer complains that his goods have not been delivered yet. The purchase form is in front of you, and you see that he signed for the goods to be delivered tomorrow morning. The customer says in an annoyed tone:

   Customer: *I bought a table from your store yesterday. You were supposed to deliver it this morning, but it's 12.30 now, and it hasn't arrived. What has happened?*

   You: ....

5. You have a meeting with your lecturer at 2.30 p.m. You arrive there at exactly 2.30 p.m., but he is cross with you, saying you promised to be there at 2.00 p.m. Your lecturer says in an annoyed tone:

   Your lecturer: *You're 30 minutes late! We agreed to meet at 2 o'clock. What happened?*

   You: ....

6. Your father left home for work at the normal time this morning. Afterwards, you happened to hear on the local radio that there was an accident on the line your father uses and the trains are running late. Later the telephone rings; it is your father's boss. He says in an annoyed tone:

   Father's boss: *I'm phoning to ask where your father is. He's supposed to be here for our team meeting, and we've all been waiting for him for about 30 minutes. What's happened to him?*

   You: ....

7. You are working in the Customer Service section of a department store. The telephone rings, and a customer complains that his goods have not been delivered yet. You know that there was a traffic accident near your warehouse, and that the road from your warehouse was closed for several hours. The customer says in an annoyed tone:

   Customer: *I bought a table from your store yesterday. You were supposed to deliver it this morning, but it's 12.30 now, and it hasn't arrived. What has happened?*

   You: ....

8. You arrange to go to a concert with a friend. You agree to meet at the ticket gate of the station near the concert hall, but you are 30 minutes late because there was an accident and your train was late. You find your friend still waiting at the ticket gate. It is still just possible to get to the concert in time. Your friend is cross with you and says in an annoyed tone:

   Your friend: *You're 30 minutes late! What happened?*

   You: ....

For each scenario, respondents provided the following contextual ratings on Likert-type 5-point scales:

When [your father's boss] says to you, '.................', at this point (i.e. before you reply)

- How annoying do you think the problem is for [your father's boss]?
  Not at all annoying   Very annoying
  1   2   3   4   5

- How far do you feel responsible for the problem occurring?
  Not at all responsible   Very responsible
  1   2   3   4   5

- How important do you think it is to try and make [your father's boss] less annoyed?
  Not at all important   Very important
  1   2   3   4   5

For each scenario, respondents were also given the opportunity to comment on their production responses and their ratings.

Japanese Version

1. 今朝、あなたの父は、（会社が従業員のために行っている）定期健康診断を受けに診療所に出かけました。一週間ほど前、あなたは父が電話で健康診断の日時を会社の上司に告げているのを聞いています。ところが、午前中にその上司から電話がかかってきました。彼は怒ったような口調で言います：

父の上司：お父さんはどちらにいらっしゃるか、伺いたくてお電話したんですが。実は、私達の部署の会議に出席なさることになっていて、皆もう３０分くらいお待ちしているんですよ。どうかされたんですか？
[答えとして言うだろうと思う言葉をそのまま書いてください。]

あなた：..

2. 友達とコンサートに行くことになりました。きちんと約束した通り、駅前で彼を待ちましたが、３０分たってもまだ現れません。あきらめて駅の中へ向かいます。その時、改札口の所にその友達が見えました。まだ開演には 間に合う時間ですが、彼は怒ったような口調で言います：

友達：３０分も遅れるなんて！　いったいどうしたんだよ？

あなた：..

3. あなたは先生と２時に会う約束をしています。行く途中で、別の先生に呼び止められ、あなたの提出したレポートのひとつに大きな問題があると言われました。その話をしていたため、着いたときには、約束の時間を３０分過ぎてしまいました。先生は怒ったような口調で言います：

先生：３０分も遅れるなんて！　いったいどうしたんだい？

あなた：..

4. あなたはデパートの顧客サービス部門で働いています。ある男性客から電話があり、頼んだ品物がまだ届かないと苦情を言われました。目の前にある「配達申込書」を見ると、その客は明日の朝に配達を指定しているのですが、彼は怒ったような口調で言います：

客：昨日おたくでテーブルを買って、今朝届けてもらうことになっていたのに、もう１２時半ですよ。いったいどうなってるんですか。

あなた：..

5. あなたはある先生と２時半に会う約束をしました。２時半ちょうどにそこへ行ったのですが、先生はあなたが遅刻したと言うのです。先生は怒ったような口調で言います：

先生：３０分も遅れるなんて！　いったいどうしたんだい？

あなた：…………………………………………………………

6. 今朝、あなたの父はいつもの時間に仕事に出かけました。その後ラジオを聞いていて、父の通勤路線で事故があり、電車が遅れているということを知りました。しばらくして、電話が鳴りました。父の上司からで、彼は怒ったような口調で言います：

父の上司：お父さんはどちらにいらっしゃるか、伺いたくてお電話したんですが。実は、私達の部署の会議に出席なさることになっていて、皆もう３０分くらいお待ちしているんですよ。どうかされたんですか？

あなた：…………………………………………………………

7. あなたはデパートの顧客サービス部門で働いています。ある男性客から電話があり、頼んだ品物がまだ届かないと苦情を言われました。実は、倉庫の近くで交通事故があり、その道が数時間通行止めになっていたのです客は怒ったような口調で言います：

客：昨日おたくでテーブルを買って、今朝届けてもらうことになっていたのに、もう１２時半ですよ。いったいどうなってるんですか。

あなた：…………………………………………………………

8. 友達とコンサートに行くことになりました。コンサートホール近くの駅の改札口で会う約束をしたのですが、事故のために電車が遅れ、３０分遅刻してしまいました。改札口の所に友達が待っています。まだ開演には間に合う時間ですが、彼は怒ったような口調で言います：

友達：３０分も遅れるなんて！　いったいどうしたんだよ？

あなた：…………………………………………………………

それぞれのシナリオに対して回答者に下記の点について５段階で評価してもらった。

[父の上司]が、「...............」と言った時点で（つまりあなたがそれに対してまだ何も言わない時点で）：

- この事態は、この[父の上司]にとって、腹立たしいことだと思いますか？
  全然腹立たしくない　　　　　　　　　　とても腹立たしい
  1　2　3　4　5

- この事態が発生したことについて、あなたには責任があると感じますか。
  全然責任はない　　　　　　　　　　とても責任がある
  1　2　3　4　5

- この[父の上司]をなだめたほうがいいと思いますか。
  全然思わない　　　　　　　　　　強く思う
  1　2　3　4　5

それぞれのシナリオに対して、コメントがあれば書いてもらう欄を設けた。

British and Chinese Reactions to Compliment Responses 5

Helen Spencer-Oatey, Patrick Ng and Li Dong

Chapter Outline

5.1 Introduction 95
5.2 Compliment response strategies 96
5.3 Research procedure 100
5.4 Evaluations of acceptance responses 101
5.5 Evaluations of rejection responses 104
5.6 Discussion 109
5.7 Concluding comments 111
Key points 112
Discussion questions 112
Notes 113
Suggestions for further reading 113
Appendix 114

5.1 Introduction

Compliments are usually intended to have a positive effect on interpersonal relations; as Holmes points out, they are typically 'social lubricants which "create or maintain rapport"' (1995: 118). However, if the compliment is interpreted negatively (for example, because the compliment is clearly untrue, because it implies envy or desire or because it assumes an unwarranted degree of intimacy), the effect on interpersonal relations is naturally less positive. Similarly, a person's response to a compliment needs to be evaluated positively, if the overall effect of the interchange is to be positive.

Many authors have identified cultural differences in complimenting behaviour (e.g. Wolfson 1981; Barnlund and Araki 1985; Herbert 1989; Lewandowska-Tomaszczyk

1989; Chen 1993; Loh 1993; Ylänne-McEwen 1993; Lorenzo-Dus 2001). However, few studies have explored the ways in which culture may affect people's interpretations of complimenting behaviour. This chapter reports a preliminary study of British, Mainland Chinese and Hong Kong (henceforth, HK) Chinese evaluative judgements of compliment responses.

5.2 Compliment response strategies

5.2.1 Taxonomies of compliment response strategies

Pomerantz (1978), in her classic study of compliment responses, drew attention to the dilemma faced by complimentees: on the one hand, there is pressure to agree with the compliment; on the other hand, there is pressure to avoid self-praise. In other words, recipients of compliments face conflicting constraints: if they uphold the maxim of agreement, they may flout the maxim of modesty; yet if they uphold the maxim of modesty, they may flout the maxim of agreement (see Leech (1983) and Chapter 2 in this book). So complimentees have to find ways of resolving this conflict, and a wide range of compliment response strategies for handling it have been identified.

Pomerantz (1978) and Holmes (1995) both suggest that for English, this wide range of strategies can be usefully divided into three broad categories: (a) acceptance, (b) rejection/deflection and (c) evasion/self-praise avoidance. Similarly, Ye (1995) uses three broad categories for compliment responses in Chinese: (a) acceptance, (b) acceptance with amendment and (c) non-acceptance. These three taxonomies are reproduced and illustrated in Table 5.1.

As can be seen, the three taxonomies differ both in the number of strategies identified, and also in the detailed categorization of strategies. Nevertheless, there is considerable agreement among them, especially in terms of the broad threefold division of strategies.

5.2.2 Compliment responses in Chinese and English

According to English etiquette books, the 'best way' to respond to a compliment is to accept it (see, for example, Hunter 1994). And as Pomerantz (1978) explains, rejection of compliments is often regarded as a symptom of a problem, such as low self-esteem. Studies which have explored compliment responses in English have found that English speakers indeed only rarely reject or disagree with a compliment, and that acceptance is much more common, as the figures in Table 5.2 show. However, it can also be seen that the frequency of acceptance responses may vary somewhat among different English-speaking countries, and that other types of responses to compliments are clearly very common.[1]

Table 5.1 Taxonomies of compliment response types in English (Pomerantz 1978; Holmes 1995) and Mandarin Chinese (Ye 1995)

Pomerantz (1978)	Holmes (1995)	Ye (1995)
1. Acceptance 1.1 Appreciation Token, e.g. A: *That's beautiful.* B: *Thank you*. 1.2 Agreement, e.g. A: *Oh it was just beautiful.* B: *Well thank you*.	**1. Accept** 1.1 Appreciation/Agreement Token, e.g. *Thanks, yes* or smile. 1.2 Agreeing Utterance, e.g. *I think it's lovely too*. 1.3 Downgrading/Qualifying Utterance, e.g. *It's not too bad, is it*? 1.4 Return Compliment, e.g. *You're looking good, too*.	**1. Acceptance** 1.1 Appreciation Token, e.g. 谢谢 $*Thanks*$ 1.2 Agreement, e.g. 我也喜欢的 $*I like it, too*$ 1.3 Pleasure, e.g. 我听了真高兴 $*I am very happy to hear that*$ 1.4 Smile
2. Self-praise Avoidance 2.1 Praise Downgrade 2.1.1 Downgraded Agreement, e.g. A: *That's beautiful.* B: *Isn't it pretty*? 2.1.2 Disagreement, e.g. A: *Good shot.* B: *Not very solid though*. 2.2 Referent Shifts 2.2.1 Reassignment, e.g. A: *You're a good rower, Honey.* B: *These are very easy to row. Very light*. 2.2.2 Return Compliment, e.g. A: *Ya' sound real nice.* B: *Yeah, you soun' real good too*.	**2. Deflect/Evade** 2.1 Shift Credit, e.g. *My mother knitted it*. 2.2 Informative Comment, e.g. *I bought it at Vibrant Knits place*. 2.3 Ignore, e.g. *It's time we were leaving, isn't it*? 2.4 Legitimate Evasion (Context needed to illustrate) 2.5 Request reassurance/repetition, e.g. *Do you really think so*?	**2. Acceptance with Amendment** 2.1 Return Compliment, e.g. 你也不错 $*You are not bad, either*$ 2.2 Downgrade, e.g. 马马虎虎 $*Just so-so*$ 2.3 Magnification, e.g. 你不看这是谁写的 $*Don't you see who wrote that?*$ 2.4 Request for Confirmation, e.g. 是吗？你真觉得不错？ $*Is it? Do you really think it's OK?*$ 2.5 Comment, e.g. 朋友送的 $*A friend gave it*$ 2.6 Transfer (switch of focus), e.g. 你喜欢吃多吃点儿 $*Have more since you like it*$

(*Continued*)

Table 5.1—cont'd

Pomerantz (1978)	Holmes (1995)	Ye (1995)
3. Rejections 3.1 Disagreement, e.g. A: *You did a great job cleaning up the house.* B: *Well, I guess you haven't seen the kids' room*.	**3. Reject** 3.1 Disagreeing Utterance, e.g. *I'm afraid I don't like it much*. 3.2 Question Accuracy, e.g. *Is beautiful the right word*? 3.3 Challenge Complimenter's Sincerity, e.g. *You don't really mean that*.	**3. Non-acceptance** 3.1 Denial (of content), e.g. 不行，不行 $*No, no*$ 3.2 Delay (of paying of compliment), e.g. 吃了再说 $*Don't comment until you've tasted it*$ 3.3 Qualification (Denial of quality), e.g. 差远了$*It's far from it*$ 3.4 Idiom, e.g. 不好意思$*I'm embarrassed*$ 3.5 Diverge (Denial by focus switch), e.g. 别逗了 $*Don't make fun of me*$ 3.6 Avoidance (of responding to compliment content), e.g. 你太客气了 $*You're being too polite*$

Table 5.2 Frequencies of selected types of compliment responses in English

	Acceptance (%)	Rejection (%)
Holmes (1986) New Zealand English	28.52	5.81
Herbert (1989) American English	36.35	9.98
Chen (1993) American English	32.45	12.70
Ylänne-McEwen (1993) British English	43	1
Loh (1993) British English	56	8.50
Herbert (1989) South African English	76.26	0

Table 5.3 Frequencies of selected types of compliment responses in Chinese

	Acceptance (%)	Rejection (%)
Chen (1993) PRC students in China	1.03	50.70
Ye (1995) PRC students in China	20.20	5.20
Yuan (1996) PRC students in China[a]	59.82	27.68
Loh (1993) HK students in Britain	41	22

[a] Unlike the other studies, Yuan's (1996) figures do not reflect mutually exclusive categories, but rather show the percentage of responses that included this semantic component.

In contrast to English, the 'best' response to compliments in Chinese is raditionally thought to be a rejection or denial. Ye (1995), for example, says that in Chinese, a denial is the routinized response to a compliment. Studies that have explored compliment responses in Chinese have indeed nearly all found that rejections are much more common than in English but, as Table 5.3 shows, most studies also found acceptance responses to be relatively frequent.

As Tables 5.2 and 5.3 indicate, 'other' types of responses to compliments (in other words, responses that are neither clear acceptances nor clear rejections) are common in both English and Chinese.

5.2.3 Evaluating compliment responses

Three Chinese researchers, Chen (1993), Ye (1995) and Yu (2003) all use Leech's (1983) Politeness Principle Maxims, and especially the Agreement and Modesty Maxims (see Chapter 2 in this book), to analyse Chinese and English responses to compliments. They all argue that the relative weightings of these two maxims in different cultural groups can account for differing response preferences, including those reported above for English and Chinese.

This leads us to the question: how do people evaluate different types of compliment responses? Since there are differences in the stereotypical beliefs about how to respond to compliments in English and Chinese, and since some differences have been found in the compliment response patterns used in the two languages, what happens when people use an unexpected response strategy? This study investigated this issue, by exploring the following questions:

1. How are people evaluated when they respond to a compliment by using an acceptance strategy?
   (a) Do others judge them to be conceited, especially if they explicitly agree with the compliment, rather than simply use an appreciation token like *thank you*? Or do they judge them to be appropriately sincere?
   (b) Are there cultural differences in the ways in which British and Chinese evaluate such responses?
2. How are people evaluated when they respond to a compliment by using a rejection strategy?
   (a) Do others judge them to be insincere and falsely modest, or do they judge them to be appropriately modest?
   (b) Are there cultural differences in the ways in which British and Chinese evaluate such responses?

5.3 Research procedure

A questionnaire (see the appendix) was used to explore these questions, so that comparable data could be obtained in Britain, HK and Mainland China. Naturally, people's evaluations of compliment responses in real life are influenced by many non-verbal and vocalization features, which a written questionnaire cannot begin to probe. Nevertheless, a questionnaire of this kind can provide a useful starting point for further more authentic research.

5.3.1 Design of the questionnaire

The questionnaire comprised five scenarios, all of which contained a compliment on someone's successful performance/achievement, such as coming top in an examination. In all cases, the person who was complimented had clearly done well, so all of the compliments that were paid appeared to be sincere. The relationship between the complimenter and complimentee varied in power and distance (teacher–student, close friends, mother–son, strangers, unfamiliar peers) across the five scenarios, in order to check for the influence of these variables.

For each scenario, five different responses were listed: two acceptance responses, two rejection responses, and one deflection response. For the acceptance responses, one was the British stereotypical rejoinder *thank you*, and the other was an explicit agreement with the compliment, such as *Yes, I'm really pleased with the mark*. For the rejection responses, one was the Chinese stereotypical rejoinder (不, 你过奖了 *bu, ni guo jiangle* $no, you're flattering me$), and the other was an explicit denial of the compliment, such as *no, I did badly*. Each scenario also included one other type of response, which seemed more like a deflection response. This was included primarily to add variety. The order in which the different types of responses were presented in each scenario was randomized.

Respondents were asked to evaluate each of the responses in terms of appropriateness, conceit, and impression conveyed (favourable/bad). Three 5-point Likert-type rating scales were listed under each compliment response, and respondents were asked to circle the numbers on these scales that corresponded to their reactions to that response. For each scenario, respondents were also asked to add some explanatory comments, if they had rated any of the responses negatively (circling numbers 1 or 2) in terms of the impression it conveyed.

Chinese and English versions of the questionnaire were produced through the collaborative efforts of six bilingual speakers, who carefully checked the developing versions of the questionnaire for equivalence of meaning. Using the decentring process suggested by Brislin (1976; see the glossary entry in this book), the scenarios and the responses were modified, until all parties (British, HK and Mainland Chinese) had agreed on Chinese and English versions that were both acceptable and equivalent in meaning.[2] The Chinese version of the questionnaire to be used in China was printed in simplified characters; the Chinese version of the questionnaire to be used in HK was printed in traditional characters.

5.3.2 The respondents

The questionnaires were completed by university students in Britain, HK and Mainland China. They were distributed during breaks in class, and filled in immediately. In Britain, only students who identified their main home language as English as well as their nationality as British were included in the sample. In HK, only students who had been brought up in HK and were ethnic Chinese were included in the sample. The numbers of students who completed the questionnaires were as follows: 172 British, 168 Mainland Chinese (67 in Guilin and 101 in Shanghai) and 158 HK Chinese. There were slightly more female respondents than male in all three regions (ranging from 54% in Mainland China to 63% in HK).

5.4 Evaluations of acceptance responses

5.4.1 Quantitative results

As explained in Section 5.3.1, respondents evaluated each of the compliment responses for appropriateness, conceit and impression conveyed (favourable/bad). The mean judgements (and standard deviations) on each of these scales for the acceptance responses, averaged across the five situations, are given in Table 5.4. Analysis of variance results showing the effect of nationality on the ratings of the acceptance responses are given in Table 5.5.

As can be seen from the figures in Table 5.4, all of the groups of respondents evaluated the acceptance responses fairly positively. Both the agreement responses, and the acceptance rejoinder (henceforth, AR) *thank you*, were judged to be appropriate responses. They were not evaluated as conceited; and they were judged as conveying a fairly favourable impression. The analysis of variance results show that nationality did not have a significant effect on people's judgements of *thank you* responses.

For the agreement responses, however, there was a tendency for the British respondents to evaluate them slightly more positively than the HK and Mainland

Table 5.4 Mean evaluations (and standard deviations) of acceptance compliment responses

	British	**Mainland Chinese**	**HK Chinese**
'Agree': appropriateness	3.83 (.59)	3.60 (.62)	3.55 (.61)
'Agree': conceit	3.44 (.65)	3.23 (.72)	3.24 (.63)
'Agree': impression	3.68 (.55)	3.53 (.66)	3.47 (.59)
Acceptance rejoinder: appropriateness	4.03 (.69)	4.15 (.56)	4.05 (.64)
Acceptance rejoinder: conceit	3.89 (.74)	3.76 (.69)	3.94 (.70)
Acceptance rejoinder: impression	3.96 (.67)	4.09 (.58)	4.03 (.63)

Note: Ratings based on a 5-point Likert-type scale from 1 (*not at all appropriate/very conceited/gives a very bad impression*) to 5 (*very appropriate/not at all conceited/gives a favourable impression*).

Table 5.5 Analysis of variance results showing the effect of nationality on the ratings of the acceptance responses

	F	**df**	*p*	**β²**
'Agree': appropriateness	9.63	2,469	<.000*	.04
'Agree': conceit	4.85	2,468	.008*	.02
'Agree': impression	5.13	2,468	.006*	.02
Acceptance rejoinder: appropriateness	1.75	2,473	.175	.01
Acceptance rejoinder: conceit	2.80	2,471	.062	.01
Acceptance rejoinder: impression	1.75	2,471	.175	.01

* Significant at the 95% level

Chinese respondents. And according to the analysis of variance results, this difference is statistically significant. On the other hand, the β^2 figures show that only 2–4 per cent of the variance is attributable to nationality, which suggests that the statistical difference is not very meaningful.

5.4.2 Qualitative results

A total of 302 respondents (89 British, 138 Mainland Chinese and 75 HK) added explanatory comments on their questionnaires. Of these, 98 people (18 British, 56 Mainland Chinese and 24 HK) made comments on one or more of the agreement responses, and 22 people (4 British, 15 Mainland Chinese and 3 HK) made comments on one or more of the AR responses.

In keeping with the positive ratings of the AR responses, there were only 30 comments (6 British, 20 Mainland Chinese and 4 HK) on the negative aspects of saying *thank you*. The most frequent criticism (made by respondents from each of the three groups) was that *thank you* showed conceit, and/or that it showed a lack of involvement because of the brevity of the response.

There were 157 comments altogether (25 British, 88 Mainland Chinese and 44 HK Chinese) on the agreement responses, indicating that agreement responses are more problematic than acceptance rejoinders. As expected, the most frequent criticism was that they conveyed too much conceit or boasting; for example:

British:	(1) *because he sounds like a smug bighead*
Mainland Chinese:	(2) 太锋芒毕露 $showing off one's abilities too much$
HK Chinese:	(3) 太自大 $too arrogant$

There were 101 comments like this (14 British, 56 Mainland Chinese and 31 HK Chinese), showing that all three groups of respondents are concerned about conceit, but in line with the quantitative data, suggesting that the Mainland and HK Chinese respondents perceived the agreement responses as conveying slightly more conceit than the British respondents did.

For the agreement responses, the other main concern, which again was shown by respondents from all three groups, was over complacency/over-confidence, sometimes with a suggestion that it was unfounded. For example, there were 31 comments (7 British, 16 Mainland Chinese and 8 HK Chinese) as follows:

British:	(4) *too self assured*
Mainland Chinese:	(5) 过与骄傲，给人感到虚有声势，长期看来不可能做常胜将军 $too conceited, sounds like bluffing; in the long run it's impossible always to be number one$
HK Chinese:	(6) 过分自满 $too complacent$

5.5 Evaluations of rejection responses

5.5.1 Quantitative results

Respondents also evaluated each of the 'rejection' compliment responses for appropriateness, conceit and impression conveyed (favourable/bad). The mean judgements (and standard deviations) of these responses, averaged across the five situations, for each of the scales are given in Table 5.6. Analysis of variance results showing the effect of nationality on the ratings of the acceptance responses are given in Table 5.7.

As can be seen from Tables 5.6 and 5.7, nationality had a much greater effect on people's evaluations of the 'rejection' compliment responses than the 'acceptance' compliment responses.

Table 5.6 Mean evaluations (and standard deviations) of rejection compliment responses

	British	Mainland Chinese	HK Chinese
'Disagree': appropriateness	2.32 (.62)	2.17 (.63)	2.97 (.70)
'Disagree': conceit	3.06 (.89)	3.21 (.87)	3.50 (.64)
'Disagree': impression	2.66 (.61)	2.36 (.63)	3.04 (.64)
Rejection rejoinder: appropriateness	2.61 (.77)	3.09 (.73)	3.98 (.66)
Rejection rejoinder: conceit	2.89 (.85)	3.47 (.69)	3.99 (.68)
Rejection rejoinder: impression	2.71 (.71)	3.18 (.71)	3.94 (.67)

Note: Ratings based on a 5-point Likert-type scale from 1 (*not at all appropriate/very conceited/gives a very bad impression*) to 5 (*very appropriate/not at all conceited/gives a favourable impression*).

Table 5.7 Analysis of variance results showing the effect of nationality on the ratings of the rejection responses

	F	df	*p*	β^2
'Disagree': appropriateness	68.73	2,473	<.001*	.23
'Disagree': conceit	11.53	2,465	<.001*	.05
'Disagree': impression	46.09	2,466	<.001*	.17
Rejection rejoinder: appropriateness	144.67	2,471	<.001*	.38
Rejection rejoinder: conceit	84.65	2,468	<.001*	.27
Rejection rejoinder: impression	123.67	2,458	<.001*	.35

* Significant at the 95% level

For the 'disagreement' responses, British and Mainland Chinese respondents judged them to be somewhat inappropriate, whereas the HK respondents had more neutral opinions. All three groups evaluated them neutrally in terms of conceit, but all three groups differed in their judgements of the impression conveyed by 'disagreement' responses. Both the Mainland Chinese and the British felt they conveyed rather negative impressions (with the Mainland Chinese judging the impression to be very significantly more negative than the British, according to further tests), whereas the HK Chinese evaluated the 'disagreement' responses neutrally in terms of impression conveyed. The analysis of variance results show that these nationality differences are statistically very significant, and the β^2 figures suggest that nationality had a meaningful effect on the respondents' evaluations of 'disagreement' compliment responses: for appropriateness, 23 per cent of the variance is attributable to nationality, and for impression, the figure is 17 per cent.

For the 'rejection rejoinder' (henceforth, RR) responses, there was even more variation among the three groups of respondents. The British respondents judged them somewhat negatively on all three scales; the Mainland Chinese respondents judged them fairly neutrally on all three scales; and the HK Chinese judged them fairly positively on all three scales.[3] The analysis of variance results show that these differences are statistically very significant, and the β^2 figures indicate that the differences are meaningful: for acceptability, 38 per cent of the variance is attributable to nationality; for conceit, 27 per cent of the variance is attributable to nationality; and for impression, the figure is 35 per cent.

5.5.2 Qualitative results

A total of 243 respondents (60 British, 129 Mainland Chinese, and 54 HK Chinese) made comments on one or more of the 'disagreement' responses, and 115 respondents (56 British, 49 Mainland Chinese and 10 HK Chinese) made comments on one or more of the RR responses.

For each of the three groups of respondents, the 'disagreement' responses attracted the largest number of comments. There were 580 comments altogether: 121 made by the British, 349 made by the Mainland Chinese and 110 made by the HK Chinese. However, unlike the comments on the acceptance responses, which showed a basically similar pattern of concerns across the three groups, there were considerable differences between the British and the Chinese comments.

As many as 40 of the British comments drew attention to the inaccuracy of the 'disagreement' responses, making remarks such as the following:

British: (7) *He thought it went well so he should admit it.*
(8) *He knows he did well – why say no?*

As comment (8) indicates, some of the British seemed to be struggling to explain why someone should disagree under such circumstances. For example, another respondent wrote:

British: (9) *John already thought it went well so why was he saying it was no good? He was being complimented, why was he so adamant it was no good?*

Many of the other British comments were attempts to explain such seemingly strange responses. A total of 36 comments explained it in confidence terms: that John was psychologically unable to accept the compliment, for example because he lacked confidence, had low self-esteem, underestimated his abilities or was just embarrassed:

British: (10) *He did play well so why say he didn't? Lack of self confidence.*
(11) *John should try to take a little credit. He needs to have higher self-esteem perhaps.*

Another interpretation was that the disagreement was strategic in some way; for example, that it was an attempt to gain further compliments. For instance, there were 12 comments as follows:

British: (12) *John knows the food was good, he is just fishing for more compliments.*

Others interpreted the 'disagreement' responses as showing conceit:

British: (13) *John knows he did well, and so the fellow student would find him conceited.*
(14) *He knows he did well – why say no?*

There were 10 comments that referred to the negative implications of a 'disagreement' response for the person giving the compliment and/or for related others:

British: (15) *basically telling his friend he doesn't know what he is talking about*
(16) *undermines other people in class*

Like the British respondents, both the Mainland and the HK Chinese respondents commented on the inaccuracy or untruthfulness of the 'disagreement' responses: there were 74 Mainland Chinese comments on this, and 27 HK Chinese comments. However, in contrast to the British, they had no apparent difficulty in understanding why such responses might be used, and clearly associated them with modesty issues. There were

120 Mainland and 29 HK Chinese comments that the 'disagreement' responses were too modest; for example:

Mainland Chinese: (17) 过分的谦虚等于骄傲 $Excessive modesty equals conceit$

(18) 在老师面前表现得过分谦虚有虚伪感 $Behaving too modestly in front of the teacher seems insincere$

HK Chinese: (19) 无需再亲人前自谦 $There's no need to denigrate yourself in front of people who are close to you$

As can be seen from the comments above, excessive modesty was associated with falseness/insincerity and with conceit. There were 117 Mainland and 35 HK Chinese comments that the 'disagreement' responses were insincere or false, and there were 48 Mainland and 4 HK Chinese comments that they showed conceit.

The above comments also show that appearing modest is very dependent on participant relations, especially in Mainland China. There were 64 Mainland and 18 HK Chinese comments that referred to role relations in evaluating the 'disagreement' responses. Some people commented that 'disagreement' responses were too formal or polite for the context (there were 15 Mainland Chinese comments like this), or that they seemed too cold or distant (there were 29 Mainland and 10 HK Chinese comments like this); for example:

Mainland Chinese: (20) 对好友的恭维过于谦虚有生疏感 $If one's too modest about a good friend's compliment, it seems too distant$

HK Chinese: (21) 我认为面对自己的母亲答案应该忠肯和直率，不需太客气 $I think one should be honest and straightforward in replying to one's mother; there's no need to sound too polite$

Compared with the British respondents, far fewer of the Chinese respondents linked a 'disagreement' response with confidence issues, although some made this connection: there were 14 Mainland and 2 HK Chinese comments that referred to lack of confidence or low self-esteem.

In terms of the negative implications of a 'disagreement' response for the person giving the compliment and/or for related others, the Mainland and HK Chinese, like the British respondents, made a few comments. There were 17 Mainland and 8 HK Chinese comments that referred to this, arguing that a 'disagreement' response could suggest poor judgement, could put others down, could make others feel uncomfortable, or could imply disrespect; for example:

Mainland Chinese: (22) 这个回答会打击 祝贺他的人的兴致和好意 $This response could attack the kind intent and interest of the person paying the compliment$

(23) 看似李明的回答很谦虚，但在他的回答中隐含了我的足球踢得很不好，你说我踢得好，你的明光可不怎么样 $It seems as though Li Ming's response is very modest, but his response implies 'I played badly, but you said I played well, so your judgement can't be very good'$

HK Chinese: (24) 令老师尷尬 $makes the teacher embarrassed$

For the RR responses, the number of comments made by the different groups of respondents reflected the differences in the mean evaluations shown in Table 5.6: the British respondents made 108 comments, the Mainland Chinese made 75 and the HK Chinese made 12.

For the British respondents, many of the comments were similar to those made for the disagreement responses: people drew attention to the inaccuracy or untruthfulness of the rejection, and once again tried to explain it either in terms of confidence or in terms of ulterior motive. For example, 19 British comments referred to psychological factors associated with lack of confidence:

British: (25) *embarrassed by good comment*
(26) *response shows lack of self-confidence*

And 12 British comments referred to an ulterior motive:

British: (27) *saying flattering is wanting more said on the subject*
(28) *Why should a teacher (authority) flatter – they wouldn't. Therefore shows some conceit and appears to be pushing for more approval.*

As the last comment indicates, some British respondents interpreted RR responses as showing conceit; in fact, there were 31 comments to that effect.

In terms of the negative implications of an RR response for the person giving the compliment and/or for related others, the British made 12 comments, covering a similar range of issues to those mentioned in relation to the DIS responses; for example:

British: (29) *seems to make the other person seem that they are lying*
(30) *Because he shouldn't accuse his close friend of sucking up to him – the friend would say the truth and he should believe it.*

In great contrast to the British evaluations, the HK respondents made very few negative comments. It seems that the only slight reservations that the HK respondents had about this response were its appropriateness for the context. Three comments said that the RR response was too distant or 'polite' for the context, and one evaluated it as too modest and four as insincere or false. The Mainland Chinese, on the other hand, were much more concerned about these contextual factors: there were 31 comments on RR responses that referred to role relations. As many as 23 comments mentioned that the RR response was too distant or 'polite', 10 comments that it was too modest and 21 comments that it sounded insincere or false.

None of the HK respondents interpreted RR responses as having any kind of negative implications for the person giving the compliment or for related others, and there were only three Mainland Chinese comments about this.

5.6 Discussion

As explained above, several Chinese researchers have argued that Leech's (1983) Politeness Principle Maxims, and especially the Modesty and Agreement Maxims (see Chapter 2), provide a suitable theoretical framework for analysing compliment responses. They argue that the relative weightings in different cultural groups of the values 'modesty' and 'agreement' can account for differing response preferences. This section discusses this claim.

5.6.1 Modesty

A number of authors (e.g. Gu 1990; Chen 1993; Yu 2003) have stressed the importance of modesty in Chinese and Japanese cultures. For example, Gu (1990: 238–9), referring to Confucian philosophy, explains that modesty is one of four essential elements of the Chinese concept of *limao* or 'politeness'. Yu (2003: 1702) argues that 'the Chinese norm is to display modesty, a culturally held value about what constitutes a good face and being polite.' Similarly, Leech (1983: 137) suggests that in Japanese society the Modesty Maxim seems to be more powerful than it usually is in English-speaking societies. To what extent, then, do the results of this study support these claims?

In Leech's (1983) Politeness Principle, he conceptualizes modesty as having two components: minimization of praise of self and maximization of self-dispraise. In discussing modesty, however, most authors (including Leech himself) seem to focus on the second element. Yet the first element, the avoidance of appearing conceited, is clearly an important component. Judging from the comments reported above, all three groups of respondents explicitly identified conceit as a negative and unacceptable trait, implying that this element of modesty is of equal importance in these three sociocultural groups. What linguistic behaviour, though, tends to give rise to judgements of 'conceit'?

Perhaps somewhat surprisingly, none of the groups of respondents evaluated any of the acceptance responses as conveying conceit. The figures given in Tables 5.4 and 5.5 show that even though the three groups differed slightly in their evaluations, the majority of each group judged them to be acceptable in terms of conceit. Conversely, the British evaluated the RR response (which is typically regarded as a strategy for conveying modesty) as tending towards conceit. For this particular RR response, however, this may be partly due to the lack of precise translation equivalence between 你过奖了 [*ni guo jiang le*] and *you're flattering me*. As comment 28 suggests, the word 'flatter' in

English has negative connotations, and is often associated with over-praising someone in order to achieve some ulterior aim. This implies that the complimentee has control of something that is desirable to the other person, and so by using such a phrase the complimentee is showing conceit by claiming power s/he does not really have. Nevertheless, even though *你过奖了 [ni guo jiang le]* does not have such implications (at least not traditionally), the comments reported in Section 5.5.2 show that 'disagreement' responses were evaluated as conceited by a fair number of Mainland Chinese, arguing that excessive modesty is equivalent to conceit. Clearly, then, it is too simplistic to regard acceptance strategies as being closely linked with conceit, and rejection strategies as being closely linked with modesty.

If we turn to the second component of Leech's (1983) conceptualization of modesty, the maximization of dispraise of self, a different picture emerges. The vast majority of the British respondents did not associate the self-denigration of the rejection responses with modesty at all: only three people mentioned it. They associated it either with a lack of confidence or with an attempt to fish for more compliments. In contrast, though, the vast majority of the Mainland and HK Chinese respondents linked the two. This suggests that the second element of modesty is very much more weakly adhered to in Britain than in China. However, once again we need to consider the strategies used for implementing this component of the strategy. Leech's wording *maximize dispraise of self* implies that the more one dispraises oneself, the more one conveys modesty. Yet the Chinese comments (especially the Mainland Chinese comments) show clearly that excessive modesty seems false and insincere, and is interpreted as conveying conceit rather than modesty. However, what counts as an appropriate degree of modesty, and what counts as an excessive degree of modesty, is clearly socially determined. With regard to HK and Mainland China, it seems that a smaller degree of self-denigration is tolerated among Mainland Chinese students than HK students. Why this should be so is unclear. Further research is obviously needed, first to check the reliability of the finding and, if it is confirmed, to explore some possible explanations.

5.6.2 Agreement and face

Disagreements are typically associated with threats to another person's face (Brown and Levinson 1987), so from this perspective, when people respond to a compliment, they have to maintain an appropriate balance between, on the one hand, upholding the other person's face by agreeing with his/her compliment, and on the other hand, avoiding sounding conceited by doing this.

The comments reported in Section 5.5 indicate that, for each of the three groups of respondents, only a relatively small number expressed concern over the effect of a rejection response on the other person's feelings. Certainly a few mentioned it, but not very many. This suggests that concern over agreeing with the complimenter is not a very powerful influence on people's choices of compliment response strategies, certainly compared with concerns about modesty/conceit. This is in keeping with Leech's (1983) own comment that there is less evidence for the Agreement Maxim than for the Modesty Maxim.

However, another perspective is to judge the use of agreement/disagreement strategies, not in relation to the complimenter's face, but in relation to the complimentee's face. If someone responds to a compliment with a rejection response, not only may it be threatening to the other person's face, but it is also potentially threatening to the respondent's own face and thus to be avoided. This seems to have been the interpretation given by a fair number of the British respondents in this study. As reported in Section 5.5.2, quite a lot of them interpreted the rejection responses as conveying a lack of confidence, an inability to accept a compliment, and so on. This is the interpretation that Pomerantz (1978) gives to the use of disagreement. However, because of the strong association between self-denigration and modesty for many of the Chinese respondents, this was not a common interpretation among those respondents.

5.6.3 Self-presentation

Ruhi (2006) and Spencer-Oatey, H. (2009) point out that Leech's (1983, 2005) and Brown and Levinson's (1987) frameworks have a bias towards 'concern for other' in their conceptualizations of 'polite' interaction, and they argue that self-presentation is another important interactional concern that needs to be incorporated into any explanatory account of the management of relations/rapport. Several of the comments reported in Section 5.5 support this claim. For example, many British and Chinese respondents evaluated the 'disagreement' responses in terms of the impression it conveys of the speaker. For example, most of the British respondents felt the speaker should present himself in a manner that is in keeping with 'the truth' (e.g. see comment 7), and were either puzzled by failure to do so or else attributed it to an ulterior motive. Similarly, many of the Chinese focused on the speaker and evaluated the 'disagreement' responses negatively, maintaining that they made the speaker sound conceited or insincere. A few of them, however, referred to the negative impact that they could have on the hearer (the person who had paid the compliment) (e.g. see comments 22–4).

This suggests that not only 'concern for other' but also self-presentation concerns are important factors that need to be incorporated into analyses of compliment responses and the management of relations/rapport.

5.7 Concluding comments

All of the scenarios used in the study made it clear that the complimentee had done genuinely well and that he was convinced of this himself. Needless to say, there are numerous occasions when this is not the case. Clearly, the findings from this study cannot be assumed to apply to other types of complimenting situations without further research.

Further research is also needed on what types of strategies are regarded as appropriate compliment responses in different contexts and for different sociocultural groups. For example, it would be interesting to know whether the self-denigration aspect of modesty only applies to distant relationships, or whether there are different strategies for upholding it in different types of relationships. There is clearly much more work that needs to be done.

KEY POINTS

1. People's strategies for responding to compliments can be usefully divided into three broad categories: (a) acceptance; (b) rejection/deflection; and (c) evasion/self-praise avoidance.
2. Previous studies have found both similarities and differences among Chinese and English speakers in their preferences for types of compliment responses. Rejection responses are much rarer in English than in Chinese.
3. This study explored British and Chinese (Mainland and Hong Kong) respondents' evaluative judgements of different types of compliment responses and found both similarities and differences.
4. All groups evaluated the acceptance responses positively, although there was a slight tendency for the British to rate them more positively than the Chinese. The British evaluated the rejection responses more negatively than the Chinese, but there were also significant differences between Mainland and Hong Kong Chinese respondents.
5. People's evaluations of compliment responses are influenced by a range of factors, including concerns for modesty, avoidance of disagreement and self-presentation.

DISCUSSION QUESTIONS

1. Jonathan is a teacher in an adult school class in the United States. After class, he speaks to Anh, one of his students who is from Vietnam:

J: Anh, your English is improving. I am pleased with your work.
A: Oh no, my English is not very good. (*looking down*)
J: Why do you say that, Anh? You're doing very well in class.
A: No, I am not a good student.
J: Anh, you're *making progress* in this class. You should be proud of your English.
A: No, it's not true. You are a good teacher, but I am not a good student.
J: (*He is surprised by her response and wonders why she thinks her English is so bad. He doesn't know what to say and wonders if he should stop giving her compliments.*)

1.1. Why is Jonathan confused/surprised by Anh's responses?
1.2. Should he stop complimenting her?
1.3. What different norms do the two speakers seem to hold regarding complimenting?
(Based on Levine, Baxter and McNulty 1987: 17)

2. An American woman received a letter from a Japanese friend who had just got married. The Japanese woman wrote in her letter, 'My husband is not very handsome. Your husband is much more handsome than mine.' The American woman was very surprised by what her friend wrote.
   2.1. Why do you think the American woman was surprised?
   2.2. Why do you think the Japanese woman wrote, 'My husband is not very handsome'?
   (Based on Levine, Baxter and McNulty 1987: 23)
3. Consider your own complimenting behaviour:
   3.1. How often do you pay compliments, and to whom?
   3.2. What do you most frequently pay people compliments about?
   3.3. Why do you pay compliments? Do your compliments always reflect your genuine opinion? Why/why not?
4. How does complimenting behaviour fit in with the conceptualization of face and rapport given in Chapter 2?
5. Look at the questionnaire used in this study. For each scenario, consider:
   5.1. Would you have complimented the person in this situation?
   5.2. Would you have used a different wording for the compliment? Why/why not?
   5.3. How would you evaluate each of the compliment responses, and why?
   5.4. How do you think you would have responded in these circumstances?

Notes

The authors would like to thank Liu Shaozhong, Xing Jianyu and Harry Wang for helping in the translation and decentring process of the development of the Chinese and English versions of the questionnaire, and Kang Qing and Liao Fengrong for administering the questionnaires in China.

1. Since each study uses slightly different categorizations of subcategories, we have made some classification adjustments for comparative purposes. 'Acceptance' includes only the strategies *appreciation token* and *agreement*; 'Rejection' includes clear non-acceptances, such as *disagreement* or *queries of accuracy.*
2. The following minor differences were deliberate: Chinese names were used in the Chinese version, and the tourist in scenario 4 spoke English rather than French.
3. Further tests showed that on all three scales, there was a very significant difference in the ratings of each of the pairs of countries ($p < 0.001$ in all cases).

Suggestions for further reading

Herbert, Robert K. (1989). The ethnography of English compliments and compliment responses: a contrastive sketch. In W. Oleksy (ed.) *Contrastive Pragmatics.* Amsterdam: John Benjamins, 3–35.

This chapter provides a clear and detailed description and analysis of compliment responses gathered ethnographically by university students in the USA and South Africa.

Herbert, R. K. (1997) The sociology of compliment work in Polish and English. In N. Coupland and A. Jaworski (eds) *Sociolinguistics: A Reader and Coursebook.* Basingstoke: Macmillan, 487–500.
This chapter provides a succinct description of compliments, especially in relation to Polish and English.

Holmes, J. (1995) *Women, Men and Politeness.* London: Longman.
Chapter 4 of this book provides an excellent overview of compliments and compliment responses.

Yu, M-c (2003) On the universality of face: evidence from Chinese compliment response behaviour. *Journal of Pragmatics*, 35: 1679–1710.
This article discusses compliment responses from a face perspective.

Ruhi, S. (2006) Politeness in compliment responses: a perspective from naturally occurring exchanges in Turkish. *Pragmatics* 16(1): 43–101.
This article considers the suitability of Brown and Levinson's (1987) face theory and Leech's (1983) Politeness Principle for analysing compliment responses, and is very useful for those who want to explore compliment responses in more detail.

Appendix

The Scenarios

1. John has just found out that he came top in an examination, after working really hard for it. After class, his teacher calls him over:

Teacher:	Congratulations, John! You did very well.
1. John:	No, no, I did badly.
2. John:	I was lucky with the questions, I guess.
3. John:	Yes, I'm really pleased with the mark.
4. John:	Thank you.
5. John:	No, you're flattering me!

2. John has just given a presentation to his class, which he feels went quite well. As he is leaving, one of his close friends, Peter, comes up:

Friend:	That was great, John. Your talk was really interesting!
1. John:	Thanks. Your presentation was excellent too.
2. John:	Yes, I thought it went quite well myself.
3. John:	No, you're flattering me!

4. John:	No, no, it was no good.
5. John:	Thanks.

3. John has just cooked an elaborate dinner for some family friends, and is pleased with how the dishes tasted. After they have gone, his mother says:

Mother:	Well done, John! The food tasted lovely.
1. John:	No, no, it was no good.
2. John:	Thanks.
3. John:	Do you really think so, mum?
4. John:	No, you're flattering me!
5. John:	Yes, the dishes turned out well, didn't they?

4. John is studying for a degree in French. One day as he is walking through the town, a French tourist asks him for directions. He answers him fluently, and afterwards the tourist comments:

Tourist:	You speak excellent French!
1. John:	No, far from it. I'm just a beginner.
2. John:	I'm studying it at university actually.
3. John:	Thank you.
4. John:	No, you're flattering me!
5. John:	I'm glad you think so!

5. John has just played in a university football match and scored a winning goal. Afterwards, a fellow student whom he knows slightly says:

Fellow student:	Congratulations! You played brilliantly!
1. John:	Thanks. I felt in good form today.
2. John:	No, you're flattering me!
3. John:	Thanks.
4. John:	Not really, it was a team effort.
5. John:	No, no I didn't play well.

For each scenario, respondents rated each of John's responses on the following Likert-type 5-point scales:

Not at all Appropriate (1)	Very Appropriate (5)
Very Conceited (1)	Not at all Conceited (5)
Gives a very bad Impression (1)	Gives a favourable Impression (5)

For each scenario, respondents were also asked to explain some of their ratings:
If you think any of John's responses give a bad impression (i.e. you have circled 1 or 2 on any of the 'impression' scales), please explain why.

Chinese Version

1. 李明刚知道，经过刻苦学习，他在考试中考的第一名。下课后，老师叫他。

   老师：　　李明，恭喜您！您考得很好！
   1. 李明：　　不不考得不好。
   2. 李明：　　我想这回我是走运罢了。
   3. 李明：　　是的，我对这次的分数很满意。
   4. 李明：　　谢谢。
   5. 李明：　　不，您过奖了。

2. 李明刚向同学们做了一次演讲，他自我感觉还不错。临走时，他的好友王洪走过来：

   王洪：　　太棒了，李明！你见得很有趣！
   1. 李明：　　你的演说也很成功呀。
   2. 李明：　　对，我也感到效果不错。。
   3. 李明：　　不，你过奖了。
   4. 李明：　　不不讲得不好。
   5. 李明：　　谢谢。

3. 李明 为来他家里的朋友做了一顿精致的晚餐，自己也感到每道菜都色香味美。等客人走后，他的母亲说：

   母亲：　　干得好，命名。
   1. 李明：　　不，不，不太好。
   2. 李明：　　谢谢。
   3. 李明：　　妈，真的吗？
   4. 李明：　　不，你过奖了。
   5. 李明：　　对，味道还不错，是不是？

4. 李明 在攻读英语专业。一天，踏上疾驶，一位英国卢克向他问路。李明很流利的回答拉的问题，于是，那位英国旅客说：

   旅客：　　您的英语好极了！
   1. 李明：　　不，还差远咧。我刚开始学。
   2. 李明：　　我在大学涅念的就是英语。
   3. 李明：　　谢谢。
   4. 李明：　　不，你过奖了。
   5. 李明：　　您这么看我很高兴。

5. 李明刚参加了一场学生足球赛，而且比赛中踢进了致胜的一球。一位不很熟悉的同学向他说：

同学：	恭贺您，踢得真好！
1. 李明：	谢谢，我今天状态不错。
2. 李明：	不，您过奖了。
3. 李明：	谢谢。
4. 李明：	不是嘛，使全队的功劳。
5. 李明：	不，不，踢得不好。

答卷人对李明在每一情景中的各种回答按 Likert 式5分级制进行打分：

恨不得提（1）	很得体（5）
很骄傲（1）	毫不骄傲（5）
给以很不好的印象（1）	给以很好的印象（5）

问卷同时要求答卷人对每一情景中的某些打分情况加以解释/进行说明：

如果您认为李明的某回答给以不好的印象（譬如您在任何一组印像级别号重拳了1哦），请您说明

6 Interactional Work in Greek and German Telephone Conversations

Theodossia-Soula Pavlidou

Chapter Outline

6.1 Introduction	118
6.2 Telephone openings	120
6.3 Telephone closings	126
6.4 Phatic communion and the relationship aspect of communication	131
Key points	133
Discussion questions	134
Notes	134
Suggestions for further reading	135

6.1 Introduction

Telephone communication has become an indispensable element of everyday life. Owing to the lack of visual information, at least in the normal use of this medium, linguistic information is foregrounded, and the role of pragmatic aspects of language becomes more crucial. Thus, telephone conversation is a challenge to anybody learning a foreign language and remains a sensitive area in intercultural encounters, even for those who have mastered the basics of a foreign language and culture. Let me illustrate this with an example from a German–Greek encounter. Recently, I (Greek) was working at home when the telephone rang; Elena, my daughter (Greek–German), also working in her room, and I both picked up the phone simultaneously, to find out that it was a close relative (German) who wanted to speak to my husband (German):[1]

{telephone rings}
Soula {in Greek} [*Ne*?]
$Yes?$
Elena {in Greek} [*Ne?*]
$Yes?$

{the rest of the conversation is in German}

Bärbel	*Ja, hier ist Barbara. Kann ich bitte den Wolfgang sprechen?* $Yes, this is Barbara speaking. Can I talk to Wolfgang please?$
Soula	{short hesitation, because of uncertainty as to which Barbara it is – we usually use the diminutive 'Bärbel' for this relative – and then a bit annoyed that she passes over Elena and me} *Ja, Bärbel, aber du kannst erst mal Elena und mir Guten Tag* [*sagen.*] $Yes, Bärbel, but you can say hello to Elena and me first.$
Elena	[{hangs up}]
Bärbel	*Ja, natürlich. Ich habe erst mal gar nix verstanden* [. . .] $Yes, of course. I did not understand a thing in the beginning [. . .]$ {although Bärbel does not speak Greek, she had hoped to at least understand the name, which she expected to hear in the very first answering turn}

The example above is one of the numerous instances indicating, if not a cultural clash, at least a temporary cultural dissonance. It illustrates the different expectations/orientations with which Greeks and Germans enter the conversational space of a telephone call: the former would expect to get some attention as partners in the conversation, before taking care of the reason for calling, the latter would expect not to be held on the phone unduly long, that is, beyond what it basically takes to handle the reason for the call. Both mean well, but *in different ways.*

Linguistic research on telephone conversation bears the distinct mark of conversation analysis, through which certain universal features of the structure of telephone calls have been established (e.g. Schegloff 1972; Schegloff and Sacks 1973; Schegloff 1994). Cultural variation has also been hypothesized (e.g. Clark and French 1981) and indeed been observed (e.g. Godard 1977; Sifianou 1989; Pavlidou 1994).[2] In this chapter, I would like to argue that this variation has to do mainly with the different norms pertaining to the relationship aspect of communication in different cultures and, consequently, with the different ways the relationship aspect of communication is attended to.

Telephone calls most commonly have a tripartite structure: an opening section, a middle section in which the main topic, that is the reason for the call,[3] is exposed and a closing section. The lion's share of the literature on telephone conversation (from the seminal studies of conversation analysts up to the most recent cross-cultural approaches) is concerned with the opening part (see e.g. Hopper 1992; Luke and Pavlidou 2002a); studies on the closing part of telephone calls are still quite rare (e.g. Button 1987, 1990). In the following, I draw on my earlier work on the opening and closing sections of telephone conversations in Greek and German (e.g. Pavlidou 1991, 1994, 1997, 1998a). Focusing mainly on the use of phatic utterances and patterns of repetition, I want to show that participants handle organizational problems in ways which reflect culture specific preferences for attending to the relationship aspect of communication.

My focus on the opening and closing sections of telephone calls is by no means intended to imply that I consider the relationship aspect of communication to be important or relevant only in these phases of the call; on the contrary, I am convinced that rapport issues never cease to be significant throughout any encounter (e.g. Pavlidou 1995, 1998b). However, the opening and closing sections of a telephone conversation pose some interesting interactional problems for the participants, such as how to counteract a possible intrusion through the telephone call, how to terminate the call without causing any bad feelings and so on. It is in this sense that Laver (1975: 217) talks of the opening and closing phases of a conversation as 'the psychologically crucial margins of interaction.'

6.2 Telephone openings

6.2.1 The data sample

My analysis of telephone openings is based on a sample of 120 Greek and 62 German telephone calls (Pavlidou 1994). All calls were initiated and tape-recorded by young adults with a university degree, the Greek ones by five women and two men and the German calls by two women and three men. None of the calls was a 'first call'; in other words, the caller phoned a person whom s/he already know. The underlying assumption for this was that, contrary to other settings, phatic utterances (which were an important focus of my research) are not used among complete strangers in the opening part of a telephone conversation. The calls were made for both social and practical reasons, and were made to people with varying degrees of closeness to the caller. The callers were not informed about the exact purpose of the research, beyond my general interest in studying telephone conversation. They were instructed to erase any part of a call, or even whole calls, which they did not want other people to hear, and they were allowed to decide how best to tell the other participant about the recording.

6.2.2 General structure of telephone openings

In the opening section of a telephone call, the physical channel has to be opened and the acoustic contact between the partners has to be established. Moreover, it must be clarified whether the person answering the phone is the one the caller wishes to talk to, before s/he can proceed to the reason for calling.

The first step, that is the establishing of physical contact, is achieved with a summons–answer sequence (see e.g. Schegloff 1972): the ringing of the telephone functions as a summons to which the person picking up the phone responds, for example by saying 'Hello?' After this very first adjacency pair, sequences of identification (self- and other-identification, either by name or telephone number), greeting and counter-greeting usually follow. Sometimes, when caller and called already know each other, ritual inquiries like 'How are you?' may appear before the partners proceed to the main section of the call. In other words, the opening section of a telephone call comprises a number of basic or constitutive sequences, which, however, may vary in their realization from context to context (cf. e.g. workplace versus home setting, business call versus private call etc.) and from culture to culture.

6.2.3 Greek openings – German openings

6.2.3.1 Some basic features

Owing to space limitations, in this section I can only point out some very general features of Greek and German telephone calls.[4] I would like to start by giving two examples of openings, one Greek and one German.

EXAMPLE 1: A Greek opening

{A (Sofia, female, 26 years old) and B (female, 28 years old)) are friends; A calls B to tell her about a lecture they wanted to go to, but after that they move on to another topic}

1.	B	*Oriste.* $Yes, please.$
2.	A	*Ja su LIA.* $Hello LIA.$
3.	B	*Ja su SOFIA.* $Hello SOPHIA.$
4.	A	*Ti jinete?* $How are you doing?$
5.	B	*Kala. Ti na jini? Isiçia. ESI ti kanis.* $Fine. Nothing special. Everything is quiet. How are YOU.$
6.	A	*Ka:la: c eɣo.* $I am fine, too.$
7.	B	*Mm.* $Hm.$
8.	A	*θimi:θi:ka: telika ti mu e:le:je:s oti iθeles na su po: . [. . .]* $I finally reme:mbe:red what you to:ld me that you wanted me to te:ll you. [. . .]$

EXAMPLE 2: A German opening[5]

{A (male, 28 years old) and B (female, 27 years old) are friends; A calls B in order to thank her for sending him some English workbooks, but after that they move on to other topics}

{telephone rings}

1.	B	*B* {name}

(Continued)

EXAMPLE 2: A German opening—cont'd

2.	A	*Tach, B hier is A.* $Hello B, this is A {name} speaking.$
3.	B	*Ah, hallo A!* $Oh, hi A!$
4.	A	*Ich wollt mich nur für die Hefte bedanken!* $I just wanted to thank you for the pamphlets!$

As indicated in the examples above, both Greeks and Germans perceive the ringing of the telephone as a summons to which they respond by picking up the receiver and taking the first turn in the conversation. Greeks usually answer the phone with utterances like *ne* ('yes'), *lejete* (say-IMPERATIVE), *embros* ('go ahead'), *malista* ('yes'), or as in the example above with *oriste* ('yes, please', literally: order-IMPERATIVE). Although Germans may sometimes also take the first turn in a similar manner and answer with, for example, *Ja bitte* ('Yes please') or *Hallo* ('hello'), it is more typical in German telephone calls for the answerer to take the first turn, as in the example above, and identify himself/herself, usually by saying his/her last name. This is then followed by the caller's self-identification, either by last or first name or both, commonly in combination with an appropriate greeting formula depending on the relationship and the time of the day.

In Greek telephone calls, on the other hand, self-identification, especially on the answerer's part indicates a work-place setting and foregrounds the speaker's orientation to an efficient completion of the call (as is common, for example, in business or institutional contexts); otherwise, Greeks when talking to friends or relatives seem to prefer covert-identification, in other words, via voice-samples, as in Example 1.[6] Greetings may be interchanged, too, as is the case in turns 2–3, of the Greek example: *ja su* ('hello', literally: health to you-T-form) or simply *ja* (literally: 'health') is the most common informal greeting formula, used also for terminating the call, especially the variant *ja xara* (literally: health joy).[7]

6.2.3.2 The use of phatic talk in Greek and German openings

The term 'phatic' was first used in linguistics in connection with the term 'communion'. The phrase 'phatic communion' was introduced by the anthropologist Malinowski (1966: 315) to describe 'a type of speech in which ties of union are created by a mere exchange of words'. As Haberland (1966: 164) emphasizes, for Malinowski (1966: 313, 316), the main contrast is between 'communion' and 'communication':

> A mere phrase of politeness, in use as much among savage tribes as in a European drawing-room, fulfils a function to which the meaning of its words is almost completely irrelevant.

Inquiries about health, comments on weather, affirmations of some supremely obvious state of things – *all such are exchanged not in order to inform, not in this case to connect people in action, certainly not in order to express any thought.* . . . [They serve] to establish bonds of personal union between people brought together by the mere need of companionship. (emphasis added)

In other words, the salience of propositional/descriptive/cognitive meaning or information content is minimized in phatic communion, while the relational aspect is positively maximized. Or, as Coupland et al. (1992: 214ff) very aptly put it, phatic communion can be associated with certain priorities in talk, that is a minimal commitment to open disclosure, seriousness, factuality, etc. and a foregrounding of positive relational goals.

Using the data set described above, I compared the use of phatic talk in the Greek and German telephone calls, focusing on the section which follows the initial answering, identification and greeting, and which precedes the mention of the reason for calling. The following utterances/features were regarded as phatic:

- Ritual questions, e.g. *How are you?*
- Comments on lack of contact, e.g. *We haven't met for ages.*
- Ritual expression of wishes, e.g. *Happy Birthday!*
- Apologies for the intrusion, e.g. *I hope I didn't wake you up.*
- Comments on the connection, e.g. *This line is very poor.*
- The joking use of the V-form among intimates, e.g. *Ti kanete ciria mu?* $What are you doing (V-form) my lady?$
- The use of phatic particles, e.g. *Na? Hast du noch Gäste?* $PARTICLE? Have you still got guests?$

Counting the number of telephone calls that had one or more of these phatic utterances, I found that more than two-thirds of the Greek telephone calls contained them, but only just over one-third of the German calls did so (see Table 6.1).

To explain this result, one might hypothesize that phatic talk is more readily deployed when people call each other primarily for social rather than transactional purposes; so

Table 6.1 Frequency of use of phatic talk in Greek and German telephone openings

	Conversations with phatic talk	Conversations without phatic talk	Total
Greek	85 (70.83%)	35 (29.17%)	120
German	23 (37.10%)	39 (62.90%)	62
			N = 182

df=1, χ^2=17.91, *p*<.001

Table 6.2 Distribution of reason for calling in Greek and German telephone calls

	Social reason	Practical reason	Total
Greek calls	38 (31.67%)	82 (68.33%)	120
German calls	15 (24.19%)	47 (75.81%)	62

df = 1, χ^2= 0.77, *p*<.5

Table 6.3 Use of phatic utterances according to reason for calling

	Use of phatic utterances	
	Greek	**German**
Calls for social reasons	34 (89.47%)	51 (62.20%)
Calls for practical reasons	9 (60%)	14 (29.79%)

df = 1, χ^2= 3.25, *p*<0.100

if Greeks reach more readily for the telephone just to chat or to arrange to meet, this might in turn explain the greater use of phatic talk in Greek openings. Although there is some evidence to support this (both Germans and Greeks used more phatic talk in social calls than in transactional calls), there is no statistically significant difference in the proportion of social and transactional phone calls in the two data sets: both Greeks and Germans made more transactional telephone calls than social calls (see Table 6.2).

Moreover, Greeks still used more phatic sequences in both types of calls than Germans, and the difference was particularly marked for the transactional calls (see Table 6.3).

Another way of explaining the findings shown in Table 6.1 would be by means of Brown and Levinson's (1987) politeness theory: if the caller wants something from the person called (which would constitute a face-threatening act to that person), s/he seeks to mitigate the threat by using phatic talk, that is a positive politeness device. Along this line, the Greeks in the sample could be hypothesized to have used more phatic utterances because they made more face-threatening calls than the Germans. But if we investigate, for example the connection between use of phatic talk and the beneficiary of the call in transactional calls, we find that Greeks deploy phatic talk to a great extent even when they are not themselves (at least not exclusively) the beneficiary of the call.

As for the connection between the type of relationship and phatic talk in transactional calls, although the results are not statistically significant, in both the Greek and

Table 6.4a Use of phatic talk in Greek telephone openings according to the relationship of the participants (transactional calls only)

Relationship	Calls with phatic talk	Calls without phatic talk	Total
Personal	16 (53.33%)	14 (46.67%)	30
Familiar	28 (73.68%)	10 (26.32%)	38
Formal	7 (50.00%)	7 (50.00%)	14
			82

$df=2$, $\chi^2=4.07$, $p<0.200$

Table 6.4b Use of phatic talk in German telephone openings according to the relationship of the participants (transactional calls only)

Relationship	Calls with phatic talk	Calls without phatic talk	Total
Personal	3 (27.28%)	8 (72.73%)	11
Familiar	10 (43.48%)	13 (56.52%)	23
Formal	1 (7.69%)	12 (92.31%)	13
			47

$df = 2$, $\chi^2=5.19$, $p<0.100$

the German samples the most extensive use of phatic utterances occurs in relationships that are neither very formal nor too personal; however, the percentage is almost twice as high in the Greek openings in comparison to the German openings, as indicated in Tables 6.4a and 6.4b.

6.2.4 Discussion

The findings reported above suggest that, at least sometimes, there are some differences in what Germans and Greeks consider to be appropriate ways of opening a telephone conversation: Greeks seem to prefer an exchange of phatic utterances before coming to the reason for calling, whereas Germans opt for a more direct path to the main section of the call.[8] While this difference can lead to cultural clashes and misunderstandings in Greek–German encounters, it can definitely not be explained away by saying either that Greeks are very considerate and Germans impolite, or vice versa (see Section 6.4 for further discussion).

6.3 Telephone closings

6.3.1 The data sample

My analysis of telephone closings is based on a sample of 45 Greek and 27 German telephone calls made between relatives or friends. They are mainly a subset of the sample used for analysing telephone openings. However, 15 of the German calls belong to the Brons-Albert (1984) corpus, and a further two are from the so-called Freiburger Korpus (TSG 1975). The full data sample used for telephone openings could not be used, either because the closings had not been recorded or else because poor sound quality (especially of the German calls) made a detailed analysis impossible.

6.3.2 General structure

Every telephone call ends unequivocally when the telephone is hung up, that is when the physical channel is interrupted. But in order to reach that point, the partners have to make clear that nothing else is left to be said and then proceed to signalling the end of the call (Schegloff and Sacks 1973: 299ff). The first is conversationally achieved by a pre-closing (an offer to close the conversation) which, if accepted by the other, allows the partners to take the last conversational step, that is the terminal sequence, usually comprising an exchange of *goodbyes*. However, as there are no linguistic means, at least in English, which exclusively serve as pre-closings, the first closing turn (the pre-closing) has to be placed after a topic (the last topic) has been closed down (Schegloff and Sacks 1973: 305). So the 'archetype closing', as Button (1987: 102) calls it, looks like the following (if preceded by a sequence in which one partner offers to close down the topic and the other accepts to do so, for example A: *Okay?* B: *All right.*, cf. Schegloff and Sacks 1973: 306):

A:	*We-ell.*	(offers to close; first close component)
B:	*O.K.*	(accepts the offer; second close component)
A:	*Goodbye.*	(first terminal utterance)
B:	*See you.*	(reciprocates; second terminal utterance)

{telephone is hung up}

However, other sequences like thanking for the call, giving regards to somebody both partners know, exchanging wishes and so on, may also be included in this last section of the call, in which conversationalists 'take-leave' (cf. Clark and French 1981) of each other.

6.3.3 Greek closings – German closings

6.3.3.1 Some basic features

Again in this section I can only limit myself to some general features of Greek and German closings and refer the reader to the relevant literature for more information.[9] Let me start with two examples of closings, one in Greek and the other in German.

EXAMPLE 3: A Greek closing

{A (female, 26 years old) calls B (male, 31 years old), a friend, to finalize the meeting point and time with other friends}

1.	B	*Ne. Stasi Aristotelus stin Tsimiski.* 'Yes. At the Aristotelous bus stop on Tsimiski street.'
2.	A	*E: endaksi. Orea. Ipe θα pari se mena i Zoi, e: θα ime eðo PANO eɣo.* 'Eh, all right. Fine. Zoe said she'll call me, eh, I'll be here UPSTAIRS.'
3.	B	*Endaksi. Ejine.* 'All right. Done.$
4.	A	*Mm. Afta.* $Mm. That was it.$
5.	B	*Ocei. θα peraso na se pa:ro: pço noris fisika=* $Okay, I'll pick you up earlier of course$
[...]		{brief moving out of closing}
10.	B	*Ocei?=* $Okay?$
11.	A	*=Ejine,ne.=* 'Done, yes.'
12.	B	*=Ejine. A[de.]* $Done. ADE.$
13.	A	*[A:]de ja.* $ADE bye.$
14.	B	*Jaxara, ja.* $Byebye, bye.$

{telephone is hung up}

EXAMPLE 4: A German closing

{A (female, 26 years old) calls an old friend B (female, 27 years old), whom she had not seen for a long time – and whom she met again only recently – to invite her to a party}

1.	A	*Gut. Dann sehen wir uns erstmal an diesem besagten Samstag.* $Good. We'll see then each other on this very Saturday.$
2.	B	*An diesem besagten. Okay.* $On this very Saturday. Okay.$
3.	A	*Gut?* $Good?$
4.	B	*Jo, bis dann.* $Yeah, till then.$
5.	A	*Bis dann. Tschüs.* $Till then. Bye.$
6.	B	*Tschüs.* $Bye.$

{telephone is hung up}

As shown in Examples 3 and 4, both closings end with equivalents of *goodbye* exchanges (this is also generally the case). In German the parting formula *tschüs* (cf. Example 4, turns 5–6) or its variations (the diminutive *tschüschen* or variants like *tschö*, *tschöho*, etc.) – some of which are dialect variants – are very commonly used in informal calls. More formal is the formula *auf Wiederhören*, which according to Werlen (1984: 257) has been formed specially for telephone communication in analogy to *auf Wiedersehen*; at the same time, however, these two formulae capture an aspect which seems to be quite important in the closing section of German telephone calls: a reference to future contact. In more informal calls, conventional phrases like *bis dann* ('till then'), *bis zum nächsten mal* ('until next time') can be used, either to refer to a specific future contact (as in Example 4, turns 4–5) or as a vague reference to future contact, that is, even when no specific arrangements have been made to meet (see Pavlidou 1997).

In Greek terminal exchanges, we find once again the formula *ja* ('bye', literally: health) and its variations *ja su* (literally: health to you-T-form), especially *ja xara* (literally: health joy), as in Example 3, turn 14. The fact that this formula can be used both in openings and closings, or more generally, both when meeting and parting, is indicative of the little, if any, lexical import that it carries. In addition, there are other expressions used among familiars when parting, like *fiʎa* (literally: kisses), *filaca* (literally: kisses-DIMINUTIVE), which shows liking and affection. Other informal parting formulae, used especially by younger people, include foreign expressions like *tsao* ('ciao') and *bai* ('bye').

Turning now to pre-closings, the German items used in this function include *also* ('so then'), *ja* ('yes'), *gut* ('good'), *okay* etc. (cf. also Werlen 1984: 255). Similarly, Greek closings are initiated with the discourse marker *lipon* ('well, so then') with falling intonation, or with expressions indicating agreement, most prominently: *ejine* ('done'), *endaksi* ('all right'), *ocei* ('okay'), but also *orea* ('nicely'), *kala* ('good') etc. Also, the particle *ade*, usually described as a hortative particle, is sometimes used as a pre-closing.

6.3.3.2 The use of repetition/redundancy in Greek and German closings

The 'archetype closing' presented in 6.3.1 can be thought of as the skeleton around which the closing section of both German and Greek telephone calls is organized. But especially in calls between familiars, 'varieties of closings' (Button 1990) are usually to be found. In such calls, as reported in Pavlidou (1997, 1998a), differentiation between Greek and German closings can be observed (e.g. a greater divergence from a dyadic structure and more repetition of agreement tokens in the Greek closings). In the following, I would like to focus on certain repetition phenomena in Greek and German closings.

Following Merritt (1994: 26), I use 'repetition' in a very general sense, covering 'all kinds of "happening again"'. But there is a very important qualification to this: there is a kind of repetition which is structurally required for the organization of conversation, as opposed to repetition that goes beyond the minimal structural necessities. For example, if somebody greets you or bids you farewell, you normally reciprocate this, for instance:

A: Hello.
B: Hello.

or

A: Goodbye.
B: Goodbye.

Taking into account the constituent sequences of the opening and closing sections of a telephone call, I consider this kind of repetition to be *conversationally required* or at least expected. On the other hand, if you respond to somebody's *Goodbye* with *Ciao, byebye* this utterance is *redundant*[10] as far as structural requirements are concerned, since from the organizational point of view either *ciao* or *byebye* would have been sufficient.

The analysis of my data sample suggests that Greek closings exhibit a greater degree of redundancy with respect to elements that are structurally required, that is terminal exchanges and closing components, than German closings. For example, in the last turn of Example 3, there are two parting formulae, although one would have sufficed. In most of the German calls I have examined, the terminal exchanges consist basically of two short turns (like turn 6 in Example 4). It is rare for such formulae to be repeated within the same turn, or within an extension of such exchanges over more than two turns, as occurs in the following Greek example (turns 4–6):

EXAMPLE 5

{Same as in Example 1: A (female, 26 years old) B (female, 28 years old)) are friends; A calls B to tell her about a lecture they wanted to go to, but after that they move on to another topic}

1.	A	*Ax kala* {hurriedly}. *Lipon. Klino ne?* $Ah, good {hurriedly}. So, then. I am hanging up, O.K.?$
2.	B	*Ejine. Ade, par esi kamɲa mera etsi?* $Done. ADE, you call me sometime, O.K.?$
3.	A	*Endaksi. Ne.=* $All right. Yes.$
4.	B	*=Ade tsao.* $ADE, ciao.$
5.	A	*Ade, ja, ja.* $ADE, bye, bye.$
6.	B	*Ade, ja, ja.* $ADE, bye, bye.$

{telephone is hung up}

Example 5 is interesting in other respects, as well:[11] it demonstrates repetition of an element, the particle *ade*, which is hardly structurally required. As mentioned in 6.3.3.1, *ade* can be employed as a pre-closing, in which case it could be considered structurally necessary. But this is not the case in Example 5, turns 2, 4–6 (nor in Example 3, turns 12–13). In fact, this particle indicates the speaker's orientation towards terminating the call and shows a desire for mutual consensus on this; it turns out to be an indispensable element of telephone closings among familiars (see e.g. Pavlidou 1998a).

Similarly, in the German closings we find repetition of the particle *ne*. This particle is derived from the modal adverb *nicht* ('not'); it functions as a tag-question with which the speaker seeks to keep the addressee involved in the conversation, or even get his/her confirmation,[12] and of course it does not play any constitutive role in the closing section. The following example[13] shows multiple recurrence of the particle *ne*:

EXAMPLE 6

{A (female, 25 years old) and B (male, 30 years old) are relatives; B called to say that his pregnant wife is not feeling well, and so they will not be coming to A's party}

1.	A	[. . .] *das kommt auf/ einn oder zwei mehr überhaupt nich an.* $[. . .] it makes really no difference if it is one or two persons more.$
2.	B	*Ja, aber wenn die schon nachmittags sacht, daß et ihr nich gut is . . . Also, wie gesagt, ne, falls . wider Erwarten . doch klappt, dann ruf ich vorher noch kurz an, ne.* $Yes, but if she says already in the afternoon, that she does not feel good . . So, as I said, NE, in case that. against our expectation. it does work, I will give you a ring before we come, NE.$
3.	A	*Hm. Bis dann, ne.* $Hm. Till then, NE.$
4.	B	*Bis dann! Tschö, A.* $Till then! Bye, A.$
5.	A	*Tschö.* $Bye.$

{telephone is hung up}

Example 6 also exhibits repetition of the formula *bis dann* in turns 3–4. Although it is frequently the case that such a formulaic expression is reciprocated (cf. also *Mach's gut* ('Take care'), *Grüss den Jürgen* ('Give my regards to Jürgen') etc.), reciprocation is not in the same sense constitutive for closing as, for example, the parting formula in the terminal exchange. Moreover, it is interesting that formulae or expressions referring to future contact are more frequently repeated than, for example, *mach's gut.*

6.3.4 Discussion

An obvious consequence of the redundancy discussed above is the greater length of the telephone closing. As already mentioned, on the whole, Greek closings exhibit a greater degree of redundancy in the use of elements that are constitutive for the closing section of the telephone call (i.e. agreement tokens and parting formulae); this means that Greek closings can be expected to be longer than the German ones. This would imply that there is a tendency for the partners to cling together in Greek closings. Moreover, the extended use of *ade* emphasizes the *locally negotiated* mutuality of the decision to terminate the call. In the German closings this mutuality of the partners' decision to close the call is negotiated by means of tag particles like *ne*, which implicitly invoke *already existing common ground*. Moreover, repetition of expressions like *bis dann*, which project the relationship into the future, suggest that Germans build up on the past of their relationship and invest in its future, whereas Greeks invest in the *hic et nunc* of their relationship.

6.4 Phatic communion and the relationship aspect of communication

In the previous sections, we examined a number of differences between openings and closings in Greek and German telephone calls. We saw, for example, that Greeks prefer an exchange of phatic utterances before coming to the reason for calling, whereas Germans opt for a more direct path to the main section of the call. In addition, Greek closings exhibit a greater degree of redundancy in the use of elements that are constitutive for the closing section of the telephone call. However, a word of caution is needed here: in cross-cultural studies there is not infrequently a tendency to rush into sweeping generalizations. It is important, therefore, to stress once more that the rapport management features which differentiate Greek and German openings or closings are not exclusive to either Greek or German conversations. In other words, there are Greek telephone calls with the 'German' characteristics, and vice versa. The findings reported here suggest that Greek and German conversationalists display different preferences for the ways in which they organize the openings and closings of their telephone calls; such preferences may be contingent on specific constellations of parameters whose importance will be revealed only under more subtle contextual considerations and in which cultural differentiation plays only a small part. So in this sense it is better to conceptualize findings like mine as motivated hypotheses for further research.

All in all, taking into account what the constitutive components of openings and closings are according to conversation analysts, we can say that Greek openings/closings differ from their German counterparts not so much in the basics of conversational organization as in the *interactional surplus* they contain. However, this should not be understood as implying that in German telephone calls there is no interactional work, since interactional work is involved even in openings or closings which comprise just the basic sequences. This becomes obvious if any of these sequences are omitted. For example, if you just pick up the phone without saying *Hello*?, although the physical channel is open, contact has not been established and the conversation cannot begin in the expected way. Alternatively, if you terminate a call by just hanging up, or even by simply saying *Goodbye*, without having properly initiated the closing section, you may unwittingly put your relationship with your telephone partner into jeopardy. What I maintain, then, is that the account of telephone openings and closings given by conversation analysts captures the *interactionally necessary work* for the conversation to start and end smoothly, and accordingly, it reflects *a minimally required attendance to the relationship aspect of communication*. However, this approach cannot account for the observed differences between Greek and German telephone calls, that is the *interactional surplus*. Any attempt to explain the differences has to be augmented by a framework which explicitly involves interactional considerations. Since I have discussed elsewhere (Pavlidou 1994) the difficulties that arise in applying Brown and Levinson's (1987) framework to my findings, I will focus here on Laver's (1975, 1981) approach, for two reasons: (a) he is explicitly concerned with the initial and closing phases of conversation which he calls 'transitional' (e.g. Laver 1975: 218), because the former leads from non-interaction to interaction and the latter 'from full interaction to departure'; (b) he focuses on the functions of phatic communion in these phases.

After an insightful analysis, Laver (1975: 236) comes to the conclusion that the functions of phatic communion 'in the crucial marginal phases of encounters when their [the participants'] psychological comfort is most at risk' are 'to establish and consolidate the interpersonal relationship between the two participants' and to ease 'the transitions to and from interaction'. Or putting the two functions together: phatic communion serves 'to facilitate the management of interpersonal relationships'. Laver's proposal is certainly helpful for interpreting my findings on Greek and German openings/closings, but only locally or partially. For example, as I have argued elsewhere using Laver's framework, in the German closings the emphasis is on the 'consolidation of the relationship', whereas Greek closings are organized toward a 'cooperative parting' (Pavlidou 1997: 160). However, an overall synthesis would be difficult to achieve for the following (*inter alia*) reasons.

Firstly, Laver's (and others') conception of phatic communion as 'applying to choices from a limited set of stereotyped phrases of greeting, parting, commonplace remarks about the weather, and small talk' (Laver 1975: 218) leads to a static understanding of a very important phenonemon.[14] As the study of the opening section of calls shows, other means such as particles like German *Na?*, playful use of V-form, and the repetition of simple greeting formula also have a phatic function. Secondly, Laver's analysis suggests, at least implicitly, that phatic communion is the only (verbal) means available for facilitating the management of interpersonal relationships. However, other means can achieve the same ends; for example, elaboration of the mutuality of the partners' decision to terminate the call (cf. Pavlidou 1998a: 92) or the playful use of the V-form (cf. Pavlidou 1994: 501). Although it is very important to recognize the significance of phatic communion and to give it a proper place in a theory of communication, it would be wrong either not to recognize that other means can facilitate the management of interpersonal relationships, or to conflate such means with phatic communion.[15]

In other words, I take phatic communion to be just one way of attending to the relationship aspect of communication. One can attend to the relationship aspect of communication not only by *doing something* (i.e. interactional work), but also by *not doing something*, which brings me back to my results. The 'Greek' way may be to exhibit an interactional surplus and build the relationship through small talk, but the 'German' way may be to refrain from keeping the partner on the phone for too long and letting him/her know pretty soon the reason for calling. Both styles may pay equally good, though different, services to the relationship aspect of communication. What I am claiming then is that there are numerous ways of attending to the relationship aspect of communication: for example phatic communion, redundancy, negative politeness, talk about the relationship itself and also strategies of directness which may result in the omission of all of the previous. Which way is opted for presumably depends not only on the phase of the conversation, but also on cultural factors.

KEY POINTS

1. This study illustrates that there may be cross-cultural differences in the way (telephone) conversations are conducted, which may in turn lead to interactional dissonance or misunderstandings in intercultural encounters.
2. Such differences, as shown in this study, may have less to do with the basic structure of conversational organization and more with an *interactional surplus*, that is with interactional investments that go beyond the work that is absolutely necessary in order to set up, unfold and end a conversation.
3. This study suggests that different cultural groups may pay equally good, though different, services to the relationship aspect of communication. For example, the more extensive use of phatic utterances before stating the reason of the call in the Greek data does not necessarily imply that Greeks are more 'polite' than Germans, who according to the data here opt for a more direct path to the main section of the call; both groups may be acting politely, but in different ways. Nor does, for example, longer leave-taking in the Greek data mean that Greeks care more for their conversational partners while Germans do not. There are numerous ways of attending to the relationship aspect of communication, and different cultural groups may have different preferences and orientations as to what strategies they employ.
4. A word of caution: it is not uncommon in cross-cultural studies to overemphasize differences and to neglect similarities, and to put forward sweeping generalizations about cultural groups without taking relevant conversational and contextual factors sufficiently into account. It is therefore important that findings as reported in this study are understood as motivated hypotheses for further research, including intra-cultural in-depth analyses of interaction.

DISCUSSION QUESTIONS

1. In your country/language, how are the opening and closing sections of telephone conversations between acquaintances usually managed (e.g. who speaks first, how is recognition accomplished, how fast do you get to the reason for calling, which linguistic items can function as pre-closings, etc.)? Do the characteristics seem more similar to the Greek or the German conversations described here?
2. In your country, what types of comments or topics are considered 'safe', and suitable for phatic talk with people you do not know well? How comfortable would you feel using each of the phrases below to a casual acquaintance you met in a corridor at university/work, and why? What other phrases might you be likely to use in this context?
   (a) *How are things?*
   (b) *Have you had lunch?*
   (c) *Where are you going?*
   (d) *It's really cold today, isn't it?*
   (e) *How's life?*
3. Try to explain the differences reported here between the German and Greek ways of attending to the relationship aspect of communication using the sociocultural interactional principles (SIPs) of equity and association in Spencer-Oatey's rapport management model (see Chapter 2). How satisfactory is this framework?

Notes

1. This particular example was written down from memory after the end of the telephone call. All the other excerpts are taken from recorded telephone calls which were later transcribed (see below for details). The Greek examples are presented in a phonetic transliteration (as close to IPA as possible), using however capital letters to indicate the beginning of a sentence or a name; stress is not marked. In translating the Greek and German excerpts into English, I tried to give an approximate English equivalent without losing totally the original linguistic form; conversational particles in Greek or German which have no exact equivalent in English are left untranslated; they appear in capitals in the English translation of the excerpt. Brackets enclosing three dots, that is [. . .] mean that part of a turn, or turn sequence, has been left out.
2. The different positions taken on this, that is universality versus cultural variation, is one of the issues discussed in the volume on telephone calls edited by Luke and Pavlidou (2002a), in particular in the introduction of the book (Luke and Pavlidou 2002b) and in the chapters by Schegloff (2002) and ten Have (2002); see also Pavlidou (2005).
3. Of course, not every telephone call is motivated by a practical or transactional reason, as we shall see below; there are also calls which are made 'just to hear how you're doing', 'just to talk'. In my view, these are equally legitimate 'reasons' for calling, serving primarily social rather than transactional purposes.
4. For more information on German openings cf. for example Henne and Rehbock 1979; Berens 1981; Brinker and Sager 1989; Liefländer-Koistinen and Neuendorff 1991; on Greek openings cf. for example Sifianou 1989; Bakakou-Orfanou 1990; and Pavlidou 1991, 1994, 1995.

5. This opening is taken from the telephone call number 22 in the Brons-Albert corpus (Brons-Albert 1984); the original transcription is retained. No information is given as to whether 'B' and 'A' are last or first names; presumably, 'B' is a last name in the first line, but a first name in the second line, since friends in Germany (who also use the T-form, as it becomes clear later on in the call) would not address each other with their last names.
6. An important element in these very first turns of telephone calls among familiars is *ela* (literally: come-IMPERATIVE) which may appear in almost every turn of the opening section with various phatic functions: from showing that the physical channel has been established up to signalling recognition of the interlocutor (cf. Pavlidou 1995, 1998b).
7. Another variant, used among strangers or when the addressee is for example older than the speaker, has a higher status etc., is *ja sas* (literally: health to you-V-form). Other greeting formulas, like *kalimera* (literally: good day), *kalispera* (literally: good evening), *çerete* (literally: rejoice-IMPERATIVE), may be used as well, but they can be understood as more formal.
8. Other studies for example Liefländer-Koistinen and Neuendorff 1991; House and Kasper 1981; Byrnes 1986; also provide some evidence in support of this conclusion.
9. For German closings, cf. Henne and Rehbock 1979; Werlen 1984; Brinker and Sager 1989; Liefländer-Koistinen and Neuendorff 1991; for Greek closings, cf. Pavlidou 1997, 1998a, 2002.
10. I owe this coinage to Sue Ervin-Tripp (personal communication, Berkeley, summer 1997).
11. It also shows repetition of markers of agreement (turn 3: *Endaksi. Ne.* $All right. Yes.$) which is not necessary from the organizational point of view.
12. There are other particles like this in German (e.g. *nö*, *ge*, *gell*, *wa*) with similar function, but usually with more restricted use according to the geographical-dialectal origin of the speaker.
13. This closing comes from telephone call number 20 in the Brons-Albert corpus (Brons-Albert 1984); it is presented here in the original transcription.
14. Cf. Also Coupland et al.'s (1992) arguments for a dynamic understanding of phatic communion.
15. It would be equally wrong to subsume any non-propositional aspect of interaction under the term 'phatic' and thus miss the important elements that the term stands for (see Section 6.2.3.2). More on this in Pavlidou (1998b).

Suggestions for further reading

Luke, K. K. and Pavlidou, T.-S. (eds) (2002) *Telephone Calls: Unity and Diversity in Conversational Structure across Languages and Cultures*. Amsterdam: Benjamins.

Suggestions for Further Reading for Part 2: Cross-Cultural Empirical Studies Involving Native Speakers

Albert, R. D. and Ha, I. A. (2004) Latino/Anglo-American differences in attributions to situations involving touch and silence. *International Journal of Intercultural Relations*, 28(3–4): 253–80.

Aukrust, V. G. and Snow, C. E. (1998) Narratives and explanations during mealtime conversations in Norway and the U.S. *Language in Society*, 27: 221–46.

Bilbow, G. (1995) Requesting strategies in the cross-cultural business meeting. *Pragmatics*, 5(1): 45–55.

Blum-Kulka, S. and House, J. (1989) Cross-cultural and situational variation in requesting behavio. In S. Blum-Kulka, J. House and G. Kasper (eds) *Cross-Cultural Pragmatics: Requests and Apologies*, Norwood, NJ, Ablix, 123–54.

Bresnahan, M. J., Ohashi, R., Liu, W. Y., Nebashi, R. and Liao, C.-C. (1999) A comparison of response styles in Singapore and Taiwan. *Journal of Cross-Cultural Psychology*, 30(3): 342–58.

Clancy, P. M., Thompson, S. A., Suzuki, R. and Tao, H. (1996) The conversational use of reactive tokens in English, Japanese, and Mandarin. *Journal of Pragmatics*, 26: 355–87.

Eslami, Z. R. (2005) Invitations in Persian and English: ostensible or genuine? *Intercultural Pragmatics*, 2(4): 453–80.

Eslamirasekh, Z. (1993) A cross-cultural comparison of the requestive speech act realization patterns in Persian and American English. In L. F. Bouton and Y. Kachru (eds) *Pragmatics and Language Learning. Monograph Series, Vol.4.* Urbana-Champaign, Division of English as an International Language, University of Illinois at Urbana-Champaign, 85–103.

Félix-Brasdefer, J. C. (2003) Declining an invitation: a cross-cultural study of pragmatic strategies in American English and Latin American Spanish. *Multilingua*, 22(3): 224–55.

Goodwin, R. and Lee, I. (1994) Taboo topics among Chinese and English friends: a cross-cultural comparison. *Journal of Cross-Cultural Psychology*, 25(3): 325–38.

Hasegawa, T. and Gudykunst, W. B. (1998) Silence in Japan and the United States. *Journal of Cross-Cultural Psychology*, 29(5): 668–84.

Heinz, B. (2003) Backchannel responses as strategic responses in [German, American English and] bilingual speakers' conversations. *Journal of Pragmatics*, 35(7): 1113–42.

Herbert, R. K. (1991) The sociology of compliment work: an ethnocontrastive study of Polish and English compliments. *Multilingua*, 10(4): 381–402. [A shortened version is reprinted in N. Coupland and A. Jaworski (eds) *Sociolinguistics. A Reader and Coursebook*, London: Macmillan.]

Holmes, J. (2005) Why tell stories? Contrasting themes and identities in the narratives of Maori and Pakeha women and men. In S. F. Kiesling and C. Bratt Paulston (eds) *Intercultural Discourse and Communication.* Oxford: Blackwell, 110–34.

Iwasaki, S. and Horie, P. I. (1998) The 'Northridge Earthquake' conversations: conversational patterns in Japanese and Thai and their cultural significance. *Discourse and Society*, 9(4): 501–29.

Jiang, X. (2006) Cross-cultural pragmatic differences in [handling of requests and refusals in] US and Chinese press conferences: the case of the North Korea nuclear crisis. *Discourse and Society*, 17(2): 237–57.

Kwon, J. (2004) Expressing refusals in Korean and in American English. *Multilingua,* 23(4): 339–64.

Lorenzo-Dus, N. (2001) Compliment responses among British and Spanish university students: a contrastive study. *Journal of Pragmatics*, 33(1): 107–27.

Márquez Reiter, R. (2002) A contrastive study of indirectness [in requests] in Spanish: evidence from Uruguayan and peninsular Spanish. *Pragmatics*, 12(2): 135–52.

Nelson, G. L., Al-Batal, M., and Echols, E. (1996) Arabic and English compliment responses: potential for pragmatic failure. *Applied Linguistics*, 17(4): 411–32.

Olshtain, E. (1989) Apologies across languages. In S. Blum-Kulka, J. House and G. Kasper (eds) *Cross-Cultural Pragmatics: Requests & Apologies.* Norwood, NJ: Ablex, 155–73.

Pearson, V. M. S. and Stephan, W. G. (1998) Preferences for styles of negotiation: a comparison of Brazil and the U.S. *International Journal of Intercultural Relations*, 22(1): 67–83.

Tryggvason, M-T. (2006) Communicative behaviour in family conversation: comparison of amount of talk in Finnish, SwedishFinnish, and Swedish families. *Journal of Pragmatics*, 38(11): 1795–1810.

Young, R. F. and Lee, J. (2004) Identifying units in interaction: reactive tokens in Korean and English conversations. *Journal of Sociolinguistics*, 8(3): 380–407.

Part 3
Processes in Intercultural Interaction

Editor's Introduction

Having read Parts 1 and 2 of this book, readers should have a clear understanding of key concepts and issues associated with rapport management, and should be aware of various types of normative differences between cultural groups in how they handle the relational aspects of communication. However, as mentioned in the introduction to Part 2, cross-cultural (i.e. comparative) studies do not tell us how people will necessarily behave or react when they take part in intercultural interactions, that is when they interact with people from one or more cultural groups. Information on the norms and interactional principles of the interlocutors' cultural groups provides useful 'baseline' data for analysing such intercultural encounters; however, we also need theoretical clarification of the range of factors that influence people's actual performance and reactions. Part 3, therefore, returns to theoretical issues.

Chapter 7, 'Pragmatic Transfer', analyses in detail how people draw on pragmatic knowledge in the communication process and how this can affect intercultural encounters. It considers this from a Relevance Theory perspective. Chapter 8, 'Communication Accommodation Theory', focuses on ways in which speakers can 'attune' their talk more or less to each other. It explains the basic tenets of the theory and describes how intercultural discourse can be analysed from this perspective. Chapter 9, 'Adaptation and Identity', deals with a very different issue – it explores the impact that life in a different culture can have on people's sense of identity. This is a very important aspect of intercultural communication, and it is very relevant to rapport because face and identity are closely interconnected (Spencer-Oatey 2007). This chapter thus takes us beyond a pragmatic approach to intercultural communication, and helps illustrate the need for the field to draw on insights from a range of disciplines.

Part 4 of the book returns to empirical studies to help illustrate the concepts and issues explained in Part 3.

7 Pragmatic Transfer

Vladimir Žegarac and Martha C. Pennington

Chapter Outline

7.1 Introduction 141
7.2 What is pragmatic transfer? 142
7.3 How can pragmatic transfer be identified? 144
7.4 How can pragmatic transfer be investigated empirically? 145
7.5 Explaining pragmatic transfer 148
7.6 Are there different types of pragmatic transfer? 155
7.7 Pragmatic transfer, pragmatic theory and second language acquisition 157
7.8 Conclusion 161
Key points 161
Discussion questions 162
Suggestions for further reading 163

7.1 Introduction

Each chapter of this book touches, more or less directly, on the ways in which culture-specific aspects of communicative competence affect what goes on in situations of communication between people from different cultural backgrounds. An insight into *pragmatic transfer* (where by 'pragmatic transfer' we mean, roughly, the carry over of pragmatic knowledge from one culture to another) is important for a good understanding of intercultural communication. This chapter aims to provide the basis for understanding pragmatic transfer by focusing on the following questions:

(a) What is pragmatic transfer?
(b) How can pragmatic transfer be identified?

(c) How can pragmatic transfer be investigated empirically?
(d) How can pragmatic transfer be explained theoretically?
(e) What is the place of pragmatic transfer in second language acquisition?

Each of these questions raises a range of issues, only some of which can be considered here. Our main aim is to provide the reader with a good vantage point for further independent investigation of pragmatic transfer in the context of intercultural communication.

There are two types of approach to *pragmatics*: the social and the cognitive. These two approaches lead to different outcomes: social pragmatics provides descriptions of communicative behaviour, whereas cognitive pragmatics explains how this behaviour is made possible by specific cognitive mechanisms (cf. Blakemore 1992: 47). Despite occasional claims to the contrary, the two approaches are not intrinsically incompatible. Some (if not most) issues relating to verbal communication can only be studied successfully from both points of view. Pragmatic transfer is a case in point. It is a cognitive phenomenon by definition, because it concerns some aspects of human knowledge, but it must also be studied descriptively from a social point of view, because the observation and analysis of communicative behaviour (whether based on naturally occurring or experimentally elicited data) present by far the most important source of evidence for pragmatic transfer. In particular, the discussion of the fourth question ('How can pragmatic transfer be explained theoretically?') explores the possibility of reconciling and combining the insights from social pragmatics (especially Brown and Levinson's (1987) work on face) with the cognitive approach of Sperber and Wilson's (1986/95) Relevance Theory.

7.2 What is pragmatic transfer?

The term 'transfer' is generally used to refer to the systematic influences of existing knowledge on the acquisition of new knowledge. People usually approach a new problem or situation with an existing *mental set*: a frame of mind involving an existing disposition to think of a problem or a situation in a particular way (see Sternberg 1995: 342–5; Holyoak and Thagard 1995). Mental sets are largely determined by culture-specific knowledge. Therefore, communication between individuals from different cultural backgrounds may be influenced by their different mental sets. For example, in some cultures an offer of coffee after a meal is generally recognized as a polite way to indicate to the guests that they ought to leave soon if they do not wish to outstay their welcome. In other cultures, an offer of coffee on a similar occasion is just an act of the host's kindness (or even an invitation to the guests to stay a little bit longer than they had intended).

If interactants from different cultural backgrounds are unaware of the differences in their respective mental sets, misunderstandings are likely to occur. Misunderstandings of this sort involve the carryover of culture-specific knowledge from a situation of intracultural communication to a situation of intercultural communication. In psychology, the term 'transfer' refers to any carryover of knowledge or skills from one problem situation to another. In the offer of coffee example, we assume that the transfer in question is pragmatic for the following reasons. The problem has to do with the way in which an offer of coffee is typically understood in the context of a particular type of situation: roughly, guests having a meal at a friend's home. A communication problem is at stake: to figure out what is the intended implicit import of the offer of coffee; and the difficulty does not lie with the linguistic meaning of the words used. (If it did, the transfer would be linguistic/semantic, rather than pragmatic.) To conclude: this example points to the reasons for studying pragmatic transfer (for instance, transfer may lead to miscommunication); it gives some indications about the possible approaches (for instance, pragmatic transfer is close to the psychological notion of transfer as a factor in general problem solving); and it provides a good basis for a fairly adequate definition of the term 'pragmatic transfer':

> Pragmatic transfer is the transfer of pragmatic knowledge in situations of intercultural communication.

This definition is rather more complex than it may seem at first sight, because some of its elements are not entirely well understood. For instance, there is no universal agreement among researchers on answers to questions like the following: What is pragmatic knowledge? How is it stored and put to use? What is the relationship between pragmatic knowledge and linguistic knowledge?, and many others. Studies of pragmatic transfer are partly guided by views on these issues, but they also provide valuable input for assessing the validity of such views. Fortunately, the starting point for investigating pragmatic transfer – the identification of situations in which transfer has occurred – does not depend on a great number of theoretically contentious premises.

Although it is customary to study pragmatic transfer in the context of second language acquisition, this is by no means necessary: as the offer of coffee example shows, pragmatic transfer is relatively independent of language because pragmatic knowledge is distinct from, although it interfaces with, linguistic knowledge. To give another illustration, Chapter 12 discusses the difficulties that East Germans have in job interviews conducted by prospective West German employers. The following is a slightly adapted version of a typical exchange in English translation (see Chapter 12, Example 6, for a detailed transcription of the German text):

(1) Interviewer:	And with your boss? Did you ever have well any argument? No?
Applicant:	Never.
Interviewer:	Because you got on with him so well?
Applicant:	No, that's got nothing to do with it. I'm respectful.

From the point of view of the East German applicant, being respectful is a very desirable quality. The pragmatic (i.e. communicative) competence of the applicant which has been shaped by life in East Germany is transferred to a situation in which successful impression management presupposes a set of cultural values which the applicant is blissfully unaware of. This is an example of pragmatic transfer within a single language.

7.3 How can pragmatic transfer be identified?

There is no fail-safe procedure for establishing that an act of communication is influenced by pragmatic transfer. However, the assumption that this type of transfer is involved may be supported by observations which focus on the communicative behaviour of learners in their first language (L1) and second language (L2), in comparison to the linguistic behaviour of native speakers of the second language. This is easiest to explain by using an example, such as responses to compliments. People from different cultures often respond to compliments in systematically different ways. Let us assume that in a particular situational context, speakers of a particular language X (LX) accept compliments without showing modesty. In such cases a speaker might accept a compliment such as 'You did a really good job' with a simple expression of 'Thanks', that is without expressing any reservations about the validity or the importance of the compliment. Let us assume further that in the same type of situation, native speakers of another language Y (LY) typically accept compliments, but play down (and are culturally expected to play down) their importance. It seems reasonable to assume that native speakers of LY who are learning LX may respond to compliments in LX in the same way as they would in LY. For example, they might respond to the compliment, 'You did a really good job' with an expression of modesty (e.g. 'You are too generous'). If this happens, we have fairly good grounds for assuming that native speakers of LY have carried over some pragmatic knowledge associated with the culture of LY to the performance of compliments in LX. In other words, they have carried over the L1 cultural knowledge that an expression of modesty is an appropriate response to a compliment, where in fact an acceptance/agreement response is more usual. This is a case of so-called negative pragmatic transfer, because the L2 learner has mistakenly generalized from pragmatic knowledge of L1 to a L2 setting. Negative transfer may, but need not, lead to miscommunication. This type of transfer is called negative, not because of its adverse effect on communicative success, but because it involves an unwarranted generalization from L1 pragmatic knowledge to a communicative situation in L2. Negative pragmatic transfer thus leads to imperfect pragmatic competence in L2, but imperfect pragmatic competence does not necessarily cause communicative failure.

For example, if native speakers of L2 realize that a non-native speaker's pragmatic knowledge of L2 is (or is likely to be) imperfect, they may make allowances (e.g. they might assume something like: *the non-native speaker is not being rude, he simply does not know that this type of answer is not appropriate in our culture*).

Just as negative transfer does not always lead to miscommunication, positive transfer does not always enhance the chances of communicative success. In some circumstances, the realization that the L2 learner is behaving like a native speaker may seem more important than what he is trying to communicate. For instance, if the L2 learner responds to compliments in the culturally appropriate way, while his L2 pragmatic competence is evidently flawed in many other respects, his appropriate communicative behaviour may be unexpected and so may be perceived as puzzling and mildly amusing. Instead of paying attention to the speaker's informative intention, the addressees may wonder about the peculiar correctness of the learner's use of L2. So positive transfer does not guarantee communicative success. This type of transfer is generally more difficult to identify than negative transfer, because the evidence for it is less direct. For example, let us assume that in both L1 and L2 compliments can be accepted with the same degree of modesty. This indicates that some aspect of a learner's L1 pragmatic knowledge is relevant to performance in L2. So if the L2 learner uses an expression of modesty in accepting compliments in L2 in roughly the same way as in L1, it is reasonable to assume that the learner's knowledge about communicating in L1 has contributed to his/her ability to communicate in L2.

7.4 How can pragmatic transfer be investigated empirically?

Like all empirical research, investigations of pragmatic transfer based on the analysis of data must take into account a wide range of factors. These studies fall into two broad categories: quantitative and qualitative. Quantitative studies involve the collection of data from a considerable number of speakers. These data are then analysed statistically, and the emerging patterns of findings are interpreted. Qualitative studies focus on the meticulous description and explanation of a sample of naturally occurring data from a small number of individuals, sometimes only one. They aim at explaining a particular aspect of one, or perhaps several, situations of communication. The best way to find out about quantitative and qualitative studies of pragmatic transfer is to read some articles based on such research, and to try to design and carry out some small-scale projects (see the studies listed at the end of Parts 2 and 4, and the chapters in Part 5). Here, a brief overview of two studies of pragmatic transfer is given in order to highlight some important aspects of such studies.

7.4.1 A quantitative study of pragmatic transfer: Yoon (1991)

Responding to a compliment is an interesting type of speech act because the communicative situation in which it is performed presents the hearer with the following problem: if s/he accepts the compliment, s/he may be seen as lacking modesty; if s/he rejects the compliment, s/he may be seen as lacking appreciation for the speaker's opinions and values. From the social point of view, neither lack of modesty nor lack of respect for the interlocutor is desirable. That is why in many societies there are communicative strategies (i.e. set ways of communicating in a particular type of situation, in this case accepting a compliment) whose purpose is to avoid this conflict.

If the verbal strategies for responding to a compliment differ across cultures, then this cultural divergence can be expected to be the locus of pragmatic transfer. Yoon (1991) investigates this possibility by comparing the speech patterns of monolingual speakers of American English and Korean, with those of bilingual Korean–English speakers, when responding to compliments. The study involved 35 native speakers of American English, 40 speakers of Korean residing in Korea, and 33 Korean–English bilingual speakers who had lived in the United States for at least 16 years. Each group was asked to complete a questionnaire in their native language; in the case of the bilingual speakers, they completed one in each language. The questionnaire was in the form of a discourse production task: *Write down quickly what you would say in the following situation:...* (where the situation involved responding to a compliment made by a speaker of slightly higher status). Despite the reservations that are sometimes expressed in the literature (e.g. see Chapter 11), the discourse completion task is still considered a valuable tool in social pragmatics; and while it is wise to exercise caution in taking the validity of the findings for granted, this method should not be rejected out of hand (see Chapter 14).

The data obtained by Yoon arguably revealed not only the presence, but also the degree and the direction of bilingual transfer. First, significant differences between the responses of American English speakers and Korean Korean speakers were observed. American English speakers' responses showed a significant preference for an agreement strategy, while Korean Korean speakers showed a marked preference for a modesty strategy. Second, Korean–English bilinguals, in their responses in English, used an agreement strategy to a lesser extent than native American English speakers, but to a greater extent than Korean Korean speakers. This finding suggests negative pragmatic transfer from Korean. Third, Korean–English bilinguals, in their responses in Korean, used a modesty strategy to a greater extent than American English speakers, but to a lesser extent than Korean Korean speakers. This finding suggests negative pragmatic transfer from American English to Korean for the bilingual speakers.

7.4.2 A qualitative study of pragmatic transfer: Tyler (1995)

Tyler (1995) points out that quantitative studies shed little light on the ways in which people who engage in communication draw upon their knowledge of their own culture. She presents a qualitative case study based on a videotaped verbal interaction between a native speaker of Korean and a native speaker of American English. The interactants engaged in communication without realizing that they had very different assumptions about their respective roles and statuses, and this led to miscommunication: each participant assumed that the other one was uncooperative. The study shows how intercultural miscommunication arises through negative pragmatic transfer.

Tyler analyses the videotape of an actual tutoring session. The tutor was a male Korean graduate in Computer and Information Science who had spent over two years in the United States. His English was reasonably good, and he had volunteered to give tutoring sessions in Computer Programming. The student was a female native speaker of American English taking an introductory computer programming course, who needed help with a programming assignment: to write a computer program for keeping score in bowling. It is important to note that both interactants were motivated to do well: the Korean computer science graduate took part in the tutoring sessions in order to improve his English communication skills. The US native-speaker student needed help on an assignment, and failure to complete the assignment would have had an adverse effect on her final grade.

At the beginning of the interaction, the student asks if the teacher knows how to keep score in bowling. The tutor's response is: 'Yeah approximately'. In fact he is very familiar with bowling, but the student interprets his response as an acknowledgement of his lack of knowledge of bowling. In the context (i.e. the set of background assumptions) readily available to the student, the hedge, 'approximately' seems relevant as an indication that the teacher is less than fully competent as a bowler (a useful study of hedges, or downgraders, is Itani 1996). The teacher is unaware of this. In the teacher's culture, the translation equivalent of 'approximately' ('com', literally 'a little') is conventionally used as a marker of modesty. In the light of his cultural background, the teacher perhaps assumes that it would be inappropriate to make an unqualified statement about his competence and, under the influence of his pragmatic knowledge of L1, opts for an expression which is inappropriate in L2. The initial misunderstanding between teacher and student leads on to pervasive miscommunication. For example, when the teacher accompanies his typing on the computer with loud comments like 'uhmm Open, spare, strike', the student thinks that the teacher is trying to work out for himself the meaning of these words, whereas the teacher is trying to help the student to learn a particular sequence of instructions. Assuming that the teacher lacks adequate knowledge of bowling, the student says: 'That has to do with the bowling game'. By stating the obvious, the student is taken to suggest that the tutor knows next to nothing about bowling. To make things worse, the student – who has previously admitted that her knowledge of bowling is limited – makes a number of incorrect assertions about the game, and challenges the teacher's views repeatedly. Given the scale of the misunderstanding, it is hardly surprising that the teacher finds the student uncooperative and aggressive, while the student thinks that the teacher is confused and incompetent.

A description of what seems to go on in instances of (mis)communication like those considered here is only a first step towards explaining pragmatic transfer. The next, and most important, step is to show how the carryover of pragmatic knowledge from one communicative situation to another can be accounted for in terms of pragmatic theory, whose primary aim is 'to describe the factors other than a knowledge of sentence meaning that affect the interpretation of utterances' (Wilson and Sperber 1986: 36).

7.5 Explaining pragmatic transfer

Good explanations of pragmatic transfer have both practical and theoretical implications: practical, because they can help understand, solve and anticipate problems in communication across cultures, and theoretical, because the possibility of explaining pragmatic transfer may provide evidence for or against the theoretical framework used in the analysis. This section provides a sketch for such a framework. First, some important questions that a pragmatic analysis needs to answer are considered. This is followed by an outline of universal production and comprehension strategies which follow from a basic pragmatic principle. Finally, the ways these strategies interact with (culture-dependent) preferences or conventions for conducting communication exchanges is examined.

7.5.1 Three questions for pragmatic analysis

Countless examples can be found to illustrate the gap between knowing what a sentence means and knowing what a particular speaker means by an utterance of that sentence on a given occasion. One of the goals of linguistics is to explain how meanings are assigned to words in context. The main goal of pragmatics is to explain how speakers use language (as well as non-verbal modes of expression) to convey information which goes beyond the meanings of the words used. In order to live up to this task, pragmatic theory needs to address three questions:

1. What did the speaker intend to say (i.e. to communicate directly)?
2. What did the speaker intend to *imply* (i.e. to communicate indirectly)?
3. What was the intended *context*?

It should be noted that the term 'context' is used more broadly in social than in cognitive approaches to pragmatics. In social approaches 'context' is the total linguistic and non-linguistic background to an act of communication. In Sperber and Wilson's (1986/95) cognitive approach, this term refers to the set of mentally represented assumptions exploited in utterance interpretation.

In deciding on the intended interpretation of the utterance, the addressee has to make some assumptions about these three questions. For example, the initial misunderstanding in Tyler's study occurs because the student did not realize what the tutor intended to say by the utterance: 'Yeah, approximately'. She thought that he was using the adverb as a way of limiting or hedging on the extent of his knowledge of bowling. But the tutor actually meant to say something like 'I know how to keep score in bowling'. By using the adverb 'approximately', he intended to indicate that he was observing a social convention about the need to show modesty, implying that he did not want to impose his authority on the student. The student was unaware of this. Given her cultural background, the context in which the tutor intended her to interpret his utterance was not available to her: the English adverb 'approximately' is not conventionally used to indicate modesty. When the tutor said: 'uhmm Open, spare, strike', the student misinterpreted his attitude towards this utterance. She thought that he was treating these instructions as mere possibilities, hoping to remember or discover the correct procedure, whereas he considered them as factual information which the student ought to learn.

To sum up: the student's failure to work out what the tutor intended to say and what he intended to imply stemmed from the teacher's inability to anticipate in which context the student was likely to interpret the teacher's utterance. What let the tutor down was not his knowledge of the English language, but his knowledge about how this language is used. This pragmatic knowledge is organized in a particular way and it is applied in communication in accordance with some basic communicative principles and strategies.

7.5.2 Pragmatic competence and pragmatic transfer

A generally accepted model of pragmatic competence does not exist, but some important insights into human communication can be brought to bear on this subject. First, communication involves information processing, which is constrained by considerations of efficiency. Second, it involves reasoning based on the interpretation of communicative signals (gestures, utterances) in context. In particular, communication cannot be reduced to the hearer's or analyst's recovery of the linguistic meaning of the words. Third, the relation between types of signals and contexts in which they are processed may be conventionalized to a greater or lesser extent. Fourth, the culture-specific conventionalized aspects of interpretation build on certain universal dispositions for the formation of specific types of concepts in the social domain.

The first and fourth points are the bread and butter of cognitive pragmatics (e.g. Grice 1989; Sperber and Wilson's 1986/95 Relevance Theory) and cognitive anthropology (see Sperber et al. 1995; Gumperz and Levinson 1996; Bloch 1998). The second point has been central to the many developments of Grice's (1989) ideas (e.g. Clark 1996; Levinson 1983; Sperber and Wilson 1986/95). The third point has received more attention in empirical research within social pragmatics (a good overview is Schiffrin 1994) than within the cognitive approach of Sperber and Wilson. It has also been studied extensively in psychology (Gibbs 1981, 1986) and in pragmatic theory and philosophy of language (see Morgan 1978; Bach and Harnish 1979/82; Searle 1996).

7.5.2.1 Communicative efficiency: relevance

Good speakers manage to communicate a lot of information in a way which does not put more strain on the cognitive resources of their addressees than is necessary. In other words, the goal of communication is not merely to convey information, but to convey it economically (see Chapter 3). This observation underlies the most important communicative principle, the principle of communicative efficiency, or, more technically, the communicative principle of relevance. Relevance (especially the tendency to minimize the expenditure of processing effort) is the driving force behind pragmatic transfer (cf. Pennington 1999). The more a new problem resembles old ones which have been solved successfully in the past, the easier it will be to solve the new problem. Since every communicative situation presents a new problem for the interlocutors, the more they can rely on their experience from previous exchanges, the easier the problem will be.

The Communicative Principle of Relevance

Every communicative signal (pointing gesture, utterance, etc.) communicates the following guarantee:

(a) the signal is worth processing (i.e. worth paying attention to), and
(b) the signal used is the most relevant one compatible with the speaker's abilities and preferences.

(A signal is relevant to the addressee to the extent that it communicates information which is worth having, and to the extent that it makes it easy for the addressee to figure out this information.)

(Adapted from Sperber and Wilson 1995: 260, 270)

It follows from the Communicative Principle of Relevance that in all genuine acts of verbal communication:

(i) the speaker should aim to produce an utterance which conveys the information s/he intends to communicate and makes it as easy as possible for the addressee to figure out the speaker's intended meaning, and
(ii) the addressee is entitled to expect the speaker's behaviour to be consistent with the communicative principle of relevance. Hence, this principle provides the basis for a production strategy, followed by the communicator, and a comprehension strategy, followed by the addressee.

Production strategy

Given your preferences and goals, choose the least effort-demanding option for the hearer.

(Žegarac 2004: 203)

Comprehension Strategy

> Begin by processing an utterance in the initial context; if necessary, discard some contextual assumptions and replace them with others, until you arrive at an interpretation which is consistent with the Principle of Relevance (or until you accept that miscommunication has occurred).
>
> (Adapted from Deirdre Wilson, lecture notes)

In the process of interpretation, then, context selection is driven by the search for relevance. The Communicative Principle of Relevance explains how successful context selection is possible: the addressee starts off with an initial context, which s/he then adjusts by discarding those contextual assumptions which seem irrelevant and by replacing them with others which seem relevant. In many cases of miscommunication involving negative pragmatic transfer, the speaker makes incorrect assumptions about the context in which the hearer is likely to interpret the utterance. The difficulties relating to context selection may lead to miscommunication when the following two conditions obtain: (a) the speaker's and the hearer's background knowledge from which the context for utterance interpretation is selected differ significantly, and (b) the speaker and the hearer are unaware of these differences.

Let us consider whether these observations on utterance understanding can provide the basis for an account of miscommunication between the teacher and the student in Tyler's (1995) study (Section 8.4.2). First, at the outset, the teacher and the student probably have different contextual assumptions about the respective roles of teacher and student in classroom interaction based on their different backgrounds. The student's context includes some assumptions to the effect that many aspects of the relationship are negotiable. By contrast, the teacher more probably assumes that in this type of situation his authority is taken for granted and cannot be questioned. Moreover, the teacher possibly mistakenly assumes that some semantic translation equivalents ('com' [Korean] – 'approximately' [English]) are also pragmatically equivalent. So it is very likely that the teacher and the student are both unaware of the differences in their initial contexts of their verbal interaction, and for this reason their exchange runs into difficulties. They cannot resolve those difficulties, because each fails to make appropriate adjustments to his or her initial context. And they fail to do this because each lacks the awareness of the other's culture. Thus, the teacher's utterance 'Yeah, approximately' seems relevant to the student in one way (namely, as communicating an admission of his incompetence), while the teacher intends it to be relevant in a different way (namely, as a modest assertion of his competence).

7.5.2.2 Speaker's preferences, context selection and sociocultural conventions

Tyler's example indicates the link between the problem of context selection, which is of central importance in cognitive accounts of utterance comprehension, and sociocultural conventions, which are the focus of social approaches to pragmatics. This link becomes particularly clear once the role of the speaker's preferences in utterance understanding is examined more closely. Consider the following exchange:

(2) A: So, it's your birthday on Monday. And how old will you be?
B: Too old to want to talk about it.

A's question makes evident which information would be relevant to her (namely, fairly precise information about B's age). B's answer is evidently not optimally relevant to A, because it does not provide this information. Instead, B communicates her preference for not talking about her age. So, B's utterance is consistent with the Communicative Principle of Relevance, because it is the best (i.e. most relevant) answer available to B, given her preferences. Now, very often, the speaker's preferences reflect, not so much individual taste, disposition towards the hearer, values, mood and so on, but rather social conventions about communication. Thus, depending on the setting in which the exchange takes place, B may well be indirectly reprimanding A for transgressing some social conventions about (not) asking personal questions (such as questions relating to age, income, etc.). But B's communicative intention will be fulfilled only if A is sufficiently aware of the social conventions that B has in mind to be able to access some assumptions about them, and to include those assumptions in the context for the interpretation.

Similarly, in the teacher–student exchange in Tyler's article, the teacher's utterance 'Yeah, approximately' seems relevant to the student in the immediately available context as the teacher's acknowledgement of his lack of knowledge of the game of bowling. The contextual assumptions about the appropriateness of the teacher conveying modesty are simply not available to the student: they are not part of her cultural background. It seems plausible to assume that, if such assumptions were available to her, the student might be able to work out (the possibility) that the teacher is being modest, even if she is not aware of a particular convention about using hedges to indicate modesty. For example, learners of English from many cultural backgrounds do not find it all that difficult to grasp that the expression 'I am afraid . . .' is readily used to indicate the speaker's regret at not being able to make a contribution which is presumed highly desirable to the hearer. This understanding follows rather intuitively from (a) an awareness that, given the immediate context, the speaker could not be intending to communicate any significant degree of fear, and (b) a universal disposition of humans to attend to particular types of needs of their fellow humans, that is face needs. Hence, if the student had been aware that from the teacher's point of view, his affirmative answer should be accompanied by some indication of modesty, and that, in a teaching situation, his knowledge is presumed to be adequate, she might also have considered the possibility that the teacher had used the adverb 'approximately' as an indication of modesty.

A detailed account of what goes on in situations of intercultural communication must, however, do more than mention the speaker's preferences. It must answer the questions: 'Why do speakers have the preferences that they have?' and 'How are particular preferences related to particular aspects of the communicative situation?'. Accommodation theory (Giles and Coupland 1991, see also Chapter 8 in this book) brings together insights from several disciplines in an attempt to explain the types of preferences that are universally observed in communicative interaction between humans, and their culture-specific realizations. According to accommodation theory, the speaker's linguistic choices reflect two sorts of pressures: (a) the tendency to conform to the needs, abilities, interests, etc., of the addressees (i.e. the tendency to attend to the addressees' face), and (b) the tendency to use a speech style which reflects the speaker's individual and social identity (i.e. the tendency to maintain the speaker's own face).

Which of these two types of pressures is prevalent on a given occasion depends on the pressures presented by the particular communicative situation. The results of Yoon's study (see Section 8.4.1) are open to two interpretations. The Korean–English bilinguals' use of agreement strategies in English and modesty strategies in Korean, which differ from both American English and Korean Korean speakers respectively, could be due to negative pragmatic transfer. Yet these findings could also be explained in terms of accommodation theory. On the one hand, the pressure to conform to the needs, abilities, interests etc. of the addressees explains why Korean–English bilinguals tend to use the agreement strategy more when communicating in English than when communicating in Korean: they adjust their linguistic choices to the expectations of their American-born interlocutors. It also explains why they tend to use a modesty strategy more when they communicate in Korean than when they communicate in English: they adjust their linguistic choices to their native Korean addressees. On the other hand, the pressure to use a speech style which reflects the speaker's group identification or individual identity explains why the same group of speakers use the agreement strategy to a lesser extent than native American English speakers: they wish to identify themselves as having an identity distinct from that of the Americans. It also explains why they use a modesty strategy to a lesser extent than native speakers of Korean based in Korea: having lived in the United States for at least 16 years, they have acquired an identity distinct from that of Koreans who live in Korea. This account is interesting because it shows that what appears to be the result of 'negative' transfer is not always caused by ignorance or lack of proficiency in a second language, but may be motivated by social psychological pressures.

In Yoon's study, the communicative strategy adopted by the Korean– English bilingual speakers conforms to considerations of face in a fairly straightforward way. Other cases of pragmatic transfer are more complicated. Let us consider the conversation described by Günthner (Chapter 10 in this book). German informal conversational style is characterized by socially accepted challenges of the interlocutor's views.

Günthner describes a conversation between two German and two Chinese students, who were meeting for the first time, in which this strategy backfires. The Chinese students perceived their German interlocutors as rude, which is hardly surprising: disagreement with one's views is understood as a direct threat to face, unless some contextual assumptions which remove the force of threat are available. In Günthner's examples such assumptions were available only to the German students, who followed the conventional wisdom of their own culture that argumentative style makes for more interesting informal conversations, but not to their Chinese interlocutors, whose cultural background does not include such assumptions for this context. Had the mutual context of the interlocutors included this assumption, the debate could have proceeded in a fairly confrontational manner without causing offence, in much the same way as academic debates often do.

It follows from this that the Chinese students should familiarize themselves with a particular convention, in the context of which the (offending) communicative behaviour of the German students would appear neither face- threatening nor rude. However, it is often claimed that knowledge without justification is not real knowledge. Pragmatic knowledge is no exception. A good grasp of particular communicative norms, strategies etc., can be achieved provided they are properly grounded in the learner's system of pragmatic knowledge. Thus, the Chinese students who wish to communicate competently in a German cultural setting need to grasp more than the convention that it is quite appropriate to adopt an argumentative style in informal conversations. They also need to have some idea of why such a convention is acceptable: to the Germans, it makes conversation more interesting and lively; it indicates that the interlocutors take each other's views seriously and so on.

The examples of pragmatic transfer considered so far have to do with the effects of the carryover of pragmatic knowledge to communicative behaviour. It seems important to note that pragmatic transfer also affects the ways in which speakers belonging to one culture interpret the communicative behaviour of those from another. For example, Greek university students studying in England often perceive English people's use of expressions of gratitude as insincere (Spencer-Oatey, personal communication). Most English people categorically deny this allegation (though, of course, expressions of gratitude, such as 'Thank you', as well as any other type of utterance for that matter, can be used insincerely). Why, then, do Greek students have this impression? It seems that the pragmatic competences of native speakers of Greek and of native speakers of English differ with respect to conventions about the circumstances in which expressions of gratitude are appropriately used. To be more precise, in English, an expression of gratitude, such as 'Thank you', is appropriate on almost any occasion in which the speaker could be described as being in the hearer's debt, no matter how small the debt might be. But the corresponding conventions about the use of the Greek language are somewhat different in that expressions of gratitude in Greek should be used only provided the action being thanked for presents a considerable imposition on the hearer (for a detailed discussion of politeness in Greek, see Sifianou 1992a). As a consequence, thanking a close friend for a small favour may easily seem odd and even impolite. If this is correct, English speakers appear insincere to Greek speakers, because the latter judge the former by their own standards for the use of expressions of gratitude. In other words, they interpret the verbal behaviour of English people in the context of Greek conventions concerning the level of gratitude required to be worth communicating. This is a case of pragmatic transfer from Greek to English, which in this instance manifests itself in the interpretation, rather than in the production, of communicative behaviour.

To conclude: utterance comprehension is driven by a principle of communicative efficiency (the Principle of Relevance) and it is constrained by the cognitive abilities of the interlocutors, in particular, the availability of the appropriate context for utterance interpretation. An important factor in context selection is the identification of the speaker's preferences. Some of these preferences follow in a more or less straightforward way from universal considerations of face and communicative efficiency, whereas others reflect the culture-specific conventions of communicative behaviour (or idiosyncratic characteristics of the speaker, which are not examined here). An important part of the speaker's task is to anticipate the set of contexts available to the addressee. An important part of the addressee's task is to figure out in which context the speaker intended the utterance to be processed. The intended context often includes some assumptions about the speaker's preferences which are rooted in sociocultural conventions of communication. These conventions relate to different aspects of the communication process.

7.6 Are there different types of pragmatic transfer?

Kasper (1992) proposes a framework for analysing pragmatic transfer which is based on Leech's (1983) distinction between pragmalinguistics and sociopragmatics. According to Leech, the term pragmalinguistics refers to 'the particular resources which a given language provides for conveying particular illocutions' (Leech 1983: 11), and Kasper (1992: 208) points out that it includes not only the resources used for conveying illocutionary meaning, but also the plethora of devices available for managing relationships. Sociopragmatics refers to the culturally-based principles or maxims that underlie interactants' performance and interpretation of linguistic action. These include both culturally-based assessments of the typical characteristics of a given communicative activity (e.g. typical degrees of distance and equality/inequality between participants, people's rights and obligations and so on) and culturally-influenced

Table 7.1 Likely pragmatic perspectives of the interlocutors in Tyler's (1995) tutoring session

	The situation from the teacher's point of view	The situation from the student's point of view
Sociopragmatics		
Characteristics of the *type* of situational setting	• The teacher has higher status than students and the general pattern of teacher–student relationship is non-negotiable. • In classroom interactions, the teacher's knowledge is presumed (by both teacher and student) to be adequate, and superior to the student's knowledge. • Assertiveness on the teacher's part in a teaching context may intimidate the student • All decisions relating to the teaching process are the teacher's responsibility.	• The teacher has higher status than students, but this does not entail that the pattern of the relationship is non-negotiable. • In classroom interactions, the details of the teacher–student role relationship are negotiated, taking into account the relevant competencies of both teacher and student.
Characteristics of the *actual* situational setting	• The primary aim of the tutoring session is to help the student with a computer programming assignment. • The teacher's expertise in all relevant aspects of the task (i.e. computer programming and bowling) is presumed by both teacher and student • The secondary aim of the session is to help the tutor develop his teaching skills in English.	• The aim of the tutoring session is to get some help with her computer programming assignment. • The teacher's knowledge of computer programming (but not his knowledge of bowling) can be presumed. • The student is entitled to help the teacher in his understanding of bowling.
Pragmalinguistics		
Markers of illocutionary force	• 'Yeah' indicates assertion.	• 'Yeah' indicates assertion • 'Approximately' is a hedge on the propositional content of the utterance.
Politeness (rapport management) indicators	• '*Com*' is a politeness indicator of modesty in Korean. • 'Approximately' is a politeness indicator of modesty in English.	

dynamic assessments of actual communicative events. Pragmatic transfer can occur in both aspects, so Kasper (1992) refers to *pragmalinguistic transfer* and *sociopragmatic transfer*.

Let us consider how the exchange between the tutor and the student from Tyler's (1995) study could be described in these terms (see Table 7.1). Recall that the student asked the teacher if he knew how to keep score in bowling and the teacher replied 'Yeah, approximately'. Miscommunication occurred because the teacher had used the adverb 'approximately' as a marker of modesty, but the student interpreted it as a hedge on the propositional content of the utterance.

It should be clear from this example that social knowledge about communication is conventionally associated with particular linguistic expressions. So the social bases of communication (i.e. sociopragmatic knowledge) and the meaning of particular expressions of the language (i.e. pragmalinguistic knowledge) are closely interrelated; for example, it is part of the conventionalized meaning of the Korean word 'com' that it is an expression of modesty. So as Kasper (1992: 210) points out, while the distinction between pragmalinguistics transfer and sociopragmatic transfer is a useful one, 'the fuzzy edges between the two pragmatic domains will be noticeable'.

7.7 Pragmatic transfer, pragmatic theory and second language acquisition

Three observations about pragmatic transfer seem particularly important from a theoretical point of view: (a) transfer of pragmatic knowledge is fundamentally different from transfer of linguistic knowledge; (b) the everyday, commonsense meaning of the term 'transfer' may be misleading because it is different from the meaning of 'transfer' as a technical term used in psychology and second language acquisition; and (c) 'transfer' may be a useful technical term, even if its theoretical content is unclear. In this section we examine these claims in more detail.

7.7.1 Pragmatic transfer and second language acquisition

Pragmatic transfer is often thought of as falling in the domain of second language acquisition (cf. Kasper 1992). In this section we want to consider some possible reasons for this view.

The notion of 'language transfer' was originally developed, and still holds a central place in applied linguistics. Knowledge of the mother tongue (or another language) is said to be transferred to the subsequent learning of another language. Thus, according to Lado (1957: 2):

> [I]ndividuals tend to transfer the forms and meanings, and the distribution of forms and meanings of their native language and culture to the foreign language and culture, both

> productively when attempting to speak the language . . . and receptively when attempting to grasp and *understand the language.* (emphasis added)

Transfer is generally seen as a process that makes links between a source language (L1), that is one that a speaker has already acquired, and a target language (L2), that is one that a learner is attempting to learn (cf. Odlin, 1989: 27). The quote from Lado (1957) above may be taken to imply that pragmatic transfer is a subtype of language transfer. This construal of Lado's observation is based on the underlying assumption that communicative success is primarily dependent on language understanding: the speaker or writer encodes certain meanings into a linguistic signal, and the listener or reader decodes the signal, thus retrieving the intended message (where encoding and decoding are processes which effect the automatic pairing of messages with signals and signals with messages, respectively). Such an approach to verbal communication entails a dubious theoretical commitment, namely the assumption that pragmatic competence is a subpart of linguistic competence. In this view, the grammatical system of a language incorporates not only phonology (the sound system of language), syntactic rules (the rules of phrase and sentence structure) and semantics (the system of meaning), but also pragmatics (the rules and principles of verbal understanding). However, this view is seriously flawed. In addition to the grammar of a language, the learner acquires competence about (a) when (not) to speak, (b) what to talk about in a particular type of situation, (c) when and where it is appropriate to talk about a particular topic, (d) in what manner the conversation should be conducted and so on. As Hudson (1980: 20) points out:

> If communicative competence is to cover all these types of ability underlying successful speech, it must include at least the whole of 'linguistic competence' plus the whole of the amorphous range of facts included under 'pragmatics' (the rules for using linguistic items in context); and it must also make close contact with 'attitudes, values and motivations' [Hymes 1971], with which linguistics generally has had little to do, even in discussions of pragmatics.

Hudson's observation that language acquisition should be seen as part of the acquisition of communicative competence is quite compelling. However, if this is the case, then it is difficult to maintain the view that pragmatic transfer falls strictly within the domain of second language acquisition.

7.7.2 Is 'pragmatic transfer' a useful term?

Pragmatic transfer occurs in a particular type of problem-solving behaviour: communication. This observation points to some possible criticisms of the term. For instance, since all communication situations present problems, and pragmatic transfer may occur among speakers of the same language, whose cultural backgrounds are similar in many respects (see Chapter 12), it seems reasonable to wonder whether the term pragmatic transfer should figure at all in analyses of intercultural communication. Would it not be better simply to explain intercultural and intracultural communication in the same way, without invoking any notion of transfer?

In fact, it seems more plausible to argue that a shift in the opposite direction is desirable, and to use the term 'pragmatic transfer' to include all situations of communication. Typical communicative problems are rather different from typical problems of language acquisition, because pragmatic knowledge is neither organized nor put to use in the same way as linguistic knowledge. The term 'language transfer' seems more appropriate if restricted to the acquisition of (the grammar of) L2, because: (a) L1 and L2 present self-contained systems of knowledge (which may be isomorphic to a greater or lesser extent); and (b) the knowledge systems involved in linguistic transfer are not amenable to introspection. In contrast to language transfer, pragmatic transfer is pertinent to all situations of communication in which new communicative problems are solved by greater or lesser reliance on existing knowledge.

The independence of, as well as the differences between, linguistic knowledge and pragmatic knowledge suggest that pragmatic transfer should not be seen as inherently linked to second language acquisition. Many observations made earlier in this chapter about pragmatic conventions (e.g. in the United States, teacher–student interaction is negotiable from a position of equality; a confrontational, argumentative style is considered to lend interest to informal conversations in German) are amenable to conscious introspection, unlike the rules of grammar. Consider the following sentences:

(3) a. Je crois avoir expliqué ce problème.
b. *I believe to have explained this problem.

Introspection does not give us access to the rules of French grammar which make (3a) grammatical in French, or to the rules of English which make (3b) ungrammatical (as indicated by an asterisk) in English. The knowledge of social norms of communication differs from linguistic knowledge in two important respects. Linguistic knowledge is a self-contained system dedicated to the production and recognition of grammatical patterns, whereas the social conventions of communication interact fairly freely with the rest of our general knowledge (about people, situations, surroundings etc.). This is illustrated by the fact that sentence (3b) is felt to be ungrammatical in any context of situation (although it may be judged acceptable if used by a foreigner), while the appropriateness of particular types of communicative act is highly context sensitive: unlike the rules of grammar, the rules for the use of expressions of modesty, gratitude etc. must make reference to the context of situation (see Chapter 2). For example, a direct request for action such as 'Give me some ice! Quickly!' will be perfectly appropriate in some circumstances (e.g. following an accident, when what matters most is to stop the swelling of the injured person's ankle), and very inappropriate in others (e.g. when ordering drinks in a pub).

Hence one might argue that it makes more sense to talk about the transfer of linguistic knowledge from L1 to L2, than to link pragmatic transfer to distinct languages and cultures. In the case of language transfer, a self-contained system of knowledge, that is the grammar of L1, affects the acquisition of another self-contained system of knowledge, that is the grammar of L2. What goes on in the development of the ability to behave in situations of (intercultural) communication is rather different. Given that pragmatic knowledge is relatively independent of linguistic knowledge, there is no reason why pragmatic transfer would not occur in a linguistically homogeneous but culturally heterogeneous community, and since, unlike linguistic knowledge (i.e. the knowledge of grammar), pragmatic competence is not a self-contained system of knowledge, there is no reason to restrict the term transfer to the description of communication problems in different cultures.

A few points should perhaps be clarified. First, we are not claiming that pragmatic knowledge is generally used in a reflective, self-conscious manner. In spontaneous communication, people rely on routinized, almost automatized, decision-making, in much the same way as competent car drivers spontaneously execute sequences of coordinated actions without rehearsing them consciously. The important point is that pragmatic knowledge is amenable to introspection and can be used reflectively when the need arises. Second, although pragmatic knowledge is an integral part of the knowledge used in interpreting human behaviour, people's knowledge about how particular aspects of communicative interaction are conducted does not consist of individually listed assumptions, but seems to be organized in various formats, such as schemas, frames and scripts (see Tyler's (1995) article for an attempt to use these categories in explaining data on pragmatic transfer; for discussions of these terms in cognitive psychology see Ringland and Duce (1988); also see Chapter 3). But however these chunks of knowledge related to different kinds of situations are stored and retrieved, pragmatic knowledge interacts fairly freely with general knowledge. Third, if, as we have claimed (a) pragmatic knowledge is not insulated, as it were, from the general belief system of the interactants, and (b) the interpretation of human communicative behaviour is a special case of the interpretation of behaviour in general (see Chapter 3) then, (c) the term pragmatic transfer seems devoid of proper theoretical content: the notion of pragmatic transfer can be reduced to the general notion of knowledge transfer in psychology. This observation may well be valid, but there may still be a good case for using 'pragmatic transfer' as a technical term: it brings together, for the purpose of description and analysis, a range of different factors specifically involved in communication within one culture, and helps us to understand their importance in communication within that culture as well as across cultural boundaries.

A further objection to the term 'pragmatic transfer' (and to the term 'transfer' in general) might be that it is used in describing processes of communication in which nothing really transfers or changes place. For example, when someone wants to transfer a sum of money, say, £1,364 from one account to another, transfer can be said to have been effected only provided the sum of £1,364 has been debited from the first account and credited to the second. Nothing of this sort seems to happen in the transfer of (pragmatic or linguistic) knowledge. The best reply to this remark is that the meaning of 'transfer' as a technical term is different from the everyday, commonsense meaning of this word. The term 'pragmatic transfer' is probably best thought of as referring to the projection of existing knowledge to new situations of communication. Another interesting difference between the technical and the everyday use of the word 'transfer' is that the reliance on existing pragmatic knowledge in solving new communication problems leads to modifications of that knowledge. The (lack of) analogy with the transfer of money is illustrative again. Thus, the assertion that a sum of £1,364 has been transferred from one account to another would not be justified if £1,364 was the sum taken from the first account, and £635 the sum paid into the second account. However, in order to assume that pragmatic transfer has taken place it is sufficient for existing pragmatic knowledge to play some role, that is to be exploited to some extent, in solving a new communication problem.

To conclude: there is an important distinction between the knowledge of the meaning of a word or larger expression (i.e. its linguistic meaning) and the knowledge about how that word or expression is used. Therefore, the view that pragmatic transfer is a type of language transfer is unfounded. Pragmatic transfer is best seen as a special case of general knowledge transfer (in the sense in which this term is used in psychology). What makes it special is that it involves a particular type of knowledge, pragmatic knowledge, and what makes it a case of general knowledge transfer is the fact that pragmatic knowledge interacts freely with general knowledge (and is, in this sense, an integral part of general knowledge).

7.8 Conclusion

Operating in a new culture and discourse system is not usually a simple matter of transferring all prior knowledge successfully to the new situation, though the closer two cultures and discourse systems are, the more a transfer strategy will offer (reasonably) effective solutions to communication problems. In all cases, some types of knowledge will transfer more successfully than others.

KEY POINTS

1. The term 'transfer' is generally used to refer to the systematic influences of existing knowledge on the acquisition of new knowledge. Pragmatic transfer is the transfer of pragmatic knowledge in situations of intercultural communication.

2. Pragmatic transfer can be identified by observing a person's communicative behaviour in the host culture and comparing it with their communicative behaviour in their home culture. If we observe that the communicative behaviour in the host culture is informed by the attitudes, values, norms and conventions of the home culture, then we have good grounds for assuming that the communicative behaviour in the host culture is partly due to pragmatic transfer.
3. The explanation of pragmatic transfer has both practical and theoretical implications: practical, because they can help us understand, solve and anticipate problems in communication across cultures, and theoretical, because the possibility of explanation of pragmatic transfer may provide evidence for or against the theoretical frameworks.
4. Pragmatic transfer may lead to miscommunication (a) when the speaker's and the hearer's background knowledge from which the context for utterance interpretation is selected differ significantly, and (b) the speaker and the hearer are unaware of these differences.

DISCUSSION QUESTIONS

1. **Culture and the perception of situations**

   Chapter 12 considers the verbal behaviour of job applicants from East and West Germany in job interviews held in a West German setting. Look at two of their data extracts: Example 4, which is an exchange between an interviewer and an East German applicant, and Example 5, which is an exchange between an interviewer and a West German applicant (see Section 12.5.2).

   1.1. Read these two exchanges carefully. Write a summary of the differences between the East German and the West German applicants' responses to the interviewer's questions.

   1.2. Does one of the applicants seem to respond 'better' than the other? If so, does negative pragmatic transfer seem to play a role in the poorer performance of one of the applicants? Discuss.

2. **Communication strategies and pragmatic transfer**

   Chapter 11 considers an exchange between a Japanese and an American co-worker, who are reviewing some advertisements. Misunderstanding occurs because the American co-worker does not realize how strongly his Japanese colleague disagrees with his view. (See Section 11.4.1, Extract 1.) Miller points out that the American employee is not aware that his Japanese superior is using particular strategies to communicate disagreement, and that miscommunication thus occurs.

   2.1. Discuss (briefly) the relation between the hearer's knowledge of particular culture-specific communication strategies and his ability to interpret correctly communicative acts which employ these strategies.

   2.2. How can pragmatic transfer make it easier or more difficult for members of one culture to learn the communicative strategies of another? Discuss with reference to examples (both from your own experience and from the literature).

3. **Creating rules of thumb for intercultural communication**
   Some suggestions for communicating with people in specific groups can be discovered by paying attention to speakers' communication patterns or by reading about those patterns in a collection such as this one. For example, based on the discussion here, the following 'rules of thumb' for communicating with Germans, Chinese and North Americans can be given:

   When speaking to a German...
   ... do not hesitate to state your opinion directly and to disagree openly
   When speaking to a Chinese ...
   ... be careful not to express direct disagreement
   When speaking to a North American ...
   ... do not be too modest about your abilities or accomplishments

   3.1. Using information provided in the contributions to this collection or using your own experiences, expand these lists; that is try to go beyond the simple prescriptions shown in the three examples above.
   3.2. Consider the value as well as the limitations of teaching 'rules of thumb' like the ones shown above when teaching pragmatic transfer and intercultural communication.

Suggestions for further reading

Blakemore, D. (1992) *Understanding Utterances: An Introduction to Pragmatics*. Oxford: Blackwell.

Kasper, G. (1992) Pragmatic transfer. *Second Language Research*, 8(3): 203–31.

Odlin, T. (1989) *Language Transfer*. Cambridge: CUP.

Wilson, D. (1994) Relevance and understanding. In G. Brown, K. Malmkjaer and A. Pollitt (eds) *Language and Understanding*. Oxford: OUP, 35–58.

Žegarac, V.(2004) Relevance theory and 'the' in second language aquisition. *Second Language Research* 20(3):193–211.

8 Communication Accommodation Theory

Virpi Ylänne

Chapter Outline

8.1 Introduction 164
8.2 Central concepts of accommodation theory 165
8.3 Accommodation research in multicultural settings: selected examples 174
8.4 Cultural difference: some dilemmas 178
Key points 182
Discussion questions 182
Notes 185
Suggestions for further reading 185

8.1 Introduction

The central insight behind the concept of communicative accommodation is rather simple – no doubt deceptively so. It is that speakers are motivated to reduce linguistic or communicative differences between themselves and their speaking partners under specifiable circumstances, principally when they want to be approved of and when they want their communication to be more effective. Correspondingly, speakers will be motivated to resist 'accommodating', and will even accentuate differences between themselves and their listeners, when approval and effectiveness are less important to them, and when they want to symbolize and emphasize difference and distance.

Building on this central idea, a large and diverse body of theoretical and empirical research has been undertaken for more than 30 years, developing what is referred to nowadays as Communication Accommodation Theory (CAT). My intention in this chapter is not to review or integrate all of this work. Indeed, this has been done in several articles and books.[1] Instead, I intend to provide, first, an introduction to the central concepts and categories used in CAT research. I illustrate the sorts of social situations and social processes which these concepts and categories can help us describe and explain. Secondly, I consider the various ways in which Accommodation Theory can be related to cultural difference and to those situations which are often described as being 'inter-cultural'. A theory which deals with social and sociolinguistic similarities and differences, and with communicative effectiveness, obviously has a direct relevance to cultural diversity and to 'intercultural communication'. But thirdly, I want to raise some difficulties and dilemmas, not least to do with the central notion of 'interculturality' and how we categorize social groups and relationships between them. In that final part of the chapter I want to suggest that CAT, but in fact any systematic approach to communication and culture, needs to be wary of generalizing too freely about the cultural identities of speakers and about the impact of communication strategies. My overall claim is that Accommodation Theory remains a rich and powerful model of how relationships between individuals and social groups are negotiated through language and discourse. But I also suggest that the theory needs to respond to large-scale social changes in how cultural groups organize themselves and in how people find meaning in cultural difference and interaction across cultural boundaries.

8.2 Central concepts of accommodation theory

The origins of Accommodation Theory are to be found in social psychology, and particularly in Howard Giles's studies of accent variation. Speech Accommodation Theory (so called at that time because accent features are specifically speech variables) was formulated by Giles (1973) when he devised a model of 'accent mobility'. The model was a reaction against assumptions made by William Labov in his seminal studies of sociolinguistic variation (e.g. 1966) in New York City. Giles proposed that a speaker's choice of a prestigious or a non-prestigious speech style need not be the result of his or her social class position or the formality or the informality of the speaking context, as Labov's approach assumed. Rather, it could be mediated by 'interpersonal accommodation processes'. Giles pointed out that the interviewees in Labov's studies may well have been responding, consciously or subconsciously, to the interviewer's own speech style; that is, they may have been 'accommodating' linguistically. For example, they could have produced casual-sounding speech because the interviewer himself had shifted style and was using a less standard accent. Alternatively, they could have been differentiating themselves from a standard-sounding interviewer. In fact, Labov's results were reliable enough to make it unlikely that any general explanation could be given along these lines. But Giles had argued convincingly that the interpersonal dimension of language use was potentially of crucial importance. In general, speech modification could be viewed not so much as determined by the social context, and more as a speaker's dynamic and subjective response to the addressee. The degree of behavioural matching between speakers needed to be analysed, and linked to social psychological factors which could explain and predict it.

The positive matching process was called *convergence* – 'a strategy whereby individuals adapt to each other's communicative behaviours in terms of a wide range of linguistic/prosodic/non-verbal features' (Giles et al. 1991: 7). As the definition suggests, convergence can operate well beyond accent variables. Speech rate and patterns of pausing, utterance length, gestures, posture, smiling, gaze and so on can all feature in acts of convergence between speakers. The basic metaphor here is one of parallel and non-parallel lines, as if speakers' trajectories can be modelled as getting closer or further apart as talk proceeds. Indeed, convergence can be almost literally demonstrated in these terms, if we are able to quantify relevant aspects of speakers' communicative behaviour relative to one another. Speakers can be shown to be converging if, for example, their measured rates of speech (perhaps measured in syllables per second) become more similar over time or, as Giles predicted, if their accents become more similar through shifts in the quality or frequency of particular features of their pronunciation.

Convergence has been established as a very robust sociolinguistic phenomenon. There is a general propensity for communicators to converge along salient dimensions of speech and non-verbal behaviour in cooperative social encounters. The psychological process at the heart of convergence and of 'being accommodative' is 'similarity attraction' (Byrne 1971). Speakers who want to cooperate and who want to be approved of will tend to converge. Correspondingly, when a speaker becomes more similar to a listener, it is generally more likely that the listener will in fact approve of him or her more strongly. These tendencies give Accommodation Theory some power to explain the *strategic* use of language codes and communication styles. Codes and styles do not merely co-vary with social groups and social situations. Rather, we can begin to see code- and style-choice as sociolinguistic strategies which individuals and groups will employ – again, whether consciously or subconsciously – to achieve the social and relational results they want. Although goals may be consciously held, the sociolinguistic means through which they are fulfilled are beyond the speaker's full consciousness. The hallmark of CAT has always been its ability to link descriptions of language in use to an appreciation of speakers' and groups' social goals and motivations.[2]

Keeping to the metaphor of parallel and non-parallel trajectories, *maintenance* and *divergence* of codes and styles are the obvious further possibilities. Maintenance simply identifies the option of a speaker or a group *not* modifying their communication relative to addressees (cf. Spencer-Oatey's 'rapport-maintenance' option, discussed in Chapter 2 of this book). Divergence refers to 'the way in which speakers accentuate speech and non-verbal differences between themselves and others' (Giles et al. 1991: 8). In CAT's treatment, the motivations associated with maintenance and divergence are more particular than those attaching to convergence. Both are specifically group-level strategies, designed to symbolize non-engagement between social or cultural groups. For example, ethnic minority community members may deliberately maintain their language or dialect code in the company of majority community members, as a symbolic act of resistance. In such a situation, increased use of the minority variety (either in terms of frequency or in some qualitative sense – e.g. using a greater number of non-standard dialect features or selecting more extreme ones) can be defined as divergence.

In the next section I consider selected instances of convergence, maintenance and divergence from CAT research in multicultural settings. But before turning to these I need to introduce some of the many refinements which have allowed accommodation research to work with more subtle concepts than the basic ones I have introduced this far. Some of them relate to the relationship between cognitive orientations and communication features. Some relate to the communication levels and dimensions through which accommodation strategies can be implemented in face-to-face communication.

As an essentially social-psychological theory, CAT has needed to distinguish carefully between *linguistic and psychological convergence and divergence.* A person's integrative orientation to others has been termed *psychological convergence*, whereas *psychological divergence* denotes a desire of commitment to achieve greater distance and distinctiveness (Thakerar et al. 1982). Although, as I have explained, an integrative psychological orientation is predictably realized through (often measurable) communicative convergence, cognitive and behavioural dimensions are in fact independent. Contextual factors may well intervene to prevent speakers realizing their convergent attitudes through their language. One obvious factor is a low facility in the requisite code or style – for example when a speaker does not command the symbolic resources to show his or her convergent intent in some particular communicative dimension. Another factor is the overriding effect of social norms, for example if a social situation imposes the use of a particular language code or register.[3] This basic distinction gives us good cause to avoid 'reading off' relational strategies directly from the evidence of language texts, without considering the potentially complex social psychology of the speaking situation (see Gallois et al. 2005 and Giles and Ogay 2006 for a more detailed account of the contexts of convergence and divergence).

CAT has also distinguished *subjective and objective accommodation. Subjective accommodation* refers to speakers' beliefs about whether they or their interlocutor are converging or diverging. *Objective convergence or divergence* is the result of direct observation or measurement by researchers. The issue here is again fundamental to a social-psychological view of communication, where verifiable facts based on researchers' analyses of data may have less explanatory value than the perceptions and beliefs of actual participants. It is important to note that 'speakers do not converge to (or diverge from) the *actual* behaviour of others, but rather to what they *think* are the communicative behaviours of their conversational partners' (Gallois et al. 1988: 161). For example, in a study by Beebe (1981), Thai–Chinese bilinguals believed they were converging towards Chinese-influenced vowel variants when being interviewed by an ethnic Chinese Thai, although this shift was actually divergent from the vowel forms produced by the interviewer. The interviewees held a stereotype of the linguistic behaviour of the group to which they saw the interviewer as belonging. They reacted to what they believed and in fact *predicted* the interviewer's speech to be like, and did this on the basis of non-speech attributes such as appearance features. Young (1988) similarly writes that it is not interlocutor ethnicity alone that causes linguistic variation, but a collection of attributes (of which one is ethnicity) by which interlocutors assess their relative similarity to each other. (I return to problems in the definition of cultural groups in the final section).

In the early days of CAT it was conventional to distinguish *upward and downward speech modifications*, where both convergence and divergence can be of either sort. Upward shifts are shifts towards a more prestigious or acrolectal variety, and downward shifts are towards a less prestigious or basilectal variety. Quantitative studies have also distinguished various extents of convergence and divergence, and cases where communication is modified only in certain modes of communication and not others (cf. Street 1982; Bilous and Krauss 1988).

Accommodation can be established to be either *symmetrical or asymmetrical*, depending on whether only one party or group (asymmetrical), or both (symmetrical), converges or diverges. This distinction can help capture the power dynamics of communication between social groups. For example, Mulac et al. (1988) found symmetrical convergence in mixed-sex dyads, in that both the female and the male participant converged more to the linguistic style of their out-group (other sex) partner than they did in an in-group (same sex) situation. Non-reciprocated convergence was illustrated in White's (1989) study of interactions between American and Japanese groups. Japanese speakers maintained the high level of backchannelling (supportive expressions such as 'mhm' and 'uh-huh') that had been observed in their within-culture situations when conversing with Americans. The American speakers, however, used significantly more backchannelling when speaking with Japanese partners than with other Americans, that is, they converged in the frequency of backchannelling behaviour whereas the Japanese speakers did not.

A lot of research attention has more recently been devoted to evaluative aspects of accommodation, and the concepts of *over-accommodation and under-accommodation* have become important (Coupland et al. 1988 and e.g. Gallois et al. 1995). There are clearly limits on (what people judge to be) the normal applicability and extent of accommodative adaptation, so that styles of talk may come to be evaluated as over-accommodative or overadapted. In multicultural contexts, talk which transcends these bounds – difficult though it is to establish empirically – is likely to be felt to be patronizing and deindividuating (treating individuals as social or cultural prototypes rather than attending to their individual competences and needs). A predictable scenario is when a member of a majority language group, possibly with a convergent psychological orientation ('with the best of intentions'), oversimplifies his or her first-language code, assuming this is a necessary adjustment for any minority language listener to be able to understand. This is the sociolinguistic territory Ferguson (1975, 1996) labelled 'foreigner talk', which can be well explicated in terms of CAT (see below).

Under-accommodation is a concept which captures equally difficult and potentially conflictual orientations between groups, for example when members of one group resolutely refuse to recognize and adapt to the conventional patterns of usage or the genuine communicative needs of another. An obvious example would be when a bilingual speaker refuses to codeswitch into the language his or her addressee is more comfortable using, or failing to conform to local cultural norms for greetings and leave-takings. Here we see how CAT needs to attend to much more than the describable properties of talk itself in its immediate context. A judgement about over- or under-accommodation can only be made relative to the norms and expectations which speakers hold about communication, and relative to their judgements of speakers' and listeners' rights and obligations in particular situations. CAT assumes that understanding the social meaning of communicative acts requires a rich appreciation of communicative context, both local and global, as it is subjectively experienced. Of course, speakers' appreciation of their own contexts of communication is often incomplete; they may, for example, be unable to predict how hearers will judge their communication strategies. This means that accommodating can often be fraught with uncertainties and, for example, miscarried attempts at convergence. Communication Accommodation Theory therefore has considerable relevance to our understanding of miscommunication (Coupland et al. 1991), particularly between social groups where normative expectations for talk are not fully shared. (I consider one instance in detail in the next section.)

Finally in this section, it is important for us to recognize how accommodation research has begun to engage with discourse analysis and pragmatics, in place of the rather mechanistic descriptions of speech and language variables that it dealt with in its early years. The early studies, and so the early development of the theory, depended on quantitative measures. Convergence and divergence were quantified as shifting values of measurable variables, such as phonological or dialect standardness and the frequency of use of specific language codes. Quantification was important in establishing the basic claims of the model, for example that linguistic convergence is regularly associated with perceived solidarity, and divergence with psychological dissociation. But it is clearly the case that 'being accommodative' is realized through a very wide range of discourse moves and strategies, and that these are fundamentally interactive in nature.

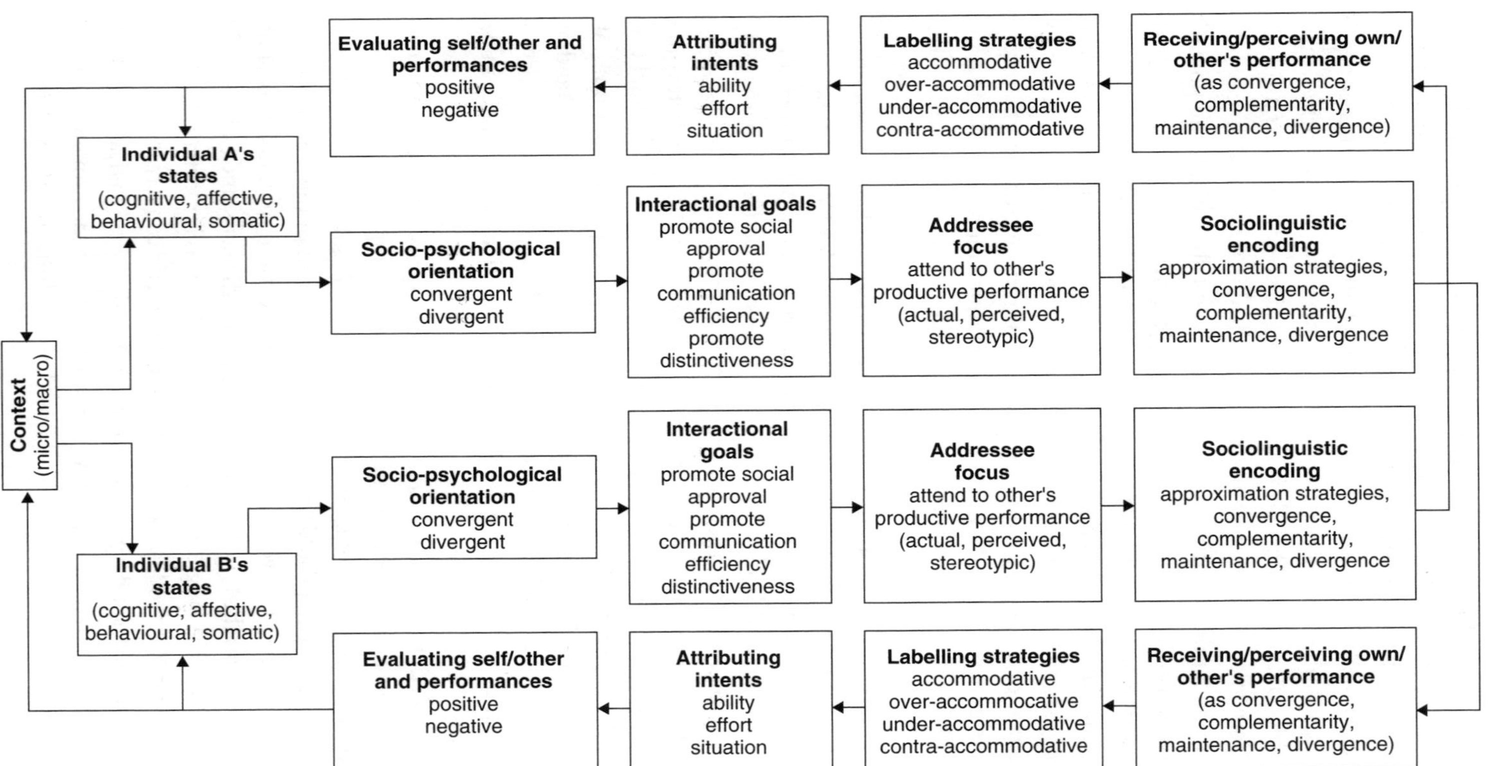

Figure 8.1 A generalized model of CAT processes.
Source: Coupland et al. (1988) Accommodating the elderly: invoking and extending a theory. *Language in Society,* 17: 1–41. (This figure is on p. 8 of the article.)

Arguing this case, Coupland et al. (1988; see also Coupland et al. 1991) proposed a significant broadening of the scope of the concept of 'communicative accommodation'. This model is schematized in Figure 8.1. It acknowledges that participants are speaker–hearers who can monitor their own performance as well as use the feedback to anticipate the receiver's attributions and evaluations of that performance in order to adjust their accommodation strategies. Listeners can label the speakers' performance as accommodative, over- accommodative, under-accommodative or contra-accommodative (conscious rendering of talk as non-accommodative) and, what is more, the speakers themselves can predict that their own performance is subject to such labelling which may or may not match their original intent. So although over-accommodation, for example, is an evaluation made most saliently by the listener, the model acknowledges the speaker's own perception of his/her behaviour and its consequences. These kinds of attributional and evaluative processes can create and alter situational and relational definitions. The model also recognizes not only that micro-level contextual factors (such as speakers' and listeners' goals and beliefs) play a part in accommodative processes, but also that macro-level factors (such as those related to the institutional roles and cultural identities of interlocutors) affect the strategies used and their evaluations. An inter-ethnic encounter in which one participant is in a gate-keeping position of some kind would be a case in point (see, for example, Roberts et al. 1992, and Chapter 12 of this book). Coupland et al. (1988) also suggest that the effects of communication accommodation strategies may transcend the boundaries of the immediate situation (in terms of psychological states and communicative actions) and have longer-term consequences in, for example, a person's degree of life-satisfaction. The 1988 study focuses specifically on intergenerational communication, but a case can equally be made regarding inter-ethnic encounters. For example, repeated experiences of being a recipient of foreigner talk, and evaluating such talk as inappropriate and over-accommodative, may arouse hostile feelings in the recipient and ultimately lead to avoidance of contact. The model represented in Figure 8.1 does not make predictions of communicative outcomes. Rather, unlike earlier work in accommodation linked to experimental work (e.g. Thakerar et al. 1982), it helps clarify communicative processes. Gallois et al. (2005) revise and synthesize the model in what they call 'phase 3' of the history of CAT: they draw attention to the 'sociohistorical context' of an interaction (highlighting intergroup history, interpersonal history and societal/cultural norms and values), the initial orientations or states (either intergroup or interpersonally oriented) of the individuals and the strategies (either accommodative or non-accommodative) that the individuals can adopt in the interaction situation.

For handling discourse data, it has been useful to identify accommodation which goes beyond approximation. Over and above convergence, maintenance and divergence (labelled '*approximation*' *strategies*), Coupland et al. (1988) identified three further

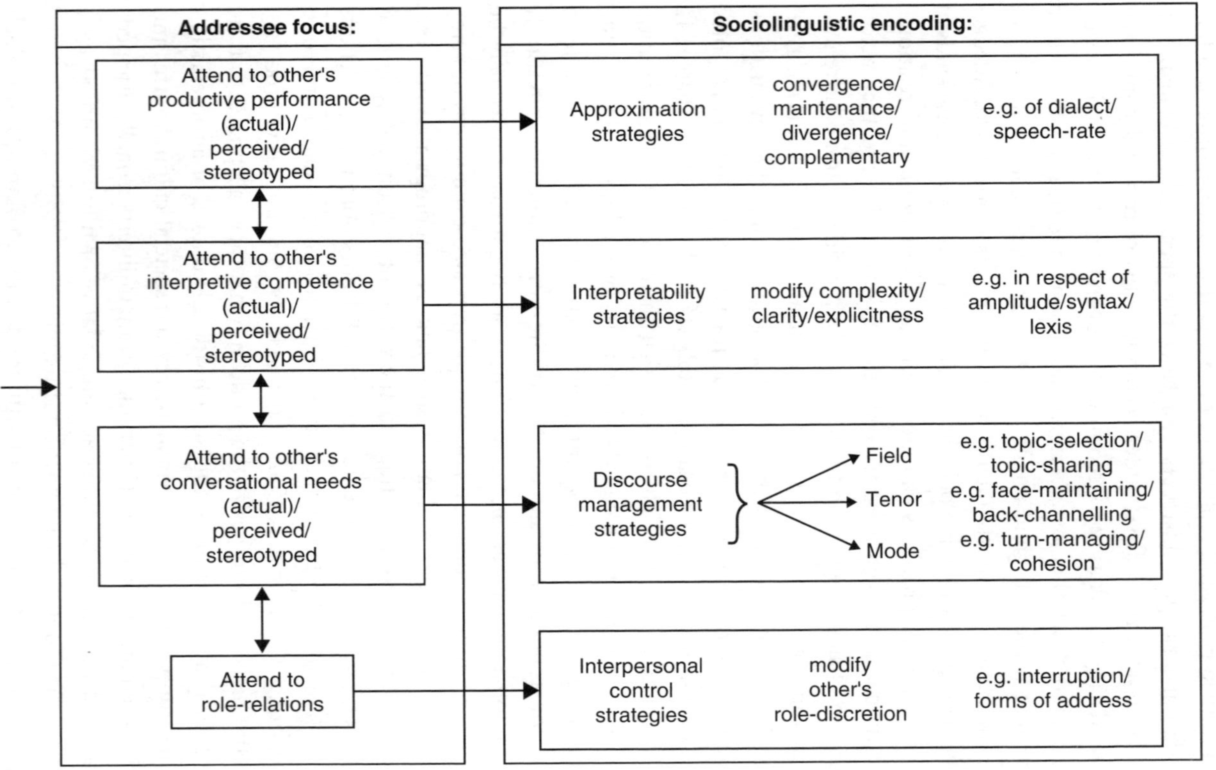

Figure 8.2 An extended model of sociolinguistic processes in CAT.

Source: Coupland et al. (1988) Accommodating the elderly: invoking and extending a theory. *Language in Society,* 17: 1–41. (This figure is on p. 28 of the article.)

broad discursive dimensions in which accommodation can be interactionally achieved: *interpretability strategies*, where speakers modify the complexity and comprehensibility of their talk, for example increasing clarity and explicitness; *discourse management strategies*, such as being facilitative in the management of turn-taking and topic selection and attending to face-wants; and *interpersonal control strategies*, allowing interlocutors discretion in the communicative roles they adopt in face-to-face talk. These four general sets of options, under the general heading of 'discourse attuning', are summarized in Figure 8.2. The different attuning strategies ('sociolinguistic encoding') are tied to different kinds of addressee focus.

First, approximation strategies arise from the speaker's focus on the interlocutor's actual productive communicative performance and degrees of similarity and difference. Secondly, interpretability strategies are linked to how the speaker perceives the other's ability to understand and deal with interaction, that is his/her receptive or interpretive competence. Foreigner talk can again be explained in this way. Ferguson originally introduced foreigner talk as an example of a 'simplified register', similar to 'baby talk', where the recipient's linguistic and cognitive abilities are perceived as somewhere below the optimal level for 'normal' fluency or syntactic complexity, for example. The CAT model explains such talk more precisely as an interactive phenomenon, for example showing how addressees' responses to foreigner talk can be *variable*, depending on normative expectations and on how the strategy is 'attributed' – what motive is ascribed to the speaker. Thirdly, discourse management strategies comprise a broad set relating to the listener's conversational needs (actual, perceived or stereotyped). A three-way classification is presented: *field* relates to the ideational/referential content construction (such as topic-selection or topic-sharing); *tenor* to the management of interpersonal positions, roles and faces (such as face-maintaining, back-channelling); *mode* to the procedural/textual dimensions that structure the interaction (such as turn-managing and cohesion) (for field, tenor and mode, see Gregory and Carroll 1978 and Halliday, e.g. 1973). Lastly, interpersonal control strategies are related to the focus on the role-relations between the participants and are realized by specific forms of address, for example. The four categories presented in Figure 8.2 can and do overlap so that, for example, tenor as a discourse management strategy can be taken to subsume control, although there is also a separate category of interpersonal control strategies in the model. It is also important to point out, as presented in Figure 8.2, that a speaker may behave accommodatively without (e.g.) converging, for example by making his/her speech more intelligible in ways that are not matched by the hearer's behaviour. In this case, the speaker would be using an interpretability strategy. Accommodation, then, is a general term which subsumes approximation strategies such as convergence or divergence, for example. This is also why terms such as over-accommodation (as opposed to over-convergence) are adopted.

As yet there have been only very few attempts to apply this more elaborate model of accommodation to sets of discourse data – and it is clearly a challenging task. The sheer range of possibilities in the selection and realization of speech acts, and in subtleties of sequencing and of interaction between speakers, in fact makes it unlikely that global quantitative measures of 'accommodativeness' can be made. On the other hand, such global assessments are routinely made by communicators themselves, and CAT has alerted us to the social impact of 'attuning' and 'counter-attuning' in social interaction.

8.3 Accommodation research in multicultural settings: selected examples

It was noted earlier that a good deal of accommodation research is concerned with group-level processes. To this extent it builds on a rich tradition of theoretical study in social psychology concerned with *intergroup communication*. We are unable to summarize this field of study here (see Giles and Coupland 1991 for a review). The central principles of intergroup theory were developed by Henri Tajfel (1974, 1978; see also Robinson 1996). A central observation is that individuals often interact with each other as representative members of social groups rather than actually as individuals, and that their communicative strategies are linked to these group orientations and to the potential gains and losses associated with them. Perhaps the strongest influence of this line of thinking on CAT is to be found in Giles and others' analyses of inter-group divergence, and the explicit link in this work with Ethnolinguistic Identity Theory (again see Giles and Coupland 1991; Giles and Johnson 1987). As we have seen, divergence is both motivated by and in many ways achieves a strong sense of in-group distinctiveness; it is one way of projecting a social and sometimes an ethnic identity through language. An individual's positive self-esteem is enhanced through the establishment of a distinct favourable social identity at the ethnic group level. Social identity is here viewed as a cognitive concept and is linguistically marked through a process of 'psycholinguistic distinctiveness'.

In this connection, it is not at all surprising that a lot of CAT research has been located in multicultural settings. These are settings where a sense of community or 'groupness' is often most marked, and where boundaries between groups, 'hard' or 'soft', permanent or shifting, are most salient in communication. Accommodation processes such as convergence and divergence are likely to be important means of marking intergroup alignments, and shifts of alignment over time. Also, 'long-term issues are of concern to researchers studying intercultural contact and adaptation by immigrants or sojourners, language rivalry or situations of long-term intergroup contact (e.g. the impact of sexism or ageism)' (Gallois and Giles 1998: 146). Some recent versions of CAT indeed make a distinction between short- and long-term convergence (Gallois et al. 1995).

Many of the early CAT studies designed to test for links between linguistic convergence and relational effects were conducted in communities with acknowledged intergroup tensions. For example, Giles et al. (1973) established that a French-Canadian speaker (in a 'matched-guise' study, where the same speaker was recorded describing a picture in four different guises which reflected increasing degrees of effort in perceived accommodation: French, mixed French-English, fluent French-Canadian accented English, and non-fluent French-Canadian accented English) was rated most favourably by bilingual English-Canadian listeners when his speech was French-Canadian accented and non-fluent. That is, he was approved of more strongly when he was seen to converge by making an effort to speak the language of the listeners. In addition, the English-Canadian subjects reciprocated the convergent accommodative strategies when given the chance in the experimental condition to communicate back to the French-Canadian man. It was suggested that 'the perception of accommodation from one speaker may be a salient cue as to whether integration and a strong desire for social approval should be features of the interaction for the other' (Giles et al. 1973: 187).

Correspondingly, divergent language shifts were shown to be particularly prominent in 'ethnically threatening' encounters, for example in Bourhis et al.'s (1979) study in Belgium of Flemish students' encounters with Francophone outgroup speakers. Again in a language laboratory setting, Flemish students were asked to respond to a Francophone speaker's (trilingual in English, French and Flemish) questions first of an emotively neutral nature, then of an ethnically threatening one. It was found that when intergroup categorization was made explicit and the subjects were told that the Francophone speaker considers their ethnolinguistic aims illegitimate, and also when the respondents believed that they would be held responsible to the group (their fellow Flemish students) later for their individual replies, a shift into Flemish was made by almost all of the respondents.

Gal's (1978/1997) study of the linguistic repertoire of a bilingual community of Oberwart (Felsöör) in Austria detailed a further intriguing case of linguistic and psychological convergence and divergence behaviour. Traditionally, both Hungarian and German are spoken in this town with about a quarter of the population (in the 1970s) being bilingual. The two language codes carry very different symbolic statuses: Hungarian symbolizes peasant status and has very negative connotations, especially for young people, whereas German symbolizes modern non-agrarian lifestyles and has a more prestigious status. Gal found that 'as speaker's networks become less and less peasant they use H[ungarian] in fewer and fewer situations. And . . . as time passes new generations use H[ungarian] in fewer and fewer situations regardless of the content of their social networks' (1997: 384). She also found striking differences in the language-choice patterns of young women and men in particular in this community.

Young women, when they diverge from peasant/agrarian female roles and work patterns, reject the use of Hungarian in preference for German, even if they have strong peasant social networks. Young men, especially those with strong peasant networks and who continue to work on the family farm, choose Hungarian in more interactions than young women and those with non-peasant networks. The young women's psychological divergence from the traditional peasant female identity has resulted in their rejection of that identity, in convergence to a more Austrian working lifestyle, and in the use of the German language in most situations. This in turn has had the general effect that more German is used in more interactions in the community. Young Oberwart women's marriage preferences also have had linguistic consequences in the community in another way: as they prefer to marry non-peasant men (another manifestation of the rejection of peasant identity), young peasant men, constituting precisely that small group most likely to be using Hungarian in various interactions, have been compelled to marry exogamously, finding wives from neighbouring monolingual German-speaking villages. The children of these marriages between bilingual Hungarian-German speaking men and monolingual German speaking women very rarely learn Hungarian, and so 'in an indirect way the present generation of young women is limiting the language possibilities of the next generation' (Gal 1978: 14).

Of course, convergence and divergence through the selection of a language code is the most obvious accommodation strategy in multilingual settings. The Gal example shows how multiple instances of divergence, while significant to individual speakers at the particular moments when they have to select a language code, can conspire to produce larger scale patterns of language shift. But accommodation processes, and particularly the subjectivities of people's expectations, judgements and attributions, can work in much less obvious ways too.

An example of this is a recent study by Bailey (1997) of interactions between immigrant Korean shop owners and sales assistants of small convenience stores in Los Angeles, USA and their African American customers. Such an encounter might open like this:

Extract 1

1	cashier:	*hi* {customer approaches counter} (2.0)
2	customer:	*how's it going partner? euh*
3	{cashier nods}	(1.0)
4	customer:	*you got them little bottles?*
5	cashier:	(*eh*?) {customer's gaze falls on the little bottles} (3.5)
6	customer:	*one seventy-fi:ve!* {customer gazes at display of bottles} (2.0)
7	customer:	*you've got no bourbon*? (1.2)
8	cashier:	*no: we don't have bourbon* (1.0)
9	customer:	*I'll get a beer then*
		{customer talks to his nephew}
10	cashier:	*two fifty* {cashier rings up purchase and bags beer} (4.5)
11	customer:	*I just moved in the area I talked to you the other day you*
12		[*remember me*]?

cashier: [*oh yesterday*] *last night*
customer: *yeah*
cashier: [(*o:h yeah?*)] {cashier smiles and nods}
customer: [*goddamn shit*][*then you don't*]
owner: [*new neighbour huh?*]
{customer turns halfway to the side towards the owner}
customer: {loudly, smiling} *then you don't KNOW me*
cashier: [(*I know you?*)] {cashier gets change from the till}
customer: [*I want you to KNOW*] *me so when I walk in here you'll know me I*
smoke Winstons your son knows me
cashier: [*ye::ah*]
customer: [*the yo*]*ung guy*
cashier: *there you go* {cashier proffers change}

(Bailey 1997: 345; transcription conventions very slightly modified. All participants are male)

In Extract 1, there are points where the African American speaker is signalling solidarity (as he perceives it to be signalled) and, hence, the cashier and, later, the shop-owner have opportunities to match this behaviour. Solidarity signalling can be seen in line 2 by the use of *partner*. Also, in line 6, the customer's reference to the price of the drink can be seen as an assessment eliciting an evaluative response and agreement from the listener. Again in lines 11 and 12, the customer discloses personal information about himself and refers to the interactants' shared history through an earlier encounter, and in lines 16 and 18 he makes a joke. In lines 20–1, he expresses very explicitly his wish to 'be known' in the shop, that is to reduce interpersonal distance. To link what is happening here to Figure 8.2, it can be said that the customer is explicitly commenting on the social distance between himself and the others by particular tenor as a discourse management strategy. All the local strategies commented on above are responded to in a minimal way by the cashier and the shop-owner (lines 3, 13, 15 and 17), and, indeed, the cashier offers transactionally salient contributions in lines 6, 10 and 24, orienting to closing the encounter, rather than accommodating to the interpersonal stance of the customer.

The participants in these encounters were found to have very different concepts of the relationship between a customer and a storekeeper in that the storekeepers showed cultural preference for 'socially minimal' service encounters and reluctance to orient to intimacy with a stranger. The customers, on the other hand, often sought to establish more 'socially expanded' relationships by introducing personal topics, using humour and making assessments, for example. The shopkeepers did on occasions display attempts at convergence towards the customer's style (see discussion question number 2 at the end of this chapter), for example by showing interest through asking questions, or smiling – but not sharing laughter – as a response to a joke. However, the degree of these shifts was minimal and the shopkeepers' different discourse management strategies (from the customer's), such as lack of backchanelling, was likely to be perceived as hostile. The customers' behaviour was in turn perceived as not very appropriate for increasing intimacy which, from the shopkeepers' point of view, would call for more silence and restraint. Bailey illustrates how the very different communicative norms and practices for displaying respect adopted by these two groups may be an important underlying cause for widely documented tensions and conflict: 'the relative restraint of immigrant Korean storekeepers . . . is perceived by many African Americans as a sign of racism, while the relatively personable involvement of African Americans is perceived by many storekeepers as disrespectful imposition' (Bailey 1997: 327). Through this example we can see that a close analysis of the accommodative orientations of interactants is a valuable means of studying interethnic tensions. In addition to these interethnic contexts, the CAT model has been explored in intergenerational contexts (Coupland et al. 1991; Giles and Ogay 2006; McCann and Giles 2006), organizational communication (Bourhis 1991) and community settings such as law enforcement (Giles et al. 2007), among others.

8.4 Cultural difference: some dilemmas

Recent developments in cultural studies and cultural theory seem to pose problems for CAT. They amount to a growing uncertainty about the definitions of culture, about the boundaries between cultural groups, and about how we should model the fundamental relationship between language and culture. It would be reasonable to say that Accommodation Theory, like most other established approaches to intergroup or 'intercultural' relations, has tended to trust the assumption that cultural groups generally have identifiable and meaningful boundaries. CAT has made this basic assumption in its research designs, in talking about 'French-Canadians', 'Welsh people', 'African-Americans' or 'Koreans', and in investigating their linguistic behaviours and their attitudes. The assumption is not that individuals will identify themselves unambiguously or consistently with such labels, but that the labels themselves 'make sense' – in social life and in social research.

But consider a different point of view, from a recent directory of key concepts in postcolonial studies:

> References to cultural diversity based on an assumption of 'pre-given cultural "contents" and customs' give rise to anodyne liberal notions of multiculturalism, cultural exchange or the culture of humanity . . . cultural authority resides not in a series of fixed and determined diverse objects but in the process of how these objects come to be known and so come into being.
>
> (Ashcroft et al. 1998: 60)

The embedded quotation is from Homi Bhabha (1988), whose theoretical writings have challenged the conventional or 'modernist' academic approaches to cultural diversity. In Bhabha's (1994) view, cultural identity always shows indeterminacy and a struggle between alternatives – what he calls 'hybridity'. He argues that 'claims to inherent originality or purity of cultures are untenable' (1994: 20).

As Riggins (1997: 4) points out (in a very useful review and compilation of recent research on cultural 'otherness'), we have tended to make the assumption that social and cultural groups share similar characteristics. Yet many studies show that individuals' membership of social categories is indeed uncertain and emergent. Riggins cites Stuart Hall's study of Afro-Caribbean identities and Hall's argument that self-identity should be conceptualized 'as a "production" which is never complete, always in process, and always constituted within, not outside representation' (Hall 1994: 392).

There is a strong flavour of social constructionism here, the argument that social realities are only fixed through discourse – through how we talk or write about them.[4] The 'critical' dimension of this stance is the argument that it is social elites who impose 'essentialist' definitions of cultural groups, and that they do this repressively, to perpetuate their own ideological values and priorities. Rampton's (1995, 1998) study of 'crossing' in the language of British urban adolescents, manifest in the use of Creole by adolescents of Anglo and Asian descent, the use of Panjabi by those of Anglo and African Caribbean descent, and the use of Indian English (stylized Asian English) by all three is worth citing in this context. The notion of crossing is a very useful perspective and challenges the essentialist assumption that a group uses 'its own' language variety. Crossing constitutes of course one set of accommodative options, even if not in an obvious sense convergent (see also Blommaert 2005, Chapter 8, for examples of 'globalized discourse').

There are also echoes of postmodernist theory (e.g. Giddens 1991) in the argument that the world has moved on and that the old, structured certainties of class and ethnic self-definition have lapsed, in a welter of reflexive and hybrid identity options. As Giddens writes, the self in (what he calls) Late or High Modernity is an identity project, rather than one transmitted from a fixed and stable social structure. We are surrounded by media and other complex imagery which offer us multiple identities, which we take up and drop more as lifestyle projects than as essential determinants of who we are.

What are we to make of this orientation to the study of culture? How should we respond to it in research on cultural difference and language? Does it perhaps make the study of 'inter-cultural' relations and communication impossible, or even reprehensible, because it fixes the notion of 'cultural group' prematurely and in ways that do not reflect how cultural identity is nowadays lived and experienced? The first necessary response is to recognize the importance of the critical and constructionist argument for research on cultural difference and identity. In 1978, Edward Said first observed that there was in the West a persistent and structured view of peoples in Asia, the Far East and Africa that one could call 'Orientalism'. Said defined it as 'the corporate institution for dealing with the Orient – dealing with it by making statements about it, authorizing views on it, describing it, by teaching it, settling it, ruling over it: in short,

Orientalism as a Western style for dominating, restructuring, and having authority over the Orient' (1978: 3; see also Karim 1997 on 'the Muslim other'). If Orientalism and similar colonial and postcolonial 'institutions' are defined partly by *teaching* them, then academic study and research are part of the process of perpetuating racial and cultural stereotypes. This is, in fact, a good example of why we can think of cultural perspectives themselves as *discourses* – as organized ways of thinking, speaking and writing about social groups. We do need to have a constant critical eye to our own studies, to make sure that the labels and categories we use, the questions we ask relating to them and the conclusions we draw, are not pre-determined by dominant ideological values and priorities.

In accommodation research, for example, it would be naïve to assume that acts of linguistic accommodation by minorities to majorities – for example adopting the majority group's language code – are no more and no less than acts of psychological convergence. To take the case of Wales and the Welsh language, there have certainly been times in the community's history when this would have been the 'natural' assumption – meaning the assumption made by a culturally and numerically dominant English-speaking elite. Bilingual speakers' linguistic convergence to English may well have realized a form of aquiescence to, or even solidarity with, an emergent cultural norm – the norm of English language usage which developed rapidly in the mid- and late-nineteenth century, as industrialization rapidly increased and as recorded numbers of Welsh speakers rapidly declined (Aitchison and Carter 1994). Correspondingly, divergence (a refusal to use English in Wales) could rightly be seen as a political act of resistance, grounded in an ideological view of Wales as an area of cultural conflict. But that interpretation of the same pattern of language use more recently would be much more controversial. In a sociolinguistic climate where the number of Welsh speakers has stabilized and where policies of genuine bilingual parity are being actively promoted through schools and regionally devolved government (the Welsh National Assembly was formed in 1999), bilingual people's 'accommodation' in using English is less easily modelled as psychological convergence to an out-group majority norm. If it is convergence, it is as likely to be convergence to a rapidly spreading ideology of linguistic parity, with different and less adversarial political bases (cf. Williams 1987).

As regards the postmodernist claim about complex and hybrid cultural identities, Wales is another relevant instance. It would be highly simplistic to assume, for example, that the half-million or so people in Wales who speak Welsh have a uniformly 'Welsh' cultural identity, while the two million or so who do not speak Welsh orient to 'English' identities. Current research is showing the highly complex and structured identities that, for example, young people in Wales recognize to be relevant to themselves and to their peers (see Garrett et al. 1999). Welsh teenagers identify radically different cultural profiles, including along the subjective dimension of 'Welshness', relating to rather fine differences in *English-language* pronunciation in Wales and the zones in which they are spoken. The cultural politics of Welshness are therefore complex, but they are also shifting. The future of the Welsh language and, as a separate but related issue, the future of Wales as a culturally distinctive zone, largely lie in how young people select from various identity options and how they articulate their felt Welshness. It would indeed be a mistake to design studies of accommodation between groups of Welsh-speaking and English-speaking young people without acknowledging the detailed subjective profiles that they use to define their own and other people's Welshness.

Yet the main point here is that processes of cultural definition and identification are entirely researchable in their own right. It is through social-psychological studies of subjective profiling that we can best confirm and fill out cultural theorists' claims about hybridity and lived cultural identities. Studies aiming to describe 'inter-cultural' communication should ideally be linked to studies of how individuals and social or cultural groups define themselves and others. In fact, this is precisely the agenda that Communication Accommodation Theory has established, aiming to locate the analysis of language within the analysis of social and cultural contexts, subjectively defined. (These relations are made explicit in Figure 8.1, above.)

The social constructionist argument is, in any case, that social and cultural reality is constituted in and through language. If this is to be more than a rather trite, universal and theoretical claim, then surely we need studies of *how* language constructs culture, in specific cases and contexts. Studying language and discourse in cultural settings offers us the best avenue to explore social construction, as situated social action. The perspective we adopt is, however, of crucial importance. We have to avoid reifying and 'essentializing' the groups we are concerned with. Being 'Welsh' or 'Iranian' or 'Malaysian', or for that matter 'European' or 'Asian', are clearly complex acts of attribution nowadays, especially in societies where these images and definitions are constantly reflected back at us – by politicians, the media and indeed by academic research – in so many selective and edited forms. We might argue that this fluidity is a source of hope that the political and military consequences of extreme nationalism will gradually become less likely. Whether or not this is the case, language will continue to be the touchstone for cultural identification – either as a symbol in its own right or as the medium through which we 'deploy' and negotiate our identities. An important part of this negotiation is specified in the concepts introduced in this chapter – acts of communicative accommodation to or away from others, but also to or away from the cultural identities they are taken to represent.

Communication Accommodation Theory runs counter to an essentialist notion of culture. By resisting notions of cultural prototypes, it helps us understand the *local* context and the process of communication.

KEY POINTS

1. Participants in interactions make verbal or non-verbal adjustments of various kinds in their communication behaviour depending on who they interact with. These adjustments might be done subconsciously or quite deliberately and the direction of the adjustment is linked to underlying motives at an interpersonal or intergroup level.
2. These adjustments or modifications are referred to as Communication Accommodation.
3. Accommodation can happen in different directions. Accommodation 'towards' some aspect(s) of the hearer's (perceived) communicative behaviour, motivated by, for example, the want to be approved of or liked or to increase communicative effectiveness is termed convergence. Convergent strategies tend to stem from interpersonal and solidary motives, when the speaker's attention is on (perceived) similarities between the participants.
4. Accommodation 'away' from some aspect(s) of the hearer's (perceived) communicative behaviour, motivated by, for example, the want to signal hostility or dislike is termed divergence. Divergent strategies (as well as communicative maintenance, non-accommodative behaviour) tend to stem from intergroup motives, when the speaker's attention is on (perceived) differences between the participants and when they wish to signal loyalty to their own in-group.
5. A speaker may over- or under-estimate the level of communicative modification necessary for satisfying or attuned communication on the basis of their perception of the hearer's needs. A speaker may either go beyond what the hearer deems necessary – for example by grammatically simplifying or by increasing the volume of their utterances. This is called over-accommodation.
6. Alternatively, a speaker may underplay some aspect of their communicative behaviour in relation to the hearer's needs – for example by not making any communicative modifications. Such behaviour may be evaluated by the hearer as under-accommodative.
7. Communication accommodation has been studied in intercultural encounters, among others. It is, however, arguable, how stable people's ethnic and cultural identities are (see Chapter 9). In relation to social interaction, the social constructionist position is that language constructs people in its use. Discourse as social action creates the people who use it, and there are different possibilities for a person to define themselves, and be defined by others, depending on the situation. From this perspective, people's cultural, ethnic and other identities are not fixed but subject to constant re-definition by people themselves as well as others. Accommodation behaviour can be seen to be linked with and be constitutive of such ongoing re-definition.

DISCUSSION QUESTIONS

1. Look back at Extract 1. Attempt (with others if possible) to outline the accommodative behaviour of the interactants in terms of Figures 8.1 and 8.2.
2. Do the same for Extract 2 below. How does the accommodative behaviour in this interaction differ from that in Extract 1? In what ways is it similar?

Extract 2

The interaction takes place in a shop between a Korean shop owner, a Korean cashier and an African American customer. The customer is a regular customer but has been away in

Chicago for a month. The participants are all male and different from those in Extract 1 (the customer enters store and goes to soda cooler).

1 Customer: [hi]
2 Owner: [how ar]e you?
{customer takes soda towards cash register and motions towards displays} (7.5)
3 Customer: wow you guys moved a lot of things around
4 Cashier: hello: {stands up from where he was hidden behind the counter}
5 heh heh how are you? {cashier retrieves customer's alcohol and moves towards the till}
6 Customer: what's going on man? {cashier gets up for customer's alcohol} (.8)
7 Customer: how've you been?
8 Cashier: sleeping
9 Customer: eh heh heh (1.8)
10 Cashier: that's it?
11 Customer: that's it {cashier rings up purchases} (1.5)
12 Customer: I haven't seen you for a while
13 Cashier: he he where you been?
14 Customer: Chicago {cashier bags purchase?}
15 Cashier: oh really?
16 Customer: [yeah]
17 Cashier: [how] long?
18 Customer: for about a MONTH (1.2)
19 Cashier: how's there
20 Customer: *CO:L!*
21 Cashier: [co:ld?]
22 Cashier: [heh] heh heh heh
23 Owner: is Chicago cold?
24 Customer: u::h! {lateral headshakes} (1.4) man I got off the plane and walked out the airport I said "OH shit" *HEH HEH HEH*
25 Owner: I thought it's gonna be nice spring season over there
26 Customer: well not now this about a month I been there I was there for about a month but you know (.) damn {lateral headshakes}
{customer moves away from cash till towards owner} (1.4)
27 Customer: too co:l' I mean this was really cold
28 Owner: (they have snowy?) season there
29 Customer: I've known it to snow on Easter Sunday (.)
{15 second discussion, not clearly audible, in which the owner asks if there are mountains in Chicago, and the customer explains that there are not}
30 Customer: see th- this- California weather almost never changes
31 {spoken slowly and clearly as for a non-native speaker} back there it's a SEASONAL change you got fall winter spring
32 Owner: mm hm
33 Customer: you know but back there the weather sshhh {lateral headshake}

34 Customer: it's cold up until *June* I mean these guys like they – wearing *lon:g john:s* from September until June
35 Owner: (it's hot season June?)
36 Customer: he- here it's hot but there it's {lateral headshake} (really?) {customer moves towards exit}
37 Owner: kay [see you later]
38 Customer: [see you later] nice talking to you

(from Bailey 1997: 340–1. Transcription conventions slightly modified.)

3. In a study to examine intergroup relations (Bourhis and Giles 1977), the following stimulus material was used: in a language laboratory setting, an RP accented English man said (on tape) to a group of adult Welsh learners of Welsh who had been asked to help in a survey on second language learning techniques:

> 'even in the boardrooms of some of your own education departments it is being said that "Welsh is dying, why can't you leave it alone? It is spoken by such a tiny proportion of people that it has one foot in the grave . . . it is on the slippery slope of extinction". . . Now as I have already said, I believe, to be realistic, that the future of Welsh appears pretty dismal . . . So could I have your opinion concerning the survival and status of the Welsh language in Wales?'
>
> (pp. 124–5)

In their replies to this question, the Welsh learners were found to broaden their Welsh accents, compared with their answers to a previous more emotionally neutral question. Some respondents introduced Welsh words and phrases into their answers. One female respondent paused for a while, then started to conjugate a socially unacceptable verb into the microphone in Welsh.

3.1. How could the learners' responses be explained by Communication Accommodation Theory?
3.2. How did the learners perceive the context?

4. In a Gambian marketplace, the vendor of local souvenirs calls out to the tourists (who are mainly British):

Vendor: that's the buck up store here Asda price Asda (.) Asda
price (.) Asda (.) yeah Asda (.) that's that's the buck up
store here (.) you buy one you get one for free Asda price

(from Jaworski et al. 2008. 'Asda' is the name of a supermarket, known in the British context for its relatively low prices)

In what way is the vendor's behaviour 'accommodative'?

Notes

An earlier version of this chapter was co-authored by Nikolas Coupland. His important input is gratefully acknowledged.

1. Overviews of Accommodation Theory include: Coupland et al. 1988; Giles et al. 1991; Giles and Coupland 1991; Coupland 1995; Niedzielski and Giles 1996; Gallois et al. 2005; and Giles and Ogay 2006. Section 2 of this chapter draws, very selectively, from these sources.
2. The accommodation strategy of gaining approval and improving communication effectiveness through reducing linguistic differences is of course similar to Brown and Levinson's (1987) notion of positive politeness, and to Spencer-Oatey's concepts (see Chapter 2) of rapport enhancement and rapport maintenance orientations. CAT also shares its strategic orientation to communication with these other approaches. Later interpretations of 'accommodation' as a set of discourse-attuning options, which we consider below (cf. Coupland et al. 1988), bring all of these concepts even closer together. See also Jones et al. 1999 for a discussion of strategies and accommodation.
3. Ball et al. (1984) have studied the link between social norms and accommodation processes.
4. Wetherell (1996: 281) summarizes a social constructionist discourse analytic position thus: 'discourse is . . . constitutive of both objects and people. Talk and writing are not merely about actions, events and situations, they are creative of those actions, events and situations . . . In talking, people are constituting their social realities and collective cultures, manufacturing and constructing their lives, and are themselves manufactured as personalities and subjects in the process. Through this negotiation, the social world becomes populated with characters which are given certain attributes. Relationships become formulated as being of certain kinds, some forms of relating become defined as problematic and some as constructive and positive, and so on. Talk is not neutrally recording. Discourse comes to constitute social life as we know it.'

Suggestions for further reading

Ashcroft, B. Griffiths, G. and Tiffin, H. (1998) *Key Concepts in Post-colonial Studies.* London and New York: Routledge.

Coupland, N. (1995) Accommodation theory. In J. Verschueren, J-O. Östman and J. Blommaert (eds) *Handbook of Pragmatics Manual.* Amsterdam: John Benjamins, 21–26.

Coupland, N., Coupland, J., Giles, H. and Henwood, K. (1988) Accommodating the elderly: invoking and extending a theory. *Language in Society,* 17: 1–41.

Gallois, C., Ogay, T. and Giles, H. (2005) Communication accommodation theory: a look back and a look ahead. In W. B. Gudykunst (ed.) *Theorizing About Intercultural Communication.* Thousand Oaks: Sage, 121–48.

Giles, H., Coupland, J. and Coupland, N. (1991) *Contexts of Accommodation: Developments in Applied Sociolinguistics.* Cambridge: Cambridge University Press, Chapter 1.

Giles, H. and Coupland, N. (1991) *Language: Contexts and Consequences.* Milton Keynes: Open University Press, Chapter 3.

Giles, H. and Ogay, T. (2006) Communication accommodation theory. In B. B. Whaley and W. Samter (eds) *Explaining Communication: Contemporary Theories and Exemplars*. Mahwah, NJ: Lawrence Erlbaum, 293–310.

Shepard, C.A., Giles, H. and Le Poire, B. (2001) Communication accommodation theory. In W. P. Robinson and H. Giles (eds) *The New Handbook of Language and Social Psychology*. Chichester: John Wiley, 33–56.

Zuengler, J. (1991) Accommodation in native-nonnative interactions: going beyond the 'what' to the 'why' in second-language research. In H. Giles, J. Coupland and N. Coupland (eds) *Contexts of Accommodation: Developments in Applied Sociolinguistics*. Cambridge: Cambridge University Press, 223–44.

9 Adaptation and Identity

Martin Fougère

Chapter Outline

9.1 Introduction: adaptation, identity and spatial metaphors 187
9.2 Identity, sensemaking and self-narrative 188
9.3 Illustrations: research procedure and context 190
9.4 Spatial metaphors and their use in identity construction 191
9.5 Conclusion 200
Key points 200
Discussion questions 201
Notes 203
Suggestions for further reading 203

9.1 Introduction: adaptation, identity and spatial metaphors

This chapter explores the impact that life in a different culture can have on people's sense of identity. It argues that spatial metaphors can be helpful in describing the sensemaking processes that people experience in such contexts.

In our globalized world which is characterized by an increasingly cosmopolitan urban population – composed of travelling professionals, expatriates, immigrants etc. – the ongoing (re)construction of cultural identities is a central issue that is of crucial concern to more and more individuals. As a result, the identity construction of individuals involved in intercultural contexts has been attracting a great deal of interest lately within contemporary cultural studies (e.g. de Certeau 1984; Gilroy 1993; Hall 1995; Hall and du Gay 1996) and works generally associated with postcolonial studies (e.g. Anzaldúa 1987; Bhabha 1994; Pratt 1992; Said 1999). Interestingly, in these latter works, identity construction is often compared to travel, and geographical metaphors seem to be at the core of the discussion, with such figurative speech as 'third space', 'the in-between', 'liminality', 'the borderlands', the 'contact zone', 'diaspora' or the analysis of stories as 'spatial practices'. One important concern is the problematization of space and place in relation to identity construction and narrative. This trend has been paralleled in the more phenomenological streams of geography by the theorization of place, and its connection with self and identity (e.g. Buttimer 1976, 1980; Casey 2001; Relph 1976; Sack 1997; Tuan 1976, 1996). As a result of these two spatial approaches on identity issues, 'cultural geographies' have emerged that claim to be at once geographic and political in their articulation of space and place in relation to identity (cf. e.g. Keith and Pile 1993; Massey and Jess 1995; Pile and Thrift 1995). In this chapter, I take this perspective, and argue that it can be fruitful to focus on spatial articulations in analysing the identity construction processes of individuals involved in intercultural interactions, in order to understand these processes better.

9.2 Identity, sensemaking and self-narrative

It is now widely agreed that the concept of identity holds little value if it is used in an essentialistic way (e.g. Bruner 1987; Gergen 1994; Hall 1995; Simon 2004) – that is, tying the individual to an unchanging understanding of who s/he is. Identities are best understood as being continually constructed through interactions and it is particularly interesting to study them in intercultural contexts because it is exactly in such contexts that people often reflect more about them.

The notion of sensemaking, as Weick (1995: 16) points out, is particularly easy to grasp since it is to be understood literally not metaphorically: 'sensemaking is what it says it is, namely, making something sensible'. What makes the use of this notion particularly appropriate for the study of identity in intercultural contexts is the idea of 'occasions for sensemaking' (Weick 1995) being brought about by 'incongruous events that do not make sense within [people's] perceptual frameworks' and thus provide them with 'opportunities to discover their blind spots' (Starbuck and Milliken 1988: 52). The role of 'surprise' is important: sensemaking can be described as 'a thinking process that uses retrospection to explain surprise' (Glanz et al. 2001: 103). Intercultural interactions can be seen as providing a context pregnant with many occasions for sensemaking, since unexpected events may occur regularly because of misunderstandings and more generally through the interactional dynamics.

Sensemaking will usually take on the form of a narrative. Narrative analysis has been understood as the very context in which individual identities are constructed, as the quotations below illustrate:

> Our present identity is not a sudden and mysterious event but a sensible result of a life story [. . .] Such creations of narrative order may be essential in giving life a sense of meaning and direction.
>
> (Gergen 1994: 187)

How individuals recount their histories – what they emphasize and omit, their stance as protagonists or victims, the relationship the story establishes between teller and audience – all shape what individuals can claim of their own lives. Personal stories are not merely a way of telling someone (or oneself) about one's life; they are the means by which identities may be fashioned (Rosenwald and Ochberg 1992: 1).

> Eventually the culturally shaped cognitive and linguistic processes that guide the self-telling of life narratives achieve the power to structure perceptual experience, to organize memory, to segment and purpose-build the very 'events' of a life. In the end, we *become* the autobiographical narratives by which we 'tell about' our lives.
>
> (Bruner 1987: 15)

In order to study the highly dynamic processes of identity construction, a number of writers have engaged in the analysis of self-narratives, understanding identity as being fashioned through personal stories, as suggested in the quotations above. The underlying argument is that self-narratives 'imitate' people's experiences, but also that their experiences in turn come to imitate their narratives – rephrasing slightly Bruner's (1987: 13) sentence: 'Narrative imitates life, life imitates narrative'. The narrative for them is thus a way to '*construct* themselves' (Bruner 1987: 24). In addition, the object of narrative can be seen as a matter of 'demistify[ing] deviations' (Bruner 2001: 30). It is easier for people to tell about such 'deviations' in self-narratives than in more structured interviews because they have time to give long accounts of the processes that led to them. In a more ordered interview setting, deviant answers are much less likely to occur. In the context of an interview that only asks an individual to talk about her/his experiences and thus to produce a self-narrative, it is possible for that individual to develop a way of examining closely the exceptional in relation to the ordinary, and to connect them by finding 'an intentional state that mitigates or at least makes comprehensible a deviation from a canonical cultural pattern' (Bruner 1990: 49–50). Now, it is precisely the ways in which intercultural contexts can be seen as providing occasions for such 'deviations' that makes them interesting contexts: how the encounter with other cultures may lead one to produce narratives somewhat emancipated from established discourses – and thus, how one may (re)construct one's identity differently.

In these stories, which to a large extent are meant to demarcate where one belongs or where one wants to escape from, the reliance on spatial metaphors has been underlined (Bruner 1987; de Certeau 1984). In particular, Bruner (1987: 25) has pointed out that the language of 'place', with a central opposition between 'home' and 'the real world', dominates the autobiography genre, by shaping and constraining the stories that the narrators tell. In self-narratives told by individuals who live and/or work in intercultural contexts, which often involve insiders and outsiders, references to space and place take up an even more central role. Examining them in detail helps us to understand the processes by which such individuals (re)construct their identity as a result of their interactions with 'others'.

9.3 Illustrations: research procedure and context

Although this chapter is primarily theoretical, I illustrate the discussion of the spatial metaphors utilized in identity construction with examples from self-narratives of four French *coopérants* (young graduates from universities, engineering or business schools who went to work for 16 months in a company abroad instead of having their military service[1]) who were in Finland in 2001 and 2002. For the purpose of this chapter these four expatriates have been (re)named Antoine, Bruno, Cyril and David respectively. All four were working in bicultural organizational contexts, meaning that they were working with both French and Finnish people, but had few if any colleagues from other countries. More specifically, three of the interviewees (Antoine, Bruno and Cyril) were working for subsidiaries of French firms in Finland, and the fourth one (David) was more isolated in the Finnish subsidiary of a big non-French multinational, but he had been a trainee within the same company in France and was working with French colleagues from that previous assignment during his stay in Finland, which also made his experience 'bicultural' to an extent.

The four long individual interviews referred to here lasted each between 90 and 120 minutes (as transcriptions, between 30 and 40 pages). These interviews were made in three different Finnish towns, in various settings, provided the place was quiet: the interviewee's home, my workplace, my hotel, the interviewee's workplace. The interviews started with what proved to be two extremely significant initial questions: why they had come as *coopérants* to Finland, on the one hand, and, what other experiences abroad they had had before, on the other hand. This allowed for an assessment of where they came from, what the place was from which their 'journey' started, making it possible to examine the articulation of their expatriation story that they narrated to me, starting from that point, which, to a certain extent, was set by me as a prerequisite, before they would start: an opportunity for them to contextualize things, indeed to place, position, situate themselves. The story *per se* was the major section of the interview (lasting, depending on the case, between 35 minutes and over one hour – all the extracts included here come from this section or an equally open concluding section at the very end of the interview), as an answer to a very general request ('I would like you to freely tell me the story of your work and life experience as a *coopérant* in Finland'[2]) and the conversational development of it, with no further predetermined structure for this section. Interestingly, this question positioned them as *coopérants* rather than anything else. One of the reasons why I opted for this was that I did not want them to focus particularly on intercultural aspects, on the culture shock, in order to preserve an inductive element. The extracts from their self-narratives that are included here have been translated from French.

9.4 Spatial metaphors and their use in identity construction

Some of the key identity issues that become particularly conspicuous to people involved in intercultural contexts relate to (1) the need for a sense of belonging, (2) the opportunity to question and learn about one's own identity and (3) the possibility of development and change. Each of these issues are illustrated below by extracts from the young expatriates' self-narratives and then connected to how spatial metaphors can be helpful in conceptualizing and describing them.

9.4.1 Sense of belonging

Belonging is an important feature of identity construction as both a collective and individual process. In this section I connect notions of (1) 'insideness' and 'outsideness', (2) competence and role fulfilment and (3) centre and periphery dynamics to some relevant extracts from the self-narratives.

9.4.1.1 Insideness and outsideness

Extract 1

So we get to a situation where the project on which I have been hired doesn't exist anymore, [the firm] is self-sufficient [. . .] So, since, clearly, there was no other work to do, since there were no new customers, then I had to find some work to do, so I was helping my technical colleagues on their maintenance jobs [. . .] So in fact I've travelled quite a bit in Finland, I've been in many, many towns, I've had many, many hours on the road, which I appreciated since because there was no work at the office, well in fact we were on the roads, it was much nicer. (Bruno)

Extract 2

Going abroad [. . .] teaches one to relativize a lot of things. It teaches one to forget the small habits that somehow, one was believing to be something universal, so to say . . . and it allows one to realize, at the end of the day, what it is to be French, I think that if one doesn't

> go abroad, one doesn't realize what it is, to be French, that is, well, what is it that says that I am really French . . . It's . . . I don't know . . . is it this sort of . . . I wouldn't say politeness but, the good manners *à la française*, is it . . . well, there's a whole lot of things, which belong to daily life and are commonplace, and which, when one goes abroad, one realizes that they're typically French. (Cyril)

Both Bruno and Cyril have, in important ways, felt as outsiders during their period spent in Finland. But interestingly, at the end of their stay they were both very enthusiastic about their Finnish experience as a whole. How can concepts of 'outsideness' and 'insideness' be useful in order to make sense of these experiences?

As Relph (1976) puts it, the essence of place, more than in anything else, lies in the experience of an 'inside' that is distinct from an 'outside'. To him, 'to be inside a place is to identify with it, and the more profoundly inside you are the stronger is this identity with the place' (Relph 1976: 49). He goes on to make the distinction between, on the one hand, 'behavioural insideness' ('physical presence in a place'), 'empathetic insideness' (involving 'emotional participation in' a place) and 'existential insideness' ('complete and unself-conscious commitment to place'), and on the other hand 'vicarious insideness' ('the experience of places through novels and other media'), 'incidental outsideness' (by which places become 'merely backgrounds for other activities'), 'objective outsideness' (with places treated as 'concepts and locations'), and 'existential outsideness' (involving 'a profound alienation from all places') (Relph 1976: 50–5). Thus, for Relph, places are understood as having more or less meaning depending on the degree that one feels 'inside' the place. According to Seamon (1984), this 'inside-outsideness continuum is an important beginning for providing a self-consciousness presentation of place experience which applies to particular places yet extends beyond them to help people understand their environmental dealings in more general, reflexive terms'.

Buttimer's (1980: 170) approach is similar, in that it underlines 'a fundamental contrast between the *insider's* ways of experiencing place and the *outsider's* conventional ways of describing them'. However, she points out that there are weaknesses in both the outsider's and the insider's viewpoints, since the former is bound to a more abstract understanding, while the latter 'may be so immersed in the particulars of everyday life and action that he or she may see no point in questioning the taken-for-granted or in seeing home in its wider spatial or social context' (Buttimer 1980: 172). There is thus a 'pedagogical challenge' for both outsider and insider, she argues. Ultimately, Buttimer's and Seamon's discussions both suggest that the empathetic insider may be the ideal mediator in interactions between insiders and outsiders, and a position that the latter should strive for is to get rid of their feeling of uprootedness, and redefine their identity thanks to a changing relationship with the 'foreign' place.

Thus, this distinction between varying degrees of insideness and outsideness in people's experiences of places can be insightful when looking at identity construction in intercultural contexts. In intercultural interactions in a given place – be it a country, a specific workplace, or some other place that takes on meanings in the social world – people will typically experience varying degrees of identification to the place: whether they feel 'at home' or 'foreign', for instance, will have a critical impact on their identity construction in this context. The examples of Bruno and Cyril above could be understood as illustrating cases where people feel both 'inside' and 'outside': Bruno engaged with the foreign place empathetically, but the fact that he did so wholeheartedly is also because being 'out of place' (both out of his normal professional position and a foreigner) made it possible for him to explore new possibilities more freely. Cyril enjoyed his time abroad but mostly because it acted as a pointer to where he *really* belongs in his view.

9.4.1.2 Competence and role fulfilment in intercultural contexts

Extract 3

So, in the mind of the managers here, I am outside of the hierarchy [. . .] I have never had hierarchical relations in Finland [. . .] [I am] someone who is bound, in fact, to become a managing executive of the company, and [. . .] who knows everybody [at the headquarters] [. . .] They know that [one of the main managers in France] is *my godfather*, so it's clear, they're not going to nitpick with me. When I decide to have a two-hour lunch break and to work late in the evening by using a laptop at home, nobody asks me questions. [. . .] I never wanted them to feel that I would be part of their hierarchy [. . .] let's say I was seconded for a limited time to Finland, and that's it. (Antoine)

As discussed above, both Bruno and Cyril in a sense felt as outsiders in Finland, yet they still found some fruitful and liberating elements in their experiences. However, it is also common for people to feel deeply rejected when they find themselves in 'outsider' situations. In Bruno's and Cyril's cases the temporary nature of their assignments probably partly explains how they managed to make sense of their experiences in a positive way. It is clear, for instance, that the need for role fulfilment for Bruno was made more flexible by the specific nature of his assignment: even though his job did not eventually correspond to his competence and what his role was supposed to be, he saw it as providing opportunities to discover other professional possibilities. Admittedly Bruno's is an extreme case. Nevertheless, it is quite common that the role fulfilment imperative is affected by the intercultural contexts people find themselves in. If intercultural situations can be at times perceived as liberating, it is partly because the professional expectations may not be as inflexible as in well-defined working situations 'at home'. Antoine's example above provides another illustration of how the need for role fulfilment can be made somewhat less pressing in an intercultural context.

In this illustration Antoine draws on his 'outsideness' as a strength, and his professional positioning 'out of position' turns out to be liberating in the sense that he does not feel much of a need for role fulfilment, because he has no easily identifiable role within the hierarchy. It should be noted that on the whole, Antoine has not appreciated his experience in Finland. What is interesting here, however, is that he has turned what he felt to be a rather hostile environment – the fact that he had no position within the local hierarchy – into a feature that has made it possible for him to liberate himself from a number of duties he could not avoid in a 'home' context. While it certainly has not been a very constructive way to cooperate, it has been his way of coping with a situation he has perceived as unfair, not well-suited to his identity as a future 'managing executive of the company'. This is an example of how even extreme outsideness can be mobilized as a strong building block for one's identity construction in an intercultural context.

9.4.1.3 Centre and periphery dynamics

Extract 4

Well, actually, when I went to, I was supposed to, in the beginning, I was supposed to go to New York, and then there were different issues . . . in fact, I, I had the choice between prioritizing, either the job or the geographic aspect [. . .] One day they tell me I'll be going to Sweden, well alright in Sweden they were friends the people there in fact, that wasn't a problem, so, and besides I was working at that moment, I mean as a trainee in the bank, so I really had something else to do than to care about the *coopération*, let's be clear. I didn't really bother about it. And one morning, arriving at work, I have one thing to sign, and they tell me "yes, you're going to Helsinki in Sweden" so, well, maybe I'm not very good in geography but . . . (laughter) I still went *tilt*! (*sic*) [. . .] and just before leaving I went to the Fnac[3] at 10 am the day before and I took a book about Finland and I looked . . . so, it wasn't my choice, I didn't even know where, I mean, I didn't know Finland, I knew nothing about Finland. (Antoine)

Extract 5

I want to have stuff to do, to be involved [. . .] When you deal with files at the European level, which are fairly important, which end up three weeks or one month later in the press, whether The Financial Times or elsewhere, you're at the heart of the economy. All the deals go through you, you tell them, you're in or you're out, you, you manage or something, but everything goes through, through you or your colleague who anyway discusses with you, so [. . .] you really have the impression . . . since the bank for which I work is quite important, you have very few deals that don't go through it, you have friends in other banks or something, you're aware of things. So, you're in the very heart of things, you open your financial newspaper, you know what it's about. Here, I've really had the impression to have been put between brackets, aside. I've really . . . ok, it's a great job, I have many friends who, who'd do everything to be, to be working in this stuff, it's well paid, it's nice, I mean it's . . . there's no denial it is. But it's just not my *trip*[4] (Antoine)

Antoine's discourse portrays someone who has already found his place, and this place should be very much at the centre, in one of the financial and economic capitals of the world, whether Paris, London, New York or Tokyo, in all of which he allegedly has had short work experiences already – or at worst in a regional capital such as

Stockholm, where he initially thought he was going to spend his *coopération* period. He describes himself as someone who knows himself perfectly and has a very clear future; his career plan is well established, and consequently, his discourse displays a great deal of 'ordering'. The problem is that, as someone who wants to be in the centre of all things, it does not feel good to find oneself in the periphery. The assignment in Finland is presented as something that happened 'by mistake'. In many ways, his narrative is an anti-narrative, insofar as he tries to minimize any major sense of journey during his time in Finland, but instead claims a fixed identity, that of an *elite* person. His story can be summarized as follows: the period he spent in Finland was a time of struggle before reclaiming his 'real' position in the centre, after having been put, by mistake or due to some adverse forces, in the periphery. Again, his outsideness, while it has been alienating him from his colleagues and Finland as a foreign place, is presented as a feature of strength rather than weakness: he would of course not want to be associated with subject positions from the periphery, since he *is* from the centre.

The most prominent postcolonial authors have, to a large extent, focused their work on the articulation of relations between centre and periphery. A key interest has been to show how the West has imposed its mark on the rest through the combined effect of territorial colonization and powerful discourses about 'others' – such as 'orientalism' (Said 1978). In these works, the West is presented as the centre, where appropriate knowledge about the whole world is produced and then imposed on the many peripheries. This spatial centre-periphery dialectic is largely about power relations that are not expressed through overt conflict but through more subtle positioning. Similarly, in the micropolitics of identity construction in intercultural contexts, issues of centre and periphery are often significant – even when there is no clear postcolonial dimension, as shown in the example above. This is particularly noticeable in bicultural organizations because centre-periphery power relations are usually deeply embedded in these organizations – for instance in the case of acquisitions or foreign subsidiaries of transnational companies.

9.4.2 Questioning and learning about self: space and place

Extract 6

I have learnt about others, about myself even though there's still a lot to learn [. . .] and then, it has taught me about what I want to do exactly, since . . . actually, no, it's not true. It has given me a few ideas on what I want to do. Well, not exactly, since I'm still wondering, but, at least, it has confirmed the choice of an international career [. . .] The international side of it, I want it, it's a choice, but, I know what I don't want to do, that is, I don't want to stay completely in technical jobs, I don't want anything too static, I don't want to be, in short, monodisciplinary [. . .] and thus in fact apart from that it leaves a very varied, wide choice, a little too much actually, that is, I want to be multidisciplinary, but which disciplines? (Bruno)

In Extract 1, it was shown that Bruno, finding out that the project he was initially hired for was not going to materialize at all, had to 'make do' with what he could find to work on. Bruno took this unfortunate turn of events as an opportunity rather than as the disaster that others could have treated it as. It allowed him to explore new spaces, both in metaphorical terms – for instance, new types of jobs – and physical terms – especially referring to the travels he had throughout Finland. Exploring these new spaces was a kind of liberating experience for him. In the citation above, about his learning experience after his 16 months in Finland, he concludes that he learnt a great deal and does feel liberated, but at the same time he ends up with many more questions than answers. However, he also claims to enjoy very much this feeling. He seems to be at once totally enthusiastic about having explored new spaces and deeply confused about what that may mean for his future – somewhat 'lost in space'. But what 'space' is referred to in this seemingly far-fetched metaphorical reformulation? Insights from humanistic geography may be helpful here.

> Place is security, space is freedom; we are attached to the one and long for the other.
>
> (Tuan 1977: 3)

This short description of space and place from Yi-Fu Tuan is useful in order to grasp the basic distinction between the two in humanistic geography: place accounts for a fixity and a familiarity, something one can get to know intimately, while space is something that one can explore, seemingly for ever, and thus represents a possible emancipation from the pressure of one's place, in a way that is at once exciting, because of the promises of new experiences it offers, and worrying, because of its unknown character. This dialectic of place and space – and Tuan's (1996) related dialectic of 'hearth' and 'cosmos' – is very reminiscent of Bruner's above mentioned opposition between home ('inside, private, forgiving, intimate, predictably safe' but also 'restricted by duties and bored') and 'real world' ('outside, demanding, anonymous, open, unpredictable, and consequently dangerous' but also 'excitement and opportunity') (Bruner 1987: 25). To make the simple place-space distinction more complete, one could add that, in the phenomenological view, 'space is a dynamic continuum in which the experiencer lives and moves and searches for meaning' (Buttimer 1976: 282), while places have meaning and 'are characterised by the beliefs of man' (Relph 1976: 3), being at once 'physical and historical, social and cultural' (Casey 2001: 683). There is thus a strong connection, a relation of 'constitutive coingredience' as Casey (2001: 684) puts it, between place and self. Similarly, the relation between place and identity has been thoroughly examined in humanistic and radical geographies (see e.g. Adams et al. 1998; Buttimer and Seamon 1980; Carter et al. 1993; Keith and Pile 1993; Low and Lawrence-Zúñiga 2003; Rose 1995).

However, place should not be misinterpreted as providing a definite sense of fixity to self or identity, since, in the postmodern world, characterized by a segmentation of places, places may become 'thinned-out' (Sack 1997: 9) and lose their meaning. This does not destroy the relation between place and self; on the contrary, as the places are segmented, so are the selves. As Sack (1997: 9) explains, 'spatial segmentation of life makes us live in a world of strangers in which experiences are often isolated', i.e. places do have meanings, but those meanings are not necessarily the same for all. This is not necessarily a bad thing, and may actually help allow for a liberation from too thick places, with too rich meanings involving more pressure. Being 'in a world of strangers' may enable one to choose with whom to interact, what meanings to give places, and ultimately one could, in theory at least, construct one's own world (Sack 1997: 10). Thus, the expatriate, as a stranger in places that have social meanings which s/he does not understand fully, may actually see this as an opportunity to gain agency and to be free to construct her/his own world. As the knowledge acquired in her/his own society has become inadequate, s/he has to 'question the "givens" of social life' (Buttimer 1976: 285–6) and it is thus an ideal 'occasion for sensemaking'.

This can also be illustrated through the experiences of Cyril, which led him to question his identity, as shown in Extract 2. His comments there present the experience as a matter of learning about oneself, about one's own cultural background. But interestingly, in this case it does not necessarily imply that Cyril has a very dynamic view of his identity. If anything, his identity seems to be more fixed after his experience abroad than before: merely a marker of 'what there was in the first place' (an alleged French cultural identity), tying Cyril to a sense of 'belonging' to his national culture more than anything else. So while there is definitely a questioning – a 'relativization' – there is also a confirmation, a reproduction of an identity imposed through a strong feeling of belonging to a (national) group.

9.4.3 Development and change

Additional insights are provided by contemporary cultural studies, especially regarding how identities have been conceptualized as fragmented in this postmodern world where meanings – among which those held by places – are contested and sometimes lost. It would be a mistake to think of spatial understandings as necessarily tying people's identities to particular places. The authors who seek to account for the fragmented and hybrid identities of today tend to articulate their views with spatial metaphors, and in the following I discuss (1) 'heterotopias' and the 'third space', and (2) the 'in-between' and 'routes' as opposed to 'roots'.

9.4.3.1 Heterotopias and the third space

Extract 7

After two weeks, we had one of those afternoons that are meant to consolidate team spirit [. . .] and there, first shock, huge cultural shock, well, I had my first sauna at that time, and, well, I started to adopt a little bit . . . the Finnish spirit regarding partying [laughs] [. . .]

> The first sauna, it was quite an experience. The day after, I had written a long e-mail to all my friends in France, explaining all the details [. . .] I'm not very modest, but, well, to be there with your boss . . . and then again the heat, it had burnt my nose, it had burnt my mouth, everything. And then the cold in the sea, because we went to bathe then, the water was around 12–13 degrees! (David)

Bicultural or multicultural organizations can potentially offer a hybrid cultural space that enables people from different cultural groups to work together in a good atmosphere, and to develop and change together. This often has to be promoted by the leadership trying to set up an atmosphere of companionship, as in the example above. Antoine, Bruno, Cyril and David have all experienced saunas with their Finnish workmates, in socializing events organized by their workplaces. All four present it as a fascinating discovery after an initial shock, and at least two of them, Cyril and David, argue that it significantly affected their whole experience at the Finnish workplace, and much enhanced their appreciation of it. The Finnish idea of sauna as a social place, where people are all equal, have nothing to hide and thus speak frankly and calmly in a spirit of togetherness, explains why it turned out to help tremendously in getting to know the Finnish workmates better. What is interesting with sauna is that Foucault (1986) described it as one example of what he calls 'heterotopia'.

Heterotopias are 'heterogeneous relational spaces' (Soja 1989: 14), or third spaces, that allow individuals to redefine themselves in relation to the new, other meanings they encounter. Foucault (1986) uses both of the terms 'place' and 'space' in relation to heterotopias: they can be seen as places that articulate an interface with others and/or otherness and they establish a space of 'borderlands' where 'the fiction of cultures as discrete, object-like phenomena occupying discrete spaces becomes implausible' (Gupta and Ferguson 2002: 66). The sauna seems to have played this role in David's experience.

However, even when certain heterotopias can be made use of, the establishment of a hybrid third space cannot be single-handedly directed by management. To a large extent any genuine intercultural interaction process in itself makes such a hybrid space emerge. Here is an illustration:

Extract 8

> We should not think 'Ok, we managed to flog that to them, they saw nothing, because [the Finns] know it [. . .] I remember smiles of complicity with them while addressing a point, saying 'yeah, well, hum, that's basically rubbish [laughs] but, well, that's the way it is for now' and the Finn, on the other side, would say 'yes, I know, but, well, it doesn't matter, we'll see that later', because we are working on a long-drawn-out project [. . .] We have common interests, I mean [. . .] so, they have this consciousness, and this intelligence, to leave certain things pending and get back to them later. (Cyril)

Despite the 'smiles of complicity', this example shows how when two groups, with clear differences both in terms of values and expectations, cooperate over a long period of time (in this case two different companies, one from Finland and the other from France, working together on the ten-year process of implementation of a product sold by the latter to the former), the development of common understandings favours the emergence of a sort of 'third culture'. This is characterized by a concern for the good of both parties and an appreciation of both viewpoints, or rather the emergence of a third viewpoint that is the result of the interaction.

9.4.3.2 Dwelling in-between: on the 'route' to intercultural personhood

Extract 9

To sum up Finnish culture, I think that . . . pragmatism, that's something they really have. Whether in their organization, in time, or whatever . . . even the way they see things. That's a quality I appreciate. Now, there are other things in French culture that are also nice. I'm not a lover of Finnish culture more than of French culture, I enjoy them both. I try to take the best from each, from all the things I know, and with a little bit of Spanish features too, since I've lived there for a little while. (David)

David seemingly took advantage of his situation in a foreign context to 'hybridize himself', especially by learning to have a more focused working day, allowing for it to be shorter and finish earlier. This enabled him to create more room for leisure, a new space that he had not had the opportunity to explore in his previous short working experiences in France and Spain. He took advantage of the fact that his work days ended usually before five in the afternoon by starting practising martial arts on a regular and frequent basis, which represented for him an additional occasion to get to know himself better, to travel 'inwards' in a new way. While he was certainly the interviewee who displayed the most sentimental attachment to the new place, he was also very much 'exploring space' at the same time, allowing himself to evolve and pragmatically adopt features from here and there, making a hybrid collage out of his identity, thanks to the ability to be 'in-between', celebrated by de Certeau (1984) and Hall (1995).

Dwelling in and exploring a sort of 'in-between space', thanks to this 'art of being in between' (de Certeau 1984: 30), is indeed critical for the outsider who needs to look for her/his place in the 'hostile' foreign environment. Hall (1995: 206–7) claims that this type of in-between position seems to characterize more and more people nowadays:

> [The 'diaspora' are people who] belong to more than one world, speak more than one language (literally and metaphorically), inhabit more than one identity, have more than one home; have learned to negotiate and translate *between* cultures, and who, because they are irrevocably the product of several interlocking histories and cultures, have learned to live with, and indeed speak from, *difference*. They speak from the 'in-between' of different cultures, always unsettling the assumptions of one culture from the perspective of another, and thus finding ways of being both *the same as* and at the same time *different from* the others amongst whom they live. [. . .] They represent new kinds of identities – new ways of 'being

> someone' – in the late-modern world. Although they are characteristic of the cultural strategies adopted by marginalized people in the latest phase of globalization, more and more people – not only ex-colonized or marginalized people – are beginning to think of themselves, of their identities and their relationship to culture and to place, in these more 'open' ways.

The idea here is that, in the 'late-modern world', identities may be better represented by 'routes' than by 'roots' (Hall 1995), or, to get back to de Certeau's vocabulary, by 'trajectories' (cf. e.g. Crang 2000: 150) more than by places. David's trajectory from France to Finland via Spain can be considered a good illustration of this. His journey is far from over, and he seems to be on his way to developing an intercultural personhood through 'a 'working through' of all cultural experiences, so as to create new constructs – that is, constructs that did not exist previously' (Kim 2001: 196). There is an interesting dialectic of stability and change here, since it is seemingly because he felt 'in place', that is, in a place with the comfortable attributes of home, he felt that he could afford to explore new spaces.

9.5 Conclusion

While a spatial understanding does not cover all aspects that may be relevant to identity construction, it is remarkable that even issues of competence and role fulfilment as part of identity are often discussed by individuals in terms of being 'at one's place' or 'where one belongs'. The professional's world is delimited by a finite space of competence that presumably prevents her/him from exploring other spaces. But for individuals who cross cultural boundaries and work in hybrid intercultural contexts, exploration can also become part of the job. Thus, the way identities are reflexively (re)constructed in intercultural contexts varies a great deal between individuals: some revert to an *originary* identity and tie themselves more strongly to 'home'; while others liberate themselves from the founding myth of an essential cultural identity to develop an intercultural personhood and become 'strangers to themselves' – dreaming of contexts where everybody would acknowledge themselves as 'foreigners, foreign to bonds and communities' (Kristeva 1988: 9; author's translation).

KEY POINTS

1. Extensive contact with members of another culture can have an impact on people's sense of identity.
2. The idea of a coherent, stable identity has been exposed as a myth in contemporary social sciences.
3. Identity can usefully be studied as a process of contextualized identity construction that is affected by social interactions.
4. Self-narratives can be seen as ways in which identities are fashioned through retrospective sensemaking.

5. Intercultural contexts provide new occasions for individual sensemaking, in that cultural identities become salient when confronted with other cultural identities. Intercultural contact can affect people's sense of belonging, it can lead them to question who they are and to start learning about themselves, and it can thereby result in development and change.
6. Spatial metaphors are often used as devices to make sense of identities in self- narratives, especially in intercultural contexts.
7. Spatial metaphors are mobilized by some narrators in order to revert to an originary identity and tie themselves more strongly to 'home'; and by others in order to liberate themselves from the founding myth of an essential cultural identity and to develop an intercultural personhood.

DISCUSSION QUESTIONS

1. Recall an encounter with another culture (for instance while staying abroad for a relatively long period) that you have had.
   1.1. To what extent did it serve as an opportunity for you to understand your own cultural identity better?
   1.2. Did you experience this process as learning about your culture, or as an opportunity to question your own assumptions and change? Discuss.
2. In Chapter 13, a number of the issues that seem to cause the Chinese business people to not feel that they are given the face they deserve can be connected to issues of space and place: the hotel itself, the spatial arrangements between 'chair' and 'audience' or the broader issue of centre and periphery perceptions on both parts. Analyse the extent to which the problem can be seen as boiling down to the fact that the Chinese do not feel they are 'in their right place'.
3. Read a passage from a travel narrative or biography of your choice, where the author reflects on her/his identity and try to focus on how spatial expressions and metaphors are used. (One possibility is given below.)
   3.1. What do they tell in terms of the author's identity construction?
   3.2. To what extent is the travel reinforcing or hybridizing the author's identity? Discuss.

Eva Hoffman was born in Poland and when she was 13, she emigrated to the United States with her family. The extract below describes some of her reflections as she learned English and adjusted to life in America.

> For my birthday, Penny gives me a diary, complete with a little lock and key to keep what I have write from the eyes of all intruders. It is that little lock – the visible symbol of the privacy in which the diary is meant to exist – that creates my dilemma. If I am indeed to write something entirely for myself, in what language do I write? Several times, I open the diary and close it again. I can't decide. Writing in Polish at this point would be a little like resorting to Latin or ancient Greek – an eccentric thing to do in a diary, in which you're supposed to

> set down your most immediate experiences and unpremeditated thoughts in the most unmediated language. Polish is becoming a dead language, the language of the untranslatable past. But writing for nobody's eyes in English? That's like doing a school exercise, or performing in front of yourself, a slightly perverse act of self-voyeurism.
>
> Because I have to choose something, I finally choose English. . . . In the solitude of this most private act, I write, in my public language, in order to update what might have been my other self. The diary is about me and not about me at all. But on one level, it allows me to make the first jump. I learn English through writing, and, in turn, writing gives me a written self. Refracted through the double distance of English and writing, this self – my English self – becomes oddly objective; more than anything, it perceives. It exists more easily in the abstract sphere of thoughts and observations than in the world. For a while, this impersonal self, this cultural negative capability, becomes the truest thing about me. When I write, I have a real existence that is proper to the activity of writing – an existence that takes place midway between me and the sphere of artifice, art, pure language. This language is beginning to invent another me. However, I discover something odd. It seems that when I write (or, for that matter, think) in English, I am unable to use the word 'I'. I do not go as far as the schizophrenic 'she' – but I am driven, as by a compulsion, to the double, the Siamese-twin 'you'.
>
> (Hoffman 1989: 120–1)

4. Read the following passage and analyse how notions of insideness and outsideness are mobilized for Zygmunt Bauman's identity construction.

> When my turn of being so honoured came, I was asked to choose between the British and the Polish anthems . . . Well, I did not find an answer easy.
>
> Britain was the country of my choice and by which I was chosen through an offer of a teaching job once I could no longer stay in Poland, the country of my birth, because my right to teach was taken away. But there, in Britain, I was an immigrant, a newcomer – not so long ago a refugee from a foreign country, an alien. I have since become a naturalized British citizen, but once a newcomer can you ever stop being a newcomer? I had no intention of passing for an Englishman and neither my students nor my colleagues ever had any doubt that I was a foreigner, a Pole to be exact. [. . .] So perhaps the Polish anthem should have been played? But that would also mean acting on false pretences: thirty-odd years before the Prague ceremony I had been stripped of Polish citizenship. My exclusion was official, initiated and confirmed by the power entitled to set apart the 'inside' from the 'outside', those who belong from those who don't – so the right to the Polish national anthem was no longer mine.
>
> Janina, my lifelong companion [. . .] found the solution: why not the European anthem? Indeed, why not? A European, no doubt, I was, had never stopped being – born in Europe, living in Europe, working in Europe, thinking European, feeling European; and what is more, there is thus far no European passport office with the authority to issue or to refuse a 'European passport', and so to confer or to deny our right to call ourselves Europeans.
>
> Our decision to ask for the European anthem to be played was simultaneously 'inclusive' and 'exclusive'. It referred to an entity that embraced both alternative reference points of my

identity, but at the same time cancelled out, as less relevant or irrelevant, the differences between them and so also a possible 'identity split'.

(Bauman and Vecchi 2004: 9–10)

Notes

1. The *coopération* format, together with French compulsory conscription, ceased to exist in 2002, and was replaced by the voluntary format named *volontariat*. Neither *coopération* nor *volontariat* is technically what is usually referred to as expatriation, since *coopérants* or *volontaires* are not sent abroad directly by a company, at least not officially (although they find this job by their own means, their applications for the peculiar status goes through French State administration).
2. Translated from the French: 'Je voudrais que vous me racontiez librement votre expérience, de travail et de vie, en tant que Coopérant en Finlande.'
3. A French chain of 'cultural stores' that sells books, CDs, DVDs, and so on.
4. In English in the original – 'c'est pas mon trip' is a common French slang expression.

Suggestions for further reading

Bauman, Z. and Vecchi, B. (2004) *Identity*. Cambridge: Polity.

Hall, S. (1995) New cultures for old. In D. Massey and P. Jess (eds) *A Place in the World?* Oxford: Oxford University Press, 175–213.

Hall, S. and du Gay, P. (eds) (1996) *Questions of Cultural Identity*. London: Sage.

Hoffman, E. (1989) *Lost in Translation: A Life in a New Language*. London: Vintage.

Said, E. W. (1999) *Out of Place: A Memoir*. New York: Viking.

Part 4
Intercultural Pragmatics: Empirical Studies

Editor's Introduction

Part 4 of the book returns once more to empirical studies. These chapters illustrate concepts and issues discussed in the theoretical chapters, both in Parts 1 and 3. They attempt to put 'flesh on the bones' and to bring the issues to life. It therefore will be useful to read these empirical chapters in conjunction with the theoretical frameworks presented in Chapters 1–3 and 7–9. In addition, it will be useful to compare the data collection and analysis procedures used in these studies with the insights and recommendations given in Chapters 14 and 15.

Chapter 10, 'Negotiating Rapport in German–Chinese Conversation', analyses an authentic conversation between German and Chinese students who meet for the first time. It illustrates how different styles and beliefs about argumentation in initial encounters can negatively affect people's evaluations of an interaction. Chapter 11, 'Negative Assessments in Japanese–American Workplace Interaction,' analyses authentic conversations between Japanese and American members of staff of Japanese companies who work together in the same offices. The analysis focuses on negative assessments, such as disagreement or disapproval, and illustrates similarities and differences in the ways in which such matters are handled and interpreted by the two groups. Chapter 12, 'Impression Management in 'Intercultural' German Job Interviews', analyses the self-presentation techniques used by East and West German applicants in job interviews conducted by West German employers, and explores the effects these have on the interviewers' assessments. Chapter 13, 'Issues of Face in a Chinese Business Visit to Britain', analyses an authentic post-sales visit to a British company by Chinese business people. It focuses on the problems that occurred, and analyses them from a face theory perspective.

Part 4 ends with a list of other papers that analyse authentic intercultural interactions. Readers may use it as a follow-up reading list if they wish.

10 Negotiating Rapport in German–Chinese Conversation

Susanne Günthner

Chapter Outline

10.1 Introduction	207
10.2 Background to the conversation	208
10.3 The interactive organization of dissent	209
10.4 Strategies to end the confrontational frame	220
10.5 Concluding remarks	223
Key points	225
Discussion questions	225
Notes	226
Suggestions for further reading	226

10.1 Introduction

This chapter deals with the question of how culturally specific expectations of communicative situations and different conventions concerning communicative activities and genres can lead to difficulties in the interactive negotiation of meaning and the constitution of rapport. Thus, it is concerned with the way language is used to construct, maintain and confirm social relationships (cf. Chapter 2).

On the basis of an in-depth analysis of a conversation between Chinese and German students who were studying at a German university, I will show what the social consequences can be when interactants have diverging communicative expectations and use different strategies across various domains (discourse domain, participation domain and stylistic domain; cf. Chapter 2). The conversation is part of a larger corpus of audiotaped data which includes 25 conversations between German native speakers and Chinese speakers of German[1] and six conversations among Chinese native speakers (in Chinese). The analysis is based on methods of interpretative sociolinguistics and the theory of contextualization (Gumperz 1982). Furthermore, I shall refer to ethnographic knowledge as well as to the interpretations of the participants themselves, and Chinese and German informants to whom I presented parts of the audiotaped conversation in later meetings. The focus of the analysis is the organization of dissent sequences and the organization of arguments and counter-arguments. Conflict activities are of special interest to the analysis of rapport management, as they demand techniques of conversational cooperation as well as strategies of confrontation and thus require a combination of discursive methods such as signalling disagreement, coherence, giving accounts for one's arguments, defending one's position and doing 'face-work'. Studies of argumentative sequences in intercultural settings not only draw attention to the fact that willingness to take part in argumentative and confrontational discourse can vary from one cultural group to another, but also that people from different cultural backgrounds may favour different ways of handling argumentative genres and activities (Naotsuka et al. 1981; Richards and Sukwiwat 1983; Günthner 1994, 2007).

10.2 Background to the conversation

The participants, two German students Doris and Andrea (both female) and two Chinese students Tan (female) and Yang (male), meet for tea. Tan and Yang, who both graduated from a university in China, were at the time of the conversation taking an M.A. course at a German university. The interaction came about for the following reasons: I had often talked to Doris about China, and she was very interested in knowing more about China and especially about the situation of women there. She asked me if I could introduce her to some Chinese students. As I knew that Tan would be very interested in meeting German students, I gave Doris her telephone number. So the two of them decided to 'meet for tea'. Both brought a friend along: Yang is a colleague of Tan and Andrea a friend of Doris.

After the conversation Tan evaluated the meeting as 'not bad', but commented that the Germans were quite 'direct', 'aggressive' and also 'rude, yes a bit offensive'. Doris mentioned that she and Andrea would not be interested in meeting the two Chinese students again as the conversation was 'just not interesting', 'the Chinese actually turned out to be boring conversationalists'. There were no further meetings between the four and the contact was broken off. What was the basis for these evaluations? The following analysis will look at the argumentative strategies used by the Chinese and German participants and will inquire into problems of rapport management in this interaction.[2]

The interaction begins with a small-talk period which accounts for the first 35 minutes. Tan serves tea and cakes, and Doris and Andrea ask about Yang's and Tan's situation in the student dormitory: how many foreign students live there, how many Chinese students, etc. Then they start talking about Chinese cuisine. Tan and Yang mention that they always cook, because they do not like the German food in the refectory.

After that the topic switches from cooking and who does the cooking in China to the topic of 'women in China and Germany'. The German participants gradually initiate a very confrontational interactive frame. As this discussion is characterized by frequent use of disagreement sequences, the analysis will concentrate on the interactive management of disagreement, and demonstrate differences in the handling of verbal confrontation.

10.3 The interactive organization of dissent

Conversation analysts typically argue that agreements are preferred activities, and that disagreements are dispreferred activities which thus tend to be avoided or at least mitigated (Pomerantz 1984a). This 'dispreference for direct disagreement' might be adequate for small talk-situations, but in argumentative sequences and confrontational discussions, disagreement is often produced in a very direct and unmitigated form (Günthner 1993; Kotthoff 1993). This direct, unmitigated use of dissent strategies even represents a constitutive feature for the construction of an argumentative sequence.

In my data, once an argumentative and confrontational frame is established, the German participants signal their dissent in such a way that the disagreement is focused and maximized.

10.3.1 Forms of dissent organization among the German participants

10.3.1.1 Dissent-formats

The term 'dissent-formats' refers to sequences where the speaker provides a (partial) repetition of the prior speaker's utterance and negates it or replaces parts of it with a contrasting element.[3] The substituted item is produced with emphatic stress and thus marked as an opposition to the replaced item:

YANG 6

8 Yang:	*das ist natürliche*
9 Andrea:	*das ist nicht NATÜRLICH.*
10	*sondern das ist eher tradiTIONELL.*
8 Yang:	this is natural
9 Andrea:	this is not NATURAL.
10	but it is actually tradiTIONAL.

Instead of mitigating the disagreement, Andrea organizes her utterance in a 'dissent-format' that consists of (i) contradiction by negation, (ii) correction by substitution and (iii) prosodic marking of the contrastive elements 'NATURAL – tradiTIONAL'. In this way, she focuses on the polarity and highlights the dissent. Thus, she openly indicates a counter-position in an aggravated fashion without giving the prior speaker the chance to correct him/herself.

The dissent formats produced by the German participants show the following features:

a. The utterance containing the disagreement repeats parts of the prior utterance and either negates it or substitutes central elements through contradictory devices.
b. The correction of the problem item is highlighted by prosodic (contrastive stress), lexico-semantic (such as antonyms; opposing categories) and/or syntactic means of contrast (syntactic parallelism).
c. The dissent is sequentially organized in a way that the speaker of the 'problem utterance' receives no possibility for self-correction.

YANG 31

6 Yang:	*ja so. wenn wenn diese Problem gelöst, dann natürlich (0.3)*
7	*die andere Problem ist leichter zu (0.3) [eh zu zu DISkutieren]*
8 Doris:	*[ne. eh ne. halt moment]*
9 Yang:	*eh zu VERSTEHEN. zu VERSTEHEN.*
10 Doris:	*ne. MOMENT. eh:m eh eh s'is für MICH kein Problem,*
11	*für mich is es KLAR*
12 Yang:	*ja.*
13 Doris:	*ehm FRAU UND MANN SIND NATÜRLICH GLEICH.*
14	*des is kein PROBLEM =*
15 Yang:	*=ja*
16 Tan:	*hihihi*
17 Doris:	*wenn DU allerdings sagst, eh::: die sind UN::gleich, NATÜRLICH UNGLEICH,*
18	*dann is es DEIN Problem, aber eh verstehst du,*
19	*des is nichts wo du drüber diskutieren kannst.*

6 Yang:	yes like this. when when this problem is solved, then of course (0.3)
7	it is easier to DIScuss (0.3) [the other problem]
8 Doris:	[no. eh no. wait a minute]
9 Yang:	eh to UNDERSTAND. to UNDERSTAND.
10 Doris:	no. WAIT A MINUTE. eh:m eh eh for ME it's no problem,
11	for me it's CLEAR
12 Yang:	yes.
13 Doris:	ehm WOMEN AND MEN ARE NATURALLY EQUAL.
14	this is not a PROBLEM =
15 Yang:	=yes
16 Tan:	hihihi
17 Doris:	however, if YOU say, eh::: they are NOT equal, NATURALLY UNEQUAL,
18	then it is YOUR problem, but eh you understand,
19	this is nothing you can discuss.

With the production of the clustered emphatic pre-elements 'no. eh no.', Doris indicates her direct, unmitigated dissent. The function of these dissent markers is to unequivocally signal disagreement and thus to bracket the entire utterance as polar in relation to the preceding turn.[4] Yang's repair (9) 'eh to UNDERSTAND. to UNDERSTAND.' is a direct response to Doris' pre-elements. Doris then uses contrastive elements and prosodic cues to mark emphasis and thus focuses on the dissent and the polarity between her utterance and the prior speaker's:

you, your	–	my
problem	–	no problem
YOUR problem	–	for ME it's no problem
WOMEN AND MEN ARE NATURALLY EQUAL	–	They are NATURALLY UNEQUAL

The polarities are constructed by a change of deictic elements ('your' – 'my'), by contrasting a referent with its negation ('problem' – 'no problem'), and by confronting a lexical item with its antonym ('equal' – 'unequal'). Instead of producing a simple negotiation 'no' as a sign of disagreement, the German speakers thus make use of rhetorical formats which take up the prior speaker's syntactic and lexical framework, negate the statement or substitute a main element of the utterance and thus highlight the polarity between the two turns.

10.3.1.2 Dissent-ties

A further strategy in the German participants' organization of dissent is what I shall call 'dissent-tying'. The speaker latches her disagreeing utterance to the prior turn and thus produces a syntactic and lexical continuation of the preceding utterance. Instead of 'unisono'-tying (in the sense of 'communicational dueting' (Falk 1979)), where the second speaker takes the floor to produce a continuation of the prior speaker's turn and thereby demonstrates concordance and camaraderie, here the second speaker ties her utterance to the prior one but then in continuing it demonstrates consequences which contradict the argumentative line of the first speaker. Tan states that in her generation housework is shared by husband and wife. It is the kind of work that just has to be 'done by one or other of them'. Andrea then ties her utterance – in the form of a sentence expansion to the right – with the pre-element 'yes' to the prior speaker's utterance (62).

YANG 5ff.

58 Tan:	*denn (0.2) es soll auch =*
59 Doris:	= (? ? ? ? [? ? ? ? ? ? ? ? ? ?)]
60 Tan:	*[ja von einem] von einem gemacht werden. JA*
61	*entweder der MANN ODER die FRAU*
62 Andrea:	*ja. und wenn der MANN keine Lust hat.*
63	*und die FRAU hat keine Lust*
64	*dann muß es die Frau machen.*

58 Tan:	then (0.2) it also should =
59 Doris:	= (? ? ? ? [? ? ? ? ? ? ? ?)]
60 Tan:	[yes be done] by one of them. YES
61	either by the HUSBAND OR the WIFE
62 Andrea:	yes. and when the HUSBAND doesn't feel like doing it.
63	and the WIFE doesn't feel like doing it
64	then the wife has to do it.

Andrea builds up a contradiction to Tan's argument that husband and wife share the housework, by taking up her turn and expanding it with the clause-combining element 'and' in a counter-argumentative direction. In order to emphasize her point, she uses rhetoric means of building up contrasts by syntactic and lexical parallelism and prosodic marking of the contrast pair (HUSBAND–WIFE):

62 Andrea:	yes. and when the HUSBAND *doesn't feel like doing it.*
63	and the WIFE *doesn't feel like doing it*
64	then the wife has to do it.

By the use of dissent-tying, Andrea at the same time achieves a 'probatio' and produces a 'refutatio': she supports her own argumentative line and tears down that of her opponent. The following transcript demonstrates the antagonistic use of 'duet'-formats:[5]

YANG 29

25 Yang:	*wenn wenn ich später von Arbeiten nach Hause ja komme*
26	*also=ich=hihihi=meine=wenn später=in=Zukunft=ja*
27	*und dann meine-meine hihi Frau hihi ist schon zu HAUS*
28	*und hat das Essen vorbereitet ja.*
29 Doris:	*und dann ist es so RICH:TIG GEMÜTLICH.*
30	*und DU SETZT dich in deinen SESSEL,*
31	*und SIE RACKERT sich ab. (-)*
32	*das glaub ich [dir gern]*
33 Andrea:	*[hihihihi]*
34 Doris:	*das finden alle MÄNNER* [*ganz TOLL*]
35 Andrea:	[*klar.*]

25 Yang:	when when I later on come home from work yes
26	well=I=hihihi=mean=when later=in=the=future=yes
27	and then my' my hihi wife hihi is already at HOME
28	and has prepared dinner yes.
29 Doris:	and then it is REA:LLY COSY.
30	and YOU SIT in your chair,
31	and SHE SLAVES AWAY for you. (-)
32	well I do believe [that]
33 Andrea:	[hihihihi]
34 Doris:	all MEN think this is [just GREAT]
35 Andrea:	[of course.]

With the conjunction 'and' Doris ties her utterance to the prior one and continues to picture Yang's wishful thinking, by presenting more concrete details to illustrate and exaggerate his imagined scene:

30	and YOU SIT in your chair,
31	and SHE SLAVES AWAY for you. (-)

The rhetorical contrast between 'you sit in your chair' and 'she slaves away' is built up by the use of syntactic parallelism and semantic oppositions (sitting – slaving away). Thus, by formally continuing his sentence and exaggerating the picture described, Doris parodies Yang's utterance and exposes him as a typical member of the category 'men': 'all MEN think this is just GREAT'.

The strategy of dissent-tying reveals how participants in argumentative discourse try to build support for their own position by undermining the opponent's argument. It is an ideal rhetorical strategy to continue the opponent's logic of argumentation in an exaggerated way and thereby illustrate its untenable consequences.

10.3.1.3 Reported speech as a strategy of confrontation

A further technique of dissent used by the German speakers is the reproduction of the opponent's prior utterance in order to oppose it. Reported speech can vary from word-by-word reproductions of the actual utterances to total misrepresentations and distortions of the original wordings. Let me present a case, where the speaker strategically distorts the original utterance. Yang argues that 'the women's problem' in China is not as severe as in Germany:

YANG 19

1 Yang:	*eh:m'::: ich ich ich, ich muß muß muß sagen,*
2	*also in Deutschland die Frauenprobleme is'*
3	*eh' (-) also is eh STÄRKER als in Schina.*
1 Yang:	eh:m'::: I I I, I must must must say,
2	well in Germany the women's problem is'
3	eh' (-) well is eh is BIGGER than in China.

About eight minutes later Doris quotes this statement. The reported speech (69–70) demonstrates the strategic transformation of the original wordings:

YANG 24a

67 Doris:	*also [ich] VERSTEH eigentlich nich unbedingt*
68 Tan:	*[hm]*
69 Doris:	*WARUM du sagst eh in in Kina gibts kein Frauenproblem.*
70	*des Problem is eigentlich das gleiche bloß daß*
71	*(-) eh:m' daß es mehr verTUSCHT wird.*
72 Yang:	*<<p> keine so stark wie hier>*

73 Doris:	*JA WEIL DIE FRAUEN HIER BEWUSSTER SIND.*

67 Doris:	well [I] don't quite UNDERSTAND
68 Tan:	[hm]
69 Doris:	WHY you say that eh in in China there aren't any women's problems
70	the problem actually is the same it's just that
71	(-) eh:m´ that it is HUSHED up much more.
72 Yang:	<<p> not as bad as here>
73 Doris:	*YES* BECAUSE WOMEN ARE MORE *CONSCIOUS* HERE

The statement: 'in Germany the women's problem is´ eh´ (-) well is eh is BIGGER than in China' now becomes strategically transformed into: 'in China there is no women's problem'. Confronted with his distorted words, Yang corrects Doris' misrepresentation in a low voice 'not as bad as here' (line 72). Shortly afterwards the conversation continues in the following way:

YANG 24b

7 Tan:	*und was denn nich gut?*
8 Andrea:	*ja ich denk, zum Beispiel*
9	*er sagt es gibt die Frauenprobleme nicht.*
10	*ich sage, es GIBT die Probleme.*
11	*aber die Frauen (-) tun nichts dagegen.*
12	*oder:´ (-) oder denken nich [darüber na:ch]*
13 Doris:	*[es kommt nicht] an d'Öffentlichkeit =*
14 Andrea:	*= ja. oder sagens nich*

7 Tan:	and what is not good?
8 Andrea:	well I think, for example
9	he says there is no women's problem.
10	I say, there ARE problems.
11	but the women (-) don't do anything about it.
12	or:´ (-) or they don't think [about them]
13 Doris:	[it is not] made a public issue=
14 Andrea:	= yes. or don't talk about them

The quoted speech (9) is again nowhere near a word-for-word reproduction of Yang's utterances (YANG 19: 1–3 and YANG 24a: 69) but plays a strategic role within the argumentative sequence: Yang, the present opponent, is now turned into a figure ('he') of Andrea's speech. Through the transformation of the original utterance: 'in Germany the women's problem is´ eh´ (-) well is eh is BIGGER than in China.' (YANG 19) into 'he says there is no women's problem.' (YANG 24b), Yang's original statement receives an illegitimate exaggeration, which provides the basis for Andrea's antithesis. This technique of distorting the quoted utterance of one's opponent by omitting his qualifications and reservations and thus simplifying and exaggerating his argument, is a strategic device suitable for building up an antagonistic counter-position and antithesis by maximizing contrasts.[6] Rhetorical means of contrast (lexical repetition, syntactic parallelism, contrasting of the two speaking subjects 'he' versus 'I' and prosodic marking) are used here again to underline the antagonism of the two opinions:

9	**he** says there is **no** women's problem.
10	**I** say, there **ARE** problems.

The trenchant formulations and simplifications organize the utterances in such a way that contrasts are built up and the rhetoric relation of thesis and antithesis are constructed.

The analysis of the strategies used by the German participants to signal dissent demonstrates that, once an argumentative or confrontational frame is established, they make use of highly aggravated forms of disagreement by employing dissent formats, distorted quotations of the opponent's utterances and forms of building up contrasts. They not only state their disagreeing opinion but at the same time make use of the opponent's utterance in order to construct contrast and heighten the polarization. This leads to the question, what kind of techniques are used by the Chinese participants to signal dissent?

10.3.2 Forms of organizing dissent among the Chinese participants

A strategy continuously used by the Chinese participants is to temporarily signal formal consent and then in the following turn to indicate a discordant position without formally marking it as a disagreement. In order to analyse Yang's and Tan's strategies of disagreement, it is necessary to follow the question 'are there natural differences between women and men' over a longer sequence of talk. When Yang argues that there are 'natural differences between women and men', Doris asks for specification:

YANG 15

79 Yang:	*das is also von der von der traditionell? oder politische?*
80	*(-) oder´, die (nur?) eh die schon (-) von Natur aus*
81	*[(???)] so natürliche´*
82 Doris:	*[ja] du glaubst es gibt eine NATÜRLICHE EINSCHRÄNKUNG?*
83	*(0.7)*
84 Yang:	*ich glau:be (-) NICHT, aber ich (hi) ich muß sagen, es gibt. (1.0) ein bißchen.*
85 Doris:	*wie meinst du das?*

79 Yang:	this is from the traditional? or political?
80	(-) or´ the (only?) eh the (-) by nature
81	[(???)] I mean natural´
82 Doris:	[well] do you believe there is a NATURAL LIMITATION?
83	(0.7)
84 Yang:	I belie:ve (-) NOT, but I (hi) I must say, there is. (1.0) a bit.
85 Doris:	what do you mean by this?

Doris' question 'do you believe there is a NATURAL LIMITATION?' (82) uses marked prosody (increase of volume and a rise of the intonation contour) to contextualize her disagreeing position. Yang answers by producing a hesitating agreement: 'I belie:ve (-) NOT'(84). However, he then utters a disagreement, introduced with 'but': 'but I (hi) I must say, there is.' As no reaction follows (the pause indicates the absence of a turn selection), Yang corrects his utterance by toning it down: 'a bit'. After Doris asks him to provide further explanations (85), the discussion on gender differences continues, and she argumentatively provides counter-examples to demonstrate that certain aspects of the life of women, which might on the surface appear to be 'natural differences' (jobs of lower status, caring for the children), do actually have social reasons (86ff.). Five minutes later Doris refocuses on Yang's thesis about 'natural differences' and asks him to restate his opinion:

YANG 17ff.

86 Doris:	*des is kein natürlicher Unterschied in meinen [Augen]*
87 Yang:	*[mhm ja] mhm*
88 Doris:	*wo siehst DU denn die NATÜRLICHEN Unterschiede? (-)*
89	*weil du hast was von natürlichen Unterschieden gere [det]*
90 Yang:	*[viel]leicht*
91	*ich habe diese eh: (1.0) eh schwer zu sagen*
......	
8 Doris:	*[du] meinst rein körperlich, jetzt?*
9 Yang:	*nein körperlich eh jetzt also*
10 Doris:	*von der Kraft her? <<p>oder wie meinst du?>*
11 Yang:	*(nich klar?) zum Beispiel die also Polizei*
12 Doris:	*POLIZEI?*
13 Yang:	*KRIMINALpolizei. das ist nicht körperlich.*
14 Doris:	*ne. das is NICH körperlich. das hat allerdings etwas damit zu tun',*
15	*was für 'n Status Frauen in der Gesellschaft habn.*
16	*MÄNNER, werden in der Gesellschaft schon mal als Autoritätspersonen*
17	*dargestellt die MEHR zu sagen haben als FRAUEN.*
18 Yang:	*ja.*
19 Doris:	*und we- DANN wirds n' natürlich problematisch*
20	*wenn so'n UNgleiches Gesellschaftsbild da ist,*
21	*da dann dann is es auch schwierig auf einmal die FRAU in die gleiche Rolle*
22	*zu setzen wie der Mann (meist?) aber wenn normalerweise*
23	*der Mann und die Frau eine gleiche Rolle hätten*
24 Yang:	*ja.*
25 Doris:	*daß eh'wenn ne Frau was sagt, das GENAUSO (-) AUTORITÄT angesehen wird,*
26	*autoritär angesehen wie en Mann*

27 Yang: *ja.*
28 Doris: *dann wär das kein Problem.*
29 *des is ein GESELLSCHAFTLICHER Unterschied*
30 *und kein (-) NATÜRLICHER.*
31 Yang: *ja(.hh)(hi)(.hh)*
32 Doris: *ja. denk ich schon. also des is kein Unterschied.*
33 *was was vielleicht stimmen könnte*
34 *[oder was]*
35 Yang: *[un und auch ein] eh eh ich meine auch*
36 *DENKWEISE von Frauen und von Männern*
37 Doris: *versuch eh was fürn Unterschied*
38 *is [das?]*
39 Yang: *[Denk]weise.*
40 Doris: *was is das fürn Unterschied? (0.6)*
41 Doris: *wie denken Frauen, [wie denken (???) Männer?]*
42 Yang: *[(? ? ? ? ? ? ? ? ? ? ? ? ? ?)]*
43 Tan: *[ich glaube das]*
44 *schon (-) auch (-) eh: wegen der Tra' dition wegen DIE Tradition =oder=so =was=*
45 Doris: *also [ich]*
46 Yang: *[viel]leicht wegen [die Tradition]*
47 Andrea: *[also die] Frauen*
48 Andrea: *können also die Frauen sind doch nich dümmer als die Männer.*
49 Yang: *nein.(-) [das is richtig]*
50 Doris: *[oder denken anders]*
51 Andrea: *du meinst die denken mehr mit Ge [FÜHL oder]*
52 Yang: *[ich glaube eh]*
53 Yang: *manchmal in in eine bestimmte Bereich ja besser als die Männer.*
54 *und die MÄNNER arbeiten in eine bestimmte Bereichen*
55 *besser als [d'] Frauen*
56 Andrea: *[mhm]*
57 Doris: *aber des is doch auch etwas was*
58 *UNHEIMLICH von der Tradition bestimmt ist*
59 *wenn Frauen nun mal IMMER in dem Bereich gearbeitet habn,*
60 *dann tun sie ihre Fähigkeiten in diesem Bereich entWICKELN.*
61 *wenn ich als FRAU immer in einem MÄNNERberuf gearbeitet hab,*
62 *dann entwickle ich meine Fähigkeiten,*
63 *die zu diesem MÄNNERBERUF gehören =*
64 Yang: *= un ich ich muß sagen, für die MÄNNER es gibt keine Grenze*
65 *für die, für die Arbeit. für die Arbeiten.*
für die Frauen es gibt Grenze.
66 Doris: *welche Grenze?*
67 Yang: *zum Beispiel die (0.3) körperliche*

86 Doris: this is not a natural difference in my [eyes]
87 Yang: [mhm yes.] mhm
88 Doris: where do YOU see NATURAL differences? (-)

89 because you mentioned something about natural differ [ences]
90 Yang: [per]haps
91 I have these eh: (1.0) eh it's difficult to say
....
8 Doris: [you] are now talking about purely physical?
9 Yang: not physical eh now well
10 Doris: concerning physical strength? <<p>or what do you mean?>
11 Yang: (not clear?) for example the police
12 Doris: POLICE?
13 Yang: CRIMINAL investigators. this is not physical.
14 Doris: no. this is NOT physical. but it does have to do´ with
15 the status of women in the society.
16 MEN can represented as authoritative figures in the society
17 who have MORE to say than WOMEN.
18 Yang: yes.
19 Doris: and wh- THEN it becomes of course problematic
20 when there is such an UNequal concept of society,
21 then then it becomes difficult to suddenly place WOMEN in the same position
22 as men (most of the time?) but if men and women
23 had the same roles
24 Yang: yes.
25 Doris: so that eh´ when a woman says something, it is treated just
26 AS (-) AUTHORITATIVE as when a man would say it
27 Yang: yes.
28 Doris: then it wouldn't be a problem.
29 this is a SOCIAL difference then
30 and not a (-) NATURAL.
31 Yang: yes (.hh) (hi) (.hh)
32 Doris: yes. I do think so. so. this is no difference then.
33 what what might be true is
34 [or what]
35 Yang: [and and also] I also think the
36 WAY OF THINKING of women and of men
37 Doris: try it eh what kind of difference
38 is [this?]
39 Yang: [way] of thinking.
40 Doris: what kind of difference do you mean? (0.6)
41 Doris: how women think, [how men (???) think]?
42 Yang: [(? ? ? ? ? ? ? ? ? ? ? ?)]
43 Tan: [I believe that] already (-) also (-) eh:
44 because of the tra(-)dition because of THE tradition or=something=like=that
45 Doris: well [I]
46 Yang: [per]haps because of [the tradition]
47 Andrea: [well] women cannot

48 Andrea: well women are not stupider than men.
49 Yang: no. (-) [this is right]
50 Doris: [or think differently]
51 Andrea: you mean they are more em[OTIONAL or what]
52 Yang: [I believe eh]
53 Yang: sometimes in certain areas they are better than men.
54 and the MEN work better in certain areas
55 than [wo]men
56 Andrea: [mhm]
57 Doris: but this is also something that is
58 VERY STRONGLY determined by tradition
59 suppose women have ALWAYS worked in one area
60 then they DEVELOP their abilities in this area.
61 when I as a WOMAN have always worked in a typical MALE profession
62 then I develop the abilities,
63 which belong to this MALE PROFESSION=
64 Yang: = and I I must say, for MEN there is no limit
65 for the, for the work. for the jobs. for women there is a limit.
66 Doris: what sort of limit?
67 Yang: for example (0.3) physical

We shall first concentrate on Yang's strategies to support his position. First of all, Doris rejects his example of the 'CRIMINAL investigators' as a socially constructed difference between women and men. Yang's recipient signals, which are produced while Doris holds the floor, are interpreted by her as 'continuers', and so she proceeds with her utterance. His 'yes'hh' and the giggling in line 31 initiates a repair on Doris' part. First she reconfirms her opinion 'yes. I do think so. so. this is no difference then.'; then she starts to formulate a possible qualification to her statement. Instead of signalling his dissent directly and marking it formally as a disagreement, Yang just provides a semantic discordant statement (35–6). His disagreeing utterance is tied to the prior one, indicating a concordant evaluation:

35 Yang: [and and also] I also think the
36 WAY OF THINKING of women and of men

Instead of taking up parts of the prior turn and opposing it, Yang lists further aspects of his position. The additive conjunction 'and' as well as the particle 'also' suggest consent. This phenomenon of producing an utterance that demonstrates dissent on the content level without formally marking it as disagreement can also be found in lines 52–5:

52 Yang: [I believe eh]
53 sometimes in certain areas they are better than men.
54 and the MEN work better in certain areas
55 than [wo] men

Doris' counter-argument (about the influence of tradition) is met with a disagreement on Yang's part; however, he contextualizes a thematic progression of Doris' statement:

64 Yang:	= and I I must say, for MEN there is no limit
65	for the, for the work. for the jobs. for women there is a limit.

Yang neither reproduces parts of his co-participants' prior turns in order to attack or de-construct them, nor does he quote their utterances in order to explicitly distance himself from them.

So far the analysis demonstrates that the Chinese and German students make use of different argumentative styles and different ways of signalling dissent.[7]

10.4 Strategies to end the confrontational frame

With the exception of the first 35 minutes of small-talk, the conversation is characterized by a confrontational frame. Verbal conflict ends when the oppositional turns cease and other activities are taken up (Vuchinich 1990: 118). As Schegloff and Sacks (1973: 297) point out, when one speaker signals his intent to close the topic, his co-participant can demonstrate in his next turn 'that he understood what a prior (speaker) aimed at, and that he is willing to go along with that'. The termination of verbal conflict also requires a consensus of the participants to go along with the closing down and to change the speech activity.

When Yang and Tan continuously employ techniques to close the verbal conflict, their German co-participants do not join these attempts, and thus the argumentation continues. We shall now consider the strategies used by the Chinese speakers to close the confrontational frame.

10.4.1 Concessions

A verbal conflict may be terminated when one participant 'gives in' and accepts the opponent's position. Since concessions signal that the speaker is not able to defend her/his position, they are potentially face-threatening acts. If the opponent accepts the concession, the conflict ends. In this conversation, the German participants, however, take the concessions of the Chinese speakers as an opportunity to focus on the contradiction between the conceding utterance and the former position of the opponent:

YANG 30

45 Yang:	*ich ich bin für Ihre Meinung.(-)daß die Frauen WIRKLICH also:: also:*
46	*nach der eh Hochschulabschluß oder (-) also: ehm:*
47	*schon als eine Er- Erwachsene und sie haben weniger Chancen oder weniger (-)*

48 *Möglichkeiten´ als die Männer*
49 Doris: *mhm*
50 Yang: *und auch die Zukunft (0.3) ist also nich so herrlich wie die Männer.*
51 Doris: *warum sagst DU, (-) daß daß du meinst eh die Frauen haben GENÜGEND Rechte.*
52 *es reicht. warum SA[GST DU DAS?]*
53 Yang: *[(? ? ? ?)hihi]*

45 Yang: I I agree with your opinion. (-) that women
46 REALLY we::ll we:ll
47 after they graduate from university or (-) we:ll ehm: as a- adults
48 they have less chances or (-) less opportunities´ than men
49 Doris: mhm
50 Yang: and also the future (0.3) is not as marvellous as the men's.
51 Doris: why do YOU say, (-) that that you think eh women have ENOUGH rights.
52 it's enough. why DO [YOU SAY THIS?]
53 Yang: [(? ? ? ? ? ? ?)hihi]

Yang (line 45ff.) agrees with Doris' position. She, however, does not accept his concession but uses it to point out the contradiction with his former position and to bring him into the situation of incompatibility. Instead of participating in the process of closing the confrontational frame, Doris thus takes the concession as an opportunity to challenge her opponent.

10.4.2 Compromises

Providing a compromise is another technique for closing down a verbal conflict. Here, the speaker offers 'a position that is *between* the opposing positions that define the dispute' (Vuchinich 1990: 126). Instead of giving in to the opponent's thesis, the speaker moves towards the other party's position and proposes a possible 'middle ground'. As s/he neither accepts the opponent's position totally nor completely gives up her/his former opinion, compromises turn out to be less face-threatening than concessions. The opposing party can either accept the proposed compromise and thus the verbal conflict can be brought to an end, or s/he can reject the compromising offer.

In the following transcript segment, Yang offers a compromise between his former position that 'in Germany the women's problem is bigger than in China' and his opponents' argument that 'women in China are just not conscious about their discrimination'. He now states that 'women and men in China have thought little about these issues so far':

YANG 33

4 Yang *sie haben auch sehr wenig darüber gedacht =überlegt=DESHALB*
5 *es gibt vielleicht in Schina ein bißchen (ruhig?)*
6 *in diese Problem. in die Frauen Problem.*
7 *das kann sein. (0.2) wir eh das' meine [zweite]*

8 Andrea:	*[mhm]*
9 Yang:	*zweite zweite Meinung. dass heißt wir können*
10	*noch viel viel tun. viel viel besser tun als[jetzt]*
11 Andrea:	*[mhm]*
12	(0.5)
13 Doris:	*mhm. also ich find es probleMATISCH ehm: ich*
14	*eh: weil ich eh es is ne´ also du denkst vielleicht*
15	*Emanzipation bedeutet (-) Frau und Mann angleichen*
16	*und daß Frau und Mann gleich SEIN*
17	*SOLLEN, aber Emanzipation bedeutet nicht (-) DAS*
18	*für mich. Emanzipation bedeutet*

4 Yang	they also have thought very little about
	this=reflected=on=this=THEREFORE
5	is it a little bit more (quiet?) in China
6	concerning this problem. concerning the women's problem.
7	this might be. (0.2) we eh the' my [second]
8 Andrea:	[mhm]
9 Yang:	second second opinion. that is there is still a lot
10	a very lot to do for us. to improve very much from[now]
11 Andrea:	[mhm]
12	(0.5)
13 Doris:	mhm. well I think it is probleMATIC ehm: I
14	eh: because I eh it is well´ you might think
15	emancipation means (-) women and men become similar
16	and that women and men SHOULD BE the same
17	however THIS is not emancipation (-)
18	for me. emancipation means

Yang's utterance (6) moves towards his opponents' position. However, instead of accepting Yang's compromising offer, Doris expands the argumentation by providing a disagreement.

10.4.3 Change of activity

One further technique to end the confrontational frame is to introduce a 'frame break' (Goffman 1986) and focus on a new verbal activity. One can achieve this for example by focusing on the local situation at hand (e.g. by inquiring 'what kind of tea is this?') or by focusing on a background aspect of the prior utterance. In the following example Tan initiates a frame break (4) by asking for personal information and thus focusing on a background aspect of the prior speaker's turn:

YANG 19

96 Andrea:	*wenn man die Arbeitkraft BRAUCHT,*
97	*dann sagt man die Frauen können*
98	*das AUCH. (-) und wenn man sie*
99	*nich [WILL] dann sagt man sie haben*

1 Tan:	*[mhm]*
2 Andrea:	*keine KRAFT. es (-) eh du siehst an anderen*
3	*[Ländern]*
4 Tan:	*[WARST] DU SCHON MAL IN TIBET?*
5 Andrea:	*ja.*
6	(0.2)
7	*un in Kina.*
8 Tan:	*eh hihi*
...	
13 Andrea:	*mhm. ich HAB ES gesehn daß daß es immer darauf ankommt,*
14	*wenn (0.2) wenn in ei'm Land eh viel harte Arbeit zu machen is*
15	*vom Klima her oder so, dann müssen alle Menschen zusammen*
16	*JEDE Arbeit machen.*

96 Andrea	when you NEED their work force,
97	then you say that women can do the SAME job.
98	(-) and when you don't WANT
99	[them] then you say that they lack
1 Tan:	[mhm]
2 Andrea:	physical ENERGY. it (-) eh you can look at other
3	[countries]
4 Tan:	[HAVE] YOU BEEN TO TIBET?
5 Andrea:	yes.
6	(0.2)
7	and to China.
8 Tan:	eh hihi
.....	
13 Andrea:	mhm.I SAW IT it always depends,
14	when (0.2) when in a country eh a lot of hard work needs to be done
15	due to the climate or so, then all people together
16	have to do ALL sort of work.

For a frame break to succeed, all participants have to orient their activities to this change of frame. In this case, the frame break is only successful for a short while: Andrea accepts it temporarily, and returns in line 13 to the argumentation.

The continuous efforts of Yang and Tan to change to a more personal conversation all fail because of the German participants' lack of cooperation. The Germans respond to the concessions by focusing on the contradiction, reject the offers of compromise and only temporarily accept the change of activities. Thus, the negotiation of a common ground of rapport fails.

10.5 Concluding remarks

The analysis above demonstrates how different discursive practices and diverging strategies of rapport management can influence social contact situations. The four students who were very willing to meet each other were confronted with culturally different conversational conventions and expectations ('pragmatic principles and conventions': see Chapter 2).[8] The two German students valued overt expressions of their opinions and cherished the idea of having a 'good argumentative exchange' – a rather typical expectation within German student culture. In this culture 'getting to know someone' means finding out what the others' opinions and positions on different issues are and perhaps debating with them. When I interviewed the participants after the interaction, Doris and Andrea mentioned that the conversation 'was not very interesting', their co-participants 'don't really have their own opinions', and therefore it was rather 'awkward and dragging'. The two Chinese students, however, had different expectations of such a meeting and of showing rapport in the situation at hand. Yang and Tan emphasized in the interview 'the much too strong willingness of the Germans to argue'. Tan explained that in China a conversation between people who meet for the first time and want to get to know each other would be totally different. Instead of 'discussing and contradicting each other all the time', one would talk about oneself and the family and ask the others about their families. Only when this kind of rapport is well established may one start to discuss social and political issues. However, Tan emphasized that both she and Yang are considered to be 'very very open' by Chinese standards. This was also the reason why the discourse style of the two Germans 'was not too much of a problem' to them.

Besides different expectations concerning the social situation, the analysis shows that the participants had differing conventions for selecting strategies in the given context, such as different ways of signalling dissent (cf. 'pragmalinguistic conventions': see Chapter 2). Furthermore, they had differing norms for attributing social meaning to discursive strategies in the particular context. Whereas the direct way of disagreeing was interpreted as 'very rude and inconsiderate behaviour' by the Chinese participants, the German students interpreted these strategies as a sign of showing argumentative 'involvement' (see Chapter 7).

Can we now conclude that the Chinese discourse style is more harmonious and indirect than the German style? Although this interaction, as well as other data stemming from informal discussions among colleagues and acquaintances, seems to confirm this,[9] it would be too simple to postulate in a context-free manner that Chinese speakers are indirect and avoid open confrontation. Likewise, it would be too general to assert that German speakers always use very direct strategies and are openly confrontational.[10] There are of course other contexts where Chinese participants demonstrate high directness, which German participants consider inappropriate (e.g. personal questions about one's income, one's marital status or asking for reasons why the German acquaintances 'do not have children'). Furthermore, for Chinese interactants who do not 'share human feelings' (*ganqing*, *renqing*), that is, who are not relatives, friends, acquaintances or do not belong to the same 'unit' (*danwei*) (i.e. are out-group rather than in-group members, see Glossary entry), other discourse conventions, directness strategies and rapport management rules apply (Pieke 1992). Thus, it is essential to ask in what communicative contexts interactants use which strategies and which contextualization cues. The interactive setting (institutional or non-institutional, degree of formality, interactive roles, etc.), the communicative genre (formal or informal discussion, political debate, small-talk, quarrelling among friends, etc.) as well as the particular speech activity (disagreement, stating an opinion, presenting a personal question, etc.) all play vital roles in the ways in which rapport is managed and thus have to be taken into account.

KEY POINTS

1. Rapport management is highly context sensitive; that is interactive settings, communicative genres and speech activities play important roles in the ways in which rapport is managed.
2. Cultural-specific expectations of communicative situations and different conventions concerning communicative activities and genres can lead to difficulties in the interactive negotiation of meaning and the constitution of rapport.
3. Conflict activities turn out to be of special interest to the analysis of rapport management, as they demand techniques of conversational co-operation as well as strategies of confrontation.
4. Studies of argumentations show that willingness to take part in argumentative and confrontational discourse can vary from culture to culture. Furthermore, people from different cultural backgrounds prefer different ways of handling argumentative activities.
5. Studies in CA (Conversation Analysis) show that there exists a 'dispreference for direct disagreement'. However, in argumentations (at least in Western cultures), disagreement is often produced in a very direct and unmitigated form. Direct, unmitigated use of dissent strategies even represents a constitutive feature for the construction of an argumentative sequence.
6. Cultural-specific strategies of rapport management (i.e. different expectations concerning 'having a good conversation and showing involvement' and differing communicative conventions of signalling disagreement) can lead to problems in intercultural communication.
7. A particular communicative genre (e.g. an argumentation) may be realized differently in different cultural groups. In informal argumentations between German and Chinese students, different preference systems concerning direct oppositional moves result in clashes.

DISCUSSION QUESTIONS

1. In your opinion, what is the strongest factor that made the German and Chinese participants react as they did to the meeting?
2. If Doris had not been such a self-conscious feminist, do you think the outcome of the meeting might have been different? Why/why not?
3. How do you think you would have felt if you had been present? Would you have been happy to debate women's issues freely, or would you have preferred discussion of a 'safer', less controversial topic?

4. In your opinion (and according to your norms), in what kind of communicative contexts is it usually appropriate to initiate and maintain a heated discussion, and in what kind of contexts is it usually inappropriate to do so?
5. What advice would you give (a) to the German students and (b) to the Chinese students, to help them become more effective/sensitive intercultural communicators?

Notes

1. As these Chinese are either teachers of German at Chinese universities or Chinese students studying at German universities their German is at an advanced level.
2. The argumentative strategies used by Chinese and German participants, which will be outlined in some detail, are also found in the other conversations; cf. Günthner (1994), where I analysed three argumentative conversations between Germans and Chinese and two between Chinese.
3. Cf. also Kotthoff (1993).
4. Cf. Goodwin (1983: 669) for children's aggravated forms of arguing.
5. As Falk (1979: 22) states, 'duet partners are speaking as if they were one person. The second's utterance is often even syntactically, lexically and prosodically a continuation of the first's.'
6. Classical rhetoric lists this among the 'dishonest argumentative strategies' (Oliver 1971).
7. It is difficult to speculate about the role of language proficiency in this interaction. However, what is striking is that in my data – contrary to assumptions that learner languages show 'politeness reductions' and lack face-saving strategies – German native speakers tend to show a more direct (and less polite) argumentative style than the Chinese learners, who show more off-record strategies.
8. Cf. Scollon and Scollon/Wong-Scollon (1991, 1995).
9. Cf. Günthner (1993); cf. also Zhan's (1992) work on politeness strategies in Chinese; Young's (1994) analysis of Chinese–American interactions; Liao's (1994, 1997) studies of directives and refusals used by Americans and Chinese.
10. As women's issues and the issue of 'men's contribution to women's oppression' are highly controversial, these topics tend to result in a highly argumentative style among German academics. Thus, I would argue that the main topic of the interaction 'women's situation in Chinese and Western societies' contributes to the confrontational style among the German participants.

Suggestions for further reading

Kotthoff, H. (1993) Disagreement and concession in disputes: on the context sensitivity of preference structures. *Language in Society*, 22: 193–216.

Pan Y. (2000) *Politeness in Chinese Face-to-Face Interaction*. Stamford: Ablex.

Rees-Miller, J. (2000) Power, severity, and context in disagreement. *Journal of Pragmatics*, 32: 1087–1111.

Van Meurs, N. and Spencer-Oatey, H. (2007) Multidisciplinary perspectives on intercultural conflict: the 'Bermuda Triangle' of conflict, culture and communication, in H. Kotthoff, and H. Spencer-Oatey (eds) *Handbook of Intercultural Communication*. Berlin: Mouton de Gruyter, 99–120.

Negative Assessments in Japanese–American Workplace Interaction

11

Laura Miller

Chapter Outline

11.1 Introduction	227
11.2 Negative assessments	228
11.3 Researching intercultural interaction	230
11.4 Negative assessments in the intercultural workplace	232
11.5 Conclusion	238
Key points	239
Discussion questions	239
Notes	239
Suggestions for further reading	240

11.1 Introduction

In the Japanese television mini-series 'Concerto' (*Kyôsôkyoku*), sultry pop idol Takuya Kimura plays the role of a struggling architect named Kakeru. In one scene Kakeru has been injured and is at home being looked after by a female neighbour when his ex-lover, who is now his boss's wife, arrives at his apartment with groceries. Surprised to find another woman there cooking for him, she leaves. The cute neighbour, Kyoko, wants Kakeru to taste the dish she is busy preparing. She says:

> *Chotto shôyu ga irimasen? Ajimi shite itadakimasu ka?*
> $Doesn't it need a little soy sauce? Won't you taste it?$

Kyoko extends a bite on a pair of chopsticks, which Kakeru obediently takes into his mouth. He immediately looks away and chews contemplatively for several seconds before answering. Finally, uttering '*gû gû*' ($good good$),[1] Kakeru makes the American 'okay' gesture and walks into another room. On the face of it this seems to be a positive endorsement. At least it isn't a negative assessment along the lines of 'Thy food is such as hath been belched on by infected lungs.'[2] Even so, the sense one gets is that Kakeru is trying hard not to hurt Kyoko's feelings by expressing his honest opinion. His delay before answering her, and the avoidance of eye contact, suggest that he's frantically searching for something kind to say. Our suspicions are confirmed in a later scene in which the ex-girlfriend describes the helpful neighbour: 'She was cooking a *really* tasteless-looking *nikujaga* (a potato and meat dish),' she informs her husband. Kakeru's problem of how to deliver an evaluation or assessment is a conversational landmine speakers in all societies face on a daily basis.

11.2 Negative assessments

In a provocative discussion of a major problem in intercultural communication, Rubin (1983) outlined the difficulties in determining when someone from another culture is saying 'no'. There is not only the issue of recognizing when denials, refusals and other negative actions are being given, but also of figuring out which of the many possible manifestations of 'no' might be appropriate to particular social situations. Saying 'no' and similar interactional sticky-patches, such as the one that confronted Kakeru, are sometimes referred to with the technical label 'dispreferred response' by conversation analysts (Levinson 1983; Pomerantz 1984a). This chapter will focus on negative assessments, which are just one type of dispreferred response.

In almost any conversation a speaker might offer evaluations of the topic of talk, their interlocutor or another person or thing. C. Goodwin and M. Goodwin (1987) caution us that the term 'assessment' may refer to a variety of phenomena. It might be used to name a structural unit of talk such as an adjective (Kakeru's '*gû gû*' (good good) in the above scene). Assessments are not limited to just lexical or syntactic units, so may be displayed through non-segmental behaviour such as intonation or gesture (Kakeru's 'okay' hand sign). Lastly, the term 'assessment' can be used to designate a type of speech act that offers an evaluation (all the features of Kakeru's response). It is this last sense that I have in mind when I examine negative assessments in interactions between Japanese and American co-workers.

Contrary to many folklinguistic theories about the respective languages, the discourse strategies most commonly used when giving negative assessments in English and Japanese are quite similar. In both languages, speakers regularly employ prefaces, qualifiers, token agreements, accounts and pausing to mute disagreements or disapproval. Yet paradoxically, this is an aspect of conversation that sometimes results in uncomfortable encounters and intercultural misunderstanding. Before examining some instances of negative assessments found in Japanese and American co-worker interactions, let me first review the common structure underlying speech acts that offer evaluations.

Pomerantz (1975, 1984a) was one of the first analysts to produce a meticulous description of the structure of assessments (and second assessments) in American English conversation. She discovered that when assessments are positive, they are usually stated clearly without delay or pausing. Negative assessments, by contrast, are delivered with all sorts of devices which serve to minimize potential conflict, risk of offense, or 'loss of face' (see Chapter 2). Instead of offering nakedly blunt evaluations, speakers typically employ one or more of the following features when doing a negative assessment:

1. Delay: responses follow silences and gaps, within a turn or between turns
2. Repair: request for a clarification or a repeat
3. Hesitation markers or fillers (uh, well, e::r)
4. Prefaces: markers that preface the response (sure but, let me see, sorta, kinda)
5. Token agreements: response framed as partial agreement followed by an assessment that modifies or downgrades it

For example, in the following segment from Pomerantz (1984a: 78) speaker D prefaces her negative assessment with a token agreement in one turn, and later with a hesitation marker in another turn:

A: D'yuh like it=
D: =(hhh) Yes I DO like it=
=although I rreally:: =
(Few seconds of intervening talk)
D: (hhh) Well I don't – I'm not a great fan of this type of a:rt

Although rarely linking their descriptions to Pomerantz's (1975, 1984a) model, many scholars nevertheless point out that certain words or interjections in Japanese are routinely used to dilute negative responses or comments (Mizutani and Mizutani 1977, 1979; Neustupný 1987; Matsumoto 1985; Kinjo 1987). Rather than categorizing these as markers or prefaces to dispreferred actions in conversation, they are described as lexical hedges or speech act qualifications that deflect the force of a sentence. Examples of hesitation markers or fillers in Japanese are *anô* (well, e::r), *mâ* (somehow, well), *sâ* (well), and *â* (uh). A paralinguistic hesitation marker characteristic of Japanese is the inbreathed fricative, (.hss), which generally indicates an inability to agree with something or an unwillingness to express one's negative opinion (Miller 1991).

Typical Japanese prefaces to dispreferred actions are phrases such as *dô deshô ne* (I wonder), *sore mo kekkô desu ga* (that's fine too, but . . . .), and *itcha nan da kedo* (a palatalized form of *itte wa nani da kado*, I hate to say it, but . . .). Perhaps the word most frequently used as a preface is *chotto* (a bit, a little, somewhat). Matsumoto (1985) has examined *chotto* in detail, observing that it may have the same function as English *sorta* or *kinda.* Often, *chotto* allows the speaker to avoid saying the negative descriptor altogether, as in:

> *Kare wa suteki kedo, koibito ni wa chotto . . .*
> $He's cool, but as a boyfriend he's sorta . . . $

Mizutani and Mizutani (1979) and Matsumoto (1985) also point out that a solitary *chotto* given as a response will function as a refusal or negative appraisal, as in:

> A: *dô omou?*
> $What do you think?$
> B: *chotto . . .*
> $It's a bit . . .$

Although the same structure for giving a negative assessment is found in English and in Japanese, speakers of one language may not always recognize the prefaces and hesitation markers of the other language. The result is that interactants, oblivious to these seemingly petty but actually critical fragments of language, may only hear the negative content of a message without the apparatus intended to soften it. Formulaic expressions that immediately signal an underlying or forthcoming negative assessment are not always recognized by non-native speakers, or else don't carry over into the target language when translated. In Japanese conversation, a few of these set phrases include *kangaete okimashô* (let's think about it) and *sore wa dô deshô ne* (I wonder about that). When speaking English, Japanese speakers may use the translated English versions of these expressions as if they had the same communicative functions, and assume that they will be interpreted as the prefacing moves to negative assessments they are intended to be. Likewise, American speakers of Japanese may also deploy inappropriate prefaces or hesitation markers when conveying negative assessments. For example, Neustupný (1987: 149) states that 'A frequent bad habit of foreigners is to hesitate by using the first person pronoun, something like *watashi wa*.. . .' Instead of indicating hesitation, *watashi wa* (as for me) as a floor-holder sounds overly forceful and direct. It is possible, therefore, that these differences in the particular modes used to pave the way for negative assessments could very well account for a few of the pitfalls in intercultural interactions.

11.3 Researching intercultural interaction

One outcome of Japan's economic prosperity in the 1970s and the 1980s was a deluge of papers on communication between Japanese and non-Japanese. These papers, primarily directed at an American audience, prototypically took the form of dichotomized lists of dos and don'ts or oppositional traits. The authors often based their description on remembered personal experiences or narratives collected from others. Yet a fundamental lesson learned from the field of descriptive linguistics is that much of our knowledge and use of language are below a level of conscious awareness. Consequently, most speakers cannot be expected to reliably produce accurate descriptions of their own or others' communicative behaviour. This fact was revealed in early sociolinguistic studies by scholars such as Labov (1966), who looked at the use of /r/ in New York City, and Gumperz (1970), who examined the linguistic behaviour of Puerto Ricans in Jersey City. For instance, when Gumperz (1970) asked participants in his study whether they spoke Spanish or English at home, they claimed to exclusively use Spanish in that setting. However, when he tape-recorded their naturally occurring speech there, he found that there was considerable, yet unconscious, 'code-switching' to English. (Code-switching is the alternation from one language to another within a single utterance or turn by one speaker, or by two or more speakers within a conversation.)

Dependence on data from consciously remembered or hypothesized instances of speech also colours many studies of intercultural communication, where we find numerous reified stereotypes, particularly of Japanese and American communication (Miller 1998). Research on Japanese and American refusals and methods for giving a negative response (Beebe et al. 1990; Ikoma and Shimura 1994; Imai 1981; Kinjo 1987; Saeki and O'Keefe 1994; Ueda 1974) has usually taken the form of comparative studies which rely on interview elicitation, questionnaires and role play rather than authentic intercultural interactions. One popular method for comparing negative answers or refusals is the 'Discourse Completion Task' (see Chapter 14). Subjects are given a description of a situation to read and a sample conversation between two people, and are then asked to decide what they themselves might say in such a situation by filling in some blanks. Beebe et al. (1990) used this method for Japanese learners of English, and Ikoma and Shimura (1994) used it to compare refusals by American learners of Japanese with those by native Japanese speakers.

While such approaches are valuable in telling us about folk models of 'proper' language, they do not necessarily describe how speakers actually use language. In an effort to remedy this, LoCastro (1986) based her contrastive study of disagreements on data from actual conversations. She had a native-speaking Japanese assistant secretly record himself asking other native speakers about food preferences, specifically whether or not they liked avocados. LoCastro then asked other native English speakers about avocados in English, and later wrote down the answers. Aside from the ethical problem of recording people without their awareness, and the faultiness of memory as a source for accurate description of contexted language use, the study is still one step away from the real locus of our present concern: conversations that actually take place *between* Japanese and non-Japanese people.

Simply collecting examples of conversations between Japanese and Americans will not guarantee that instances of negative assessment will surface. Luckily, I was able to record naturally occurring talk at two advertising agencies in Tokyo, workplaces in which we would expect that co-workers will sometimes offer opinions of work in progress.[3] These conversations were audiotaped or videotaped openly with the full knowledge and consent of participants, who will be identified in the following data segments with pseudonyms. All of the participants spoke each other's languages with various degrees of proficiency. The tapes provide empirical documentation of what, in fact, actually happens in these intercultural interactions.[4] By 'naturally occurring' talk I mean that people were not in artificial speech situations, but were in their normal work habitats doing their usual routines. I didn't create or elicit any particular type of talk, but rather taped workers engaged in everyday business with each other. As Kottak (1999: 8) states about those people anthropologists attempt to study, 'It is not part of ethnographic procedure to manipulate them, control their environments, or experimentally induce certain behaviours.' The value of having such recordings is that they may reveal instances of problematic talk that will go unnoticed by participants, and therefore remain inaccessible through self-report methods of data collection.

11.4 Negative assessments in the intercultural workplace

The snippets of talk which follow illustrate co-workers who use the linguistic resources available to them to accomplish mutual work. Even when they have disagreements to resolve or complaints to air, all of them are ultimately working toward cooperation, consensus and resolution. These are not adversaries at the trade negotiation table or joint venture meeting, but fellow members of the same firm who sit next to each other day by day. Too much of our prior research on Japanese–American communication focuses on what happens between virtual strangers trying to wrangle deals out of each other. The result is a list of 'cultural' traits or behaviours which are supposed to characterize members of each group. But a model like that falls very short of describing what is actually seen and heard in authentic encounters. These social actors are embedded in a work environment in which all of them, Japanese and American alike, equivocate and waffle, or alternatively blurt out cheeky asides and direct requests or complaints. What concerns us about their identities as Japanese or American is whether or not they hold different linguistic and/or cultural assumptions about *specific* settings, tasks, or behaviours which will produce interpretations that differ from other interactants.

For instance, in addition to the problems associated with recognition of the linguistic forms in which negative assessments are delivered, cultural assumptions about the nature of an interaction, and the social relationships of the participants, will add other dimensions of complexity. In this first segment we see how all these possibilities come together to produce mutually negative interpretations. In this conversation an

American copywriter named Ember (E) and one of his Japanese co-workers named Nakada (N) are reviewing some advertisements for which Ember has provided the English copy. As an account executive, Nakada is in a position of more authority in this firm. Here they are talking about one ad in particular:

Extract 1

1	E	I mean yuh can see through it right
2		you don't have to use your imagination you can
3		see every little thing so–(it's?) right
4		(it?) plays off of the–the visual
5		(leaves?) nothing <<wh> to the imagination>
6		(0.5)
7	N	(.hss) Is that so?
8		(0.2)
9	N	idea is cl-very clear to me [now]
10	E	[no:w]
11	N	this video can do everything=
12	E	=do everything
13		(0.8)
14	N	But too much pitch for the vi(hihi)sual
15	E	too (hihi) much? [No no no no]
16	N	[too much visual]no?
17	E	no (.) no I don't think so
18		(0.2)
19	N	{smacks lips} (.hhh) maybe
20	E	(maybe?)
21	N	ye[ahh]
22	E	[I thin] I think it's okay

After Ember describes what the advertisement is about in lines 1–5, we would expect an assessment of some sort from Nakada. Instead, there is a silence in line 6, followed in line 7 by Nakada giving an inbreathed fricative or <.hss>, and a repair initiator 'Is that so?' This in turn is followed by a weak agreement preface in lines 9 and 11, after which he actually gives his negative assessment in line 14. Here we have a classic example of a negative assessment as proposed by Pomerantz (1984a). So why is there a problem?

At the conclusion of this conversation (not transcribed here) Nakada tells Ember to 'think about' this ad copy a little longer. As mentioned already, *kangaete okimashô* (let's think about it) is a formulaic preface in Japanese for a negative assessment that, when used alone, signals that something 'won't do' or 'isn't right'. By telling Ember to 'think about it' Nakada is using this English phrase as if it has the same communicative function as it does in Japanese, and that it will be interpreted accordingly (as a rejection). Yet a few days later Ember was surprised when he found out that this particular copy had been excluded from the campaign. He had most likely understood Nakada's 'maybe' in Line 19 and 'yeah' of Line 21 as showing a type of agreement, and therefore didn't identify Nakada's negative assessment to 'think about it' as a type of refusal.

Nakada's comment to Ember also brings to light another misinterpretation present during their conversation. This relates to what sort of communicative task each participant assumes is in progress. I spoke with the participants later, and found out that Ember thought the meeting with Nakada was simply in order for him to explain his ideas for the ads. Nakada, on the other hand, saw the meeting as an occasion for a senior (himself) to tell a subordinate (Ember) which ad copy had been selected for use and which had been retracted. Because of Ember's assumptions about the situation, he gave his personal opinions freely, disagreeing with Nakada's negative assessment and producing his own assessment in line 22, 'I think it's okay'. From Nakada's perspective, Ember's expression of a differing opinion would be inappropriate, not seen as the exchange of ideas intended but as an uncooperative reluctance to accept his decision. Nakada interpreted Ember's behaviour as churlishly argumentative, while Ember thought Nakada had deliberately misled him by not stating his wishes clearly.

Interpretations of negative assessments, even when offered in 'correctly' encoded forms, will critically depend on whether or not the offering of a disagreement or disapproval is even considered appropriate at all in that setting, or between those participants. In the next segment we find that an American who offers a negative assessment to his Japanese co-workers, although delicately coded in hedged forms, is still interpreted as 'too direct'. Another copywriter named Moran has been asked to edit and check the English translation of a Japanese script for use in subtitling a television commercial. He is explaining to the two creators of the commercial and a division head why he has changed their direct translation of the Japanese text. Here Moran is concerned about the line in the translation that says 'We brush our teeth together but we use different toothpaste'. When delivering his negative assessment of this scene, which contains images and text pertaining to teeth brushing in a commercial which is not about toothpaste, Moran delicately dances around the problem:

Extract 2

. . . so you see the shot of the toothbrush with the different kinds
of toothpaste on them and you talk about that and you immediately
understand but you've never said 'well we brush our teeth differently'
ahh which is kinda a s::tra::nge–I mean its jus not a–
(0.3)
(hhh)
(0.2)
it's not a pleasant image (hhh) to start a commercial with necessarily
ahh so: I ahh don't say it directly since you have a visual but

He prefaces his negative evaluation of this image with many pauses, qualifiers ('kinda' and 'necessarily'), outbreaths, stretched syllables ('s::tra::nge' and 'so:'), hesitation markers and self-interruptions. Even so, his Japanese co-workers later characterized him as directly expressing inappropriate disagreement because they had a different assumption about why they were meeting. They thought the conference with Moran was simply to have him check the grammatical correctness of their English, not to offer his advice on a better or more culturally appropriate translation. His offering of a negative assessment, no matter that it was indirectly produced, was therefore seen as too straightforward an expression of opinion.

These next two segments concern 'second assessments' (Pomerantz 1984a), wherein a speaker's assessment of something or someone invites a second assessment from the recipient. In each of the following cases, the Americans use a form of sarcasm for their second assessments, strategies that do not function in the ways intended. Sarcasm is here understood in Haiman's (1998) sense of communication which encodes the metamessage 'I don't mean this'. According to both Haiman (1998) and Adachi (1996), Japanese and English employ many of the same linguistic strategies for marking an utterance in the sarcastive modality. For instance, both languages use hyperformality, exaggerated pitch, repetition, stylized intonation and other indexing features. Even so, speakers of one language do not necessarily recognize when sarcasm is being performed in another language. Sarcastic assessments such as 'whatever', commonly found in American English, are often interpreted literally. In addition, sarcasm, like compliments and other speech actions, are not always used the same way in both cultures. In this segment a clerk named Fuji (F) approaches two co-workers, a Japanese, Makino (M) and an American, Crane (C), to get advice on how to write a wedding salutation in English for someone who is getting married. She asks them, 'What's a cute and cool thing to say in English?'

Extract 3

1 M	*are okurun no? dempô?*
	$are you sending that? telegram?$
2 F	*ya-anô kâdo kaiten no, ima*
	$ah-well I'm writing a card now$
3 M	congratulations *de iin ja nai*
	$isn't 'congratulations' okay?$
4 F	congratulations *nan ka sa ajikenai ja nai*
	$But isn't it that something like um 'congratulations' is bland?$
5 C	whaddiya want, poetry?
6 F	poetry, un

After Makino suggests 'congratulations', Fuji gives a negative assessment of this candidate greeting as lacking flavour (line 4). Crane then gives a sarcastic assessment of her display of disapproval, as if she's expecting too much for something as trivial as a card. Yet Fuji accepts his formulation innocently with the agreement token 'un' as if he's posing a legitimate question rather than the sarcasm intended. After her happy response Crane must have regretted his wisecrack, because he immediately crafted a detailed greeting for her to use. The next example of American sarcasm, however, simply added to the already existing tension and confusion.

In this segment an American account executive named Penn (P) is the recipient of implied criticism from another account executive, Muramoto (M), who has more seniority in the firm and often 'checks' his work. A third co-worker named Aoyama had previously complained to Muramoto that Penn is spending too much time with the client from one account (Mr. Jones), while neglecting their client from another account (Mr. Adams), so Muramoto talks to Penn about modifying his behaviour. After Penn receives Muramoto's critique, he produces a sarcastic quip disguised as gratitude:

Extract 4

1 M	it's okay to go in an around with Mr. Jones, but now also now you should,
2	na-be good friends with Mr. Adams at K-company
3 P	oh
4 M	so, un, don't focus on Mr. Jones only, *wakatta*? ($got it?$)
5 P	Thank Aoyama-*san* ($Mr.$) for arranging my social calendar for me

Penn does not respond to Muramoto's negative assessment and request with an agreement token or compliance token, but rather with a flat, free-standing 'oh'. This 'oh' simply acknowledges receipt of Muramoto's words, but does not invite further explanation or elaboration (Heritage 1984). Muramoto pursues a compliance response from Penn by upgrading the suggestion (now you should . . .) into something like an order (don't focus on . . .) in line 4. The Japanese tag here, *wakatta*? (got it?), especially when issued by a senior, is intended to elicit strong compliance such as 'yes'. Instead, using a completely flat intonation and a deadpan facial expression, Penn produces his oblique dig. This sarcasm deflects and masks his discomfort at both Aoyama for snitching on him, and Muramoto for criticizing him and telling him what to do, all of which may be seen as threats to his face (see Chapter 2). Muramoto, too, was left feeling frustrated that the issue was unresolved. She was annoyed by Penn's lack of consciousness and respect for the hierarchical relations between them, which would be a threat to her face (see also Chapter 13).

An interesting and more successful tactic for dealing with negative assessments unique to settings like these in which two languages are available for communication is to switch from one language to the other language. Those unaccustomed to it may find the constant code-switching between Japanese and English odd or discordant. Yet both intersentential and intrasentential switching are very common, and serve a multitude of functions. For instance, code-switching may help buttress solidarity and identity (Miller 1995). In the next bit of talk, Crane (C) and Ono (O) are looking over a heap of photographs for use in an advertisement layout. Ono selects one from the pile and sets it in front of Crane, who examines it and then rejects it as 'a bit boring'.

Extract 5a

1 C	*kono shashin wa chotto tsumaranai*
	$this photo is a bit boring$
2 O	*tsumaranai?*
	$boring?$
3 C	*unn*
4 O	*kochi wa ii ja nai*
	$here is nice isn't it?$

Crane's first negative assessment *tsumaranai* (boring) is mitigated nicely with the preface marker *chotto* (a bit). Ono doesn't really agree with him (she does a repeat), but the two of them continue to look through the pile, searching for more candidate photos. Ono picks out another and suggests a specific placement in the layout for it (line 5). Crane rejects this photo too, but switches to English when giving this second negative assessment:

Extract 5b

5 O	*ja kochi mô ii wa? kore to kore to (.) kochi no hô ga ii yo*
	$ah then here is also okay? this and this and (.) HERE is better$
6 C	It's easy to see the cracks on the cover

Crane nixes Ono's selection of the first photo in Japanese, while he rejects the second selection in English. The code-switching serves to distance or buffer the subsequent negative observation. Speakers display a reluctance to deliver too many negative assessments in a row, and so, in essence, begin a new series in the other language. This pattern is also characteristic of the next example.

In this segment, members of an account team are talking about what media markets to use in order to reach an audience of upscale young women. The possible media under consideration are train station posters, radio spots and magazines. Tanaka (T) prefers the magazine choices, Cosmo (Cosmopolitan) or Abbey Road, over the other two options. The American, Penn (P), however, is attracted to the idea of spending money on train station posters:

Extract 6

1 P	okay you guys figure it out please recommend magazine Cosmo or Abbey Road
2 T	Cosmo or Abbey Road, *hai*
	$right$
3 P	or radio or more posters

4 T	poster enough I think enough
5 P	maybe Nagoya
6 T	*Nagoya mô ii*
	$Nagoya is fine already$
7 P	*dame?*
	$no good?$
8T	Nagoya is country town

In line 4, Tanaka gives a negative assessment of the idea of more train station posters in English, but when Penn suggests adding Nagoya station in line 5, Tanaka switches to Japanese to deliver his next negative assessment. When Penn challenges this with a repair initiator in line 7, Tanaka code-switches back to English. His use of 'country town' is how he translated the Japanese word *inaka*, which means something closer to 'outback' or 'boondocks'. Speakers in both instances have 'used up' their opportunities for delivering a series of negative assessments in one language, and switch to the other language in order to maintain goodwill.

I might also note that in these segments, as well as in other intercultural conversations in the data, participants' speech sometimes shades into 'foreigner talk',[5] a simplified form of language produced for non-native speakers. One potential for further study is to determine whether or not the use of a foreigner talk register results in stripped-down utterances in which crucial bits such as prefaces and hesitation markers are refined away as dross, leaving the remaining assessments and other dispreferred speech actions unnaturally bald.

11.5 Conclusion

As the last two examples illustrate, talk between Japanese and American co-workers is not always fraught with difficulty and misunderstanding. The exchange of negative assessments may seamlessly unfold without participants becoming miffed or uncomfortable. But when there are misunderstandings, folk theory and popular stereotypes would lead us to blame Clint Eastwood-style Americans who blast their way through every conversation, or compromisingly ambiguous Japanese who produce a trail of uncertainty in their wakes. But none of the humans who speak in these tapes refrain from expressing their ideas or opinions, and each of them struggles to produce speech in which negative assessments are moderated or cushioned. Even so, misinterpretations sometimes bubble up into the tiny crevices of talk. Prefaces and hesitation markers intended to pillow negative assessments are not 'heard' as such by colleagues, or else there is a mismatch in cultural assumptions about when or to whom assessments should be offered at all. It is here in the finely tuned traces of everyday talk that recurring misinterpretations and patterned misunderstandings arise and, eventually, assume the guise of grand characterizations of entire populations and ethnic groups.

KEY POINTS

1. Carrying out refusals, denials and other negative conversational actions often result in misunderstandings in interethnic interaction.
2. The discourse strategies used for giving negative assessments (refusals, denials, negative opinions, etc.) are similar in Japanese and English conversation.
3. In both languages, speakers often deliver negative assessments with delays, hesitations, and prefacing to minimize the risk of offense, yet speakers may not be able to identify or recognize these strategies in cross-language interactions.
4. Speakers may interpret discourse strategies for giving negative assessments differently because of assumptions about the nature of the interaction.
5. Interpretations of negative assessments are also dependent on understandings of the task at hand, the participants and other features of the context.

DISCUSSION QUESTIONS

1. Why are negative assessments potentially face-threatening? What aspect(s) of face do they threaten?
2. Under what circumstances do you find it particularly difficult to give a negative assessment? Under what circumstances (if any) do you find it relatively easy to give a negative assessment? Try and explain the factors that give rise to the difference.
3. Look again at Extracts 1 and 2, and consider the cultural factors that led to the communicative problems. How do these differences correspond to the description given in Chapter 2, section 2.9, of potential areas of cultural variation that can affect rapport?
4. During the course of one day, consciously attend to and keep track of every time you refuse a request or invitation, or someone else refuses a request or invitation you issue. Are any of the strategies you find similar to those used in negative assessments? (e.g. delay, pausing, hesitation markers, prefaces, repair).

Notes

1. The Japanese word *gû* (good) is a loanword borrowed from English. For a review and analysis of the incorporation of English into the Japanese language, see Miller (1997).
2. From the play of William Shakespeare, *Pericles: Prince of Tyre*, Act 4 Scene 6, edited by Louis Wright and Virginia Lamar, 1968 edition, p. 80. New York: Pocket Books.
3. Moeran (1996) has written an excellent ethnographic description of a Japanese advertising agency.
4. Discussion of these naturally occurring interactions are also found in Miller (1995, 1994a, 1994b, 1991). Although a few of the transcribed segments presented here are also found in these prior studies, the remainder were recently transcribed and analysed for this chapter.
5. The concept of a foreigner talk register was first proposed by Ferguson (1971). Studies of foreigner talk in Japanese include Iino (1996) and Skoutarides (1986).

Suggestions for further reading

Goddard, C. (ed.) (2006) Ethnopragmatics: *Understanding Discourse in Cultural Context.* Berlin: Mouton de Gruyter.

Haugh, M. (2005) The importance of 'place' in Japanese politeness: implications for cross-cultural and intercultural analyses. *Intercultural Pragmatics* 2(1): 41–68.

Kotani, M. (2002) Expressing gratitude and indebtedness: Japanese speakers' use of "I'm Sorry" in English conversation. *Research on Language and Social Interaction*, 35(1): 39–72.

Lerner, G. (ed.) (2004) *Conversation Analysis: Studies from the First Generation.* Amsterdam/Philadelphia: John Benjamins.

Richards, K. and Seedhouse, P. (eds) (2005) *Applying Conversation Analysis.* Basingstoke: Palgrave Macmillan.

Schegloff, E. (2007) *Sequence Organization in Interaction: A Primer in Conversation Analysis.* Cambridge: CUP.

Impression Management in 'Intercultural' German Job Interviews

12

Karin Birkner and Friederike Kern

Chapter Outline

12.1 Introduction 241
12.2 Theoretical and methodological preliminaries 242
12.3 Data 243
12.4 Typical features of job interviews 243
12.5 Linguistic differences between East and West Germans in job interviews 244
12.6 Conclusion 255
Key points 255
Discussion questions 256
Notes 257
Suggestions for further reading 257

12.1 Introduction

The fall of the Berlin Wall on 9 November 1989 represented, among other repercussions, a stroke of luck for social sciences and linguistics in particular. After 40-odd years of living in separate communities with almost opposing weltanschauung, East and West Germans reverted to political unity. The social upheaval that accompanied this process was reflected in language, and quite a number of linguistic issues have arisen since unification (for an overview see Schwitalla 2001; Stevenson and Theobald 2000; and Stevenson 2002, who also gives an historic account of the current language situation). The process of unification created the opportunity to study language contact in a unique environment, with the need mostly for East Germans to accommodate and adapt to new communicative practices resulting in instances of intercultural communication, and with constant negotiation and stereotyping of membership categories.

All these can be interpreted as elements of a hegemonic struggle about the validity of social and linguistic norms.

Talk-at-work and, more specifically, the job interview is a significant domain where linguistic differences can result in social participation or marginalization of speakers. What happens if someone who until very recently belonged to a separate speech community suddenly has to compete with members of a different, (more or less) unknown speech community in a highly competitive labour market (defined by the rules of the latter) and finds himself or herself confronted with stylistic and interpretative patterns of a largely unfamiliar communicative genre? Based on a selection of authentic job interviews, as well as 11 narrative interviews with personnel managers conducted by us we investigate differences in impression management between applicants from the former GDR and FRG.[1]

This chapter will explore several aspects of German–German communication in job interviews with regard to their cultural specificity. Firstly, we will give an overview of the theoretical and methodological approach that our study is based on. Secondly, we will present some typical features of job interviews. We will then discuss two main areas of differences between East and West Germans in language use in job interviews: the use of self- and other perspectives and the expression of agreement/disagreement.

12.2 Theoretical and methodological preliminaries

Our approach is largely inspired by conversation analysis (henceforth CA; for an overview see Levinson 1983). CA postulates that no external categories should be used in analysis. Instead, analytical categories are obtained empirically and derived directly from data, and need to correspond as closely as possible to those that the participants themselves can be proved to orient to in interaction (participation categories). Forms and structures of language are understood to be intersubjectively produced in discourse and are investigated in terms of their interactive function. As a consequence, much attention is paid to how the interaction proceeds and the participants' contribution to it.

However, there are limits to data analysis if CA's postulates are followed strictly. For example, it is difficult to include situational factors into the analysis, such as the role of participants, distribution of speakers' rights, and so on, which could explain the participants' selection of specific communicative styles. Hence, we have included the notion of communicative genre (see Chapter 2) to account for such situational elements. Furthermore, we considered it appropriate to include ethnographic information such as interviewers' accounts and interpretations of specific verbal behaviour, since we consider these to be part of the participants' knowledge as competent speech community members.

12.3 Data

The study described here is based on two types of data.[2] First, 41 authentic job interviews (22 with East and 19 with West Germans) were recorded in seven companies in 1994–5. Secondly, we interviewed 11 staff members from personnel departments of different companies to gain a certain understanding of job interviews and to collect ethnographic data on common stereotypes of East and West Germans and their respective linguistic behaviour. We also recorded several discussions of interviewer teams evaluating candidates immediately after a job interview.

12.4 Typical features of job interviews

One of the main reasons why job interviews were chosen as the focus of this study is that they were a comparatively unknown communicative genre in East Germany. In the former GDR the allocation of jobs, especially for leading positions, was based on different selection procedures. In the West, job interviews are important gate-keeping situations and determine social participation or marginalization – even more so in times of increasing unemployment and economic crisis. In the Western social and cultural context, they are closely associated with rules of Western economic discourse in which existing hierarchies are often downplayed and the notion of competition plays an important role. However, the changing social realities in Germany 'after the wall' have forced Eastern speakers to adjust to such new forms of communication to at least a certain extent.

Impression management and positive self-presentation are the applicants' main goals in a job interview. We understand strategies of self-presentation as elements of positive facework and part of the construction of a speaker's social identity. In job interviews constructions of identity are at least partly coordinated with genre-specific goals and function to present the applicants as suitable candidates for the job in question. However, applicants want to present themselves not only as suitable candidates, but also as friendly and likeable people. Likewise, interviewers evaluate the applicants' answers not only by *what* is being said but also by *how* it is said (cf. Adelswärd 1988).

The sharp asymmetry between applicant and interviewer is reflected in one of the main features of job interviews: their so-called *hidden agenda* (Adelswärd 1988: 77: 'the explicit and implicit criterion of success'; cf. Roberts 1985). Interviewers often have some sort of checklist of job allocation criteria which the applicants are not told about: 'So the whole interviewer's "agenda" is hidden from the candidate. The interviewer's line of questioning has a hidden purpose that the candidate may not pick up on' (cf. Roberts 1985: 37). While questioning the applicants the interviewers try to elicit statements relevant to the hidden agenda without making this explicit.

Nevertheless interviewers often make an effort to let job interviews seem relaxed, informal and equal conversations. This can be seen in the formulations at the beginning of many interviews where participants are informed about what is going to follow (e.g. 'let's keep this informal and just get to know one another'). However, applicants have to be aware that they are the sole object of an omnipresent evaluation. They try to present themselves as positively as possible in order to influence the interviewers' impressions of them, as the interviewers have the right to select whom they want. On the other hand, the interviewer's main concern is to find out 'if it is put on, (. . .) is he just a good actor and pulling the wool over our eyes, or is he for real?' (in the words of one personnel manager). Consequently, we must distinguish two semantic levels: a surface level with an explicit agenda, where the interlocutors talk about facts and dates (biographies, qualifications, the enterprise, etc.), and a hidden level, where the utterances are always related to hidden aims, messages and interpretative foils.

Because of the hidden agenda, experienced applicants have a clear advantage over inexperienced ones (cf. Roberts 1985; Sarangi 1994: 171 'situational literacy'). Indeed studies by Gumperz et al. (1979), Gumperz (1992b), Akinnaso and Seabrook Ajirotutu (1982) and Sarangi (1994) demonstrate that lack of knowledge of the rules of the genre, and especially of the hidden dimensions, may contribute to discrimination of minority members: 'The job interview is one of the most culture-specific events we all have to face' (Roberts and Sayers 1987: 114).

Knowing what makes a job interview a job interview, that is familiarity with the genre's special conditions and constraints, is part of the shared knowledge of a community. The Western genre follows Western linguistic norms of positive self-presentation, and frequently these norms are not shared by East German applicants. In our study divergent understandings of the genre prove to be a major factor in the different courses which job interviews take with East and West German applicants (Birkner 2001, 2004).

12.5 Linguistic differences between East and West Germans in job interviews

There are many facets to impression management and positive self-presentation in job interviews, and these vary according to levels of linguistic choice. In our project, we compared similar question–answer sequences in order to gain an understanding of the ways in which cultural factors may influence strategies of linguistic self-presentation in East and West German candidates. In the following sections, we will take a closer look at two such strategies. One will concern the constitution of self- and other perspectives in talk and their pragmatic impact. The second will have to do with the discursive organization of agreement and disagreement.

12.5.1 Self- and other perspectives

The notion of perspective is a relational, dynamic and evaluative concept which refers to somebody's standpoint, or point of view or mode of perception (cf. Graumann 1989). Common to all conceptions of 'perspective' is the view that sensual and cognitive perception is constituted in relation to a person's spatio-temporal or cognitive standpoint. The notion of 'perspectivization' focuses on the dynamic aspect and thus refers to how perspectives are co-established and signalled in discourse. In language, the ability to set and take perspectives (or standpoints) is understood to be a basic communicative competence (cf. Graumann 1989). Interlocutors mutually produce and fix subjective and objective perspectives in the course of interaction; they share and/or negotiate them.

In contextualized dialogue, the use of perspectives depends furthermore on general, genre-specific goals and intentions on the one hand (cf. Linell and Jönsson 1991) and on various local context conditions on the other. Adelswärd (1988: 116) argues that the candidates' ability to take specific perspectives on themselves is one of the main criteria for their success or failure in job interviews: 'A successful applicant positions herself when telling her life-story at the perfect distance, she is neither too impersonal nor too personal'.

More specifically, candidates should clearly set their personal perspectives on certain issues so as to inform the interviewer of their interests and preferences, especially when asked about their motive for applying. Thus, positive self-presentation is partially dependent on foregrounding the individual and stating personal views on certain topics.

In the following section, we will look closely at the various ways speakers verbally express and focus on subjective and objective perspectives. For the purpose of this chapter, we will concentrate mainly on the use of personal pronouns that – as deictic expressions – play an important role for the structuring and presentation of perspectives (see Kern 2000 for further reading on perspectivization in East-West German job interviews).

EXAMPLE 1: Eastern applicant

I: *WAS: war der ANlass; dass sie sich (.) grade auf diese stelle bewErben? (.)*
und eh: wi:e eh was GLAUben sie aufgrund ihrer bisherigen TÄtigkeit (.)
eh für dieses stelle MITbringen zu können.
{Auslassung 9 Zeilen}
A: *ja und von den QUELlen her, und von den (.) archiVArien die im stadtarchiv*
llegen, (.) <<acc> doch das IS (also/eine?) DACHte ich mir is eine sehr
interessante> AUFgabe? (.) SEIN KÖNnte? (.) für JEmanden der das
archiv=beARbeitet? (1) das SCHRIFTgut?

(Continued)

EXAMPLE 1: Eastern applicant—cont'd

I: *WHY have you appLIED for this job of all jobs? (.)*
and how eh: wha:t eh do you THINK you can BRING to this job because
of your present work?
{9 lines left out}
A: well and because of the SOUrces and because of the (.) ARchive files that are in the
archive (.)<<acc> indeed that is (well/a?) *I THOUGHT to myself is a very*
interesting> JOB? (.) COULD be? (.) for SOMEone who WORKS
at the archive? (1) the WRItings?

The interviewer explicitly asked for the applicant's perspective on the matter; he wanted to find out about his motivation for applying ('why have you applied for this job of all jobs'). However, by shifting to a different perspective, the candidate does not answer the question from the requested point of view.

A first notable change happens when the candidate turns an objective fact ('is a very interesting task') into a hypothesis ('could be an interesting task') by self-repairing from 'is' (*realis*) to 'could be' (*irrealis*). This, of course, communicates a major limit to his motivation – he does not even seem sure whether it is an interesting job he is applying for. Additionally, the applicant places himself in this hypothetical world by setting his own perspective ('I thought to myself') but then initiates a significant perspectival shift by using the impersonal pronoun 'someone'. Consequently, the candidate expresses his personal perspective on the subject, that is to say that the job would be interesting for an archivist, only by indirect reference to himself. He backgrounds his own personal perspective more and more, and replaces it with an unspecified other's perspective. His account is consequently transferred from an individual, personal mode of presentation to a general one. In the context of a job interview, where interviewers regularly want to find out about the applicants' personal opinions and motivations, this is not a successful linguistic strategy. Indeed, the candidate's presentation of his reasons for the application has remarkable consequences for the interview. In his next turn, the interviewer immediately challenges the applicant's suitability for the job in a face-threatening way. His reaction indicates that the candidate's self-presentation has not succeeded in convincing him of his suitability.

As the next example shows, perspectives are not always discussed explicitly but are nevertheless oriented to and therefore of interactive importance to both speaker and listener. See the following extract, in which the interviewer asks the candidate to give a hypothetical other evaluation of her positive qualities.

EXAMPLE 2: Eastern applicant

1 I2: *und wie haben=sie=sich mit ihren kollEgen und kollEginnen denn verstanden?*
2 I3: *{räuspert sich}*
3 B1: *sehr GUT.*
4 I2: *ja,*
5 B1: *ja.*
6 *(1)*
7 I2: *was: (.) konnten die so; (0.5) oder was würden DIE SAgen, wenn wir sie*
8 *FRAgen würden, was sie besonders an ihnen SCHÄtzen?*

1 I2: and how did you get on then with your COlleagues?
2 I3: {clears her throat}
3 A: very well
4 I2: yes,
5 A: yes.
6 (1)
7 I2: *wha:t (.) did they; (0.5) or what would they SAY if we ASKed them what they*
8 *particularly LIKE about you.*

The interviewer carefully constructs a hypothetical scene with a set of perspectives, including the candidate's former colleagues' ('what would *they* say') and his fellow interviewers' ('if *we* asked them') perspectives. So instead of asking 'what do you think makes you an amiable colleague?', the candidate is asked what her former colleagues thought of her. It is now her interactively established task to adopt this hypothetical perspective and discuss her own qualities from her former colleagues' standpoint. However, the applicant does not do this. Instead she initiates a complex perspectival shift that allows her to answer the question from a different point of view. Let's take a look at her response:

EXAMPLE 3: Eastern applicant (continues Example 2)

9 A: *(hh) (0.5) joa. (1) das is(=ne) gute FRAge; (1) {schnalzt} man muß EIgntlich,*
10 *wie jesacht, wie alle anderen AUch, PÜNKTlich sein, man muß na[türlich, (hh)*
11 I2: [<<p> mhm,>
12 *(0.5) wie jeSACHT, weil ja auch jeder seine arbeit HAT, seine KUNden, dass man*
13 *dran intressIERT is, diese alle ANzurufen,*

9 A (hh) (0.5) well (1) that's a good QUESTion; (1) {clicks tongue} one has to be,
10 as I said, LIKE everybody ELse, be on TIME, one has to of [course (hh)
11 I2 [<<p> mhm,>
12 (0.5) as I SAID, because everybody HAS their job, their CLIents, and one is
13 INterested, wants to RING them all,

After an introductory remark ('that's a good question'), the candidate introduces a change of perspectives by shifting to the impersonal pronoun 'one'. The applicant does not speak from her colleagues' point of view, rather she refers to generalized 'common sense knowledge' about intergroup behaviour and relates this to a sense of moral obligation ('one has to'). Thus, the candidate does not take up the specific 'other' perspective of her former colleagues as requested, but instead draws on some higher authority to take an unspecified third person perspective. This shift in perspective allows her to discuss her own positive qualities indirectly and more generally.

During the next few minutes, the interviewer makes several further attempts to elicit 'other' perspectives on the candidate's qualities. Again, the candidate shifts to a general perspective by introducing some higher moral authority as a reference point: one does not ask other people what they think about oneself. Thus, she refuses more or less directly to answer the question. A dramatic divergence of perspectives develops until finally the interviewer drops the topic.

The cultural dimension of the constitution and expression of perspectives in the job interviews has already been hinted at. The results show that West and East German candidates' conversational styles differ with respect to perspectivization when they present themselves in job interviews. The examples point to a recurrent pattern in establishing perspectives in dialogue that is possibly culturally bound. Eastern candidates display a tendency to shift to unspecified, generalized perspectives in a variety of contexts. The examples given illustrate that (a) the subjective perspective is replaced by an unspecified impersonal one and (b) requests for an individual perspective are answered with a generalized one referring to a higher authority.

If we look at the West German use of perspectives in similar contexts, a different picture emerges. Even though in comparable contexts, West Germans do not always establish their personal views directly and also refer to other's perspectives,[3] they do not shift to impersonalized, general perspectives based upon common sense to back up their argument.

Interviews with members from personnel departments confirm the observed differences. Many interviewees took the issue of the candidates' openness concerning especially personal characteristics (such as one's qualities and weaknesses) to be one of the striking distinctions between East and West Germans. They found East German applicants to be more evasive on the matter, talking in 'general phrases' and in 'expressions concerning the collective', whereas they considered the West Germans to be more accurate 'saying more precisely that and that I want and I mean it (. . .)'.

Few researchers have addressed the issue of diverging perspectives in conversation (cf. for example, Linell and Jönsson 1991; Shea 1994; Liebscher 2006). The use of perspectives, however, may be ruled by culturally divergent linguistic norms. Assuming we are dealing with two distinct cultural perspectives here, we can construct two sets of perspectivization rules. As far as East Germans are concerned, a rule might exist according to which questions about personal qualities, goals or ambitions are answered by reference to impersonalized perspectives. West German applicants, on the contrary, might be said to follow a rule that allows them to state their subjective perspectives more openly or, alternatively, relate to individualized others' perspectives.

However, such rules only concern linguistic practices; even though they might be tied to or shaped by a sociocultural norm about the value of modesty, it is difficult to find evidence in the data alone for genuine differences in values. In any case, the analyst must be careful when using such external categories as explanatory devices for linguistic differences.

12.5.2 Disagreement

We will now look at how applicants deal with agreement and disagreement in job interviews (see Chapter 10 for dissent organization of (West) Germans). Overt disagreement on the part of an applicant is not very common in a job interview; however, interviewers are more likely to disturb the harmony and to express disagreement. This can be related to the participants' differing goals: the applicant aims to give a positive impression, while the interviewer wants to evaluate candidates and select the best.

To ensure a certain comparability of East and West Germans we looked at applicants' reactions to 'critical questions' by interviewers (Birkner 2001: 151f). By 'critical questions', as you will see in the examples, interviewers implicitly or explicitly bring out an inconsistency in the applicant's self-presentation. In order to not jeopardize their goal of presenting themselves as suitable candidates, applicants must disagree. Expressing disagreement, however, is conversationally precarious since it contradicts the preference system for agreement (cf. Sacks 1987; Pomerantz 1984a; Kotthoff 1993). How applicants react to the conflicting demands of global agreement versus local disagreement is illustrated by the following two examples.

EXAMPLE 4: Eastern applicant

{Kontext: der Bewerber macht sein Abitur in Abendkursen nach}
I1: *<<p> mhm,> (3) beLAStet das nich? also so (.) so abiTUR und*
AR[beiten?
A: *[(gut?) der (.) TACH is ziemlich VOLLjepackt; aber ich WOHne*
noch zuhause, un[d
I1: *[mhm;*
A: *(1) gehe MORgens aus=dem haus, und komme ABends; (0.5) gegen ZEHN*
wieder, (2) ESse noch was;
I1: *<<p> abends [um zehn wieder> ach so <<f>dann; (0.5) von der*
A: *[(???)*
I1: *SCHUle> dann [schon.*
A: *[ja ja geNAU. [(????)*

(Continued)

EXAMPLE 4: Eastern applicant—cont'd

I1: *[is das JEden abend.*
A: *JEden abend.*
I1: *(1) <<p> oijoijoi. (1.5) puh (0.5) MEIne GÜte.> (0.5) eh (0.5) MEInen*
sie nicht; dass das vielleicht (.) probLEme bereiten könnte, wenn man
sich irgendwo neu EINarbeitet. (2) also jetzt in SO einer phase zu WECHseln.
A: *wäre (.) MÖGlich. ja.*
(2)
I1: *<<p> mhm>*
A: *(aber?) eh:*
I1: *(0.5) {schnalzt} also dass letztendlich dann durch dadurch ihr abiTUR leidet.*
A: *neu EINarbeiten (0.5) würd ich (0.5) verGLEIchen mit der entwicklung*
eines (.) komplexen neuen proJEKtes. (0.5) wie ich=s letztes jahr geMACHT habe.
(1.2)
I1: *<<p> mhm.> (1) (hh) (1) ja GUT. aber das is eh (0.5) so oder SO. (0.5)*
es is natürlich immer beLAStung. nich,
A: <<pp> mhm,>
I1: *und es geht immer nur auf KOSten (.) oder es geht MEIst immer auf kosten*
von irgndeiner sache dann. (hh) (2) <<pp> mhm> (2.2) {schnalzt} eh: (0.5)
zu WANN (.) würden sie denn zur verFÜgung stehn.

{context: the applicant is preparing for his A-levels in evening classes}
I1: <<p> mhm,> (3) isn't that STRESSful? I mean (.) A levels and
WORK[ing?
A: [(okay?) the (.) DAY is pretty FULL; but I still LIVE at home,
an[d
I1: [mhm;
A: (1) leave the house in the MORNing, and come back again in
the evening; (0.5) at about ten, (2) have something to eat;
I1: <<p>in the evening [at ten> oh I see <<f> then; (0.5) from
A: [(? ? ?)
I1: SCHO[ol>
A: [yes yes right. [(? ? ?)
I1: [that's EVery evening.
A: EVery evening.
I1: (1) <<p> wow (1.5) huh (0.5) MY GOODness.> (0.5) eh (0.5) don't
you THINK; that could possibly (.) cause problems, if you're just starting
on a new JOB somewhere. (2) I mean to CHANGE jobs in a situation like that.
A: might be (.) POSSible. yes.
(2)
I1: <<p> mhm>
A: (but?) eh:
I1: (0.5) {clicks tongue} I mean that ultimately your A levels would suffer.
A: starting out on a new JOB (0.5) I would (0.5) comPARE to developing a (.)
complex new PROject. (0.5) like I DID last year.
(1.2)
I1: <<p> mhm.> (1) (hh) (1) oKAY. but it's either eh (0.5) one thing or another.

EXAMPLE 4: Eastern applicant—cont'd

(0.5) of course it's always stressful. isn't it,
A: <<pp> mhm,>
I1: and something is always going to SUffer (.) or ALmost always something's
going to suffer. (hh) (2) <<pp> mhm> (2.2) {clicks tongue} eh: (0.5)
WHEN (.) would you be aVAIlable then.

Upon being asked about his employment goals, the East German applicant mentions that he is taking evening classes (data not shown). The leading question 'isn't that stressful? I mean (.) A levels and working?' could prima facie express empathy, whereas in fact the interviewer is trying to find out if his future employee will be able to start a new job involving additional strain. In this context a clear expression of disagreement from the applicant is needed. But instead he produces an agreement preface (cf. Pomerantz 1978: 99) '(okay) the (.) day is pretty full', followed by an adversative 'but', which introduces a contrasting statement. This contrast, however, remains implicit: 'but I still live at home'. Then he goes on to outline his daily routine. Even though he is making an effort to express the opposite, he seems to lead a rather stressful lifestyle, especially if you take into account the importance that many interviewers assign to hobbies and recreational activities.

The emphatic reaction of the interviewer signals his disagreeing conclusion 'wow (1.5) huh (0.5) my goodness'. In the next leading question the interviewer's doubts about the candidate's suitability are more apparent. But again, instead of a clear contradiction the applicant produces a 'weak agreement': 'might be (.) possible. yes.'. The falling final intonation (orthographically marked by a full stop in the transcription) indicates that he has nothing to add, but the interviewer's reactions (a quiet continuer, produced after a pause of 2 seconds, and a precision) show that he is not satisfied with the answer. The applicant continues: 'starting out on a new job (0.5) I would (0.5) compare to developing a (.) complex new project. (0.5) like I did last year'. Again, the argumentative reference remains implicit and he fails to explain that despite evening classes he managed the job well; nor does he refute the negative implications of the interviewer's leading question.

The interviewer's final comment indicates that his doubts have not been dispelled. What he previously articulated as questions ('isn't that stressful? . . .' and 'don't you think; that . . .'), he now asserts directly: 'of course it's always stressful' and 'something is always going to suffer (.) or ALmost always'. The subject then changes, and the applicant's opportunities for a counter-argument are exhausted.

If we review the applicant's answers as a whole, we detect a tendency to avoid disagreement and to communicate indirectly. Possibly he does not relate the interviewer's questions to the job on offer, but rather interprets them as everyday topics.

He clearly does not foresee the negative implications of his utterances and even when the interviewer becomes more explicit about them, he fails to clarify his position.

The next example illustrates a conversational strategy of a different kind.

EXAMPLE 5: Western applicant

{Der Bewerber berichtet von einem Gespräch mit potentiellen Vorgesetzten während einer Betriebsführung}

B: *und dann <<all>die ham mich natürlich AUCH gefragt; ob ich mich das>*
mir das VORstellen könnte;
I2: *mhm,*
B: *=<<p>sowas zu tun;>*
I2: *(0.5) und da ham sie gesagt SELbstverständlich. <<all>produkTION*
ANwendungstechnik und MARketing mach ich. (0.5) aber sie können ja
nich ALles machen.>
B: *(0.5) nee; des hab ich NICH gesagt.*
I2: *was HAM sie gesagt?*
B: *(0.5) ich hab gesagt dass ich mir im AUgenblick, (.) nich so gut VORstellen*
kann. (0.5) <<all> sondern dass ich=s eigentlich ganz GUT finde; dass man
hier zuNÄchst in der forschung eingestellt wird.> {fährt fort}

{The applicant is telling about a conversation he had with potential superiors during a tour through the plant}

B: and then <<all> naturally they ALso asked me
if I> could imagine that;
I2: mhm,
B: =<<p> to do something like that>
I2: (0.5) and then you said of COURSE. <<all> I do technical proDUCTion
application and MARketing. (0.5) but you can't
do EVerything.>
B: (0.5) no; I didn't say that.
I2: what did you say?
B: (0.5) I said that at the moment, I really can't
imagine, (0.5) <<all> but what I find GOOD is that one is inITially
hired for research.> {continues}

In this 'critical question' the interviewer contrasts two positions: one that is presented as an applicant's statement about his prospective fields of activity and another one that doubts the practicability of these aspirations. This contradiction should be resolved by the applicant in order to avoid damaging a consistent self-presentation.

In fact, the applicant counters with a strong disagreement. He rejects the claim 'put into his mouth' by the interviewer, using a 'contrastive opposite', which has been described by Goodwin (1983: 672, see also Pomerantz 1978: 93) as the most aggravated form of disagreement. It is characterized by showing neither dispreference markers nor accounts or justifications, but solely displaying a position of opposition (note the opposition preface 'no'). Strong cohesion is obtained by using the 'opposition format' rhetorical device (Kotthoff 1993: 201ff; M.H. Goodwin and C. Goodwin 1987), which consists of citing the preceding utterance in great part but negating it at the same time. The concatenation of several syntagmas 'then you said – I did not say – what did you say – I said' (even more obvious in the German original) intensifies the disagreement format. This form of 'dissent-tying' (see Chapter 10) is structurally reminiscent of the 'he-said-she-said' events which Goodwin (1980) described in a group of adolescent girls. But despite being such a strong counter reaction, it does not lead into overt dissent between the interactants; rather the applicant gains the floor for a self-repair and to formulate his own point of view.

In our material we observed a general tendency for negative impressions to result from applicants agreeing with 'critical questions' (cf. Birkner 2001). The East German applicants, who mostly make use of this conversational style, have difficulty afterwards in maintaining a positive self-presentation. With the West Germans, however, who more frequently use conversational strategies characterized by overt disagreement, the critical topic is typically dropped. The ethnographic data seem to confirm these findings. In one ethnographic interview, for example, a personnel manager (who also took part in the job interviews) commented: 'If we count assertiveness and conflict management as elements of team work, it's true that they are a bit more reserved, the East Germans.' Later he assesses East Germans as 'very submissive, at times, what the boss says goes and you don't question it'. Asked for the causes he assumes 'because they never had to or it wasn't allowed'. This indicates that some interviewers perceive East Germans as submissive and servile and even assume that they lack the ability to deal with conflict successfully. West Germans, on the other hand, are considered more self-confident and better prepared to handle conflict. From an analytical point of view, this judgement of East German employees could be a result of differences in conversational style. If we take into account that most employers consider assertiveness a key qualification because of its association with teamwork, we could argue that East Germans have to make greater effort to achieve successful self-presentations than West Germans do, because of the East Germans' conversational preference for downgrading disagreement.

However, in job interviews, the candidates' assertiveness is not only judged by their linguistic behaviour; it is also discussed explicitly. In our data we find an example of an Eastern applicant who is asked if she has ever had an argument with a superior.

EXAMPLE 6: Eastern applicant

1 I2: *and mit ihrem CHEF? ham=se auch mal, (0.5) so=n paar~*
2 A: *{empört} NE:IN;*
3 I2: *(0.5) disKURse gehabt, NEIN?*
4 A: *=nie.*

(Continued)

EXAMPLE 6: Eastern applicant—cont'd

5 12: *weil s=sich so gut mit dem verSTANden haben.*
6 A: *(0.5) nee das hat damit nischt zu [TUN; (da hab ich?) reschPEKT.*
7 12: *[nee,*
8 A: *(hi[hi)*
9 12: *[sie haben resPEKT.*
10 A: *ja; resPEKT;*

1 12: and with your BOSS? did you ever, have (0.5) well any~
2 A: {indignant} NO:;
3 12: (0.5) ARgument, {lit. 'discourses'} NO?
4 A: =never.
5 12: because you got ON with him so well.
6 A: (0.5) no that's got nothing to DO with [it; (I'm?) resPECTful.
7 12: [no,
8 A: (hi[hi)
9 12: [you are resPECTful.
10 A: yes; resPECTful;

The applicant emphatically denies having had any conflicts with a superior, and gives 'respect' as the reason. The team of interviewers come back to this in their post-interview evaluation, and it seems to be an important factor in their judgement of her:

EXAMPLE 7: Interviewers' evaluation

I2: Conflicts are something she has problems with, because she also has (0.5) as we have seen in the course of the interviews, the eastern mentality, that she keeps quiet about them, no question.
I1: (. . .) she probably isn't able to cope with conflicts with her team colleagues. We have clear evidence that she can't easily handle conflict with management.

The interviewers' assessment of the applicant corresponds with our findings in the ethnographic interviews. However, looking more closely at the job interview with the applicant concerned, we find a narrative later on where, discussing something else, she gives a detailed account of how she once confronted her boss who had been criticizing her performance behind her back. It is a perfect example of using initiative in dealing with conflict with a superior.

This suggests that although Eastern applicants' communicative norms differ from Western ones in job interviews, their behaviour in real life may in fact be quite similar. In the interviews, Eastern applicants seem to orient much more to the asymmetry of the encounter, whereas West Germans (interviewers as well as applicants) tend to downplay it. This would account for the lack of disagreement shown by East Germans in the interview situation as well as for their apparent rejection of assertiveness. Example 7 also points to another observation: in job interviews the candidates do not seem to get a second chance, as the interviewers obviously missed her narrative about a successfully handled conflict with a boss. Yet this might also suggest that interviewers are blinded by stereotypical expectations about the East German way of dealing with conflicts (see also Roth 2005 for stereotypes of East and West Germans).

12.6 Conclusion

The empirical findings we have reported here show clearly that candidates and interviewers have very different ideas about the suitability and practicability of particular communicative and linguistic resources in job interviews. Conversations among East and West German speakers are potential sites for intercultural encounters (Auer and Kern 2001). Even though one has to avoid the common shortcut in intercultural communication research to equate intercultural communication and misunderstanding (ten Thije 2006), the comparison of East and West German candidates' impression management in job interviews reveals that specific strategies of linguistic self-presentation can lead to unfavourable outcomes for East Germans in job interviews with West German interviewers (Birkner 2001; Kern 2000). Indeed, there are many such instances recurring in our data.

We argue, therefore, that cultural miscommunication does not always arise as a result of deficient linguistic proficiency but concerns the knowledge of rules and conventions of language use which are widely acknowledged to be a substantial part of culture (cf. Gumperz 1982, 1996; Auer 2000). Hence, the principles of potential differences in impression management in intercultural interviews remain a relevant issue for research into intercultural communication. The areas of linguistic diversity that we have covered in our chapter are likely to be relevant not only in German–German discourse but also in encounters with people from other cultural backgrounds, as for example Shea's (1994) study on the use of perspectives in intercultural encounters, Günthner's (1994) study of different agreement/disagreement strategies in German–Chinese encounters and Shing-Lung's (2003) research into differences in German–Chinese job interviews.

KEY POINTS

1. The study compares the linguistic strategies of self-presentation used by East and West German applicants in job interviews with West German interviewers. It reveals that East German candidates and West German interviewers have very different ideas about the suitability and impact of particular communicative and linguistic resources.

2. It illustrates that when West and East German candidates present themselves in job interviews, their conversational styles differ with respect to perspectivization. Eastern candidates display a tendency to shift to unspecified, generalized perspectives in a variety of contexts, while West Germans do not change to such impersonalized, general perspectives to express their own views.
3. According to culturally shaped norms about what suits positive self-presentation in job interviews, East Germans tend to avoid direct disagreement and to downplay their readiness for conflict when asked about this. This often leads to the interaction developing in unfavourable ways.
4. The study argues that intercultural miscommunication need not arise from deficient linguistic proficiency but can result from people's knowledge of differing rules and conventions of language use.

DISCUSSION QUESTIONS

1. Find a job advertisement that could be interesting for you and imagine being invited for an interview. The interviewer asks: why have you applied for this job of all jobs?
   1.1. Note down five possible answers.
   1.2. Compare them with the answers your fellow students have found. Order them according to semantic similarity. Can you recognize argumentative patterns?
   1.3. Discuss the pros and cons of the respective argumentative patterns.
2. The next question you are asked is: What are your strong points and what are your weak points?
   2.1. Note down two or three possible strong and two or three possible weak points.
   2.2. Collect the answers in class and make a list of frequency. Can you recognize what sort of answers people prefer to give?
   2.3. What sort of answers do people tend to avoid giving, and why?
3. Read the following extract from an authentic job interview.

Example (1) Application for telephone marketing

```
I3:   what do you enjoy about retailing?
B:    (1) well (.) enjoy (.) hm – (.h) what do I enjoy?
I3:   (1) because you just said I WOULD LIKE that (somehow?).
B:    yes I want to earn money; yes, (.) well if one (has has to?) earn money in a wa:y
      [what ] (.) I can't go [there ] and (stand there?)
I3:   [mhm,]                 [mhm,]
B:    and say – well folks I'm just doing it for fun. – I certainly [won't do that.
I3:                                                                  [mhm,
B:    e:h eh just (.) for fun. I wanna earn somethin too. 'h
```

3.1. Evaluate the answer from the perspective of an employer.

Now read the next example.

Example (2) Application for telephone marketing

```
I2:   =mhm, – what was especially attractive to you in selling; what did you enjoy about
      it;
B:    (1) if someone didn't want to buy anything; and did in the end anyway
I2:   aha,
```

3.2. Evaluate the answer from the perspective of an employer and compare it with the first applicant's answer. Which of the two would you hire? Why?
3.3. Ask people with different cultural background how they evaluate the two answers. Does everybody agree that the reason 'enjoying your work' is a convincing argument to show positive motivation?
3.4. To what extent might the use of specific arguments (e.g. strong and weak points) be linked to culturally bound linguistic practices?

Notes

1. The findings presented are drawn from the research project 'Impression Management in East and West German Job Interviews' funded by the German Research Foundation.
2. We also collected 27 role-played interviews for the project. That data are not considered here.
3. A Western candidate is asked the same question as the Eastern candidate in example (2) with the same complex play of perspectives. She replies from the required point of view, giving her colleagues' hypothetical views on herself.

Suggestions for further reading

Auer, P. and Kern, F. (2001) Three ways of analysing communication between East and West Germans as intercultural communication. In A. di Luzio, S. Günthner and F. Orletti (eds) *Culture in Communication. Analyses of Intercultural Situations*. Amsterdam and Philadelphia: Benjamins, 89–116.

Birkner, K. (2004) Hegemonic Struggles or Transfer of Knowledge? East and West Germans in job interviews. *Journal of Language and Politics* 3, 293–322.

Gumperz, J. and Roberts, C. (1991) Understanding in intercultural encounters. In J. Blommaert and J. Verschueren (eds) *The Pragmatics of International and Intercultural Communication.* Amsterdam: John Benjamins, 51–90.

Kerekes, J. (2003) Distrust. A determining factor in the outcomes of gatekeeping encounters. In J. House, G. Kasper and S. Ross (eds) *Misunderstanding in Social Life. Discourse Approaches to Problematic Talk.* London: Longman, 227–57.

Roberts, C. and Sayers, P. (1998) Keeping the gate: how judgements are made in interethnic interviews. In P. Trudgill and J. Cheshire (eds) *The Sociolinguistics Reader. Vol.1. Multilingualism and Variation.* London: Arnold, 25–43.

Sarangi, S. (1994) Accounting for mismatches in intercultural selection interviews. *Multilingua*, 13 (1/2): 163–94.

13 Issues of Face in a Chinese Business Visit to Britain

Helen Spencer-Oatey and Jianyu Xing

Chapter Outline

13.1 Introduction	258
13.2 Background information	259
13.3 Problematic occurrences	259
13.4 A face perspective on the problematic occurrences	264
13.5 Discussion	266
13.6 Implications for face and rapport management theory	270
Key points	272
Discussion questions	272
Note	273
Suggestions for further reading	273

13.1 Introduction

This chapter explores the face issues that arose during a ten-day visit to a British company by a group of six Chinese business people who were customers of the British company. This company had previously hosted many such delegations, yet this particular visit turned out to be particularly problematic: the visitors cancelled all the training sessions that had been arranged, they asked to change hotels twice and were dissatisfied with the sightseeing programme. On the last day of the visit, they challenged their hosts over the spending money they were given, and argued that the British company had broken the terms of the contract. What should have been a harmonious and enjoyable visit turned out to be acrimonious and unpleasant.

Needless to say, neither side was pleased. The Chinese felt that they had not been hosted appropriately, while the British felt that the visitors were very 'demanding', 'hadn't any ethics' and 'had no due respect for their hosts'.

What actually went wrong? This chapter explores the events from a face perspective.

13.2 Background information

13.2.1 The business background

The British company designs, manufactures and sells an engineering product that is used in industrial plants throughout the world. In every contract signed in China, they agree to host a delegation of up to six people who are involved in some way in the deal. The official purpose of the visit is to inspect the products purchased, to receive technical training and to have a good time sightseeing. In reality, though, the products have typically already been shipped and installed, so the visitors are unable to inspect the goods. The British company handles all the administration associated with the visit, and prepares a programme of events which includes a welcome meeting, training sessions, local business visits, sightseeing, shopping and social activities, and ends with a close-out meeting.

The costs of the visit are paid by the Chinese, and included in the contract as a package deal. If the expenses incurred during the visit are less than the sum paid, then the balance is given to the visitors as 'pocket money' at the end of the visit.

13.2.2 Research procedure

Two types of data were collected for analysis: (1) video recordings of all the official meetings between the British and Chinese business people, and (2) comments made by the participants during follow-up interviews and playback sessions. The British and Chinese participants were interviewed separately, and were asked to watch the recordings and to comment on anything they found strange or annoying. All these sessions were audio recorded.

In all aspects of the data collection, we endeavoured to maximize the validity and reliability of the data. Over the last few years, we have developed very good relations with staff at the host company. During the visit, one of us spent as much time as possible socially with the Chinese visitors in order to build up a good rapport with them (e.g. accompanying them on sightseeing trips). We did this deliberately, so that both British and Chinese participants would have confidence in us, so that they would not feel too uneasy about the recording, and so that they would be honest and open with us in the interviews and playback sessions. We were very satisfied with the ways in which they seemed to 'conduct their business as normal' and with their cooperation during the follow-up sessions.

13.3 Problematic occurrences

During the first 24 hours of the visit, a number of problems arose and as a result, negative attitudes began to emerge.

13.3.1 Hotel arrangements

The British company took the visiting delegation to an inexpensive hotel which they had previously used with other Chinese delegations. They assumed that the visitors would prefer to stay in relatively cheap accommodation, so that they would have more pocket money at the end of the trip. However, the Chinese visitors felt the hotel was not good enough, and complained that the rooms were small and the carpets old and worn out. They claimed that when they were on business trips in China, they would stay in at least four-star hotels, and felt that this poor quality hotel was beneath their status. They asked the host company there and then to arrange for them to stay in a different hotel, and were moved to a better quality family-run hotel the next morning.

13.3.2 The welcome meeting: seating arrangements

The welcome meeting took place that next morning in the host company's conference room. Six Chinese visitors were present, and six British hosts, along with a local interpreter (of Chinese nationality). The room was rather small in size, and had a large oblong table placed in the middle of the room. There were four chairs on either side, and a fifth at one end of the table (the end that was further away from the door). Four Chinese visitors sat on one side (facing the door) and two sat on the other side with the interpreter. One seat was left empty. The British chairman of the meeting sat at the end of the table, and the other British staff were located away from the table, with most either standing or sitting behind the Chinese visitors (see Figure 13.1).

The room arrangements made it physically difficult for people to move around to shake hands and to present business cards, and both British and Chinese participants felt that the venue for the meeting was inappropriate. However, while the British chairman noted that it was 'bad organization' and 'genuine chaos', the Chinese attributed much greater significance to the seating arrangements. In the follow-up interview, the delegation leader commented as follows, with other members chorusing agreement:

Comment 1 (Chinese Delegation Leader)[1]

It shouldn't have been that he was the chair and we were seated along the sides of the table. With equal status, they should sit along this side and we should sit along that side.

In other words, the Chinese felt that since the two teams were of equal status, they should have sat on opposite sides of the table, with the heads of each side sitting in the middle. They interpreted the different arrangements as conveying a significant 'status' message:

Comment 2 (Chinese Delegation Leader)

They were chairing, and we were audience, which naturally means that you do what you are told to . . . They were, right from the start, they were commanding, in control, contemptuous. In actual fact we should have been given equal status.

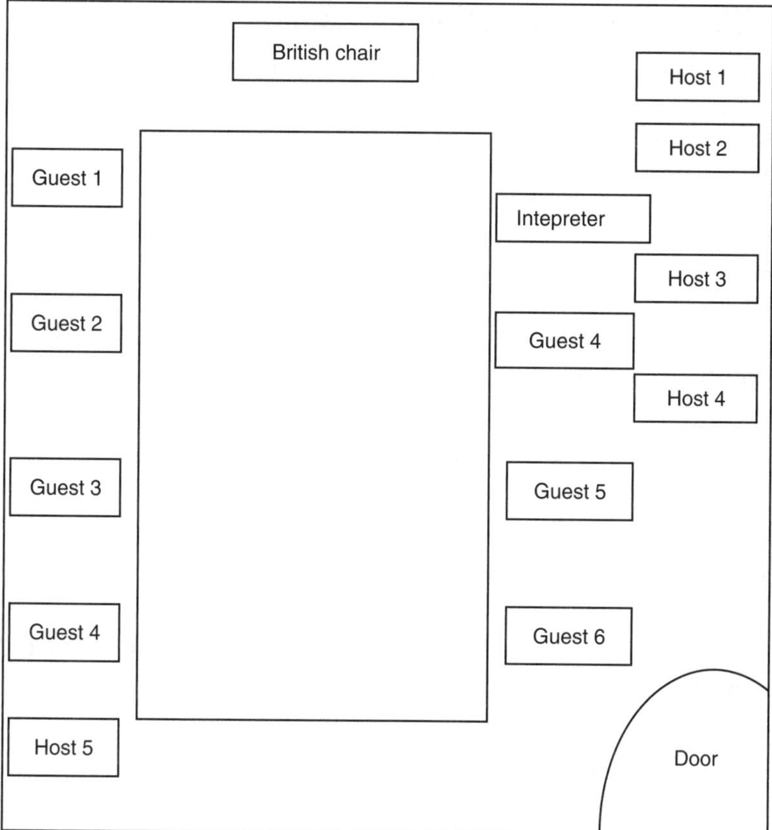

Figure 13.1 Seating arrangements at the meeting.

The British, on the other hand, clearly had no idea that this was the impression they had conveyed. While they acknowledged that the room was too small, the chairman explained that they had previously taken a more formal approach, but that the visitors on successive delegations had got younger and younger and now do not want to have very formal meetings:

Comment 3 (British chairman)

Several of our people have been to China and gone through their banquets and the welcome ceremonies and everything else, and that's the perception they got, that's what we replicated. Now over time, we discovered that the groups were not really interested, er, they just want to get in say [???] find out how things go, agree with the programme, and get on with it. It seems to be a lot more of the cash in their approach now. . . . It seems that we get younger and younger people now, and I think to a certain degree these younger and younger people are much more exposed to say Western cultures, so there seems to be more, some of them seem to be a lot more familiar with Western cultures, where to begin with, some of the party, some of the gentlemen that came over, er, it was a completely different group.

13.3.3 The welcome meeting: discourse issues

The welcome meeting had the following general structure:

- preliminaries (everyone shaking hands, and giving out business cards)
- welcome (British chairman)
- introductions (British staff and Chinese visitors in turn)
- introduction to the company (British chairman)

In his welcome comments, the British chairman drew attention to the importance of the Chinese contracts to his company, and expressed his company's hope that the good relationship between the two parties would continue in the future:

Extract 1 (Welcome Meeting)
It is extremely important for us at (company) to make a special effort to welcome all of our Chinese friends and colleagues, as you and your company are very important to us. We we've over the last probably four or five years had quite quite a good relationship with with China, and have people from (company) and (place) and and the the various (industrial plants) in the various provinces of China, and we hope this will continue in the future.

Later on, he gave some background information on his company, and made the following comments:

Extract 2 (Welcome Meeting)
So we are obviously very experienced eh in the design and the manufacture of these products. . . . A lot of our trade now obviously goes to China and to the other Eastern countries, because that is obviously where a lot of the world trade now is and will be in the future.

In the follow-up interview with the British chairman, he pointed out that his company wanted to make the visit memorable for the Chinese visitors, so that they would have a good impression of his company and remember them on their return. The Chinese, on the other hand, felt that his comments on the Sino–British relationship had not been weighty enough. They had heard on the Chinese grapevine that the British company was in serious financial difficulties, and they believed it was the Chinese contracts that had saved them from bankruptcy. (This was denied by the British company.) So they felt that the British hosts should have expressed their sincere gratitude to them for helping them so significantly.

Comment 4 (Chinese Sales Manager)
It is understandable for them to praise their own products, but by doing so they in fact made a big mistake. Why? Because, you see, because for a company when they haven't got new orders for their products for several years it is a serious problem, to them, but they didn't talk about it. . . . he should have said that you have made great efforts regarding [the sale of] our products, right? And hope you continue. They should have said more in this respect. He didn't mention our orders. So in fact this is a very important matter. It is not just a matter of receiving us.

After the chairman finished giving his welcome comments, the British staff introduced themselves, and then the chairman asked the Chinese delegation members to introduce themselves. The head of the delegation took it as an invitation to deliver a return speech, and started to express the group's appreciation to the hosts. However, he was cut short by the interpreter, who explained that they had been asked to introduce themselves, not give a return speech. After several minutes of uncomfortable discussion in Chinese by the visitors, each delegation member introduced himself.

Once again, the British and Chinese participants interpreted the issue very differently. In the follow-up interview with the Chinese, they all argued that it was normal and polite for the head of the delegation to 'say a few words of appreciation', and then introduce himself and each member of the delegation. The head of the Chinese delegation explained it as follows:

Comment 5 (Head of Chinese Delegation)

According to our home customs and protocol, speech is delivered on the basis of reciprocity. He has made his speech and I am expected to say something. . . . Condescension was implied. In fact I was reluctant to speak, and I had nothing to say. But I had to, to say a few words. Right for the occasion, right? But he had finished his speech, and he didn't give me the opportunity, and they each introduced themselves, wasn't this clearly implied that they do look down upon us Chinese.

Clearly, he and his colleagues were bitterly hurt by not being given the chance to deliver a return speech. Yet in the interview with the British chairman, he once again claimed that current delegations are different from earlier ones, saying that they used to have return speeches, but that as the Chinese have become more familiar with them, 'formalities have really eroded and sort of drifted away'.

13.3.4 Programme of activities

The original programme included one-and-a-half day's on-site training (a manufacturing review, an engineering review and a quality assurance review), and six days' local sightseeing trips and shopping tours. However, the visitors cancelled the training sessions, saying that they wanted more time for sightseeing and shopping. Yet they showed little interest in the tourist attractions they were taken to, and became impatient for more opportunities for shopping.

The British hosts were offended by this, and in the follow-up interview commented that the group showed no interest at all in their products and manufacturing, and that 'they haven't any ethics, had no due respect for their hosts'.

13.3.5 Attempts to meet with the China Sales Manager

After a few days, the visitors decided they wanted to have more time in London, and to stay in London for a night. They had asked the staff accompanying them on different trips about this, but had received no definite response. This irritated them, and so they decided to try and talk with Tim, the China Sales Manager. Two of the visitors regarded Tim as a friend, as they had previously met him during his visits to China, and they thought he would make the arrangements for them.

Tim was away on an overseas trip when the visitors arrived, and was due back during the middle of their visit. The Chinese visitors expected that, since he was their friend, he would make contact with them immediately after he got back, either officially in the office, or unofficially at their hotel or at least telephone them. But when Tim made no contact with them on the day of his return, they were annoyed. They repeatedly asked, and at one stage even demanded, the accompanying personnel to contact Tim, and to be given his home telephone number. This continued for the next few days, including the weekend.

Eventually, Tim arranged a meeting with them the following Monday, one day before their departure. In the follow-up interview, Tim explained that he needed to spend time with his family, since he had been away on a long trip. But from the Chinese point of view, he had failed to act as a genuine friend.

13.4 A face perspective on the problematic occurrences

As argued in Chapter 2, face is a universal phenomenon that is concerned with people's sense of worth, dignity and identity, and that is associated with issues such as respect, honour, status, reputation and competence (cf. Ting-Toomey and Kurogi 1998). In this section, we examine the problematic occurrences from a face perspective.

13.4.1 Aspects of face

Brown and Levinson (1987), in their classic work on politeness, maintain that there are two types of face concern: concern about autonomy, independence and freedom from imposition (negative face) and concern for approval and appreciation (positive face). However, other theorists (e.g. Matsumoto 1988, 1989; Lim and Bowers 1991; Lim 1994; Mao 1994) have criticized this specification. Tracy and Baratz (1994), for example, argue that this twofold distinction is too general to capture the dynamic face concerns that people have in different contexts, and in line with this, Spencer-Oatey (2007; Chapter 2 in this book) argues that people's face sensitivities are best analysed from an attribute perspective. People experience a sense of face threat/loss/gain when there is a mismatch between an attribute that they are claiming and an attribute they perceive to be ascribed by others.

How, then, do face attributes relate to the concerns of the Chinese and British business people in this case study?

During the ten-day visit, the problematic events for the Chinese primarily revolved around their concerns over their status and prestige. They regarded themselves as being extremely important to the British company, and thus as having high status. However, they felt that the British hosts failed to acknowledge this attribute sufficiently, and so failed to give them the face they deserved. Several of the incidents became face-threatening in this way.

- When they were taken to a cheap hotel, their face was threatened, because they were used to staying in four-star hotels, and expected to receive at least comparable treatment in Britain.
- When they were welcomed in a cramped room in which they were seated in a 'superior–subordinate' arrangement (from their perspective), their face was threatened once again, because they regarded themselves as being at least equal with their hosts.
- When the British chairman failed to express deep-felt gratitude towards them for helping to save his company financially, they felt that their importance to the company had been underestimated and unacknowledged, and that their face had thus been insufficiently honoured.
- When the chairman omitted to allow the Chinese delegation leader to give a return speech, they felt that they had been regarded with disdain and treated as inferiors, thus threatening their face once more.

Another attribute that the visitors claimed was friendship and closeness with the China Sales Manager. So when the latter failed to make contact with them as soon as he arrived back from his trip, this was face-threatening to them because it challenged their claim to a friendship.

All of these problematic events (apart from the last one) took place within the delegation's first 24 hours in Britain, so it is not really surprising that negative attitudes began to arise so early. The cancellation of the training sessions, the demanding approach over arrangements for sightseeing and shopping and the arguments over money and costs were presumably the Chinese visitors' ways of attempting to redress the balance. Unfortunately, however, the British hosts were oblivious (apart from knowing that they were dissatisfied with the hotel) to the Chinese concerns over status and to the offence they felt from the threats to their face.

13.4.2 Group as well as individual face

In defining face, most theorists seem to emphasize the personal or individual scope of face through using terms such as *image of self* (Goffman 1972), *self-image* (Brown and Levinson 1987), and *self-worth* (Ting-Toomey and Kurogi 1998).

However, face concerns are not always individual; sometimes they can be group concerns as well. Gao (1996: 96), for example, argues as follows:

> 'Face need' is not only a personal concern but, more important, a collective concern (King and Bond 1985). As King and Myers (1977) indicate, face is more a concern to the family than to the person and face-losing or face-gaining acts reflect both on persons themselves

and on their families. To illustrate, one's failure threatens the face of the family; one's accomplishment, however, gains face for the family.

During the delegation visit, the face concerns of both the British and the Chinese participants seemed to be group oriented. The British were concerned about their company's reputation: they wanted the visitors to learn more about their company, and to go back to China with a deep and positive impression, firstly of the company and secondly of Britain. Although this naturally involved individual staff members behaving appropriately, the focus of concern seemed to be more on the company than on people's individual face. See, for example, Extract 1 (above) and Extract 3:

Extract 3 (British administrator, Close-out Meeting)
Would you explain to them that [company] has entertained many groups here. It is very difficult to guess to make provision for them various visits. We could only I would assume that this would be best for them.

Similarly, the Chinese delegation presented themselves as a group, and were concerned about the group's face, and the reputation of Chinese people in general:

Extract 4 (Chinese delegation member, Close-out Meeting)
You just tell him. Is it so easy to bully us Chinese so easy to fool us? This money is what we've been saving on our food. We've had instant noodles every day just to save money and now they've grabbed it. Is that fair?

13.5 Discussion

Although the British hosts were keen to create a positive impression on their Chinese visitors, they inadvertently threatened the visitors' face and the consequences were very negative. Why then did the British host's positive intentions (their rapport enhancement and rapport maintenance orientation) result in a negative interpretation (rapport neglect and rapport threat)?

13.5.1 Anticipating preferences

The British hosts had formed the impression from previous delegations that the visitors' preferences would be as follows:

- to stay in a cheaper hotel so that they could have more personal 'pocket money' at the end of the visit
- to have an informal atmosphere in the meetings
- to have a mixture of training, sightseeing and shopping

During earlier visits that we recorded and analysed, it seems that the Chinese were fairly satisfied with the arrangements made for them. So the British hosts' anticipation of preferences seems to have been reasonable. Perhaps, though, this group was different in composition from earlier groups.

13.5.2 Judging the importance of the visitors

To the British company, this delegation's ten-day stay was just another customary visit under a standard contract. They did not regard the group as being any different from previous groups, and commented that although the Chinese visitors regarded themselves as important, 'they were not much higher ranking' than other visitors. The British believed that most of the delegation members were engineers, and that they would therefore be interested in receiving technical training. In fact, however, unlike most previous delegations, nearly all of these visitors were sales managers. In China sales managers are much richer than engineers, and also typically regard themselves as much more important. So from a Chinese perspective, this delegation was significantly different from previous groups.

It seems, therefore, that the British had difficulty identifying the roles/ positions of the visitors, and assessing their relative importance. One reason for this could be the way in which jobs and positions are often identified in Chinese and translated into English.

It is common practice in China for a person to have two titles on his/her name card, an 'expertise' (technical) title, and a 'position' (job) title. The former shows the area/ field s/he is skilled or trained in, and the latter shows the position s/he holds within the organization. So a person, for example, may be trained as an engineer but working as a sales manager. The British hosts were only given information on the delegation members' 'expertise' titles, not their 'position' titles. In other words, they did not receive the full information given in Table 13.1; they only received that shown in columns one and two (along with company affiliations).

Table 13.1 The Chinese visitors' 'expertise' and 'position' titles

Name	'Expertise' title	'Position' title
Mr FJY	Senior Engineer	Head of Delegation [position title not given on card]. Design Department, [W] Company
Mr YZY	Engineer	Sales Manager, International Sales and Planning, [W] Company
Mr XZB	Senior Engineer	Director, [X] Project
Mr LT	Engineer	Director of [Y] Company; Manager of [Z] Company
Mr WFS	Assistant Economist	Head of Equipment Section, [X] Project
Mr HP	Economist	General Manager of [A] Company and [B] Company

It is not surprising, therefore, that the British hosts thought the visitors would be interested in technical training, and failed to realize the important roles they played in concluding contracts. However, the British chairman did sense there was something a little strange, as can be seen from one of his comments in the follow-up interview. When he was asked whether he realized that most of the guests were involved in sales, he replied as follows:

Comment 6 (British chairman)

One of the things that happened is that when you read their job titles, and explain what they do within the company sometimes it doesn't seem to stack out. Sometimes it doesn't seem to be believable, eh, because sometimes you'll get for example a title like senior project engineer, and a project engineer, but you'll find the project engineer is actually more senior than the senior project engineer. So sometimes their titles and their job descriptions don't actually tie up with what they do. So maybe I didn't I didn't pick up the fact that they were all in sales.

Clearly, it was difficult for the British company to judge accurately the status, decision-making power and professional interests of the delegation members.

13.5.3 Managing practical constraints

However, even if the British hosts had gained an accurate understanding of the relative importance of the visitors, they would still have faced difficulties, because there were practical constraints on them, both in terms of the venue and the resources.

13.5.3.1 The venue

The only large room which the company could use for formal welcome and close-out meetings was the cafeteria. During this particular visit, the cafeteria was not available for use, so even if they had wanted to provide a better setting, they would have had difficulty doing so.

13.5.3.2 Resources (financial and staff)

In terms of the financial as well as the staff resources, the hosts had little room to manoeuvre. Under the terms of the contract, the Chinese side had paid a fixed sum of money to cover the expenses incurred by each member of the visiting group. Unlike in China where members of staff involved in receiving foreign visitors normally each have an entertainment budget, the British staff had no such extra allowance. They had to stay strictly within the fixed sum included in the contract and at the same time allow a certain amount to be given back to the visitors as spending money.

The hosts were also having difficulty providing staff to accompany the visitors on sightseeing and shopping trips. It meant people having to take time off from busy schedules; it meant starting early in the morning, getting back late in the evenings and going out at weekends. Many people were reluctant to be involved, and this put the hosts under great pressure; in fact, they had to ask retired former employees to help out.

13.5.4 Understanding cultural conventions

Another major source of problems was the lack of mutual understanding of cultural conventions.

In Britain, there is an increasing move towards informality (for example, in the use of terms of address, and in the conduct of meetings) and an implicit assumption that everyone finds informality more comfortable than formality. Moreover, there is a preference for minimizing hierarchical differences and for stressing equality (at least superficially). However, in China people more normally regard formal protocol as natural, and as a way of displaying respect for all concerned, and especially for those with high status. And, as is common in high power distance societies (see Chapter 1, and Spencer-Oatey 1997), status differences are usually explicitly acknowledged. So people may pay great attention to issues such as seating arrangements, the use of formal titles, the appropriate presentation of business cards and speech turn-taking. Clearly, both British and Chinese participants were unaware of each other's different conventions regarding preferences for formality/informality and the management of hierarchy issues in relationships.

Another area of unfamiliarity concerns the rights and obligations of the host–guest relationship. Gao and Ting-Toomey (1998: 46) claim that in the Chinese host–guest relationship, 'the host demonstrates *ke qi* (politeness) by doing everything to make the guest "feel at home", and the guest returns *ke qi* by not imposing on the host'. During this visit, however, the visitors clearly thought the British had failed in their responsibilities as hosts. They knew that their airfare and hotel bills would be taken out of the money that they had paid, but they assumed that the cost of other events, such as welcome dinners, sightseeing trips and so on, would be met by the hosts from a different budget. They could not understand how the British could be 'hosts' if the Chinese had to pay for everything, including the expenses (such as meals) of accompanying British staff. As soon as they realized at the close-out meeting that this was how the costs had been calculated, they protested vehemently, and demanded that the figures be re-calculated. While these host–guest obligations are understandable to British people for 'personal' visits, in a British business context, it is normal to add them in to the contract price because the hosting costs have to be recovered from somewhere. Once again, each side seemed unable to grasp the other's cultural norms in this respect.

13.6 Implications for face and rapport management theory

Tracy and Baratz (1994: 293) argue for a case study approach to the study of face and facework:

> A case study approach would enable researchers to develop a better understanding of the following: How do interactants in a particular setting want to be seen or *not* want to be seen? How do these interactants get this across or try to get this across? What is the relationship between certain communicative behaviors and attributions of identity? What misunderstandings, problems, and/or contradictions arise in the setting that relate to facework?

What implications, then, does this case study have for face theory/rapport management theory?

13.6.1 Face, identity and attributes

Firstly, this case study offers support for the arguments that face sensitivities can be helpfully conceptualized in terms of claims to specific identity attributes. During this particular business visit, 'status/prestige' was an especially sensitive attribute.

Simon's (2004) 'Self-Aspect Model of Identity' proposes that a person's self-concept comprises beliefs about his/her own attributes or self-characteristics. These can be huge in number, and typically include elements such as personality traits (e.g. shy), abilities (e.g. poor dancer), physical features (e.g. curly hair, slim), behavioural characteristics (e.g. usually gets up early), religious beliefs (e.g. Christian, atheist), social roles (e.g. mother, lecturer), language affiliation(s) (e.g. English, Chinese) and group memberships (e.g. female, academic, Christian). However, this should not be interpreted as meaning that people have a fixed conception of their identity; on the contrary, people construe their identity attributes in dynamic ways. The relative salience of different identity attributes can vary not only across individuals but also across contexts. Just as an anti-virus program may run unnoticed in the background for the majority of the time but will capture the user's attention the moment a problem arises, so people may be unaware of the identity attributes they are claiming until they are challenged in some way in an interaction.

In this case study, the Chinese visitors became very conscious of the status/prestige they were claiming because they perceived a mismatch between their own evaluations and those they felt their British hosts were conveying. Analysing their face concerns in terms of identity attributes helps us gain a much richer and more granular understanding of them than if we simply used Brown and Levinson's (1987) twofold distinction between positive and negative face.

13.6.2 Independent and interdependent face

Ting-Toomey and Kurogi (1998) argue for a distinction between 'I-identity' and 'We-identity' facework, which derives from the difference between independent self-construal and interdependent self-construal. They argue that independent–interdependent self-construal is the mediating factor between individualism–collectivism (a culture-level factor; see Chapter 1) and behaviour (e.g. facework), and they explain independent and interdependent self-construal as follows:

> Individuals with high independent self-construals tend to view themselves as unique and distinctive from others. They use their own personal attributes and abilities as motivational bases for action rather than the thoughts and feelings of others. Individuals who view themselves as independents value 'I-identity', personal achievement, self-direction and competition. When communicating with others, high independents believe in striving for personal goals, being in control of the agenda and expressing their positions assertively. Overall, independent self-construal types tend to be more self-face oriented than other-face oriented. ... The interdependent construal of self, on the other hand, involves an emphasis on the importance of relational connectedness (Markus and Kitayama 1991). People who have an interdependent self-construal want to fit in with others, act appropriately, promote others' goals and value relational collaboration. The self-in-relation guides the behavior of high interdependents in social situations. When communicating with others, high interdependents value other-face and mutual-face concerns. They are eager to appeal to other-face concerns in vulnerable interpersonal situations in order to preserve relational harmony.
>
> (Ting-Toomey and Kurogi 1998: 196–7)

Ting-Toomey and Kurogi's discussion revolves round the distinction between individual rights/interests/concerns, and group rights/interests/concerns. However, there is no mention of multiparty inter-group communication, and how this fits into their characterization.

In our case study, as explained in Section 13.4.2, we found group face to be an important concept. Both groups (British hosts and Chinese visitors) seemed to be more concerned about group face than individual face, and so using Ting-Toomey and Kurogi's terminology, they each had interdependent face concerns. However, their group concerns seem slightly different from the concept of independence–interdependence discussed by Ting-Toomey and Kurogi (1998). It seems that Communication Accommodation Theory (see Chapter 8 and Gallois et al. 1995, 2005) provides a clearer set of concepts for describing their orientations. The British and Chinese participants seemed to take an intergroup orientation, rather than an interpersonal orientation (in other words, they each had a kind of corporate identity), and because of this their concerns were primarily for group face rather than personal face.

The question of independence–interdependence relates to another issue that is included in Communication Accommodation Theory: socio-psychological orientation. Interdependent self-construal seems associated with a convergent orientation, while independent self-construal seems associated with a divergent or maintainance orientation. People with a convergent orientation show concern for mutual face (mutual interpersonal and/or intergroup face), while people with a divergent (or maintenance) orientation show concern for self-face (individual and/or own in-group face).

Clearly rapport management theory needs more case studies which explore the genuine concerns about face, sociality rights and interactional goals that arise in different types of interactions and different cultural settings. Such studies are necessary in order to check and validate theoretical concepts, and they may also help (where appropriate) to integrate different theoretical perspectives.

KEY POINTS

1. People develop expectations regarding the types of behaviour (verbal, non-verbal and general arrangements) that they expect to experience in certain contexts, yet in intercultural contexts these are not always easy to predict.
2. People (unconsciously) claim certain identity attributes in their interactions with others, such as status, competence, friendship relations, and if they perceive a mismatch between the attributes they are claiming and the attributes they perceive others are ascribing to them, they will experience this as face-threatening.
3. People's concerns about face not only relate to them as individuals but also to the groups that they are members of.
4. To avoid inadvertent face threats, people need to be mindful – to pay great attention to subtle cues that could indicate differences in expectations and potential threats to face.
5. A case study approach to face, which gathers different types of data including post-event comments, allows face to be studied from a rich, interactional perspective.

DISCUSSION QUESTIONS

1. List all the problems that occurred between the hosts and the visitors during the visit (from both British and Chinese perspectives). For each of them, consider:
   1.1. How far do you think the British hosts were responsible and how far do you think the Chinese visitors were responsible for the problems that occurred?
   1.2. How upsetting or annoying was each of the problems for the people concerned? Do you think it was an infringement of sociality rights (equity and/or association rights), a threat to face and/or a hindering of interactional goals (see Chapter 2)?
2. Identify the background assumptions of (a) the hosts and (b) the visitors which played important roles in the misunderstandings (see Chapter 7). Write a summary of the ways in which the background assumptions you identified led to miscommunication.

3. To what extent can the problems that arose during the visit be explained in terms of negative pragmatic transfer (see Chapter 7), and to what extent can they be explained in terms of under- or contra-accommodation (see Chapter 8)? (Do not expect to find clear-cut answers to these questions!)
4. How do you think the problems described in this chapter can best be overcome and/or avoided on future occasions?

Note

1. Translations of Chinese extracts are by Jianyu Xing.

Suggestions for further reading

Spencer-Oatey, H. (2007) Theories of identity and the analysis of face. *Journal of Pragmatics*, 39: 639–56.

Spencer-Oatey, H. and Xing, J. (2003) Managing rapport in intercultural business interactions: a comparison of two Chinese–British welcome meetings. *Journal of Intercultural Studies*, 24(1): 33–46.

Spencer-Oatey, H. and Xing, J. (2004) Rapport management problems in Chinese–British business interactions: a case study. In J. House and J. Rehbein (eds) *Multilingual Communication*. Amsterdam: Benjamins, 197–221.

Spencer-Oatey, H. and Xing, J. (2005) Managing talk and non-talk in intercultural interactions: insights from two Chinese–British business meetings. *Multilingua*, 24: 55–74.

Suggestions for Further Reading for Part 4: Studies which Analyse Intercultural Interactions

Axelson, E. (2007) Vocatives: a double-edged strategy in intercultural discourse among graduate students. *Pragmatics*, 17(1): 95–122.

Bailey, B. (1997) Communication of respect in interethnic service encounters. *Language in Society*, 26: 327–56.

Bailey, B. (2000) Communicative behaviour and conflict between African–American customers and Korean immigrant retailers in Los Angeles. *Discourse and Society*, 11(1): 86–108.

Belz, J. A. (2005) Intercultural questioning, discovery and tension in internet-mediated language learning partnerships. *Language and Intercultural Communication*, 5(1): 3–39.

Bjørge, A. K. (2007) Power distance in English lingua franca email communication. *International Journal of Applied Linguistics*, 17(1): 60–80.

Chen, Y., Tjosvold, D. and Su, S.F. (2005) Goal interdependence for working across cultural boundaries: Chinese employees with foreign managers. *International Journal of Intercultural Relations*, 29(4): 429–47.

Clyne, M. (1994) *Intercultural Communication at Work*. Cambridge: CUP.

Cutrone, P. (2005) A case study examining backchannels in conversations between Japanese–British dyads. *Multilingua*, 24(3): 237–74.

Gershenson, O. (2003) Misunderstanding between Israelis and Soviet immigrants: linguistic and cultural factors. *Multilingua*, 22(3): 275–290.

Halmari, H. (1993) Intercultural business telephone conversations: a case of Finns vs. Anglo-Americans. *Applied Linguistics*, 4(4): 408–30.

Halualani, R. T., Chitgopekar, A., Morrison, J. J. T. A. and Dodge, P.W.-W. (2004) Who's interacting? And what are they talking about? – intercultural contact and interaction among multicultural university students. *International Journal of Intercultural Relations*, 28(5): 353–72.

Jenkins, S. (2000) Cultural and linguistic miscues: a case study of international teaching assistant and academic faculty miscommunication. *International Journal of Intercultural Relations*, 24(4): 477–501.

Kerekes, J. A. (2006) Winning an interviewer's trust in a gatekeeping encounter. *Language in Society*, 35: 27–57.

Li, W., Zhu, H. and Li, Y. (2001) Conversational management and involvement in Chinese–English business talk. *Language and Intercultural Communication*, 1(2): 135–50.

Liu, J. (2002) Negotiating silence in American classrooms: three case studies. *Language and Intercultural Communication*, 2(1): 37–54.

Marriott, H. E. (1990) Intercultural business negotiations: the problem of norm discrepancy. *ARAL Series S*, 7: 33–65.

Miller, L. (1991) Verbal listening behavior in conversations between Japanese and Americans. In J. Blommaert and J. Verschueren (eds) *The Pragmatics of International and Intercultural Communication*. Amsterdam: John Benjamins, 111–30.

Miller, L. (1995) Two aspects of Japanese and American co-worker interaction: giving instructions and creating rapport. *Journal of Applied Behavioral Science*, 31(2): 141–61.

Mori, J. (2003) The construction of interculturality: a study of initial encounters between Japanese and American students. *Research on Language and Social Interaction*, 36(2): 143–84.

Nakane, I. (2006) Silence and politeness in intercultural communication in university seminars. *Journal of Pragmatics*, 38(11): 1811–35.

Poncini, G. (2003) Multicultural business meetings and the role of languages other than English. *Journal of Intercultural Studies*, 24(1): 17–32.

Rogerson-Revell, P. (2007) Humour in business: a double-edged sword. A study of humour and style shifting in intercultural business meetings. *Journal of Pragmatics*, 39(1): 4–28.

Ryoo, H.-K. (2005) Achieving friendly interactions: a study of service encounters between Korean shopkeepers and African–American customers. *Discourse and Society*, 16(1): 79–105.

Ryoo, H.-K. (2007) Interculturality serving multiple interactional goals in African American and Korean service encounters. *Pragmatics*, 17(1): 23–47.

Sarangi, S. (1994) Accounting for mismatches in intercultural selection interviews. *Multilingua*, 13(1–2): 163–94.

Shigemasu, E. and Ikeda, J. (2006) Face threatening act avoidance and relationship satisfaction between international students and Japanese host students. *International Journal of Intercultural Relations*, 30(4): 439–55.

Spencer-Oatey, H. and Xing, J. (2004) Rapport management problems in Chinese–British business interactions: a case study. In J. House and J. Rehbein (eds) *Multilingual Communication*. Amsterdam: John Benjamins, 197–221.

Spencer-Oatey, H. and Xing, J. (2005) Managing talk and non-talk in intercultural interactions: insights from two Chinese–British business meetings. *Multilingua*, 24(1–2): 55–74.

Steinberg, S. and Bar-On, D. (2002) An analysis of the group process in encounters between Jews and Palestinians using a typology for discourse classification. *International Journal of Intercultural Relations*, 26(2): 199–214.

Stephens, K. (1997) Cultural stereotyping and intercultural communication: working with students from the People's Republic of China. *Language and Education*, 11(2): 113–24.

Tyler, A. (1995) The coconstruction of cross-cultural miscommunication. *Studies in Second Language Acquisition*, 17(2): 129–52.

Ulijn, J. M. and Li, X. (1995) Is interrupting impolite? Some temporal aspects of turn-taking in Chinese–Western and other intercultural business encounters. *Text*, 15(4): 589–627.

Zimmerman, E. (2007) Constructing Korean and Japanese interculturality in talk: ethnic membership categorization among users of Japanese. *Pragmatics*, 17(1): 71–94.

Part 5
Methodology

Editor's Introduction

Part 5 discusses methodological issues and is applicable to all other parts of the book. It has the following aims:

- to provide readers with background information on research design and analysis which can inform their understanding of the empirical chapters in this book and of other cross-cultural and intercultural studies that they read;
- to help readers start (or continue) exploring the field for themselves by providing them with some useful background information and advice; and
- to suggest some ideas for projects in cross-cultural and intercultural pragmatics.

Chapter 14, 'Data Collection in Pragmatics Research', focuses on the collection of pragmatic data, describing the different procedures that can be used for collecting such data, and evaluating their relative strengths and weaknesses. It emphasizes two fundamental points: that data collection methods need to be decided in relation to the research questions posed, and that the researcher's own ontological and epistemological stance will influence what is researched and how. Chapter 15, 'Recording and Analysing Talk across Cultures', argues that the cultural element of cross-cultural and intercultural research introduces challenges and complexities for both data collection and interpretation. Drawing on insights and experiences gained through the 'Language in the Workplace' project at the University of Wellington, the paper explains the nature of such complexities and suggests ways of handling them. Chapter 16, 'Projects', suggests some cross-cultural and intercultural pragmatics topics that could be researched, and provides some brief reminders about questions to think about in carrying out such projects.

Needless to say, these methodology chapters cannot provide a comprehensive treatment of research issues; they can only touch on aspects that are particularly pertinent to cross-cultural and intercultural pragmatics. Readers are recommended to consult specialized research methodology books for broader discussion and advice.

14 Data Collection in Pragmatics Research

Gabriele Kasper

Chapter Outline

14.1 Introduction 279
14.2 Interaction 281
14.3 Questionnaires 291
14.4 Interviews 296
14.5 Diaries 297
14.6 Verbal report 298
14.7 Conclusion 300
Key points 301
Discussion questions 302
Note 302
Suggestions for Further Reading 302

14.1 Introduction

In the years since the original version of this chapter was written, methods of collecting data on pragmatic objects and topics have become more diverse, and the emphasis on methodological choices has shifted. In the past, some form of questionnaire was the dominating tool for gathering data, especially in cross-cultural and interlanguage pragmatics, and questionnaires continue to be a standard data collection instrument. However, the analysis of authentic data of situated interactions has been gaining ground, and new genres and media as habitats for pragmatic phenomena have entered the literature. The pull towards authentic data has a counterpart in data collection methods that afford tighter experimental control, and such methods have made their way into interlanguage pragmatics research as well. To some extent, changes in research methods have arrived on the back of technological advancements. As computers, the internet, and digital video technology are becoming more widespread and affordable, data types and methods of data gathering have not only expanded the scope but raised expectations as to the quality of pragmatics research. Another strong influence on changes in the landscape of pragmatics research is the theoretical sources that researchers draw on. Pragmatics research has always engaged theories and methodologies from a range of social sciences (Kasper and Rose 2002). In recent years, however, a stronger orientation is visible towards incorporating theoretical perspectives from cognitive psychology and psycholinguistics on the one hand, and sociology on the other, and the different theoretical stances privilege particular kinds of data and analytical strategies.

There has also been a growing recognition that methodological problems cannot adequately be solved by considering 'methods' in a theoretical vacuum, as mere 'neutral techniques' with no metaphysical strings attached. It is generally accepted that methods need to be chosen so that they optimally answer the research questions. What appeared to be less considered in cross-cultural and interlanguage pragmatics research is how the objects for investigation, and the questions asked about them, are shaped by the researcher's ontological and epistemological stance towards them. For instance, under a rationalist model of politeness (Brown and Levinson 1987), actors compute the politeness investment for doing a particular face-threatening act by assessing three contextual factors: power, distance and imposition. On the basis of this calculation actors select politeness strategies suitable for offsetting the imminent face-threat. This model has generated standard questions such as how members of different speech communities assess the context factors in varying social scenes, and what strategies they choose under different variable constellations, other things being equal. The last qualification is perhaps the defining feature in politeness research under a rationalist model (though not necessarily in Brown and Levinson's theory, cf. Arundale 1999, 2005), as it conceptualizes the relation between social context and politeness as a static unidirectional effect of independent on dependent variables. Commensurate with a deterministic model are such data collection methods as scaled response instruments, multiple choice and discourse completion questionnaires, and indeed these have predominantly been used in the literature. Alternative conceptualizations of politeness spawn different questions and require different methods to investigate them. When politeness is viewed as emergent, interactionally constituted and co-constructed by the participants in practical activities (e.g. contributions in Kasper 2006a), researchers have examined, *inter alia*, how interlocutors attend to face through preference organization (Lerner 1996; Golato and Taleghani-Nikazm 2006), how they construct variable social identities, relationships and member status in communities of practice (Cook 2006; Locher 2006), and how they orient to institutional mandates (Kasper 2006b; Piirainen-Marsh 2006). When politeness is viewed as locally produced and reflexively constituted by the participants in the details of their interactional conduct, it cannot be investigated in abstraction from situated practical activities. Consequently, a discursive-constructionist perspective requires records of natural interaction as data – unless a 'staged' interaction, such as an experiment or role play, becomes the research topic itself. In the past, records of natural interaction were limited to video- or audio-taped talk exchanges and transcripts, but documents of online interactions are becoming increasingly common as well.

The example of politeness studies illustrates two different metatheoretical stances that have been discussed extensively in the research methodological literature. Within the current landscape of research paradigms in the social sciences, politeness research under the rationalist model has a good fit with post-positivism (Guba and Lincoln 2005; Silverman 2006), whereas the discursive perspective on politeness aligns itself with constructionism (Schwandt 2003; Silverman 2006) and ethnomethodology (ten Have 2003). And just as the concept of politeness as an object for research and the questions one might ask about it are shaped by paradigmatic assumptions, so is the problem of what constitutes relevant data and how the data may be collected and analysed. While all scientists have to probe the implicit assumptions and consequences of their methods, pragmaticians are especially well equipped to do so because collecting and analysing data in pragmatics, as in social research generally, critically involves talk and text (Cicourel 1982). Pragmaticians can, and should, turn their professional expertise on their own research methods, making them the topic of, and not only a resource for, pragmatic inquiry.

As in the original version of this chapter, I will limit the discussion to methods of data *collection* because strategies and practices for the analysis of data collected in pragmatics have been discussed extensively in the literature on research methodology and in the context of specific research traditions, for instance in different schools of discourse analysis. Examples from the research literature will primarily be drawn from cross-cultural and interlanguage pragmatic studies. The methods to be considered below will be grouped into three categories: interaction (authentic discourse, elicited conversation, role play), questionnaires (discourse completion, multiple-choice, scaled response) and written and oral forms of self-report not based on questionnaires (diaries and verbal protocols). These groupings are not without a hitch and alternatives are possible.

14.2 Interaction

Authentic talk, elicited conversation, and open-ended role play or simulation are different forms of interaction that allow researchers to examine a wide range of discourse phenomena, including the overall structuring of talk activities, the distribution of turns at talk, turn structures and their composition through linguistic and other resources, the sequencing of conversational contributions, speaker–listener coordination, participants' joint accomplishment of action within the discourse context, and participants' understandings of the interlocutor's contributions. Although participants are engaged 'online' (i.e. the interaction is current) in all three forms of interactional discourse, neither of the two elicited data types can unproblematically be treated as 'the same' as authentic conversation – in fact, in order to evaluate their usefulness for the research purpose, close attention needs to be paid to participants' constructions of their interaction *as* staged.

14.2.1 Authentic discourse

Discourse type. For the most part, pragmaticists are interested in collecting substantial quantities of data about a specific phenomenon. Some phenomena are ubiquitous in any kind of non-specialized everyday talk and others are more closely related to specific occasions. Participants take turns, display recipientship through listener tokens (Gardner 2001) or structure the interaction through discourse markers (Schiffrin 1987) in any kind of ordinary conversation, but many conversations may go by without such actions as complaints or refusals. Questions, requests or compliment sequences are not bound to specific types of conversation, yet some activities get done through such sequences. Studies of various groups of speakers have shown that getting-to-know activities in initial encounters are typically accomplished through question–answer sequences (Mori 2003; Svennevig 1999); family dinner talk generates requests for verbal and non-verbal action (Blum-Kulka 1997), and dinner parties at someone's house provide numerous occasions for compliments and compliment responses (Golato 2005).

Discourse analysts frequently distinguish between ordinary conversation and institutional interaction (Drew and Heritage 1992). Although this categorization is by no means clear-cut, it is helpful in the present context because the two types of discourse afford partly different opportunities for collecting data on pragmatics. 'Conversational' and 'institutional' are hypernymic categories for a possibly infinite number of heterogeneous forms of interactions, but despite the large within-category diversity, each has certain characteristics that are consequential for pragmatics research. *Ordinary conversation* among friends, family members, acquaintances and strangers provide a rich data source for the study of pragmatics and discourse, enabling researchers to identify activities, episodes, actions and semiotic resources – linguistic, non-verbal and non-vocal – that allow comparison between different groups (Fox, Hayashi and Jasperson 1996) or to examine repeated occurrences of the target phenomenon in activities shared by participants from different linguistic and cultural backgrounds (Cheng 2003). In peer conversation in particular, participants have equal discursive rights and obligations, self-manage turn-taking, take shifting discourse roles, and contingently co-construct identities and develop topics without a pre-given agenda. In contrast, *institutional interaction* is structured through institution-specific tasks and goals, which make certain institutional roles, topics, and actions available and impose constraints on others. As bounded, and often scheduled, events that evolve through distinct phases, institutional activities enable participants to accomplish their goals in an efficient and timely manner. Compared to mundane conversation, institutional discourse is often more predictable and therefore offers abundant opportunities for cross-cultural and intercultural comparison, and well as for developmental interlanguage pragmatic research. For Bardovi-Harlig and Hartford (2005a), institutional discourse has the advantage of a natural experiment: it is partially pre-structured or 'controlled', but by the participants' orientation to the institutional activity rather than the researcher. At the same time, unlike researcher-manipulated data, institutional interaction is context-embedded and socially consequential for the participants (Bardovi-Harlig and Hartford 2005b; Kerekes 2007). These two critical properties are absent in data arranged for research purposes.

Medium. Interaction, in its primordial form, takes place among spatially and temporally co-present participants. As such, face-to-face interaction is the most commonly studied type of interaction. Because participants have full visual access to each other, they make use of non-vocal resources as well as vocal (non-verbal and linguistic) repertoires (McNeill 2000). By contrast, interaction conducted on the telephone relies exclusively on talk without any visual access. Particularly well-researched are the methods by which the parties open and close telephone calls in the standard auditory medium. Studies have shown both cross-culturally and cross-linguistically stable and variable practices (Luke and Pavlidou 2002; Thüne and Leonardi 2003). As the rapidly developing technologies for telephone- and computer-mediated communication enable a wider range of semiotic resources, better access to direct participation, and greater user mobility, questions arise about the impact of technological innovation on discourse-pragmatic practices in the new media. Comparative studies of interaction in different electronically mediated environments show that participants carry over the fundamental practices of talk-in-interaction to the new media while also dealing with medium-specific constraints and affordances. For instance, comparisons of telephone conversations via mobile phones and landlines in British English (Hutchby and Barnett 2005) and Finnish (Arminen and Leinonen 2006) reveal that answers to summons in opening exchanges are more variable on the cell phone because the summons identifies the caller/number (a feature also available on landlines with caller ID), and that the co-participants orient to their mobility in space ('Where are you?'). However these modifications appear to indicate that participants recalibrate their interactional competencies from talk-in-interaction to the affordances of mobile phone technology rather than abandoning and re-inventing the norms and practices of face-to-face and conventional telephone discourse. Similar findings are reported from comparisons of repair (Schönfeldt and Golato 2003) and request and assessment sequences in Web chats (Golato and Taleghani-Nikazm 2006). Although the temporal adjacency of turns is often interrupted in multiparty interactions in synchronic Web chats, participants still orient to the normative sequential structure of co-present interaction in their organization of response turns (Gonzales-Lloret in press; Schönfeldt and Golato 2003). Likewise, participants draw on linguistic, orthographic and pictorial resources (smiley faces) as indices of social solidarity (Golato and Taleghani-Nikazm 2006). On a similar line, longitudinal studies of telecollaborations between students of French and German as foreign languages and native speakers of those languages have registered how the students become increasingly more adept at using the affiliative *tu/Du* forms of address, a critical part of their pragmatic competence that is quite difficult to achieve in foreign classrooms alone (Belz and Kinginger 2002). In order to explicate how participants attune their pragmatic abilities to the distinctive affordances of communication technologies, comparison is needed between different electronically mediated forms of interaction, such as between landlines and mobile phones, or between synchronous and asynchronous chat formats, and between face-to-face interaction and electronically mediated communication.

Recording authentic talk. The wide range of communication technologies requires equally diverse methods of data collection. Text-based computer-mediated communication, such as email, discussion groups or various chat forms, allows uncomplicated collection of the stored postings from a consenting participant, whereas voice and visual access require more complex technology and arrangements for recording (Markham 2004). Rather than exploring the various forms of technologically mediated interaction as sites for pragmatic research, I will consider how interaction in ordinary face-to-face encounters can be recorded. For the study of speech acts, three recording techniques have been used: field notes, audio recording and video recording. Although there is substantial variation in the scope, delicacy and quantity of what these techniques allow to be recorded, they are all subject to the law that observation and recording is necessarily perspectival, partial and selective (Duranti 1997).

Recording observations through *field notes*, a standard ethnographic technique (Sanjek 1990; Spradley 1979), was frequently adopted in the earlier speech act research; for instance, in studies of compliments and compliment responses (Manes and Wolfson 1981; Wolfson 1983; Holmes 1988; Herbert 1989, 1991), invitations (Wolfson, D'Amico-Reisner and Huber 1983), and apologies and apology responses (Holmes 1990). The speech act corpora collected through the note-taking technique are impressively large: Manes and Wolfson's (1981) collection on compliments in East-Coast American English included 'well over twelve hundred examples' (Wolfson 1989: 110), Herbert's (1991) Polish corpus consisted of 400 compliment exchanges, Holmes' (1988) New Zealand English corpus comprised 484 compliments and 440 responses. These corpora proved a useful basis for establishing the realization strategies of compliments and compliment responses, the linguistic formulae routinely used in their implementation, and their distribution according to such variables as interlocutors' status and gender (Holmes 1988). Rose (1999) designed a data collection worksheet for recording requests that could be adapted to other speech acts. While field notes in pragmatics research can be valuable as a supplementary data source, two caveats have to be registered. First, borrowing the field-note technique from ethnography does not make a study ethnographic. Speech acts have been the object of classic ethnographic research (see Frake 1964, on asking for a drink in Subanun, or Irvine 1974 on greetings in Wolof), but in this work they were 'thickly' described as part of comprehensive ethnographies. In the speech act research of the 1980s and 1990s, by contrast, socio-cultural contextualization and grounded interpretation, based on extensive, multiple analytically interconnected data sources, are virtually non-existent. Secondly, what can be recorded by researcher's observation and subsequent field notes is constrained by human cognitive capacities. People's short term memory is not an effective device for recording interaction because attention is selective and memory content decays rapidly. Consequently, the only speech acts that may be reliably recorded through classic ethnographic observation are limited to single-turn, short, high-frequency 'semantic formulae', such as greetings, leave-takings, and (some forms of) compliments (e.g. Wolfson 1989). A speech act's sequential structure – how the focal action is occasioned, how it is responded to, how it unfolds over perhaps multiple turns – loses shape in memory, as does its temporal and prosodic organization. However, participants in interaction do things not only with 'words', but also through non-linguistic semiotic resources and interrelated forms of interactional organization. So there is a need for technology that can register and preserve this information for repeated listening and viewing.

Approaches to pragmatics as socially situated interaction – conversation analysis (Sacks 1992), interactional sociolinguistics (Gumperz 1982) and ethnographic micro-analysis (Erickson 1992) – would not have been possible without *audio recording.* Interactional sociolinguists in particular emphasize the role of prosody as a critical contextualization cue (Gumperz 1992a). Conversation analysts note that temporal phenomena are systematically employed as resources in interaction. For instance, a recurrent practice by which speakers attend to 'face' is to delay disaffiliative or face-threatening actions, as in the response to the invitation shown in Example 1.

EXAMPLE 1: [from Davidson 1984: 125]

1. A: So if you guys want a place tuh sta:y
2. (0.3)
3. B: 't 'hhh Oh well *th*ank you but you we ha- yihknow *Th*omas

B's account for not accepting the invitation (which can be heard as a rejection) is delayed through a series of practices – (1) a gap of silence before B takes her turn, (2) turn-initial perturbations, (3) a receipt token, (4) a *well*-preface, (5) a thanking formula, and (6) the adversive marker *but*. The account is also internally stretched out through (7) a self-repair and a mitigator (yihknow). While speakers may combine delay practices in various ways, they are all regularly deployed social methods for postponing the production of a disaffiliative response (Davidson 1984; Lerner 1996). Speech act research that only focuses on the semantic formulae of refusal, rejection or other face-threatening speech acts fails to grasp a fundamental property of interaction, that is, preference organization (Pomerantz 1984b).

Video recording enables yet more comprehensive analysis of interaction. As non-vocal forms of conduct – gaze, facial expression, gestures, body movement, positioning in space and manipulation of artefacts – interact with vocal practices in face-to-face encounters, audio recordings miss out aspects of interaction that video can show to be demonstrably relevant for the participants (Heath 2004; ten Have 2007). Visual data afford access to the physical setting, which in turn enables inferences regarding the social, cultural and institutional organization of the setting, personal and social relationships, and participant attributes. In multiparty interactions, they facilitate speaker identification, and their relative permanence allows repeated viewing to examine specific episodes or sequences (DuFon 2002). Different genres of videotaped data for pragmatic research may be distinguished according to whether or not the researcher participates in the setting. Examples of the participatory version are Blum-Kulka's (1997) investigation of pragmatic socialization during family dinners in three cultures and DuFon's (2000, 2006) studies of the socialization of politeness in Indonesian as a second language. Iino (1996) and Cook (2006) collected video data of interactions between host families and sojourning students in Japan by means of the 'remote observation method', an example of non-participatory recording. Which participation status is preferable would depend on the research goals as well as theoretical and methodological considerations.

Conversation analysts insist on authentic interaction data as a legitimate data source, whereas discourse and pragmatics researchers in other traditions accept a wider variety of interactional arrangements. One problem that researchers may face in collecting authentic discourse data is access to the research site, for a sufficiently long time, and to be able to video or audio record. Other difficulties may be the time it takes to collect sufficient instances of the focal pragmatic phenomenon, or to obtain comparable data from groups of speakers with different characteristics (languages, language proficiency or other participant factors). For these reasons, researchers may opt for various forms of specifically arranged interaction. We will consider two main categories, elicited conversation and role play.

14.2.2 Elicited conversation

The term *elicited conversation* refers to any conversation staged for the purpose of data collection. In contrast to role plays, participants do not take on different social roles from their own; however, they may assume discourse roles assigned by the researcher. We can distinguish two varieties of elicited conversation.

In *conversation tasks*, participants are requested to converse about a topic or jointly reach a particular goal determined by the researcher. Instructions can be as vague as asking participants to get to know each other (e.g. Scarcella 1983; Svennevig 1999; White 1989), or they can be as specific as requiring them to respond to troubles tellings (Kerekes 1992). Data elicited through conversation tasks have been found useful for studying various aspects of conversational management (Scarcella 1983), listener responses (White 1989), the use of indexicals such as the Japanese interactional particle *ne* (Yoshimi 1999) and the effects of pragmatic transfer on the use of discourse markers and strategies. Even though conversation tasks can be designed to include symmetric or asymmetric participant configurations, studies have predominantly investigated equal status encounters.

In this regard, conversation tasks are systematically different from another type of elicited conversation, the *sociolinguistic interview.* As any kind of interview, the sociolinguistic interview is an asymmetrical speech event in which 'one party asks the questions and the other party gives the answers' (Schegloff 1992: 118). Unlike the conversation task, sociolinguistic interviews have a genre-specific structure. As part of the standard repertoire in sociolinguistic data collection (Labov 1984; Schiffrin 1987), the interviewer asks the informant about her life history, experiences and attitudes. In Labov's original design, one important function of the sociolinguistic interview was to ask the informant about highly emotional experiences under the assumption that such topics would trigger vernacular speech. In a second language context, topic investment has been shown to affect interlanguage performance (Eisenstein and Starbuck 1989). Sociolinguistic interviews with L2 learners have served as data sources for a range of discourse phenomena: conversational management and repair (Færch and Kasper 1982), the acquisition of the Japanese interactional particle *ne* (Sawyer 1992), and retroactive transfer in the listener responses of L1 speakers of Mandarin Chinese from their L2 English (Tao and Thompson 1991).

Elicited conversations can display a range of discursive configurations that is rather camouflaged by the generic category name. Although they are arranged for research purposes, under certain conditions the interactions may resemble authentic ordinary conversation quite closely. Naturalness may be significantly enhanced if the interaction is consequential for the participants (Bardovi-Harlig and Hartford 2005a). For a study on getting-acquainted talk, Svennevig (1999) recruited participants who had not met each other but were going to have regular future contact in a common social network. Schiffrin (1987) studied discourse markers through sociolinguistic group interviews among long-term neighbours. The arrangement of the interviews as multiparty rather than dyadic events, the participants' orientation to their shared history and the consequentiality of their talk for future social relations transformed the speech exchange system of interview into that of ordinary conversation. Svennevig's and Schiffrin's accounts of their data collection procedures are particularly helpful for design decisions on elicited conversation.

Although elicited conversations have the capacity to shed light on a wide range of interactional resources and practices, some research purposes require that investigators exert experimental control over participant roles, contextual factors and communicative activities. A data collection format that affords more tightly pre-structured interaction is the role play.

14.2.3 Role play

Role plays are simulations of communicative encounters, usually (but not necessarily) conducted in dyads on the basis of role descriptions or instructions. Role plays have been defined as 'a social or human activity in which participants 'take on' and 'act out' specified 'roles', often within a predefined social framework or situational blueprint (a 'scenario')' (Crookall and Saunders 1989: 15–16).

In behavioural assessment, different types of role play are distinguished according to participant involvement and extent of interaction. In spontaneous role plays, participants retain their own identities. In mimetic-replicating roleplays, participants play the role of a visually presented model, while in mimetic-pretending role plays, actors assume a different identity (Kipper 1988). Useful as these categories are as a first rough distinction, they are too broad to capture other potentially important variables that might affect the extent to which role plays resemble authentic interaction. For instance, a particular type of spontaneous role play is the idiographic role play, in which participants recall and re-run specific, recent and personally relevant extended interactions (Kern 1991). Proponents of idiographic role play argue that participants can rely on recent episodic memory, which helps to reduce the cognitive load associated with having to invent the action spontaneously.

Role plays also differ in the extent of the interaction. In interlanguage pragmatics, a distinction has been suggested between closed and open role plays (Kasper and Dahl 1991). In closed role plays, the actor responds to the description of a situation and, depending on the communicative act under study, to a standardized initiation produced by a confederate. The response is organized as a single-turn speech act. This procedure has been used to elicit speech acts such as requests (Rintell 1981; Rintell and Mitchell 1989), suggestions (Rintell 1981) and apologies (Cohen and Olshtain 1981;

Rintell and Mitchell 1989). Because the format does not allow speech act sequences to occur over multiple turns, the applicability of closed role plays is quite limited. In open role plays, on the other hand, the course and outcome of the interaction are jointly and contingently produced by the participants, on the basis of prompts specifying the initial situational context. Depending on the purpose of the investigation, open role plays can be designed to make variable demands on the participants' pragmatic and interactional abilities. At the low end of a complexity continuum, open role plays may require actors to achieve converging goals in familiar, pre-structured, routine activities, with formulaic linguistic resources. A role play of high complexity may confront the actors with diverging goals in unfamiliar, non-prestructured activities that require contingent negotiation and instantaneous use of unprepackaged resources. In interlanguage pragmatics, role plays involving contexts or practices specific to the target culture may be more challenging to second language speakers than situations that are culturally shared (Eisenstein and Bodman 1993). For instance, a fairly complex interaction could be one with an inbuilt goal conflict and interpersonal difficulties, as in the prompt in Example 2, which is designed to elicit a refusal of an offer.

EXAMPLE 2

You are at the home of your host family, the Sumners. Both the children, Charlie and Kern Sumner, have short, very ugly haircuts. At one point, they ask you how you like their hair. You answer politely that it looks very cool and comfortable. Mrs. Sumners announces proudly that she cuts their hair herself. And because you like the style, she will be glad to cut your hair to look like theirs. "Now where are my scissors . . .? , she asks.

(Gass and Houck 1999: 208)

Unlike closed role plays, open role plays that are elicited by prompts of this type evolve over many turns and different discourse phases. For their study of interlanguage refusals, Gass and Houck (1999) collected videotaped role play interactions that enabled them to examine the sequential structure of the refusal events, speaker–listener coordination through listener responses and non-verbal actions and politeness. As Fant (1992) notes, open role plays allow researchers to observe generic resources and structures of conversation that are fairly independent of particular contexts and goals, but unlike authentic discourse and elicited conversation, they also permit researchers to design contexts and roles that are likely to elicit specific speech events and communicative acts. Researchers working within Brown and Levinson's (1987) politeness theory have found open role plays effective for examining how context factors such as power, distance, and imposition influence the selection and realization of communicative acts and how the values of these factors may be changed through conversational negotiation. The potential of role plays to elicit pragmatic and sociolinguistic features in their full discourse context has been shown in cross-cultural and interlanguage pragmatics research on communicative acts such as requests (Hassall 2001; Márquez Reiter et al. 2005), expressions of gratitude (Eisenstein and Bodman 1993), apologies (García 1989), complaints (Trosborg 1995), refusals (Gass and Houck 1999; Widjaja 1997), and various face-threatening acts (Piirainen-Marsh 1995), (mis)understanding in service encounters and institutional discourse (Bremer et al. 1996), discourse cohesion (Stemmer 1981), gambits (Wildner-Bassett 1984, 1994); conversational organization and maintenance (Edmondson et al. 1984), routine formulae (Tateyama et al. 1997) and pragmatic fluency (House 1996).

As the literature indicates, open role plays can generate all aspects of conversation, but whether they provide valid representations of conversational practices in authentic contexts is another matter. Whereas external validity is a central concern in behavioural assessment and other social sciences that use role play as a research tool, only a few studies have examined the external validity of role play in pragmatics. The few studies that do exist (Edmondson and House 1991; Sasaki 1998) have mostly compared different role plays with other forms of elicited data, especially with written discourse completion questionnaires (for a summary, see Kasper and Rose 2002). Though not methodological in focus, Eisenstein and Bodman's (1993) study of expression of gratitude by native and non-native speakers of English sheds light on the effects of three data collection procedures: discourse completion questionnaires, open-ended role plays, and field notes on expressions of gratitude occurring in authentic interactions. All three data types yielded the same words and expressions, yet they differed in length and complexity. The questionnaire data were the shortest and least complex, the authentic data the longest and most complex, with the role play data coming in between. The oral data included more restatements of thanks and discussions about the received gift or service. Both role play and authentic data showed that thanking is collaboratively enacted, involving the giver as much as the receiver. In Turnbull's (2001) multimethod comparison of refusals, the role plays, while largely similar to the authentic data, contained interruptions of the requester and more repetitions, giving the role play data a 'long-winded' quality. Discussing simulated discourse in interactional sociolinguistic research, Gumperz and Cook-Gumperz (1982: 11) make the important point that the validity of role play does not hinge on an exact match between a person's action in simulated and authentic contexts. In their view,

> Experience with a wide range of natural situations can serve as the basis for recreating socially realistic experimental conditions where individuals are asked to reenact events such as job interviews with which they have become familiar in everyday life. If these naturalistic situations are skillfully constructed and not too carefully predetermined, rhetorical strategies will emerge automatically without conscious planning, as such strategies are so deeply imbedded in the participants' practices. Since it is these rhetorical devices we want to analyze, eliciting such constructed texts does not necessarily entail a loss of validity.

A critical condition for researchers to consider, then, is whether the simulated activity is grounded in participants' social experience. When this condition obtains, simulations fall under the category of idiographic role plays (Kern 1991), the type of role play recommended for its good validity in behavioural assessment research. In a comparative study of authentic and simulated employment interviews, Grieshaber (1987) found that without an experiential basis in the activity, actors produced a much reduced and stumbling version of authentic job interviews. A good example of how to anchor role played situations in participants' experience is offered by Gass and Houck (1999). For their study of interlanguage refusals, they chose as participants students from Japan who had recently been on homestay in a particular location in North America. All of the role play situations in the study were episodes in such homestay contexts (cf. Example 2 above), many of them created on the basis of 'true stories'. While researchers have a range of design options to help role play interaction approximate to authentic discourse, they have to consider carefully whether role plays are actually an effective choice for the investigative purpose. Second language speakers with limited target language proficiency may be faced with an additional difficulty if they are required to interact in an imagined context with no real-life history and consequences. It is therefore possible that in comparison to other data sources, role plays may underrepresent L2 learners' pragmatic and interactional abilities.

14.3 Questionnaires

Questionnaires are standard research instruments in the social sciences, and pragmatics is no exception. Compared with the collection of different forms of spoken interaction, questionnaires support a more limited range of investigative purposes in pragmatics research. Questionnaires produce offline responses, that is, respondents are not currently engaged in the activity addressed in the questionnaire. Excluded from study are precisely those pragmatic features that are specific to spoken interactional discourse – any aspect related to interactional contingencies, turn-taking, sequencing of actions, speaker–listener coordination, features of speech production that may have pragmatic import, such as hesitation, and all paralinguistic and non-verbal resources. What, then, can questionnaires examine in pragmatics? To answer this question, it is helpful to consider the generic properties of questionnaires. First, questionnaires are texts that have to be read, understood, and responded to. Survey research shows that respondents may understand questionnaire items in widely different ways (Belson 1981). Although careful instrument development (Brown 2001b) may improve clarity and ease of comprehension to some extent, reading is always an active interpretive process and therefore variable understandings cannot be completely eliminated. Secondly, questionnaire responses are self-reports. They provide information about what respondents believe, think, feel, or know, but not about what they do in their social life (Babbie 1998). This property of questionnaires has perhaps the most profound consequences for research in pragmatics. In order to find out how people *do* language-mediated actions, they have to be observed. Thirdly, questionnaires decontextualize their object of study and as a consequence, respondents tend to elaborate abstract items in ways that make sense to them. Questionnaire designers sometimes try to offset the variable interpretability of questionnaire items by providing more specific descriptions of the scenarios. However, there are limits to how long a text prompt can be, and a longer prompt also increases reading time and possible problems for less than completely fluent readers. From an ontological perspective on pragmatics that distinguishes between underlying decontextualized pragmalinguistic and sociopragmatic knowledge and contextualized language use, questionnaires can be seen as mediating tools to access pragmatic knowledge. However, if pragmatics is conceptualized as discursively constituted situated practices, the knowledge–use dichotomy is not sustainable and consequently a place for questionnaires in pragmatics research would seem more difficult to locate.

The three most widely used types of questionnaire in pragmatics are discourse completion tasks (DCT), multiple choice and rating scale questionnaire. They differ from each other in the type of elicited response. DCTs require a constructive, that is, participant-generated textual response that is coherent with the context specified in the stimulus item. Multiple choice and scaled response questionnaires provide fixed response alternatives from which the participant has to choose the most appropriate one.

14.3.1 Discourse completion tasks

Items in a **Discourse completion task** (DCT) include a situational description and a brief dialogue which has one turn as an open slot. The context given in the scenario is designed to constrain the open turn so that it elicits the desired communicative act.

In the classic DCT format, a rejoinder is provided to terminate the exchange; the rejoinder can be positive or negative. The open turn can also be prefaced by an interlocutor initiation (see Example 3).

EXAMPLE 3: In the lobby of a university library

Jim and Charlie have agreed to meet at six o'clock to work on a joint project. Charlie arrives on time and Jim is an hour late.

Charlie: I almost gave up on you!

Jim:_________________________

Charlie: O.K. Let's start working.

(Blum-Kulka et al. 1989)

The basic format has been variously modified (see Kasper 2000 for example items). In dialogue construction and open response formats, no rejoinder is provided.

In dialogue construction (Bardovi-Harlig and Hartford 1993; Bergman and Kasper 1993), the respondent may have to supply the second pair part to a provided first pair part or to both contributions. The open response formats may require a verbal response (Eisenstein and Bodman 1993; Olshtain and Weinbach 1993; Robinson 1992) or allow a verbal, non-verbal or no response (Beebe and Takahashi 1989b; Steinberg Du 1995; Takahashi and Beebe 1993). The choice to 'opt out' makes it possible to identify perceived sociopragmatic differences in the appropriateness of communicative acts (Bonikowska 1988), not only their format.

As DCTs are widely used in the pragmatics literature, researchers have tried to determine whether specific design features generate instrument effects, whether delivery mode affects responses and how DCT data measure up against data collected by other means. Comparing DCTs which provide a description of the situation and an opening conversational turn with ones which provide only a description of the situation, Bardovi-Harlig and Hartford (1993) found that L1 respondents were largely indifferent to this variation, whereas the L2 participants' responses showed a closer match with responses in authentic interaction when an opening turn was included. With regard to the effect of rejoinders, studies come to different conclusions. In a comparison of request items with and without rejoinder, Rose (1992) reports no significant differences between item formats. In contrast, examining the effects of absent, preferred and dispreferred rejoinders on requests, apologies and complaints, Johnston, Kasper and Ross (1998) reported that the differences in rejoinder did influence strategy choices, and that item format had different effects on the three speech acts. The observed method effect implies that results from DCTs with different item formats may not be directly comparable. A further variable feature of DCTs is the amount of information provided in the situational description that prefaces the dialogue segment. Billmyer and Varghese (2000) compared response effects of short descriptions and content-enriched descriptions on L1 and L2 speakers' request realizations. No differences between versions were found for directness levels and internal modification of the head act, but the enhanced prompt elicited longer responses and more external modification, suggesting that the enhanced descriptions provided accounts for the request that respondents could readily incorporate in their response. Several studies document that DCT responses are affected by mode and medium of delivery (Brown 2001a; Eisenstein and Bodman 1993; Kuha 1997; Rintell and Mitchell 1989; Turnbull 2001; Yuan 2001), and the presence and type of such method effects may vary between respondents of different language backgrounds and target language proficiency.

Comparisons of written DCTs with authentic data (Hartford and Bardovi-Harlig 1992; Beebe and Cummings 1996; Golato 2003; Turnbull 2001; Yuan 2001) show substantial overlap in speech act strategies and linguistic resources deployed for implementing the focal speech act, but they also register critical differences in both categories. One striking example is Golato's (2003) study of compliment responses in German.

Whereas the DCT respondents offered appreciation tokens (*danke* 'thank you') in 12.4% of their compliment responses, they did not use them at all when they participated in authentic compliment events. On the other hand, only 1 of 217 DCT responses featured an assessment + agreement pursuit (*super ne*? 'super isn't it'), a response type occurring in 12% of the authentic interactions. The comparative research supports the view that DCTs and other questionnaire formats elicit intuitional data rather than data on language use and behaviour (Golato 2003; Kasper 2000; Kasper and Rose 2002; Turnbull 2001). Pragmatic intuition can be a legitimate object of research; for instance, in studies of pragmatic development or language testing. As long as there is a clear understanding of what DCT data can and cannot deliver, DCTs remain a valuable instrument in the researcher's toolkit.

14.3.2 Multiple choice

Multiple choice (MC) has been used to examine people's preferences for speech act strategies and forms, comprehension and metapragmatic judgements. Like DCTs, MC items specify the situational context and include a prompt for a response, but rather than requiring the participant to actively construct a response, MC presents several response alternatives from which one has to be chosen (see Example 4 from a request study below).

EXAMPLE 4

You are having dinner with your friend's family. The food that your friend's mother has prepared is delicious, and you want some more. What would you say or do?

A. I would wait until the mother saw my empty plate and offered more food.
B. 'Please give me more food.'
C. 'This food sure is delicious.'
D. 'Could I have some more please?'

(Rose 1994)

While MC has been used occasionally to investigate choices of speech act strategies (Hinkel 1997; Fukushima 2000; Rose 1994; Rose and Ono 1995), research on the testing of pragmatics sounds a note of caution. Several studies have found poor reliability scores of MC questionnaires targeting strategy selection (Brown 2001a; Röver 2005; Yamashita 1996). The unreliability appears to indicate a fact of pragmatic life, namely that many speech acts can be done in a variety of context-appropriate ways. In addition, selecting possible appropriate combinations of strategies and linguistic forms in a principled manner is a daunting task for instrument designers unless the research focuses on a very narrow object. For other investigative targets, MC fares much better.

Röver (2005) shows that MCs requiring the selection of situational routines and examining how respondents understand speech acts and implicature (Bouton 1994; Carrell 1981; Koike 1989) can be constructed with satisfactory degrees of consistency.

14.3.3 Rating scales

Rating scales are the instrument of choice for investigating 'attitudinal objects' in social research and for eliciting acceptability judgments in linguistics. In pragmatics, a voluminous literature examines how appropriate, polite, deferential and so forth people assess strategies of communicative action and their linguistic realizations to be, usually in specific scenarios constructed to operationalize theoretically defined variables. Studies of 'pragmalinguistic assessment' can be theoretically derived from Hymes' theory of communicative competence (e.g. Hinkel 1996). Another type of question asks how people assess the values and weights of the contextual variables that influence strategic and linguistic choices, such as participants' relative power, social distance and the degree of imposition involved in a linguistic act. Such questions articulate sociopragmatic problems and are usually motivated by Brown and Levinson's politeness theory (see Spencer-Oatey 1996 for a comprehensive discussion of participant variables and Spencer-Oatey 1993 for a cross-cultural study).

Metapragmatic assessments can be obtained for several purposes: as a research issue in its own right; as an additional resource to help interpret performance data; as a preliminary step towards developing the instrument for the main study; or as a combination of the above. In studies using controlled data elicitation formats, researchers need to know how respondents assess the context variables built into the stimulus scenarios. Such information should not be based on researcher's intuition. Sociopragmatic assessments of possible contexts elicited in a pre-study enable researchers to ground their contextual constructions empirically and thus to improve control over contextual variables. Several works document instrument development through a sequence of pre-studies using sociopragmatic and pragmalinguistic assessments (Fukushima 2000; Hagiwara 2005; Takahashi 1995, 1996; Tokuda 2001; see also Chapter 5 in this book for a questionnaire with pragmalinguistic-oriented rating scales, and Chapter 4 for a questionnaire with sociopragmatic-oriented rating scales.)

The sociometric and psychometric literature offers a wealth of advice on how to construct scaled response instruments (e.g. Bernard 2000; Miller and Salkind 2002). In order to maximize the informativeness, reliability and validity of a scaled response instrument, social research sources recommend the following practices: 1. Composite constructs (such as 'power' or 'imposition') are unfolded into their underlying dimensions (e.g. for 'imposition' in apologizing: severity of offence, obligation to apologize, likelihood of apology acceptance, offender's face-loss; Bergman and Kasper, 1993). 2. Each dimension is operationalized by at least two indicators (e.g. for severity of offence: 'How serious is John's offence?', 'How great is the damage done to Paul by John?').

3. Rating scales have five to seven points. 4. If the instrument is prepared in different languages, the stimulus material must be cross-linguistically equivalent. The most widely used method to achieve this is backtranslation (Behling and Law 2000; also see the glossary entry in this book).

The practice of measuring 'attitudinal objects' through different types of scale is consistent with a rationalist view of pragmatics, which often includes cognitivist interpretations of Hymes' theory of communicative competence (Canale and Swain 1980). From an epistemic position that investigates social-psychological topics as matters of discursive construction rather than as intrapsychological states and processes, the question would be how participants engage evaluative pragmatic categories for practical social purposes, how they enable inferences (for the co-participants) on pragmatic evaluation, and how they make aspects of social context relevant in their interaction.

14.4 Interviews

Metapragmatic interviews – that is, interviews whose topic is a pragmatic object – can have several functions in pragmatics research. They can serve as an initial exploration of a research issue, as a means to triangulate the researcher's interpretation of authentic discourse data, as one among several data types in a multimethod approach, and as the main data source. In order to appreciate the structure and process of interviews, it is useful to consider them from a discursive and cognitive perspective. Because interviews are organized as question–answer sequences, interview respondents' answers are always shaped by the question, and at the very least in that sense, interview responses are co-constructed by default. It is therefore problematic to treat them as externalizations of stable, decontextualized belief and knowledge states. Silverman (2004) offers a useful discussion of how interviews are conceptualized in different research paradigms. Some types and applications of interviews in pragmatics can be illustrated by Knapp, Hopper, and Bell's (1984) and Miles' (1994) studies on compliments in American English. Knapp et al. conducted a large-scale survey interview with partly closed-ended questions and brief responses, focusing primarily on the forms of compliments and compliment responses. Data were content-analysed and frequencies reported. Miles' qualitative study was based on the observation of compliment exchanges in authentic discourse, aiming at compliment forms and their distribution, and on interviews in order to understand the social meanings and functions of complimenting from the community members' perspectives. The questions were open-ended and respondents engaged in extensive narratives and commentary. Data were analysed interpretively, with particular attention to the respondents' discursive constructions. The methodological differences between Knapp et al.'s and Miles' studies resulted in remarkable discrepancies in substantive outcomes. One such difference is the preferred response pattern identified in the two studies. According to the observational part of Miles' study, only 7 per cent of the recipients expressed agreement with the compliment, whereas Knapp et al. registered 46 per cent of the compliment responses as agreements, of which only 16 per cent were minimized. Miles' findings concur with the outcomes of other observational studies on complimenting in American English (for a recent review, see Golato 2005), suggesting that the interview responses in Knapp et al.'s study were guided by prescriptive pragmatic norms and ideologies. The different methods used in the compliment research illustrate well that self-reports, whether DCT or interviews, cannot substitute recorded observation if the investigative goal is to establish pragmatic practices.

Researchers' interest in social life from the participants' perspective, and especially in the relationship of identity, language and language learning in multilingual societies, has fuelled an upsurge of qualitative interview studies in the social sciences. Judging by the published literature, for many investigators the royal road to the participants' perspective is the qualitative interview. The risk of engaging a research tool that bears a strong family resemblance to a common activity type in ordinary social life is that it does not appear to invite the critical scrutiny given to other data collection methods. But as the comprehensive literature on research interviews shows, different ontological and epistemological stances on interviews result in distinct methods for analysis and consequently in different research outcomes. Reports of failed qualitative interviews (Boxer 1996; Briggs 1986) encourage researchers to turn their disciplinary knowledge on research interviews and to consult the literature on the topic (e.g. Gubrium and Holstein 2002).

14.5 Diaries

Diary studies are investigations whose primary data are one or several persons' journal entries about their experiences relating to the topic of the study. Diaries are the least pre-structured type of self-report, and it is this property that allows them to combine most of the features characteristic of the self-report categories discussed in the preceding sections. Similar to scaled response instruments and interviews, they may provide data on past experiences and subjective theories, but they can also include retrospective reports on specific recent events. Irrespective of their focus, diaries are usually textual constructions and therefore they need to be analysed from an explicit text analytical perspective. Two types of diary study can be distinguished: the self-study, in which the diarist and the researcher are the same person, and the commissioned diary study, in which the researcher requests participants to keep a journal that is then submitted to and analysed by the researcher, with or without participant collaboration. Diaries distinguish themselves from other forms of self-report in that they are – in the self-study variety at least – participant-directed, since the diarist decides on the topics, form and timing of entries without being constrained by a response format or particular type of social interaction.

Because of the in-built participant perspective of personal journals, diary studies in second language research have primarily investigated individual differences, learner strategies, teachers' and students' experiences of second language classroom learning and teaching and sojourners' and immigrants' perceptions of second language learning and communication in particular social and institutional contexts. Although diaries have a long history as a research method in second language acquisition (Schumann 1998), they gained renewed interest with the advent of post-structuralist theories in second language studies. Diaries have been advocated as a particularly suitable medium to study learner subjectivity and investment (Peirce 1994). Published diary studies on L2 pragmatic development include self-studies on the diarist's classroom learning of Japanese pragmatics (Cohen 1997), learning how to take leave in Indonesian during an in-country sojourn (Hassall (2006) and the socialization of taste during dinner-table conversations in Indonesia (DuFon 2006)). Commissioned diaries vary considerably in the extent to which they mandate that entries be made on particular topics and according to a fixed schedule. For an analytical perspective that considers diaries as autobiographic narrative constructions, Pavlenko (2007) offers comprehensive discussion and recommendations.

14.6 Verbal report

The self-report methods considered so far generate data about past events, hypothetical scenarios or participants' views on various topics. In contrast, verbal report (VR) protocols are verbalizations of thought processes that a person entertains while doing a task. VR were developed for discipline-specific purposes in many social sciences, among them cognitive psychology, literacy studies and interactional sociolinguistics. The most influential work is *Protocol Analysis: Verbal Report as Data* (Ericsson and Simon 1993). On the basis of an information-processing theory of memory, the book lays out a theoretical framework for predicting the conditions under which verbal reports provide valid accounts of thought processes and offers detailed instructions for creating such experimental conditions.

In a nutshell, the theory proposes that information processed in short-term memory while a participant is carrying out a task is reportable and veridical. In contrast, information that is not processed in short-term memory, such as perceptual processes, motor processes and all automated processes, are not available for report. Veridical report is also possible immediately after task completion, when the attended information is still in short-term memory. Once out of short-term memory, information will be lost or encoded in long-term memory. Since storage in and retrieval from long-term memory entails further processing, the most valid reports are concurrent or immediately consecutive verbalizations. Delayed retrospective protocols may only have a tenuous relationship to the original attended information. In addition to type of information and recency of processing, the instruction to participants for verbalization may critically influence the quality of the report. Prompts should only request participants to say what they are thinking; they should not be asked to describe, explain or hypothesize because such requests will prompt different cognitive processes than those required by the task and will interfere with the task-related processes.

Applications of verbal protocols in second language research follow Ericsson's and Simon's (1993) theory more or less consistently (Cohen 1996, 1998; Færch and Kasper 1987; Gass and Mackey 2000). In interlanguage pragmatics, a study conducted by Robinson (1992) illustrates different types of verbal protocol and raises important design issues. Robinson (1992) asked intermediate and advanced Japanese learners of English to think aloud while completing a DCT on refusals. In accordance with Ericsson and Simon's (1993) prescriptions, participants were requested to verbalize whatever they were thinking while focusing on the task, in the language they were thinking in, and they were given a practice session. The think-aloud protocol was immediately followed by a consecutive verbal report based on play-back of the audio-recorded concurrent protocol. Against the theory's predictions, the concurrent and consecutive reports turned out quite differently. The concurrent reports were task-focused and identified the information that the participant was attending to, the planning decisions, considerations of alternatives, the consulted pragmalinguistic and sociopragmatic knowledge and the difficulties experienced in deciding on a response. In the consecutive reports, despite the stimulated recall, participants often had difficulties remembering their task-related thoughts. Yet in some cases, they provided more complete reports than in the concurrent verbalization and added informative details about the reasoning for their planning decisions and the sources of their L1 and L2 pragmatic knowledge.

The main controversy surrounding VR methodology has centred upon the validity and completeness of verbal protocols, without questioning their theoretical foundation. But literacy researchers in particular have also raised issue with the notion that VR is non-social and insensitive to context (Witte and Cherry 1994). Smagorinsky (1998, 2001) has proposed reconceptualizing VR from the ontological perspective of cultural-historical activity theory. From a Bakhtinian perspective, he argues that all forms of speech are inherently dialogical and addressee oriented (see also the response by Ericsson and Simon 1998). Taking the question of recipient-design in VR to interlanguage pragmatics, Sasaki (2003) asked respondents to a scaled response questionnaire to think aloud while rating the appropriacy of contextualized English refusals. As in Robinson's (1992) study, the participants were proficient L2 speakers of English and L1 speakers of Japanese. Although the researchers encouraged the participants in both studies to verbalize their thoughts in either or both languages, the respondents in Robinson's study used English consistently, whereas seven of the eight participants in Sasaki's study only used Japanese or switched between Japanese and English. Through their language choice, the participants oriented to the investigators' status as L1 speakers of either English or Japanese. Furthermore, the Japanese-speaking respondents in Sasaki's study displayed their orientation to the researcher through direct address, shifts to a more formal speech style (*-desu/-masu*) and the use of interactional particles. As Sasaki's study shows, recipient design is systematic in VR, but it may escape researchers' attention if the data are content-analysed rather than examined through a detailed discourse analysis.

The combination of authentic or simulated interaction with retrospective interviews is a common procedure in interactional sociolinguistics. For studies of miscommunication in interethnic encounters, Gumperz and Cook-Gumperz (1982: 19) recommended stimulated recall of a preceding recorded conversation as a technique for evaluating 'how participants reflexively address the social activity that is being constituted by their ongoing talk'. In the European Science Foundation Project on Second Language Acquisition by Adult Immigrants, different types of authentic and simulated spoken discourse were supplemented by feedback sessions focusing on participants' understanding of the recorded interaction, their attitudes, intentions and experience (Bremer et al. 1996). Fiksdal (1990) used microanalysis and focused playback to examine the temporal organization and uncomfortable moments in cross-cultural gatekeeping interviews. Participants first watched the videotaped interaction they participated in and provided any commentary they wished to make. In a second viewing, the researcher stopped the tape and asked the participants for comments 'at all moments that seemed uncomfortable because of the topic or because of specific comments of the participants while viewing it; and (...) at all moments of postural change' (Fiksdal 1990: 66–7). The comments during the playback session provided a crucial source of information about participants' understanding and intent at those particular points in the discourse. In several respects, the use of retrospective interviews in interactional sociolinguistics and ethnographic microanalysis is more akin to analytic induction than to protocol analysis in the information processing approach (see Smagorinsky 1998 and Ericsson and Simon 1998 for discussion).

14.7 Conclusion

For reasons of exposition, this chapter has focused on the design features of individual data-collection procedures and their applications in pragmatic research. But as mentioned several times in passing, studies often combine two or more methods. A multi-method approach is standard in ethnographic studies, including participant observation, audio- and video-recordings of interactions, interviews and collection of documents. Researchers in different disciplinary traditions advocate the use of multiple data collection procedures as a means to offset inherent instrument or observer bias. Material collected by means of complementary methods and from different sources allows triangulation, which may be necessary or desirable in order to increase the validity and reliability of a study.

The data collection methods discussed in this chapter have generated a wealth of knowledge about pragmatics and discourse and will continue to do so. Innovative forms of data gathering, especially those utilizing advances in communication technology, open new perspectives for theory and research. As video recording of interaction becomes increasingly more standard, proposals to reconsider the interrelations of language and embodied action are most likely to gain ground, and with them the concept of language as a system with a separate existence from gesture may become increasingly questionable. In comparative and developmental pragmatics, researchers will continue to borrow from neighbour disciplines, while also developing their own methods suitable for investigating different research objects and questions. But progress in the field depends in no small measure on discourse analysts' and pragmaticians' willingness to reflexively examine their work tools with the theoretical and analytical apparatus of their disciplines. Such critical examination is more than an interesting exercise. By gaining a theoretical perspective on data collection and analysis formats and their ontological and epistemological underpinnings, researchers are better equipped to design studies whose metatheoretical and theoretical positions are coherently extended into method.

KEY POINTS

1. Methods of data collection and analysis extend research paradigms and theories into research practice. Methodological choices have to be compatible with the paradigmatic and theoretical stances adopted in a study, and they should enable researchers to optimally meet the investigative purpose.
2. Video- and audio-recorded authentic interaction in ordinary conversation and institutional settings provides an inexhaustible resource for pragmatic and discourse studies. Such studies also provide a basis for comparison with electronically mediated interaction and other data sources.
3. As an expanding and increasingly important environment of social interaction, electronically mediated communication invites research from a range of pragmatic and discourse-analytical perspectives.
4. Talk elicited through conversation tasks and role plays can be a useful alternative to authentic interaction. However, elicited forms of interaction should be chosen because they are more appropriate for the research purpose. Whether the phenomena under investigation are structurally similar to those in authentic interaction is an empirical matter and needs to be examined.
5. Questionnaires should be used if and when they are better suited to meet the purpose of a study than other methods of data collection, not because they seem to be the easier option. Questionnaires generate decontextualized self-report data and cannot replace observation and recording if pragmatic and discourse practices are the research goal. If the goal is to find out what people say or write they know about discourse practices and if general structural patterns and tendencies rather than contextual specifics and locally generated meanings are of interest, well-designed questionnaires are an appropriate and effective means of collecting data. The literature on surveys and social measurement offers assistance with designing a questionnaire that is valid and reliable for its purpose.
6. Like questionnaires, interviews, diaries and verbal report protocols are self-report data. They show how the interview respondent, diarist or reporter describes, explains or otherwise makes sense of pragmatic objects and events. The literature on research interviews, autobiographic and narrative analysis and

verbal report provides theoretical perspectives and practical guidance for conducting pragmatic research in these genres.

7. A reflexive stance on methods of data collection and analysis, together with technical skill, enhances the quality of research in cross-cultural and interlanguage pragmatics.

DISCUSSION QUESTIONS

1. According to empirical studies, how (and to what extent) does the procedure for collecting spoken data influence the language that is produced?
2. If you want to investigate spoken interaction, what are the relative strengths and weaknesses of using authentic discourse, elicited conversation or role play?
3. What issues should you take into account when devising a DCT for cross-cultural research?
4. Audiotape a conversation between yourself and another person, first obtaining permission to do so. Try to transcribe a few minutes of talk on the tape. What are some of the problems you have in your efforts to make a transcription? Are there aspects of the talk you find on the tape which surprise you? Were there features of your own speech you were not previously aware of?
5. After a few weeks, listen to the tape again and compare what you hear with your transcription. Are there differences? Revise your transcript, being careful not to 'normalize' it. In other words, don't change what you hear into something that makes better sense or is grammatically correct. How is this authentic talk different from what you might find in a novel as an example of 'conversation'?[1]
6. Look at each of the empirical chapters in this book and, for each one, note the data collection procedure(s) that were used. Why do you think the researchers chose those methods? What are the strengths and weaknesses of these procedures for the research issue(s) they were designed to investigate?

Note

1. Discussion questions 4 and 5 were contributed by Laura Miller.

Suggestions for further reading

Bardovi-Harlig, K., and Hartford, B. (eds) (2005). *Interlanguage Pragmatics. Exploring Institutional Talk.* Mahwah, NJ: Lawrence Erlbaum.

Félix-Brasdefer, C. (2003). Validity in data collection methods in pragmatics research, in P. Kempchinsky and C.-E. Piñeros (Eds) *Theory, Practice, and Acquisition: Papers from the 6th Hispanic Linguistics Symposium and the 5th Conference on the Acquisition of Spanish and Portuguese.* Somerville, MA: Cascadilla Press, 239–57.

Golato, A. (2005). *Compliments and Compliment Responses*. Amsterdam: Benjamins.

Kasper, G. (2006). Speech acts in interaction: towards discursive pragmatics, in K. Bardovi-Harlig, C. Félix-Brasdefer, and A. Omar (eds), *Pragmatics and Language Learning, Vol. 11*. Honolulu, HI: National Foreign Language Resource Center, 281–314.

Silverman, D. (ed.) (2004). *Qualitative Research*. 2nd edition. London: Sage.

Silverman, D. (2006). *Interpreting Qualitative Data*. 3rd edition. London: Sage.

15 Recording and Analysing Talk Across Cultures

Meredith Marra

Chapter Outline

15.1 Introduction 304
15.2 Using authentic data to research workplace communication 306
15.3 Researching in Māori workplaces 309
15.4 Adapting the LWP methodology for working with Māori organizations 311
15.5 Conclusion 317
Key points 319
Discussion questions 320
Notes 320
Suggestions for further reading 321

15.1 Introduction

Successfully collecting and analysing naturally occurring data from busy workplaces involves considerable thought and reflection. When the Language in the Workplace (LWP) project team at Victoria University of Wellington began investigating effective workplace talk in the mid-1990s, a research priority was the collection and analysis of authentic data; we were interested in exploring what people actually did when they talked together at work. This approach contrasted with many of the existing studies which used interview and survey data, that is self-report data where informants typically report what they think they do. As well as recording and analysing naturally occurring talk, it was also a goal to focus on workplace communication specifically in our local New Zealand community, with an assumption that there are potentially important differences based on a distinctive New Zealand culture. And although many New Zealand workplaces appear to orient to some kind of national culture which mirrors the dominant group in society, this is by no means the case for all workplaces. This chapter describes some of the issues that arise when researchers work with groups who consciously foster attention to minority cultural norms and ethnically distinctive ways of doing things in the workplace. I document how working with an ethnically different group inevitably introduces challenges and complexities to the research process which invite investigation.

Over the last decade, the original methodology used by the research team when it began in 1996 has, from necessity and by design, evolved to handle new kinds of workplaces and new technical, logistical and ethical issues. Throughout the project, however, the methodology has consistently followed two important principles: (i) identifying issues of interest to both the organizations and the researchers, who cooperate in developing agreed research objectives; and (ii) building strong relationships with volunteers in organizations and then handing over control of what is recorded to these participants (Stubbe 2001; Holmes and Stubbe 2003). The participatory research design (see Stubbe 1998) takes up the call to negotiate research motivations and outcomes with participants. As argued by Cameron, our goal is to 'break down the division between the researcher and the community' (1985: 2), to avoid researching *on*, and instead to research *with* our participants.[1]

The approach also takes account of Celia Roberts' (2003) argument that applied research of this nature needs to address concerns which are not only practically relevant but also have goals and methods that are developed collaboratively with the participants in an ongoing relationship.[2] As a number of researchers have noted, research is a form of social relationship, and one which is ongoing (Cameron et al. 1992; Garner, Raschka and Sercombe 2006; Sarangi 2006). This means in practice that our research design involves co-participation from the outset and, with the academic researchers' support, the workplace participants themselves collect the spoken data. With technical advice, volunteers audio-record and video-record their everyday workplace interactions. This process is entirely within the volunteers' control, and the involvement of the academic researchers is systematically minimized. Indicative of the continuing nature of the research process, we return to the workplaces at intervals for de-briefing interviews and focus-group discussions which have proved fruitful in yielding valuable material for interpretation.

This data collection methodology proved comparatively straightforward to operationalize in the white collar workplaces where we began our research. We felt relatively confident and comfortable because the cultures of the organizations were similar to our personal workplace experiences. When the data collection expanded beyond these government departments and corporate organizations into factory, medical and IT settings, our task was more difficult, although still fairly manageable. We needed to take into account logistical factors relating to the different ways of working which are specific to these environments, whether it was the loud machinery and the mobile workforce of the factory, or the peripatetic doctors and nurses who interacted with immobile patients in hospitals or even the integral role that the computer played in the communication patterns of the IT workers. In each case, consulting throughout with the workplace participants, we made practical decisions on ways of adapting the data collection procedures to meet the challenges identified, while still adhering to the underlining research philosophy.

In each of the 20 workplaces covered by the description above, the cultural orientation of the workplaces could be considered as Pākehā, that is the dominant 'European-based' culture of New Zealand. The most recent phase of the LWP research, however, compares the leadership styles at work of Pākehā and Māori (the indigenous people of New Zealand who constitute approximately 15 per cent of the population), and one of our particular aims is to explore what effective Māori leaders do that might be overlooked when their leadership and communication styles are viewed through a mainstream lens. Collecting data from workplaces where Māori *tikanga* (ways of doing things) prevails has provided interesting challenges beyond any faced in our research to date. Māori researchers have been at pains to point out the abuses suffered by indigenous peoples in the name of research in previous decades, and have actively advocated ways of researching with Māori partners which are 'respectful, ethical, sympathetic and useful' (Smith 1999: 9).

In this chapter, we outline some of the central methodological and analytical issues raised by our cross-cultural research.[3] This involves unpacking the Pākehā assumptions we have made in devising our methodology, and relating them to important ethical and cultural aspects of the *Māori Kaupapa* research design which has been advocated for research involving Māori issues and people. We describe our efforts to adapt the LWP methodology in appropriate ways while we attempt to 'amplify others' voices' (Pringle 2005).[4]

15.2 Using authentic data to research workplace communication

The first step in adapting procedures for working with Māori organizations was to identify the philosophy which informed the existing methodological design. The aim of this process was to make explicit the assumptions that we were inevitably making as Pākehā researchers.

15.2.1 Basic methodological principles

As described in the introduction, one overriding principle that shapes our research is that control should remain with the volunteers who record their interactions for our research. The result is the participatory methodology which has been developed over the course of the project's life, which includes working with all participants in articulating jointly agreed research goals and in developing appropriate research practices (see Stubbe 1998). The advantage of this philosophy is the trust that steadily builds between the team members, that is the academic participants and the workplace participants, and the productive ongoing relationships which are thus formed with various workplaces.

Unavoidably, this philosophy also has some disadvantages. For example, it is the workplace participants who decide what is recorded, how much is recorded and when this recording takes place. The composition of the corpus cannot be predetermined, and instead evolves naturally as data is collected. Indeed, we have to rely on the volunteers to give us data that they feel is representative of their workplace interaction. One way of overcoming this disadvantage, however, is ensuring that all participants accept that our focus is on the positive, on what works, rather than the on negative and unproductive. With a focus on effective workplace communication, the project team adopts an 'appreciative inquiry' approach (Hammond 1996), consistently seeking to identify features of successful communication at work. This means that we actively select organizations, teams and individuals who are recommended to us (by other organizations, colleagues or employees) as good models of effective communication. The value of our philosophy is that workplace participants feel confident in providing their data to us, and among the practical benefits is the fact that the quality of the data has been routinely high.

15.2.2 Data collection procedures

The LWP team uses a methodology developed within a broadly ethnographic framework. As well as collecting recordings of naturally occurring workplace talk, we also use participant observation, debriefing interviews and focus groups, as appropriate. This ensures that we gather information from a wide range of communication channels and contexts within each workplace to provide a basis for a thorough description of the communication practices of the workplace participants.

The first step in the process, once an organization and individuals have been recommended as exemplary, is to make contact with senior management. In most cases, we have used personal contacts to facilitate this stage of the research process. This has the added benefit of providing an insider who can support our work and vouch for our standing and trustworthiness, giving us increased credibility with our workplace participants. The task of persuading organizations that working with us offered genuine advantages to them became easier as our research progressed and our reputation was built (we could provide publications for them to read, for example). But the involvement of internal support nonetheless remains one of the key indicators of the success of the data collection process; where we have had enthusiastic insiders sponsoring our cause with senior management and other employees, the task of convincing an organization of the worth of the research is infinitely easier.

Once we have organizational permission, we typically give an open presentation to interested staff members, and provide ideas regarding possible benefits of the proposed research to the organization. This is an effective way of promoting discussion of the form of the organizations' research goals which will eventually be integrated with our own. We similarly provide a description of our typical data collection procedures, and invite comment and feedback on ways in which these may need to be adapted or changed to suit particular workplace contexts. The practising workplace is not a sterile experimental site, and for employees their main task is their work, not the recording that may be going on around them; while data collection might be our primary focus, it is not the primary focus of those we record. Thus begins our negotiations and the building of a working relationship: ensuring that workplace participants give genuine informed consent and understand their right to delete material; providing a commitment to report preliminary findings as soon as possible; guaranteeing confidentiality, not only as a component of the ethical requirements of working with people, but also to ensure that people feel confident and comfortable about the process and that they do not fear negative consequences.

With data collection procedures agreed upon by all parties, volunteers record a range of their everyday interactions using lapel mikes and individual audio recorders (originally a cassette walkman, but now using MiniDisc and digital recording devices). In general, volunteers record approximately 4 hours of data over two to three weeks, all the time retaining complete control over what they do and do not record. Along with the recordings, each volunteer fills out a background information sheet providing ethnographic details, and they sign a consent form permitting us to use the data for research purposes. To supplement the audio recordings, we also video-record a series of meetings using small fixed cameras.

After a period of three to six months, depending on the amount of data involved, the research team goes back into the participating workplaces to report on progress and findings, and to collect further feedback from workplace participants. Typically our relationship with workplaces continues through personal contacts, and in a number of cases participants from the workplaces have become more directly involved in particular aspects of the analysis as Research Associates. During this preliminary analysis, certain topics and interactions emerge as potentially fruitful for further research, and these become the focus of continuing in-depth analysis, often with insightful input from these Research Associates and with the support of the workplace participants.

Our aim has always been to operate in ways considered objectively ethical (i.e. in line with the principles of any Research Ethics Committee), and more importantly in ways in which we as researchers are also personally comfortable. As we began working with Māori workplaces, it became apparent that the principles guiding our approach to workplace research were consistent with those considered acceptable by researchers engaged with Māori issues, but there were crucial differences in the ways in which the respect and control we were espousing were enacted in practice in Māori research contexts.

15.3 Researching in Māori workplaces

After the 1970s, there was a period in New Zealand where research on the Māori population seemed to cease altogether, despite the growing recognition of the importance of this cultural group as New Zealand's indigenous population. Critical reasons for this implicit ban were a growing understanding of the effects of the power differential between the typically Pākehā researchers and those being researched, a recognition of the exploitative nature of much previous research, and a challenge by Māori researchers to the claims of objectivity by Pākehā researchers in Māori contexts (Smith 1999, Pringle 2005). A result of this backlash, which originated largely from the Māori population themselves, was the significant support given to Kaupapa Māori research, an approach which calls for a 'decolonization' of methodologies (Smith 1999).

At its most basic, this approach argues that ethically responsible Māori research should be carried out in a way which is culturally framed, and which acknowledges a Māori worldview; it gives 'primacy to an Indigenous Māori paradigm' and forces the researcher to approach topics 'from an alternate [Māori] philosophic orientation' (Ruwhiu and Wolfgramm 2006: 51). In seminal work on Kaupapa Māori research, Linda Tuhiwai Smith (1999: 120) set out a framework prescribing the adoption of culturally specific ideas:

1. Aroha ki te tangata (a respect for people).
2. Kanohi kitea (the seen face, that is present yourself to people face to face).
3. Titoro, whakarongo . . . korero (look, listen . . . speak).
4. Manaaki ki te tangata (share and host people, be generous).
5. Kia tupato (be cautious).
6. Kaua e takahia te mana o te tangata (do not trample over the *mana*[5] of people).
7. [K]aua e mahaki (don't flaunt your knowledge).

These guidelines draw on various cultural values, and are, significantly, expressed in recognizable proverbs (an important form of expression with high currency in Māori culture[6]). As noted above, on the surface these guidelines, which largely advocate respect and engagement, appear to be reasonable and obvious goals for any ethical researcher. Their application in Māori settings, however, requires a deeper understanding of the subtle messages conveyed by proverbs deeply embedded in Māori culture and expressing fundamental Māori values.

For us, as Pākehā researchers, the largest obstacle was undoubtedly our own cultural background. As James Ritchie, a much-admired and respected (by both Māori and Pākehā) New Zealand sociologist, noted in his discussion of becoming bicultural, '[in] the Māori world I am an outsider, a visitor, and always will be' (1992: 51). This is a factor we acknowledge as one of our limitations. Nevertheless we are committed to finding mutually beneficial ways of working with Māori people in Māori organizations. The practical reality is that although the ideal research model for indigenous groups involves only indigenous people as researchers on indigenous topics, there are simply not as yet sufficient numbers of trained indigenous researchers to undertake the research that Māori people have identified as desirable. Smith acknowledges this problem, and recognizes the necessity that in many cases Pākehā researchers have needed to act as 'mentors' in the research process (Smith 1999: 178).

However, bicultural methodology carries with it many inherent challenges. These include developing a productive and acceptable balance between the analytical perspectives of the non-indigenous outsider on the one hand, and the insights and perceptions of the indigenous insiders concerning the meaning and significance of research material. One fruitful way forward is suggested by Garner et al. (2006). Developing a framework introduced by Fiske (1992), they propose 'a social relations approach' to ethical research with minority groups. The model comprises four dimensions which Fiske (1992: 690ff) labels (i) an equality matching relationship, (ii) a market pricing relationship, (iii) an authority ranking relationship and (iv) a communal sharing relationship. These dimensions are defined along two parameters: equality-inequality; independence-interdependence.

While the labels are not appealing, Fiske's concepts are useful. Simplifying slightly, we can make use of this model to examine our research relationships from the point of view of (i) solidarity relationships (ii) costs and benefits (including economic, social and cultural) (iii) authority and power relations and (iv) information and skill sharing based on different strengths. Thus, from our perspective, the model provides a way of evaluating the kinds of social relationships which we inevitably engage in when we work with Māori participants as co-researchers. It provides a way of drawing our attention to areas of potential problems and misunderstanding due to the taken- for-granted nature of many aspects of the research process for us as academics. For example, what kind of social relationships do we establish with the workplace participants and with our Māori research assistants? Are they colleagues, friends, advisors, experts? How do these relationships develop over time? What are the costs and benefits of participating in the research for each party? The commitment of some participants, for instance, may be directly related to who is paying them for what, rather than to less tangible rewards or costs. Who has power and authority in different situations? Who decides, for instance, what will be recorded and for how long? And what are the academic researchers expected to contribute to the workplaces where they are working? What social and professional obligations do they incur from their workplace participants' perspectives? What skills are they expected to develop and share?

One particular strength of the model from our perspective is that it takes account of the fact that the social relationship between the academic researchers and the workplace participants is not fixed, but is rather a developing one which is constantly negotiated as the research progresses, and moreover, that the perspectives of each about what is important at any particular point may differ (Garner et al. 2006: 70).

With this in mind, in collaboration with the workplace participants, we believe that we have found ways of adapting our approach to meet the challenges of working ethically with Māori people in Māori organizations. I turn now to a detailed description of how data on the ways in which people communicate in Māori organizations was gathered.

15.4 Adapting the LWP methodology for working with Māori organizations

The most important factor helping us to meet our goal of ethical responsibility in relation to working with Māori organizations has been the growing role of a Māori research team within the wider research group.[7] Even during earlier phases of our research, when our focus was on effective communication in New Zealand workplaces more generally, we were fortunate to have the support of Māori advisors and colleagues. Harima Fraser (Te Arawa) from Te Puni Kōkiri (Ministry of Māori Development), for example, and Mike Hollings (Ngati Raukawa) who has worked at three different government organizations during the period of our research, have both been involved in the planning of this project from its inception. An invaluable team of advisors, research associates and research assistants continue to provide guidance in all aspects of the methodological design, ensuring that we approach, interact and consult with Māori workplaces in culturally appropriate ways.

15.4.1 Addressing Māori Kaupapa philosophies

In an earlier section, I listed Smith's (1999) description of an appropriate methodology for investigating Māori topics and for working with Māori people: [show] respect for people; present yourself to people face to face; look, listen . . .speak; share and host people; be cautious; do not trample over the mana of people; don't flaunt your knowledge. There I commented on the superficial similarity between these translations of Māori sayings and good ethical practice. To gain a better understanding of these cultural beliefs, we need to explore the deeper meaning behind the translations.

The Māori workplace participants with whom we have worked typically use English as their principle working language. Because they are using the same native variety as is used by the majority of workplaces in New Zealand, there is understandably a common (mistaken) belief for many New Zealanders that everyone interprets English from the same cultural perspective. This opens up the potential for extensive miscommunication, that is there is an assumption that if I believe I understand the words that you use, we should understand each other. This was the impetus for Metge and Kinloch's *Talking Past Each Other* (1978). The same issue arises when we try to interpret Smith's outline for ethical Māori research; we risk misinterpreting the concept by taking the maxims at a literal level.

In practice, enacting these principles meant that every step in our research process required some kind of adaptation. The principles speak to the very heart of the research motivation, and cannot simply be addressed by minor tweaking to the research methods which emerge from a Western worldview (Ruwhiu and Wolfgramm 2006). For example, to show respect in our Pākehā organizations, we aimed to be unobtrusive or negatively polite in Brown and Levinson's (1987) terms. Our goal was always to avoid imposing on busy participants; we aimed to be practically invisible in the data collection phase, following our sociolinguistic assumptions regarding the importance of minimizing observer effects. In Smith's outline of Kaupapa Māori research, however, this behaviour could be considered disrespectful. To show respect we needed to address issues of positive politeness and make efforts to build solidarity with our workplace colleagues. This meant 'fronting up' in the organizations to show our commitment to the research goals of benefiting Māori, by being visible and available, being involved, as well as accepting hospitality and reciprocating in turn. To be accepted takes time, and respect is earned through displays of appropriate behaviour. In every way our goal was to become accepted group members.

To elucidate how these differences are manifest in the modified research design, I revisit the four steps which form the basis of our methodology: make contact – negotiate goals and procedures; volunteers record their own interaction; initial feedback given to workplace participants; in-depth analysis by the research team. In each step there were modifications. These modifications can be usefully understood as a form of decentring (cf Brislin 1976; see Chapters 4, 5 and the Glossary); instead of translating the language used in the research, our task was to adapt the research procedures in culturally appropriate ways.

Make contact

Step one is generally a quick and simple negotiation in Pākehā organizations that takes place in a formal meeting using past practices as a starting point for discussion. In Māori workplaces, however, our introduction to the organization typically occurs over a longer period of time. Although we used the first staff meeting of one organization as a chance to ensure that everyone understood the procedures that would be followed, this presentation was preceded by extensive interaction between the research team and various individuals and groups, as well as collaborative discussions within the organization. By the time of the formal presentation, everyone was already in agreement and the chance was taken to formally welcome us into their group. At the end of this first recording session, food and drink was provided – a very typical and ethnically appropriate indication of acceptance in this large group meeting in a Māori workplace (Metge 2001). In a second Māori organization, the CEO escorted us around the organization, introducing us individually to each staff member, and ensuring everyone was fully informed about the research. In both cases, it was clear from the outset that we would be involved in the organization rather than remaining as 'researchers'.

Volunteers' record

The individual data collection process remained relatively similar in both cultures. However, when it came to following up with volunteers in order to organize the collection of filled tapes and completed consent forms, we made a point of doing this by telephone rather than email, and preferably in person, that is following the second principle of presenting ourselves face to face. There are any numbers of benefits in this small change: not only are you showing your ongoing commitment by being present in the workplace, but as researchers we also gained invaluable 'by the by' ethnographic information that is otherwise inaccessible.

Initial feedback

Whereas in Pākehā organizations the first official feedback session is a time for us to present our 'expert' analysis of the data, and that is precisely what the organization expects, in the Māori organizations the sessions typically become interactive workshops where the research participants and workplace participants negotiate understandings and knowledge-sharing occurs. For example, instead of making claims about what constitutes an effective Māori workplace based on data analysis, our most satisfying interactions have been those where the discussion has been built around asking workplace participants about what they consider important, and also asking if possible interpretations we can postulate based on the discourse are credible or even possible. This practice recognizes the various types of information and skills that we all bring to the table. The results are a richer and more culturally sensitive set of interpretations.

In-depth analysis

These feedback workshops also help identify what is considered worthy of further investigation by our Māori co-participants. If our goal is to demonstrate and explicate what can be misunderstood when minority group communication is viewed through a mainstream lens, then we need to recognize the important information that our workplace participants have from experiencing these misunderstandings. Our analyses are also informed by the very fruitful discussions we have enjoyed with workplace participants when we take our academic findings back for discussion and, to a certain extent, validation.

In all four steps, the mutually beneficial relationships that develop are paramount to the success of the research, and these are built on deep mutual respect which is established in ongoing practice. This requires a certain degree of accommodation from all parties, but recognizing the differences goes a long way to addressing them.

It is also important to note that there are many interesting features of the data we have collected which remain the same regardless of the cultural orientation of the group. As just one example, once they had agreed to become co-participants in the research, volunteers took great pleasure in competing to collect data, and on more than one occasion two participants actually recorded the same interaction. The following extract, which was recorded in a Māori organization, could just as easily have been recorded in a Pākehā organization. Ants and Daniel, two senior leaders, recorded their interactions in the same period. Daniel describes Ants' speed in being the first to bring out his recorder using the analogy of participating in a gun fight in the Wild West!

EXAMPLE 1

Context: Regular reporting meeting of a team of seven people in a Māori organization

Ants: I didn't bring it to this session cos I knew I I
Daniel: no he's a fast draw
we had a meeting last week . . .
he pulled his one out before I could put mine up
[laughter]

Irrespective of cultural orientation, the first time the video cameras are used in an organization, the novelty of the situation uniformly results in humour. Female participants typically joke about their need for lipstick, new dresses and new hairstyles; male colleagues are teased about their choice of attire: *I wondered why Caleb was in early this morning with a full length mirror under his arm.* Those that are shy tend to be explicit about avoiding being 'in shot', and their behaviour becomes the focus of humour: *Well they're gonna see the back of your head – 'spose they're getting your best side!*[8]

In Māori workplaces, these kinds of comments acquire additional significance which must be borne in mind in interpretation and analysis. An important cultural value for Māori is the expectation of modesty (*whakaiti*) and the avoidance of appearing to boast (*whakahihi*). Yvonne, a leader in a Māori workplace, regularly refers to this value as the basis for a humorous comment. At the first meeting we recorded in her organization, the cameras prompted humorous reactions, as they always do. Yvonne commented that she predicted the room would divide into those who 'performed' for the cameras, showing off and boasting (*whakahihi*), and those who took a back seat and kept a low profile (*whakaiti*).

EXAMPLE 2[9]

Context: The first video-recorded staff meeting in a Māori organization. Gretel is about to deliver her monthly report. There is laughter throughout this excerpt.

Gretel: do you want me to read it
Lilian: yeah
General laughter
David: are you shy
Zara: talk to the camera babe
Gretel: talk to the camera
General laughter
Lillian: I'm Lillian by the way
General laughter
Gretel: I'm ready for my close-up now um
Yvonne: (*smiling broadly*) I told them beforehand the room will divide easily into the whakahihi and the whakaiti

While the point is made humorously in this context, it nonetheless provides evidence of the pervasive significance of Māori cultural values in this workplace.

15.4.2 Analysis

Using a range of discourse analytic techniques, earlier analyses of our large corpus of workplace interactions relied heavily on knowledge developed by the researchers as members of the relevant speech community, or alternatively inferred as on-going participant observers in the specific settings and local contexts in which the data was collected. As analysts working within a new cultural frame of reference, interpretation is much more demanding; differences are often very subtle, and can easily be overlooked or underestimated, one of the very reasons that misunderstandings occur.

When interpreting the social meaning of workplace talk in Pākehā organizations, there is a large body of research based on majority group norms available to support our analyses. This is simply not the case for Māori organizations. While linguists have identified a number of linguistic features, pragmatic particles and discourse patterns associated with Māori English, the name given to an ethnically marked variety of New Zealand English (see Benton 1991; Kennedy and Yamazaki 1999; Macalister 2003; Holmes 1997, 2005), research on Māori communication patterns is sparse. This partly reflects the relative dearth of research in the 1980s and 1990s resulting from the reaction to research by majority group members on indigenous groups. However, the work of two researchers in the area of (social) anthropology provides particularly useful starting points. Anne Salmond's important study of Māori ceremony (Salmond 1975) included influential work on rituals of encounter (Salmond 1974) which has informed much of our analysis of meeting openings and closings. Joan Metge has produced a number of groundbreaking 'handbooks' to make potential sources of cultural misunderstanding between Māori and Pākehā explicit, in particular *Talking Past Each Other* (with Patricia Kinloch in 1978) and more recently *Talking Together* (Metge 2001). However, with only a small number of published scholarly resources on which to draw for corroboration, our interpretations must be tentative.

With these limitations in mind, an important aspect of the process of interpretation has been ongoing consultation with Māori researchers and advisors, as well as participants in the interactions, in order to check the accuracy of meanings inferred from the specific cultural context in which the interactions take place. As a short and humorous example of what this means in practice, consider the following brief interaction between two senior managers at a Māori organization. When we encountered this interaction, we could identify from the participants' reactions and tone of voice that there was humorous content, but naïvely we were looking for some deeper significance in their talk.

EXAMPLE 3

Context: Frank and Daniel share a quiet aside during a large meeting where another team member is presenting to the group.

Frank: and what's [in Māori]: Maraetai: mean?
Daniel: mm?
Frank: what's [in Māori]: Maraetai: mean?
Daniel: it's by your left eye
Frank: mm?
Daniel: it's by your left eye

Initial thoughts were that *eye* might in fact be *ae*, the Māori word for 'yes', or that Frank and Daniel were actually referring to something that was physically beside Frank's left eye. One of our Māori research assistants let us in on the joke. Although Maraetai is recognizable as a Māori place name in New Zealand, Frank (unwittingly we think) provided the first line of a well-rehearsed Māori joke. Daniel responds with the punch line; the humour is a pun based on the similarities in pronunciation between the place name and this English phrase when pronounced in a broad New Zealand English accent: *What does 'my right eye' mean? It's by your left eye!* This is a trivial example, but it highlights the importance of insider knowledge when interpreting interaction.

Sensitively analysing data provided by people from culturally different backgrounds is a complex matter requiring considerable thought and care. Our main task when analysing the Māori data is to explore what exactly contributes to effective interaction in Māori workplaces. There are many answers to this beguilingly simple-looking question. As sociolinguists we argue that the precise form that effective communication takes depends on who is talking to whom, and in what kind of context; it depends on what each is trying to achieve in the interaction; and it depends on their workplace culture or the taken-for-granted interactional norms which provide a framework for workplace talk.

One method for dealing with such a daunting task has been to restrict the context in which we make our interpretations. A particularly useful tool has been the Community of Practice framework (Wenger 1998). Researchers have argued for the value of the concept of gendered communities of practice (see Eckert and McConnell-Ginet 1992; Holmes and Meyerhoff 1999); we propose the concept of 'ethnicized' communities of practice where the participants construct their group membership in ways which are consistent with cultural and ethnic norms (Schnurr, Marra and Holmes 2007). Drawing on our knowledge of fundamental cultural values and beliefs, we identify linguistic evidence for ways in which these norms play out in interaction. This framework draws on our skills as discourse analysts and in this context our outsider status provides some benefits in enabling us to identify possible cultural mismatches with the potential for cross-cultural misunderstanding (e.g. Holmes 2007; Marra 2006).

15.5 Conclusion

This chapter has described the methodological challenges we have faced in recording and analysing interactions from New Zealand workplaces. A particular focus has been the ethical and practical questions we have encountered in our investigation of Māori workplaces, where our position as Pākehā researchers has the potential to result in an uneasy insider/outsider standoff. In his book on research methods, Nunan notes that '[u]nfortunately, published research is all too often presented in neat, unproblematic packages, and critical skills are needed to get beneath the surface and evaluate the reliability and validity of research outcomes' (Nunan 1992: xi). It is clear that in reality researchers, no matter how careful their methodological design, almost always encounter (often unforeseen) issues along the way. Similarly in her doctoral thesis, Mary Roberts acknowledges the importance of making problems transparent for the aid of future studies (1999). She endorses claims by McEntegart and Le Page who espouse 'reporting defects and failures as fully as space permits for the benefit of further research in sociolinguistics' (1982: 105 as cited in Roberts 1999: 161). We have identified our 'defects' (the unavoidable problems facing majority group researchers engaged in research involving minority group participants) in order to critically problematize issues of cross-cultural methodology, and to identify a role for a collaborative approach between insiders and outsiders.

Overall the LWP approach was intentionally designed to be 'sufficiently flexible and adaptable to evolve with the project' (Stubbe 1998: 2), and it is this flexibility which allows for the constant modifications that result from negotiating research processes with different workplaces. Our greatest challenge in working with non-Pākehā organizations has been recognizing the modifications needed to work sensitively and respectfully with co-participants from a different cultural background. We benefited from explanations of the principles of Kaupapa Māori research promoted for use by those involved in research with indigenous people, but a deep understanding of these principles and appropriate application of this understanding will always remain a challenge. Differences are often very subtle. For example, as illustrated, what counts as showing respect for busy workplace participants in a Pākehā context, can potentially be seen as a disrespectful lack of engagement in a Māori context. This demonstrates that similarities at a conceptual level do not necessarily work out as similarities in the application of principles.

We remain committed to the benefits of close discourse analysis to our understanding of workplace communication. This is especially important for challenging naïve Pākehā interpretations of what is going on, and exhibiting the potential benefits of understanding different cultural frames. In a perfect world, the kind of investigations we propose would be carried out by Māori researchers trained in discourse analytic techniques. As Pākehā researchers we can offer skills in exploring workplace interaction, and in highlighting differences, and we work with Māori research assistants as much as possible to share those skills. In practice, however, at the interpretation stage in particular, we are heavily reliant on the generosity of insiders in providing potential explanations and insights into cultural norms.[10]

Following Garner et al.'s (2006) model for sociolinguists, we have critically examined the research relationship we have with our workplace participants and advisors. Despite consistently operating with a philosophy of building ongoing relationships with organizations, the relationships that have developed differ. In Pākehā workplaces we recognize that we typically highlight the costs and benefits for the organization; the benefits for us as researchers are treated as so obvious they are never mentioned. Members of participating organizations typically benefit by gaining some insights into their communicative behaviour. In the case of our research with New Zealand factories, a resource kit for teaching successful communication skills was one tangible practical outcome (Stubbe and Brown 2002). Resource materials for a targeted English language course for professional migrants has been another valuable practical outcome of our research. In the contexts in which the data which led to these outcomes was collected, whether large multinational corporations, small commercial workplaces or productive factories, we were seen as experts with knowledge to impart in exchange for their cooperation, and with obvious potential for the kind of practical applications described.

In Māori workplaces, the research relationship has been very different. Applying a methodology which was as consistent with Kaupapa Māori research as possible and highlighted the importance of mutual respect and engagement, the ongoing relationship placed much greater emphasis on solidarity between all involved. The benefits are still being explored, though skill and knowledge sharing, and greater understanding and respect, are among the most obvious. Recognizing our position as inevitable outsiders, and recognizing the skills and strengths of all participants, has resulted in a research design which we hope has proved as satisfying and empowering for the organizations as it has been for us.

KEY POINTS

1. Researching in cultures other than your own introduces challenges and complexities for both data collection and interpretation.
2. To illustrate the complexities, this paper reflects on the most recent phase of research by the LWP team, who use authentic data to explore effective workplace communication. The methodology has developed within a broadly ethnographic framework and while the primary data source is audio and video recordings of naturally-occurring interactions, the recordings are supplemented by interviews, focus groups and participant observation.
3. The standard LWP research philosophy emphasizes the importance of an ongoing relationship with participants. Working with Māori workplaces highlights differences in these relationships; the LWP team are cultural outsiders and must make their Pākehā assumptions explicit when adapting their approach.
4. Māori people have argued that early research (by Pākehā researchers) was unacceptable because it was exploitative and lacked necessary sensitivity regarding cultural differences. An appropriate approach for ethically responsible research is Māori Kaupapa research, which is culturally framed and recognizes the importance of a Māori worldview.
5. Linda Tuhiwai Smith (1999) describes an appropriate methodology for investigating Māori topics and for working with Māori people: [show] respect for people; present yourself to people face to face; look, listen . . . speak; share and host people; be cautious; do not trample over the mana of people; don't flaunt your knowledge.
6. The LWP team has attempted to find ways of researching which are consistent with a Māori Kaupapa approach. This has meant some small but significant changes in the application of the research philosophy and methodology. Nevertheless, the mutually beneficial relationships that develop remain central to the success of the research, and these are built on deep mutual respect which is established in ongoing practice.
7. An important aspect of the process of interpretation is ongoing consultation with Māori researchers and advisors, as well as participants in the interactions, in order to check the accuracy of meanings inferred from the specific cultural context in which the interactions take place.
8. The author encourages researchers to find a productive and acceptable balance between the analytical perspectives of the non-indigenous outsider, and the insights and perceptions of the indigenous insiders. As an analyst working within a new cultural frame of reference, interpretation is much more demanding; differences are often very subtle, and can easily be overlooked or underestimated resulting in misunderstanding.
9. Recognizing cultural differences goes a long way to addressing them.

DISCUSSION QUESTIONS

1. Consider your own culture and another culture with which you are familiar.
   1a. Which of the approaches described in this chapter would be most appropriate in each culture?

1b. What changes you would you need to make in order to behave appropriately and ethically for these cultures?

2. Think about a Community of Practice of which you are a member (remembering the three distinguishing characteristics of mutual engagement, joint enterprise and a shared repertoire of linguistic resources built up over time).

   2a. Identify examples of things an outsider would need to know in order to understand what is going on.

   For example:

   - Are there unique names for things/people which are important to the group?
   - Are there any running jokes or shared stories?
   - Is there a special jargon or any shortcuts to communication?

3. The LWP Project uses an ethnographic approach to collecting and analysing workplace data.

   3a. List other approaches you could use to investigate workplace communication. What are their relative advantages and disadvantages?

   3b. How universal are these approaches, i.e. could they be used with a number of organizations or would they need to be adapted for each individual workplace?

Notes

The cross-cultural research described here is funded by a Marsden grant from the Royal Society of New Zealand. Previously the LWP project has received grants from the New Zealand Foundation for Research, Science and Technology and Victoria University of Wellington.

1. I would like to express my extreme gratitude to the many workplaces and participants who have worked with me over the life of the project, and thank them for allowing me access to their thoughts not to mention their words. The core LWP team currently includes the author (Research Fellow), Professor Janet Holmes (Project Director) and Dr Bernadette Vine (Corpus Manager). We also acknowledge the important contributions made by former Research Fellow Maria Stubbe who was integrally involved in the conception of the original participatory methodology (see for example Stubbe (1998) for a discussion of the methodological model, Stubbe (2001) for a description of adapting the methodology for the factory environment, and Holmes and Stubbe (2003) for a summary of the overall methodology). I also thank the many research assistants who have painstakingly collected and transcribed many hours of data for us.
2. See the in-depth theoretical discussion in Sarangi (2006), Sarangi and Candlin (2003) and our discussion of the role of the applied (socio)linguist in Holmes, Joe, Marra, Newton, Riddiford and Vine (forthcoming).
3. 'Cross-cultural' refers to our comparison of Māori and Pākehā workplaces; in each workplace we are investigating intra-cultural communication.
4. This choice of phrase is deliberate. Garner et al. (2006: 68) note that even ethically sensitive researchers have talked of 'giving a voice' to their 'subjects' (Cameron et al. 1992: 25), illustrating the insidious effect of the language of empowerment in the research context.
5. *Mana* can be loosely translated as power, prestige or authority which is earned (not assigned) and is closely related to respect. This term is used widely in New Zealand English, although its complexities are not typically carried over.

6. One of our participants commented on the importance of proverbs and the difficulty of using them in English (as opposed to Māori). She noted that she uses proverbs frequently in Māori because they express so much, based on shared cultural understandings. When translated into English, however, she described them as sounding 'daggy'.
7. As we argue, without the involvement of a group of Māori researchers and advisors at all levels within the project, our research would not be possible. We express our gratitude to them here: Harima Fraser who has been involved as a Research Associate since the first stages of the LWP research; Mike Hollings and Brian Morris who have provided ongoing support and encouragement; and Mary Boyce whose life as a Pākehā immersed in a Māori workplace, has enabled her to share invaluable insights with us. We are also fortunate to have had a number of very able and enthusiastic Māori research assistants: We thank Paranihia Walker, a key team member, who contributed to the project in many ways for many years. We also acknowledge the work of our Māori research assistants, past (Maika Te Amo and Crystal Parata) and present (Te Atawhai Kumar, Te Rangimarie Williams and Reuben Tipoki) who have been generous with their knowledge and skills.
8. In defence of this apparent evidence of a weakness in our methodology, where our stated aim is to be unobtrusive, we note that after the first 15 minutes or so of any meeting the cameras are generally ignored completely. We expect this reaction and this was a strong motivation for collecting a series of meetings (which has proved very effective). All the evidence indicates, and participants confirm, that the cameras are rapidly perceived as part of the furniture.
9. This example is discussed in more detail in Holmes (2007).
10. Interestingly, in discussions with a Japanese doctoral student who was attempting to interpret data from a Pākehā workplace, it was clear that the project team brought to bear a great deal of implicit background knowledge as they interpreted the workplace data. This included knowledge gained through the experience of physically being in the organization, e.g. we had observed building activity outside the workplace that was going on at the time of recording and which appeared as a topic intermittently in the talk. However, it also included knowledge about Pākehā communication patterns and indicators of discourse structure, e.g. the Pākehā norm for meeting openings (see Marra 1998). This might simply involve identifying appropriate opening discourse markers (typically *okay*), or in the case of one particular workplace *shoot Rog*, which signalled to the group that the meeting had started. As an outsider, this information was far from obvious to the Japanese student.

Suggestions for further reading

Smith, Linda Tuhiwai (1999) *Decolonizing Methodologies: Research and Indigenous Peoples*. Dunedin: University of Otago Press.

Corder, S. and Meyerhoff, M. (2007) Communities of practice in the analysis of intercultural communication. In H. Kotthoff and H. Spencer-Oatey (eds) *Handbook of Intercultural Communication* (Handbooks of Applied Linguistics 7). Berlin and New York: Mouton de Gruyter, 441–461.

Clyne, M. 1994. *Inter-cultural Communication at Work. Cultural Values in Discourse*. Cambridge: Cambridge University Press.

House, J. and Rehbein, J. (eds) (2004) *Multilingual Communication*. Amsterdam: John Benjamins.

House, J., Kasper, G. and Ross, S. (eds) (2003) *Misunderstanding in Social Life. Discourse Approaches to Problematic Talk*. London: Pearson.

16 Projects

Helen Spencer-Oatey

Chapter Outline

16.1 Ideas for projects 322

16.2 Things to think about 324

Suggestions for further reading 325

This brief chapter presents some ideas for projects, lists some things to consider in relation to them and provides some suggestions for further reading.

16.1 Ideas for projects

One of the best ways to get ideas for projects is to read what other people have done. The empirical chapters in this book may stimulate your thinking, and reading some of the studies listed at the end of Part 2 and Part 4 will also be very helpful. However, a few possibilities are listed here. They are divided into two groups: cross-cultural/comparative studies and intercultural interaction studies. In fact, both types of study are needed for a more comprehensive understanding of intercultural pragmatics because the findings from one type of study will be useful for informing similar studies of the other type. However, unless the research project is a very large one, it is not usually feasible to include both types within one study.

16.1.1 Cross-cultural pragmatics

Cross-cultural pragmatics projects compare the pragmatic use of language by members of two or more cultural groups. Some possible projects are as follows:

a. Choose a speech act (e.g. disagreement, refusals, apologies, invitations, compliments, compliment responses) and compare how two different groups of speakers implement them in given contexts.

b. Choose an activity type that is common in two different cultural groups (e.g. a lecture, a service encounter) and collect some examples from each group. Using the framework given in Section 2.6.4, analyse the two sets of data for their similarities and differences.
c. Collect data on the use of terms of address in given contexts by two different groups of speakers. Compare the similarities and differences between the two sets of data, and discuss the impact of contextual factors.
d. Identify two different groups of speakers, and record some mealtime conversations within each of the groups. Compare the two sets of data for turn-taking patterns and use of listener responses.
e. Collect a few examples (e.g. audio or video extracts) of verbal/non-verbal interaction that you find noticeably polite or impolite. Present these examples to speakers from two different cultural/linguistic backgrounds and investigate how similar or different their reactions are.
f. [For those who are brave!] Choose an interactional norm that is widespread in your country and try breaking it. Some examples for Britain could be queue jumping, bumping into people, talking to strangers on a commuter train/bus (for some more examples, see Fox, K. 2004). Note down how people react and whether they say anything. If possible, do the same with a different cultural group and compare the two sets of data.

16.1.2 Intercultural interaction

Intercultural interaction projects examine the use of verbal and non-verbal behaviour by members of two or more cultural groups as they interact with each other. They may also research broader issues of identity and adaptation, since these factors are often of great concern to the participants and can have a significant impact on intercultural interaction.

g. Collect some ethnographic-type examples of interactions when rapport is damaged in some way. (They could be examples that you personally experience, or you could ask other people to collect examples of their experiences.) For each one, collect information on what happened, where it occurred, and why the person felt annoyed/upset/embarrassed etc. Try to analyse the data using the rapport management framework presented in Chapter 2, and discuss how suitable the framework is for this purpose.
h. Identify a group of people (e.g. a university seminar group, a workplace team) who comprise a mixture of cultural backgrounds, and try to obtain one or more recordings of their interactions. Analyse the interaction(s) for features that seem pertinent; e.g. turn-taking, silence, topic content.
i. Collect some jokes from speakers of two different cultural groups and translate them into the other language. Try the translated jokes out on native speakers, and explore the extent to which they found them amusing. Discuss the factors that affect the perception of humour across cultures.
j. Find some people who have moved to a different cultural context. Interview them about the adjustments they needed to make, asking them to 'tell you their story' of their experiences. Analyse their accounts using the metaphors of space and place reported in Chapter 9, and discuss the extent to which those metaphors are helpful/unhelpful.
k. Find some people who have recently moved to a different cultural context and collect some data from them (e.g. through interviews or by asking them to keep diaries) about the interactional/

communication successes and difficulties they have experienced. Analyse this data and make some recommendations for both the host nationals and the newcomers.

l. Collect some advertisements which seem to require a significant amount of culturally based background knowledge in order to understand them. Show them to a number of people, including both native speakers and non-native speakers, and ask them to explain the advertisements to you. Analyse your data using the Relevance Theory framework explained in Chapter 3.

16.2 Things to think about

To carry out any of these projects, you will need to think carefully about issues such as the following:

a. The feature of language use that you want to study; for example the performance of a type of speech act like apologies or compliments, turn-taking, reactive tokens, humour, terms of address, proxemics (i.e. the use of space, e.g. how close people stand to each other);
b. Whether you are going to focus on productive language use and/or interpretive language use (i.e. how people evaluate/react to what is said);
c. What contexts of language use will enable you to collect the kind of communicative behaviour you want to study;
d. What data collection method(s) you will use; for example discourse completion questionnaire, role play, interview, ethnographic collection of naturalistic data; audio/video recordings of (authentic) interaction;
e. How much data you will need to collect;
f. Which groups of respondents you will study and how you will get access to them;
g. What ethical issues you will need to consider;
h. What language(s) you will use during the data collection process;
i. For cross-cultural studies, how you will ensure equivalence of your data sets, for example in terms of equivalence of the features of language use (do the languages use similar resources for your chosen aspect of language use, or do they use different resources for it?), and conceptual and linguistic equivalence of the data collection instruments;
j. Whether you need to collaborate with a colleague for data collection and analysis purposes, for example someone who is very familiar with the other culture/language;
k. How and when you will pilot your data collection method(s);
l. What software (if any) you will need for analysing the data; for example statistical software or qualitative data analysis software;
m. How you will process your data to get it ready for analysis, for example transcribe it or enter it into a statistical software package;
n. Procedures you will use for analysing the data;
o. How valid it will be to generalize from the data;
p. How you will report your project findings and to whom.

Suggestions for further reading

There are not many publications that discuss methodological issues in cross-cultural and intercultural research from a linguistic/pragmatic perspective. One of the few is the following:

Hall, J.K. (2002) *Teaching and Researching Language and Culture.* London: Longman. Section III, 'Researching language and culture', is particularly relevant.

Several psychology books address the issue, and although they usually take a different approach from most work in pragmatics and applied linguistics, the following include some useful information on concepts such as equivalence, decentring, backtranslation, etc.

Triandis, H. (1994) *Culture and Social Behavior.* New York: McGraw-Hill. Chapter 3: How to study cultures.

Brislin, R. (2000) *Understanding Culture's Influence on Behavior.* 2nd edition. Fort Worth: Harcourt College Publishers. Chapter 3: Some methodological concerns in intercultural and cross-cultural research.

Matsumoto, D. and Juang, L. (2007) *Culture and Psychology.* 4th edition. Belmont, CA: Wadsworth. Chapter 2: Cross-cultural research methods.

Two useful books on research methods in general in applied linguistics are as follows:

Dornyei, Z. (2007) *Research Methods in Applied Linguistics.* Oxford: Oxford University Press.

Richards, K. (2003) *Qualitative Inquiry in TESOL.* Basingstoke: Palgrave Macmillan.

The following books all provide useful information on small-scale research in the social sciences, including project work:

Kane, E. and O'Reilly De Brun, M. (2001) *Doing your Own Research.* London: Marion Boyars Publishers.

Bell, J. (2005) *Doing Your Research Project: A Guide for First-Time Researchers in Education, Health and Social Science.* 4th edition. Buckingham: Open University Press.

Punch, K.F. (2006) *Developing Effective Research Proposals.* 2nd edition. London: Sage.

Denscombe, M. (2007) *The Good Research Guide for Small-Scale Social Research Projects.* 3rd edition. Buckingham: Open University Press.

Glossary

Accommodation: see Communication Accommodation.

Activity type: This is a type of communicative event, such as a job interview, a service encounter or a dinner party, that has culturally based constraints on how it should be carried out. The notion was proposed by Levinson (1979).

Backtranslation: This is a procedure frequently used in cross-linguistic research to ensure that the research instruments, such as questionnaires, are linguistically equivalent in meaning. It involves the following steps: (i) one person translates the research instrument into the target language; (ii) another person translates the target language version back into the original language; (iii) the two versions are compared, and if there are no discrepancies, the two instruments are regarded as equivalent. If there are some differences, the procedure is repeated until all discrepancies are eradicated (cf. *Decentring*).

Cognitive pragmatics: see Pragmatics.

Communication accommodation: This refers to the verbal or non-verbal adjustment of communicative behaviours between participants in an interaction in order either to reduce linguistic or communicative differences between themselves or to accentuate any such differences. These adjustments might be done subconsciously or quite deliberately and the direction of the adjustment is linked to underlying motives at an interpersonal or intergroup level.

Communication style: A communication style (also sometimes known as a 'communicative style') is a manner of language use and behavioural interaction that conveys an overall impression, such as of warmth, distance, directness, formality and so on. People's communication style is subject to contextual variation and, in that sense, it is similar to the term 'register'. However, the concept also incorporates the notion of personal preference, which interacts with contextual variation. When many people share or use similar communication styles, it results in an interactional ethos. (See *Interactional ethos*.)

Communicative genre: Communicative genres are historically and culturally specific, pre-patterned and complex solutions to recurrent communicative problems. They comprise the communicative conventions and ideals according to which speakers compose talk or texts and recipients interpret it. In choosing a particular genre, a speaker makes use of culturally segmented solutions to communicative problems, and at the same time – due to their pre-patterning – genres not only 'relieve' the speaker, but also assist the recipients in limiting the interpretative possibilities of utterances by relating them to the specific genre. Genre analysis provides a useful analytical tool for describing communicative patterns both in everyday interactions and in intercultural communication.

Communicative principle of relevance: see Relevance.

Community of practice: The concept of a 'Community of Practice' was originally introduced by Lave and Wenger (1991) as a context for situated learning. It focuses on how we learn to behave appropriately in a community by demonstrating our identity as peripheral and then core members. The framework describes the ongoing negotiation of groups who have a common goal and who regularly interact together using a set of shared linguistic resources developed over time; that is the group is defined by its practices.

Constructionism: Constructionism comprises a range of theories developed across the social sciences. Although many different versions of constructionism have been proposed, they share the assumption that the social world and what can be known about it is constructed in social practices, notably in discourse. In contrast to realist views (cf. *Essentialism*), social constructionism insists that social institutions, identities and relationships are not fixed but subject to constant re-definition by people themselves as well as others. With respect to identities, the focus is on how the self is talked about, rather than seeing the self as an entity. Instead of asking what the true nature of the self is, the focus is on the methods that people use for constructing the self. Accommodation behaviour can be seen to be linked with, and constitutive of, such ongoing re-definition.

Context: The set of assumptions (drawn from general knowledge, perception, previous communication etc.) which are used in the interpretation of a communicative act.

Contextual knowledge: The general world knowledge about a person, situation, topic, and so on, which is part of the context in communication about that person, situation, topic, and so on.

Conventionalization: This is the process which leads to a particular form of words being used regularly with a particular meaning that departs from the literal meaning of the words. Conventionalization can be seen as a matter of degree. In some cases, the literal meaning may not be lost but is retained alongside the conventionalized meaning. For example, an interrogative utterance such as 'Can you help me with my homework?' is conventionally used as a request for action (i.e. a request for help), rather than a request for information about the speaker's ability to help the hearer with their homework, but it can still be used in its literal meaning. In other cases, the conventionalized meaning has replaced the literal meaning which is completely or almost completely lost. For example, the form of words 'How do you do?' is a (somewhat old-fashioned) greeting, which cannot be used literally as a question about the hearer's well-being.

Convergence: This is a concept within Communication Accommodation Theory that refers to accommodation 'towards' some aspect(s) of the hearer's (perceived) communicative behaviour, motivated by, for example, the want to be approved of or liked or to increase communicative effectiveness. Convergent strategies tend to stem from interpersonal and solidary motives, when the speaker's attention is on (perceived) similarities between the interactants. (See also *Divergence*.)

Conversation analysis: Conversation analysis (CA) is an approach to studying talk in interaction. Using detailed transcription of machine-recorded, naturally occurring conversations, analysts look for and document the sequential patterns and organization found in conversation. Of particular interest is how turn-taking and identifying and repairing problems are accomplished through talk. Some well-known conversation analysts include Harold Garfinkel, Harvey Sacks, Emanuel Schegloff and Gail Jefferson.

Culture: Culture is notoriously difficult to define. Some key characteristics assumed in this book are: culture is manifested through different types of regularities, some of which are more explicit than others; culture is associated with social groups, but no two individuals within a group share exactly the same cultural characteristics; culture affects people's behaviour and interpretations of behaviour; and culture is acquired and/or constructed through involvement with others.

Decentring: In cross-cultural and intercultural research, there is a high risk that data collection and analysis is conducted from the cultural viewpoint of the researcher and hence may be culturally biased. The term 'decentring' refers to the process of moving away from the researcher's perspective so that more equal weight is given to various cultural perspectives. The term was originally used by Brislin (1976) in relation to the development of cross-culturally equivalent research instruments. During the back-translation process, it may emerge that certain concepts or meanings have no close linguistic or cultural equivalents in the target language/culture. The original instrument is thus adjusted, and so 'decentred' away from the original language/culture in which it was conceptualized (cf. *Backtranslation*).

Directness–Indirectness: a distinction relating to the extent to which the meaning of an utterance is determined by the words used, as opposed to being determined by the context. The more the message is determined by the words used, the more directly communicated it is said to be; and conversely, the less the message is determined by the words used, the more indirectly communicated it is. Directness–indirectness can be considered from three perspectives: linguistic (explicitness–implicitness), interpersonal (bluntness/baldness–hedging) and pragmatic inferential (communicative strength–weakness).

Divergence: This is a concept within Communication Accommodation Theory that refers to accommodation 'away' from some aspect(s) of the hearer's (perceived) communicative behaviour, motivated by, for example, the want to signal hostility or dislike. Divergent strategies (as well as communicative maintenance and non-accommodative behaviour) tend to stem from intergroup motives, when the speaker's attention is on (perceived) differences between the interactants and when they wish to signal loyalty to their own in-group. (See also *Convergence.*)

Epistemology: In philosophy, epistemology asks how we can come to know about things in the world, what the nature of knowledge is, and how to view the relationship between knowable objects and the knower. For instance, is it possible to know the world objectively, independently of the investigator, or does the investigator shape the object of investigation? From the position of epistemological realism, objective knowledge is possible. Theories have the status of testable statements about and explanations of the world. From the perspective of epistemological relativism, all knowledge is perspectival and theory-dependent. What one sees depends on why, where, how and how long one looks.

Essentialism: Essentialism, as it relates to the concept of identity, views identity as part of our fixed, 'true', 'authentic', primordial, essential being which is not amenable to change by, for example, history, culture or political methods.

Ethnography: Ethnography is a method for studying human behaviour through long-term immersion in the ongoing everyday activities of those being studied. Through fieldwork and participation in the life of the society, the researcher aims to understand and systematically document the meaningful social contexts, relationships and processes of a particular culture.

Face: According to Goffman's (1967: 5) classic definition, face is 'the positive social value a person effectively claims for himself by the line others assume he has taken during a particular contact. Face is an image of self delineated in terms of approved social attributes'. In other words, face is associated with people's sense of self. People typically claim certain positive qualities for themselves in interaction and they want other people to acknowledge those qualities. Brown and Levinson (1987) maintain that face sensitivity is the motivational force underlying politeness, but other linguists (e.g. Watts 2003; Spencer-Oatey 2005) draw a conceptual distinction between face and politeness. (See also *Face threatening acts* and *Politeness.*)

Face threatening acts (FTAs): Face is affectively sensitive – people can lose face (feel embarrassed or humiliated) or they can gain face (feel their reputation or self-image has been enhanced), depending on whether the qualities they are claiming are upheld or denied by others. When people's verbal or non-verbal behaviour challenges or brings into doubt someone else's face-sensitive attributes, this is known as a face threatening act (FTA). Brown and Levinson (1987) argue that certain speech acts (e.g. requests, compliments, disagreement, criticism) intrinsically threaten face; other linguists maintain that face threat is a subjective perception and that certain speech acts (e.g. requests) or behaviour could be face threatening on some occasions, yet face enhancing on others.

Focus groups: At one level, focus group discussions can be described as interactive group interviews where a trained moderator facilitates a conversation with multiple (6–10) interviewees. As a research tool for collecting opinions and attitudes, focus groups also have the advantage of obtaining negotiated and collaborative information in an environment which is more natural than a standard one-to-one interview. Although traditionally used for market research, focus groups have become increasingly popular for qualitative research in the social sciences.

Frame: Frames are basic cognitive structures that guide how we perceive what is going on around us. They influence which things we pay attention to, and how we interpret them. Members of social and cultural communities use particular 'framing devices' to indicate which frames should be selected for interpreting their language/behaviour. For example, English speakers may use the words 'Once upon a time' as a framing device to indicate that hearers should perceive, or frame, the following story as a fairy tale. The concept of 'frame' is particularly associated with Erving Goffman (1986).

Gatekeeping: Gatekeeping occurs in situations where judgements are made and/or decisions are taken as to what or who can pass through the 'gateway'. In journalism, it refers to the process by which ideas and information are filtered for publication. In interactional linguistics, it refers to communicative activities such as counselling interviews and job interviews that can have long-lasting consequences for one of the participants (cf. Erickson and Shultz 1982). In the case of job interviews, the interviewer acts as the gatekeeper who decides the applicants' access to the political, social and economic resources of a society.

Heterotopias: Heterotopias or heterotopic spaces were first discussed by Michel Foucault (1986) in a 1967 lecture. Foucault did not define the notion very sharply but it has been used by him and some other social scientists to designate 'different' places which take on ambivalent social meanings that may vary depending on the context, where different rules apply than in the rest of society and where it is thus possible to redefine identities and relations between people. To use a Finnish sauna as an example, going to sauna can be a matter of cleaning oneself, having a work meeting, doing both at once and/or doing many other things, from the almost sacred to the very profane.

Hybridity: Widely used within postcolonial theory, the notion of cultural hybridity was initially connected to cross-breeding cultural processes that were the result of colonization, such as creolization – giving birth to creole languages or creole cuisine, for instance. While the use of the term in the colonial context was rather pejorative, contemporary postcolonial uses (in line with Bhabha 1994) emphasize the fact that there can be a liberating promise in the recognition of the inherently hybrid nature of cultures and intercultural interactions: the possibility to escape the binarisms that have until now characterized our understanding of culture. (See also *Third Space.*)

Identity: Identity refers to a person's or a group's sense of self. It has always been an ambivalent notion, in that it can refer to both the set of characteristics that distinguishes an individual from others and those characteristics by which s/he is recognizable as a member of a group. Thus a distinction is traditionally drawn between individual and social identity, but these can be seen to be inter-linked in that a person has a sense of self both as a unique individual and also as a member of various social groups. Senses of identity can be seen as processes of identification and they cover domains such as geographical location, ethnic and ethnolinguistic origin, occupation, gender, sexual orientation, age and others. Today, many theorists argue that individuals take on different identities in different contexts, constructing new identities in their interactions with others; such constructionist views contrast with essentialist perspectives on identity (cf. *Essentialism*). The notion of *originary identity* refers to the cultural origins of a person; it is usually an idealization of a cultural identity that was lost and is contrasted with 'newer' identities that can be the result of individual journeys or broader cultural changes in society – for instance, within a postcolonial context.

Illocutionary force indicating device (IFID): This is the utterance, or part of an utterance, that conveys the speaker's communicative intention. It is often formulaic and routinized. For example, if someone says 'I'm sorry I'm late. The traffic was very heavy', the phrase 'I'm sorry I'm late' is the IFID and indicates that the communicative intention of the utterance is an apology. (See also *Speech Act.*)

Impression management: Impression management, or self-presentation, refers to the process by which people try to control or influence the impressions that others form of them. The sociologist Erving Goffman was one of the first to study it systematically, and his book *The Presentation of Self in Everyday Life* is a classic in the field. People manage impressions for a variety of reasons, such as to bolster or protect their self-image, or to please or influence significant audiences. They may do this consciously or unconsciously. In the case of job interviews, applicants usually attempt to present themselves as the best or most suitable candidate for the post.

Independent–interdependent self-construals: This is a social psychological construct proposed by Markus and Kitayama (1991). An independent construal of self emphasizes autonomy and separateness from others, while an interdependent construal of self emphasizes one's relatedness to others. People's dynamic construals of self can influence various aspects of rapport, including the relative emphasis they give to sociality obligations compared with to sociality rights, and how sensitive people are to face threats to groups they are members of.

In-group/out-group: This is a distinction used very widely in social psychology. It refers to people's subjective categorization of others as either belonging or not belonging to their group. In-group relationships are typically characterized by some degree of familiarity, intimacy and trust, whereas out-group relationships do not have this. A bond of some kind exists among in-group members, whereas no such bond exists with out-group people. Many social psychologists argue that the in-group/out-group distinction is stronger and less fuzzy in societies where collectivism is highly valued than in societies where individualism predominates.

Interactional ethos: Brown and Levinson (1987) use this term to refer to the affective quality of interaction that is characteristic of members of a given society; it derives from people's preferred communication styles (see Communication style). At present, there is no agreement as to how different qualities of interactional ethos are best distinguished and labelled. Distinctions widely referred to in linguistics and communication studies include positive politeness–negative politeness/involvement–independence/associative expressiveness–restraint; directness–indirectness; self-enhancing–self-effacing.

Interactional sociolinguistics: Developed by John Gumperz in the 1970s, interactional sociolinguistics examines language use in social interaction. On its theory of situated interpretation, understanding in discourse is inferential, tentative and co-constructed. Critical interpretive resources are linguistic, paralinguistic, or gestural signs that index dimensions of context, and construct social identities and relationships. As contextualization cues emerge from interactional practices and cultural relevancies, they are often not interculturally shared. Interactional-sociolinguistic research shows that different practices of using and interpreting contextualization cues can be a source of miscommunication, resulting in unfavourable social attributions and unsuccessful interactional outcomes. Such undesirable consequences are particularly harmful in gatekeeping encounters (cf. *Gatekeeping*).

Intercultural personhood: The term 'intercultural personhood' was introduced by Young Yun Kim (2001) to refer to individuals who, as a result of prolonged intercultural interactions and/or acculturation to a host society, have developed an ability to move beyond their cultural heritage and embrace two or more cultural identities at once.

Maxims: The sub-principles of Grice's (1989) Co-operative Principle and Leech's (1983) Politeness Principle are labelled as maxims. They refer to regularities or norms in communicative interaction that speakers can be observed to follow, unless overridden by other factor(s). More recently, Leech (2005, 2007) argues that 'constraint' is a more suitable term, because 'maxim' is too easily misconstrued as implying some kind of moral imperative. Spencer-Oatey (Spencer-Oatey and Jiang 2003; Chapter 2 in this book) maintains that people often develop prescriptive or proscriptive expectations in relation to interactional norms and that failure to fulfil the expectations can then have a significant impact on rapport. She thus retains a value-based element, and labels them 'sociopragmatic interactional principles (SIPs)'

Metapragmatic: This term describes the self-reflexive processes associated with contextualized language use. For example, when people make judgements about the factors influencing their choice of language (e.g. the power and distance between the interlocutors), they are making metapragmatic assessments.

Negative transfer: see Transfer

Observer's paradox: see Participant observer

Ontology: In philosophy, ontology asks what things exist in the world, and what their structure and properties are. Depending on how these questions are answered, objects are conceptualized differently. One of the most important ontological differences is whether to view social phenomena as objective facts (realism) or social constructions (constructionism). For example, on a realist view, language is a rule system that exists independently of its users. In constructionist perspective, language exists only through its use in discourse. (See *Constructionism.*)

Orientalism: The term 'orientalism' initially referred to the study of near-Eastern and far-Eastern cultures by Western scholars. Edward Said (1978) has shown how these allegedly neutral academic studies of 'the Orient' were in fact far from neutral, expressing colonial power relations in their representation of oriental cultures and people as the negative of their Western counterparts, and establishing this biased representation as though it was objective knowledge.

Out-group: see In-group

Over-accommodation/Under-accommodation: A speaker may over- or underestimate the level of communicative modification necessary for satisfying or attuned communication, on the basis of their perception of the hearer's needs. A speaker may either go beyond what the hearer deems necessary (over-accommodation) – for example by grammatically simplifying or by increasing the volume of their utterances too much. Alternatively, a speaker may underplay some aspect of their communicative behaviour in relation to the hearer's needs (under-accommodation) – for example by not making any communicative modifications when they are needed.

Participant observer: A common concern for sociolinguistic researchers is the effect an observer has on the research participants' language and communicative behaviour. To overcome this 'observer's paradox' (Labov 1966), fieldworkers may choose to become longer-term participants in the community they are investigating. This reduces the impact of the observer's presence on the data (under the assumption that, over time, participants become less aware of the attention to their speech). It also improves interpretation because the researcher gains an insider's perspective on the data.

Perspective/perspectivization: The notion of perspective refers to the subjective point of view, standpoint or mode of perception of a discourse participant. 'Perspective' is a relational, dynamic and evaluative concept, and in the context of talk-in-interaction, 'perspectivization' refers to the ways in which perspectives are co-established and signalled in discourse.

Phatic talk/phatic utterances/phatic communion: The term 'phatic communion' was first introduced in the 1920s by the anthropologist Malinowski to describe 'a type of speech in which ties of union are created by a mere exchange of words' (1966: 315), such as when inquiring about the interlocutor's well-being, exchanging comments about the weather, or deploying other forms of small talk. In such cases, the informational content of the phrases is secondary and the relational aspect is forefronted. Some forty years later, the term 'phatic' entered linguistics through Jakobson who applied it to the use of language to open up channels of communication and to establish and maintain contact.

Politeness/impoliteness: Linguists use the term 'politeness' in a variety of ways, for example as the means of minimizing or avoiding conflict, as the use of language to maintain smooth and harmonious interpersonal relations, as the use of socially appropriate behaviour, and to refer to an evaluative judgement regarding social appropriateness. For example, in Brown and Levinson's (1987) framework, politeness is regarded as the performance of redressive action to minimize face threat (see *Face*, and *face threatening acts*). Yet according to Fraser (1990), no behaviour is intrinsically polite or impolite; rather (im)politeness is a subjective judgement that is made by the hearer. (See also *Face.*)

Positive transfer: see Transfer

Pragmalinguistics: Leech (1983: 11), drawing on earlier work by Thomas (1981), suggests that pragmatics can have both a linguistic focus and a sociocultural focus. The linguistic focus interfaces with the grammar of the language and it explores how people use the particular resources of a given language to convey given pragmatic meanings. This focus to pragmatics is known as pragmalinguistics. (See also *Sociopragmatics.*)

Pragmatic transfer: see Transfer

Pragmatics: On one view, pragmatics is the study of the relation between various signs (including utterances and texts) and their use for any purpose (including communication). However, the most common definitions of pragmatics characterize it as the discipline concerned with the study of those aspects of the meaning of communicative acts which are not determined by the meanings of the signal independently of the context, but follow from the interpretation of the signal in context. *Cognitive pragmatics* is concerned with the study of the cognitive mechanisms and principles involved in the production and comprehension of communicative acts. *Social pragmatics* focuses on the description and analysis of the systematic relations between types of communicative act, particular contextual features (e.g. the relationship between the participants, the topic, the purpose of communication, etc.) and their impact on the success of communication in general, and the rapport between the participants, in particular.

Rapport: Spencer-Oatey (2005; Chapter 2 in this book) uses the term 'rapport' to refer to people's subjective perceptions of (dis)harmony or smoothness–turbulence in interpersonal relations. She proposes that there are three key factors that influence rapport – interactional goals, face sensitivities and sociality rights and obligations – and that people's handling of these affect perceived rapport. *Rapport management* refers to the verbal and non-verbal strategies that people use in (mis)handling these elements.

Rapport management 'domains': Brown and Levinson's (1987) classic model of politeness places particular emphasis on the performance of speech acts in relation to politeness. However, Spencer-Oatey (see Chapter 2) argues that rapport is managed across all aspects of communicative behaviour, including discourse content and structure, participation procedures, stylistic choices and non-verbal behaviour. She groups these elements into a number of fuzzy categories and labels them 'rapport management 'domains'.'

Rapport orientation: Brown and Levinson (1987) propose that people generally cooperate with each other in interaction to maintain each other's face, yet others (e.g. Culpeper 2005) argue that impoliteness can be deliberate and intentional. Spencer-Oatey (see Chapter 2) maintains that it is helpful to distinguish different rapport orientations – that people may sometimes want to enhance harmonious relations or to maintain them, but they may also sometimes prefer to ignore them or damage them.

Relevance: In pragmatics, relevance is defined as a property of inputs to cognitive processing. The input to a cognitive process (e.g. an utterance) is more relevant if processing it mentally leads to more cognitive effects and if the mental effort required for deriving these cognitive effects is small. Cognitive effects are the product of processing the communicative act in context. The *Communicative Principle of Relevance* is a generalization about communicative acts: a communicative act makes evident the communicator's guarantee (or presumption) that the act is optimally relevant (where a communicative act is optimally relevant if processing it leads to enough cognitive effects to offset the processing effort required for deriving these effects). Putting it very informally, the Communicative Principle states that by claiming the addressee's attention the communicator makes it evident that in his/her view the communicative act worth the addressee's attention, that paying attention to the communicative act and interpreting it will be worth the addressee's while.

Schema (plural: *schemata*, occasionally the plural form 'schemas' is also used): This is a mental structure in which our knowledge of the world is organized so that it can be efficiently used in thinking, communication, etc.

Scripts: This is a mental structure in which our knowledge about events is organized so it can be efficiently used in thinking, communication, and so on. A script is a type of schema.

Self-presentation: see Impression Management

Social constructionism: see Constructionism

Social pragmatics: see Pragmatics

Sociality rights and obligations: According to Spencer-Oatey (see Chapter 2), there are three key factors that affect rapport: interactional goals, face sensitivities and sociality rights and obligations. The latter refers to the fundamental social entitlements that people effectively claim for themselves in their interactions with others. They can be based on a range of factors, including contractual agreements, role specifications and interactional norms.

Sociocultural interactional principles (SIPs): see Maxims

Sociopragmatics: Leech (1983: 11), drawing on earlier work by Thomas (1981), suggests that pragmatics can have both a linguistic focus and a sociocultural focus. The sociocultural focus interfaces with social psychology and sociology and it explores how people's performance and interpretation of linguistic behaviour is influenced by socioculturally-based principles. This focus to pragmatics is known as sociopragmatics. (See also *Pragmalinguistics.*)

Speech acts: The notion of speech acts refers to the insight that language can be viewed as action. The concept is particularly associated with the philosopher John L. Austin, who identified three types of acts: locutionary acts (uttering words that have meaning), illocutionary acts (performing communicative intentions such as greetings, requests and compliments) and perlocutionary acts (the effect of an act on the hearer). Nowadays, the term 'speech acts' is often used to mean the same as 'illocutionary acts'.

Stereotypes: This is a fixed set of widely held beliefs about a group, based on an actual or imaginary feature shared by the group's members.

Third space: Originally introduced in Fredric Jameson's works on postmodernism, the notion of 'third space' has been imported and used by a variety of scholars from different disciplines, and taken on different meanings. For the postcolonial theorist Homi Bhabha (1994), the third space is the space that is set up by an encounter with an other, the space in which communication with that other, and thus negotiation and translation from one perspective to the other, take place. In this meaning of the term, any intercultural interaction gives birth to a 'third space'. In Bhabha's view, it is crucial to recognize this in-between, hybrid character of the space set up by the encounter, as it helps to avoid conflict – what Bhabha calls the 'politics of polarity' – and develop new, liberating identities. (See also hybridity.)

Transfer: The carryover of knowledge from solving problems relating to one type of situation to solving problems in another type of situation. When this carryover of knowledge is warranted the transfer is described as *positive* and when it is not warranted, the transfer is described as *negative*. Pragmatic transfer is the carryover of pragmatic knowledge from one type of situation of communication to another.

Under-accommodation: see Over-accommodation.

References

Abe, K. and Ohama, R. (2006) 'Shazai' no nicchuu hikaku – shazai no hitsuyoo ga shoojita jijoo no sai ni chakumoku shite. *Shakai gengo kagaku kai* No.17, conference proceedings.

Adachi, T. (1996) Sarcasm in Japanese. *Studies in Language*, 20(1): 1–36.

Adams, P. C., Hoelscher, S. and Till, K. E. (eds) (1998) *Textures of Place – Exploring Humanist Geographies*. Minneapolis: University of Minnesota Press.

Adelswärd, V. (1988) *Styles of Success: On Impression Management as Collaborative Action in Job Interviews*. Linköping University, Schweden: VTT-Grafiska Vimmerby: Linköping Studies in Arts and Science.

Aitchison, J. and Carter, H. (1994) *A Geography of the Welsh Language 1961–1991*. Cardiff: University of Wales Press.

Akinnaso, F. N. and Seabrook Ajirotutu, C. (1982) Performance and ethnic style in job interviews. In J. J. Gumperz (ed.) *Language and Social Identity*, Cambridge: Cambridge University Press, 119–44.

Andersen, P. A., Hecht, M. L., Hoobler, G. D. and Smallwood, M. (2002) Nonverbal communication across cultures. In W. B. Gudykunst and B. Mody (eds) *Handbook of International and Intercultural Communication*. 2nd edition. Thousand Oaks: Sage, 89–106.

Anzaldúa, G. E. (1987) *Borderlands/La Frontera: The New Mestiza*. San Francisco: Spinsters/Aunt Lute.

Apte, M. (1994) Language in sociocultural context. In R. E. Asher (ed.) *The Encyclopedia of Language and Linguistics Vol.4*. Oxford: Pergamon Press, 2000–10.

Arminen, I. and Leinonen, M. (2006) Mobile phone call openings: tailoring answers to personalized summonses. *Discourse Studies*, 8: 339–68.

Arundale, R. B. (1999) An alternative model and ideology of communication for an alternative politeness theory. *Pragmatics*, 9: 119–53.

Arundale, R. B. (2005) Pragmatics, conversational implicature, and conversation. In Kirsten L. Fitch and Robert E. Sanders (eds) *Handbook of Language and Social Interaction*. Mahwah, NJ: Lawrence Erlbaum, 41–63.

Ashcroft, B., Griffiths, G. and Tiffin, H. (1998) *Key Concepts in Post-Colonial Studies*. London and New York: Routledge.

Auer, P. (2000) Changing communicative practices among East Germans. In P. Stevenson and J. Theobald (eds) *Relocating Germanness: Discursive Disunity in Unified Germany*. London: Macmillan, 167–88.

Auer, P. and Kern, F. (2001) Three ways of analysing communication between East and West Germans as intercultural communication. In A. di Luzio, S. Günthner and F. Orletti (eds) *Culture in Communication: Analyses of intercultural situations*. Amsterdam and Philadelphia: Benjamins, 89–116.

Augustinos, M and Walker, I. (1995) *Social Cognition: An Integrated Introduction*. London: Sage Publications.

Babbie, E. (1998) *The Practice of Social Research*. 8th edition. Belmont, CA: Wadsworth.

Bach, K. and Harnish, R. M. (1979/1982) *Linguistic Communication and Speech Acts.* Cambridge, Massachusetts: MIT Press.

Bailey, B. (1997) Communication of respect in interethnic service encounters. *Language in Society*, 26: 327–56.

Bakakou-Orfanou, A. (1990) [in Greek]. Telephone communication: utterance variation of requests forgetting connected with the person called. Paper presented at the Glossologia 7–8 (1988–1989).

Ball, P., Giles, H., Byrne, J. L. and Berechree, P. (1984) Situational constraints on the evaluative significance of speech accommodation: some Australian data. *International Journal of the Sociology of Language*, 46: 115–30.

Bardovi-Harlig, K. and Hartford, B. S. (1993) Refining the DCT: comparing open questionnaires and dialogue completion tasks. In L. F. Bouton and Y. Kachru (eds) *Pragmatics and Language Learning, Vol. 4.* Urbana: Division of English as an International Language, University of Illinois at Urbana-Champaign, 143–65.

Bardovi-Harlig, K. and Hartford, B. S. (2005a) Institutional discourse and interlanguage pragmatics research. In K. Bardovi-Harlig and B. S. Hartford (eds) *Interlanguage Pragmatics: Exploring Institutional Talk.* Mahwah, NJ: Lawrence Erlbaum, 7–36.

Bardovi-Harlig, K. and Hartford, B. S. (eds) (2005b) *Interlanguage Pragmatics: Exploring Institutional Talk.* Mahwah, NJ: Lawrence Erlbaum.

Barnlund, D. C. and Araki, S. (1985) Intercultural encounters. The management of compliments by Japanese and Americans. *Journal of Cross-Cultural Psychology*, 16(1): 9–26.

Barnlund, D. C. and Yoshioka, M. (1990) Apologies: Japanese and American styles. *International Journal of Intercultural Relations*, 14: 193–206.

Baxter, L. A. (1984) An investigation of compliance-gaining as politeness. *Human Communication Research*, 10(3): 427–56.

Beebe, L. (1981) Social and situational factors affecting communicative strategy of dialect code- switching. *International Journal of the Sociology of Language*, 32: 139–49.

Beebe, L. M. and Cummings, M. C. (1996) Natural speech act data versus written questionnaire data: how data collection method affects speech act performance. In S. M. Gass and J. Neu (eds) *Speech Acts across Cultures.* Berlin: Mouton de Gruyter, 65–86. (Original version 1985)

Beebe, L. M. and Takahashi, T. (1989a) Do you have a bag?: social status and patterned variation in second language acquisition. In S. Gass, C. Madden, D. Preston and L. Selinker (eds) *Variation in Second Language Acquisition. Vol.1: Discourse and Pragmatics.* Clevedon: Multilingual Matters, 103–25.

Beebe, L. M. and Takahashi, T. (1989b) Sociolinguistic variation in face-threatening speech acts. In M. Eisenstein (ed.) *The Dynamic Interlanguage.* New York: Plenum, 199–218.

Beebe, L. M., Takahashi, T. and Uliss-Weltz, R. (1990) Pragmatic transfer in ESL refusals. In R. C. Scarella, E. Anderson and S. C. Krashen (eds) *On the Development of Communicative Competence in a Second Language.* New York: Newbury House, 55–73.

Beekman, J. and Callow, J. (1974) *Translating the Word of God*, Vol. 1. Grand Rapids, Michigan: Zondervan.

Behling, O., and Law, K. S. (2000) *Translating Questionnaires and Other Research Instruments.* Thousand Oaks, CA: Sage.

Belson, A. (1981) *The Design and Understanding of Survey Questions.* Hants, England: Gower.

Belz, J. A. and Kinginger, C. (2002) The cross-linguistic development of address form use in telecollaborative language learning: two case studies. *Canadian Modern Language Review/Revue canadienne des langues vivantes*, 59(2): 189–214.

Benton, R. (1991) 'Māori English': A New Zealand Myth? In J. Cheshire (ed.) *English Around the World: Sociolinguistic Perspectives.* Cambridge: Cambridge University Press, 187–99.

Berens, F. J. (1981) Dialogeröffnung in Telefongesprächen: Handlungen und Handlungsschemata der Herstellung sozialer und kommunikativer Beziehungen. In P. Schröder and H. Steger (eds) *Jahrbuch 1980 des Instituts für Deutsche Sprache*. Düsseldorf: Schwann, 402–17.

Bergman, M. L. and Kasper, G. (1993) Perception and performance in native and nonnative apology. In G. Kasper and S. Blum-Kulka (eds) *Interlanguage Pragmatics*. New York: Oxford University Press, 82–107.

Bernard, H. R. (2000) *Social Research Methods*. Thousand Oaks: Sage.

Bhabha, H. K. (1988) The commitment to theory. *New Foundations*, 5: 5–23.

Bhabha, H. K. (1994) *The Location of Culture*. London: Routledge.

Billmyer, K., and Varghese, M. (2000) Investigating instrument-based pragmatic variability: effects of enhancing discourse completion tests. *Applied Linguistics*, 21: 517–52.

Bilous, F. R. and Krauss, R. M. (1988) Dominance and accommodation in the conversational behaviours of same- and mixed-gender dyads. *Language and Communication*, 8: 183–94.

Birkner, K. (2001) *Ost- und Westdeutsche im Bewerbungsgespräch. Eine kommunikative Gattung in Zeiten gesellschaftlichen Wandels*. Niemeyer: Tübingen.

Birkner, K. (2004) Hegemonic Struggles or Transfer of Knowledge? East and West Germans in Job Interviews. *Journal of Language and Politics*, 3: 293–322.

Blakemore, D. (1992) *Understanding Utterances: An Introduction to Pragmatics*. Oxford: Blackwell.

Bloch, M. E. F. (1998) *How We Think They Think*. Oxford: Westview Press.

Blommaert, J. (2005) *Discourse*. Cambridge: Cambridge University Press.

Blum-Kulka, S. (1997) *Dinner Talk*. Mahwah, NJ: Erlbaum.

Blum-Kulka, S., Danet, B. and Gherson, R. (1985) The language of requesting in Israeli society. In J. P. Forgas (ed.) *Language and Social Situations*. New York: Springer-Verlag, 113–39.

Blum-Kulka, S., House, J., and Kasper, G. (eds) (1989) *Cross-Cultural Pragmatics: Requests and Apologies*. Norwood, NJ: Ablex.

Bonikowska, M. P. (1988) The choice of opting out. *Applied Linguistics*, 9: 69–181.

Bourhis, R. Y. (1991) Organisational communication and accommodation: toward some conceptual and empirical links. In H. Giles, N. Coupland and J. Coupland (eds) *Contexts of Accommodation: Developments in Applied Sociolinguistics*. Cambridge: Cambridge University Press, 270–303.

Bourhis, R. Y. and Giles, H. (1977) The language of intergroup distinctiveness. In H. Giles (ed.) *Language, Ethnicity and Intergroup Relations*. London, New York and San Francisco: Academic Press in co-operation with European Association of Experimental Social Psychology, 119–35.

Bourhis, R. Y., Giles, H., Leyens, J. P. and Tajfel, H. (1979) Psycholinguistic distinctiveness: language divergence in Belgium. In H. Giles and R. S. Clair (eds) *Language and Social Psychology*. Oxford: Blackwell, 158–85.

Bouton, L. F. (1994) Conversational implicature in the second language: learned slowly when not deliberately taught. *Journal of Pragmatics*, 22: 157–67.

Boxer, D. (1996) Ethnographic interviewing as a research tool in speech act analysis: the case of complaints. In S. Gass and J. Neu (eds) *Speech Acts across Cultures*. Berlin: Mouton de Gruyter, 217–39.

Bremer, K., Roberts, C., Vasseur, M.-T., Simonot, M. and Broeder, P. (1996) *Achieving Understanding*. London: Longman.

Briggs, C. L. (1986) *Learning How to Ask*. Cambridge: Cambridge University Press.

Brinker, K. and Sager, S. E. (1989) *Linguistische Gesprächsanalyse. Eine Einführung*. Berlin: Erich Schmidt.

Brislin, R. (1976) *Translation: Application and Research*. New York: Gardner.

Brons-Albert, R. (1984) *Gesprochenes Standarddeutsch. Telefondialoge*. Tübingen: Günter Narr.

Brown, G. and Yule, G. (1983) *Teaching the Spoken Language*. Cambridge: Cambridge University Press.

Brown, J. (2001a) Pragmatics tests: different purposes, different tests. In K. Rose and G. Kasper (eds) *Pragmatics in Language Teaching*. Cambridge: Cambridge University Press, 301–25.

Brown, J. (2001b) *Using Surveys in Language Programs*. Cambridge: Cambridge University Press.

Brown, P. and Levinson, S. C. (1987) *Politeness. Some Universals in Language Usage*. Cambridge: Cambridge University Press. Originally published as 'Universals in language usage: politeness phenomenon', in E. Goody (ed.) (1978) *Questions and Politeness: Strategies in Social Interaction*. New York: Cambridge University Press.

Brown, R. and Gilman, A. (1960) Pronouns of power and solidarity. In T. A. Sebeok (ed.) *Style in Language*. Cambridge, MA: MIT Press, 253–76. [Reprinted in P. Giglioli (ed.) (1972) *Language and Social Context*. Harmondsworth: Penguin Books, 252–82.]

Brown, R. and Gilman, A. (1989) Politeness theory and Shakespeare's four major tragedies. *Language in Society*, 18: 159–212.

Bruner, J. (1987) Life as narrative. *Social Research*, 54(1): 11–32.

Bruner, J. (1990) *Acts of Meaning*. Cambridge: Harvard University Press.

Bruner, J. (2001) Self-making and world-making. In J. Brockmeier (ed.) *Narrative and Identity: Studies in Autobiography, Self and Culture*. Philadelphia: John Benjamins Publishing Company, 25–37.

Buttimer, A. (1976) Grasping the dynamism of lifeworld. *Annals of the Association of American Geographers*, 66(2): 277–92.

Buttimer, A. (1980) Home, reach, and the sense of place. In A. Buttimer and D. Seamon (eds) *The Human Experience of Space and Place*. London: Croom Helm, 166–87.

Buttimer, A. and Seamon, D. (eds) (1980) *The Human Experience of Space and Place*. London: Croom Helm.

Button, G. (1987) Moving out of closings. In G. Button and J. R. E. Lee (eds) *Talk and Social Organization*. Clevedon: Multilingual Matters, 101–51.

Button, G. (1990) On varieties of closings. In G. Psathas (ed.) *Studies in Ethnomethodology and Conversation Analysis*. Lanham: University Press of America, 93–148.

Byrne, D. (1971) *The Attraction Paradigm*. New York: Academic Press.

Byrnes, H. (1986) Interactional style in German and American conversation. *Text*, 6(2): 189–206.

Cameron, D. (1985) 'Respect, please!' – subjects and objects in sociolinguistics. Unpublished manuscript.

Cameron, D., Frazer, E., Harvey, P. Rampton, B. and Richardson, K. (1992) *Researching Language. Issues of Power and Method*. London: Routledge.

Canale, M., and Swain, M. (1980) Theoretical bases of communicative approaches to second language teaching and testing. *Applied Linguistics*, 1: 1–47.

Carrell, P. (1981) Relative difficulty of request forms in L1/L2 comprehension. In M. Hines and W. Rutherford (eds) *On TESOL '81*. Washington, DC: TESOL, 141–52.

Carston, R. (2002) *Thoughts and Utterances: The Pragmatics of Explicit Communication*. Oxford: Blackwell.

Carter, E., Donald, J. and Squires, J. (eds) (1993) *Space and Place – Theories of Identity and Location*. London: Lawrence and Wishart.

Casey, E. S. (2001) Between Geography and Philosophy: what does it mean to be in the place-world? *Annals of the Association of American Geographers*, 91(4): 683–93.

Chen, R. (1993) Responding to compliments: a contrastive study of politeness strategies between American English and Chinese speakers. *Journal of Pragmatics*, 20: 49–75.

Cheng, W. (2003) *Intercultural Conversation*. Amsterdam: Benjamins.

Cicourel, A. (1982) Interviews, surveys, and the problem of ecological validity. *The American Sociologist*, 17: 11–20.

Clark, H. C. and French, W. J. (1981) Telephone goodbyes. *Language in Society*, 10: 1–19.

Clark, H. H. (1996) *Using Language*. Cambridge: Cambridge University Press.

Clyne, M. (1994) *Intercultural Communication at Work: Cultural Values in Discourse*. Cambridge: Cambridge University Press.

Cohen, A. D. (1996) Developing the ability to perform speech acts. *Studies in Second Language Acquisition*, 18: 253–67.

Cohen, A. D. (1997) Developing pragmatic ability: insights from the accelerated study of Japanese. In H. M. Cook, K. Hijirida and M. Tahara (eds) *New Trends and Issues in Teaching Japanese Language and Culture (Technical Report #15)*. Honolulu: University of Hawai'i, Second Language Teaching and Curriculum Center, 133–59.

Cohen, A. D. (1998) *Strategies in Learning and Using a Second Language*. London: Longman.

Cohen, A. D. and Olshtain, E. (1981) Developing a measure of sociocultural competence: the case of apology. *Language Learning*, 31: 113–34.

Cook, H. M. (2006) Joint construction of folk beliefs by JFL learners and Japanese host families. In M. A. DuFon and E. Churchill (eds) *Language Learners in Study Abroad Contexts*. Clevedon, UK: Multilingual Matters, 120–50.

Coupland, J., Coupland, N. and Robinson, J. D. (1992) 'How are you?': negotiating phatic communion. *Language in Society*, 21: 207–30.

Coupland, N. (1995) Accommodation theory. In J. Verschueren, J.-O. Östman and J. Blommaert (eds) *Handbook of Pragmatics Manual*. Amsterdam: John Benjamins, 21–26.

Coupland, N., Coupland, J. and Giles, H. (1991) *Language, Society and the Elderly: Discourse, Identity and Ageing*. Oxford: Blackwell.

Coupland, N., Coupland, J., Giles, H. and Henwood, K. (1988) Accommodating the elderly: invoking and extending a theory. *Language in Society*, 17: 1–41.

Coupland, N., Giles, H. and Wiemann, J. M. (eds) (1991) *'Miscommunication' and Problematic Talk*. Newbury Park, CA: Sage.

Crang, M. (2000) Relics, Places and Unwritten Geographies in the Work of Michel de Certeau (1925–86). In M. Crang and N. Thrift (eds) *Thinking Space*. London: Routledge, 136–53.

Crookall, D. and Saunders, D. (1989) *Communication and Simulation*. Clevedon: Multilingual Matters.

Culpeper, J. (1996) Towards an anatomy of impoliteness. *Journal of Pragmatics*, 25: 349–67.

Culpeper, J. (2005) Impoliteness and entertainment in the television quiz show: the weakest link. *Journal of Politeness Research*, 1(1): 35–72.

Davidson, J. (1984) Subsequent versions of invitations, offers, requests, and proposals dealing with potential or actual rejection. In J. M. Atkinson and J. Heritage (eds) *Structures of Social Action*. Cambridge, UK: Cambridge University Press, 102–28.

De Certeau, M. (1984) *The Practice of Everyday Life*. Berkeley: University of California Press.

Drew, P. and Heritage, J. (eds) (1992) *Talk at Work: Interaction in Institutional Settings*. Cambridge: Cambridge University Press.

DuFon, M. A. (2000) The acquisition of negative responses to experience questions in Indonesian as a second language by sojourners in naturalistic interactions. In B. Swierzbin, F. Morris, M. Anderson, C. A. Klee and E. Tarone (eds) *Social and Cognitive Factors in Second Language Acquisition*. Somerville, MA: Cascadilla Press, 77–97.

DuFon, M. A. (2002) Video recording in ethnographic SLA research: Some issues of validity in data collection. *Language Learning and Technology*, 6: 40–59.

DuFon, M. A. (2006) The socialization of taste during study abroad in Indonesia. In M. A. DuFon and E. Churchill (eds) *Language Learners in Study Abroad Contexts.* Clevedon, UK: Multilingual Matters, 91–119.

Duranti, A. (1997) *Linguistic Anthropology.* Cambridge: Cambridge University Press.

Eckert, P. and McConnell-Ginet, S. (1992) Think practically and look locally: language and gender as community-based practice. *Annual Review of Anthropology*, 21: 461–90.

Edmondson, W. J. and House, J. (1991) Do learners talk too much? The waffle phenomenon in interlanguage pragmatics. In R. Phillipson, E. Kellerman, L. Selinker, M. S. Smith and M. Swain (eds) *Foreign/Second Language Pedagogy Research.* Clevedon, UK: Multilingual Matters, 273–86.

Edmondson, W. J., House, J., Kasper, G. and Stemmer, B. (1984) Learning the pragmatics of discourse: a project report. *Applied Linguistics*, 5: 113–27.

Eisenstein, M. and Bodman, J. W. (1986) 'I very appreciate': expressions of gratitude by native and non-native speakers of American English. *Applied Linguistics*, 7(2): 167–85.

Eisenstein, M. and Bodman, J. W. (1993) Expressing gratitude in American English. In G. Kasper and S. Blum-Kulka (eds) *Interlanguage Pragmatics*, New York: Oxford University Press, 64–81.

Eisenstein, M. and Starbuck, R. J. (1989) The effect of emotional investment on L2 production. In S. Gass, C. Madden, D. Preston and L. Selinker (eds) *Variation in Second Language Acquisition: Psycholinguistic Issues.* Clevedon: Multilingual Matters, 125–37.

Erickson, F. (1992) Ethnographic microanalysis of interaction. In M. D. LeCompte, W. Millroy and J. Preissle (eds) *The Handbook of Qualitative Research in Education.* New York: Academic Press, 201–25.

Erickson, F. and Shultz, J. (1982) *The Counselor as Gatekeeper. Social Interaction in Interviews.* New York: Academic Press.

Ericsson, K. A. and Simon, H. A. (1993) *Protocol Analysis.* Cambridge, MA: Bradford/MIT Press. First edition 1984.

Ericsson, K. A. and Simon, H. A. (1998) How to study thinking in everyday life: contrasting think-aloud protocols with descriptions and explanations of thinking. *Mind, Culture, and Activity*, 5: 178–86.

Færch, C. and Kasper, G. (1982) Phatic, metalingual and metacommunicative functions in discourse: gambits and repair. In N. E. Enkvist (ed.) *Impromptu Speech.* Åbo: Åbo Akademi, 71–103.

Færch, C. and Kasper, G. (eds) (1987) *Introspection in Second Language Research.* Clevedon, UK: Multilingual Matters.

Falk, J. (1979) The duet as a conversational process. Dissertation, Princeton University.

Fant, L. (1992) Analyzing negotiation talk – authentic data vs. role play. In A. Grindsted and J. Wagner (eds) *Communication for Specific Purposes.* Tübingen: Narr, 164–75.

Ferguson, C. (1971) Absence of copula and the notion of simplicity: a study of normal speech, baby talk, foreigner talk, and pidgins. In D. Hymes (ed.) *Pidginization and Creolozation of Languages.* Cambridge: Cambridge University Press, 141–50.

Ferguson, C. (1975) Towards a characterization of English foreigner talk. *Anthropological Linguistics*, 17: 1–14.

Ferguson, C. (1996) *Sociolinguistic Perspectives: Papers on Language in Society, 1959–1994*, ed. T. Huebner. New York and Oxford: Oxford University Press.

Fiksdal, S. (1990) *The Right Time and Pace: A Microanalysis of Cross-Cultural Gatekeeping Interviews.* Norwood, NJ: Ablex.

Fiske, A. P. (1992) The four elementary forms of sociality: framework for a unified theory of social relations. *Psychological Review*, 99:689–723.

FitzGerald, H. (2003) *How Different Are We? Spoken Discourse in Intercultural Communication.* Clevedon: Multilingual Matters.

Foucault, M. (1986) Of other spaces. *Diacritics*, 16(1): 22–7.

Fox, B. A., Hayashi, M., and Jasperson, R. (1996) Resources and repair: a cross-linguistic study of syntax and repair. In E. Ochs, E. A. Schegloff and S. A. Thompson (eds) *Interaction and Grammar*. Cambridge: Cambridge University Press, 185–237.

Fox, K. (2004) *Watching the English*. London: Hodder and Stoughton.

Frake, C. O. (1964) How to ask for a drink in Subanun. *American Anthropologist*, 66: 127–32.

Fraser, B. (1990) Perspectives on politeness. *Journal of Pragmatics*, 14(2): 219–36.

Fraser, B. and Nolan, W. (1981) The association of deference with linguistic form. In J. Walters (ed.) *The Sociolinguistics of Deference and Politeness*, The Hague: Mouton, 27: 93–111.

French, J. R. P. and Raven, B. (1959) The bases of social power. In D. Cartwright (ed.) *Studies in Social Power*, Ann Arbor: University of Michigan, 150–67.

Fukushima, S. (2000) *Requests and Culture*. Bern: Peter Lang.

Gal, S. (1997) Language change and sex roles in a bilingual community. In N. Coupland and A. Jaworski (eds) *Sociolinguistics. A Reader and Coursebook*. Basingstoke and London: Macmillan, 376–90. (A shortened version of Gal, S. 1978. Peasant men can't get wives: Language change and roles in a bilingual community. *Language in Society*, 7(1): 1–16).

Gallois, C. and Giles, H. (1998) Accommodating mutual influence in intergroup encounters. In M. T. Palmer and G. A. Barnett (eds) *Mutual Influence in Interpersonal Communication: Theory and Research in Cognition, Affect, and Behavior (Progress in Communication Sciences, Volume XIV)*. Stamford, Connecticut and London, England: Ablex, 135–62.

Gallois, C., Franklyn-Stokes, A., Giles, H. and Coupland, H. (1988) Communication accommodation in intercultural encounters. In Y. Y. Kim and W. B. Gudykunst (eds) *Theories in Intercultural Communication*, Newbury Park: Sage, 157–85.

Gallois, C., Giles, H., Jones, E., Cargile, A. C. and Ota, H. (1995) Accommodating intercultural encounters. Elaborations and extensions. In R. L. Wiseman (ed.) *Intercultural Communication Theory. International and Intercultural Communication Annual Volume XIX*. Thousand Oaks, London and New Delhi: Sage, 115–47.

Gallois, C., Ogay, T. and Giles, H. (2005) Communication accommodation theory: a look back and a look ahead. In W. B. Gudykunst (ed.) *Theorizing about Intercultural Communication*. Thousand Oaks: Sage, 121–48.

Gao, G. (1996) Self and other: a Chinese perspective on interpersonal relationships. In W. B. Gudykunst, S. Ting-Toomey and T. Nishida (eds) *Communication in Personal Relationships across Cultures*. London: Sage, 81–101.

Gao, G. and Ting-Toomey, S. (1998) *Communicating Effectively with the Chinese*. London: Sage.

García, C. (1989) Apologizing in English: politeness strategies used by native and non-native speakers. *Multilingua*, 8: 3–20.

Gardner, R. (2001) *When Listeners Talk. Response Tokens and Listener Stance*. Amsterdam: Benjamins.

Garner, M., Raschka, C. and Sercombe, P. (2006) Sociolinguistic minorities, research, and social relationships. *Journal of Multilingual and Multicultural Development*, 27(1): 61–78.

Garrett, P., Coupland, N. and Williams, A. (1999) Evaluating dialect in discourse: teachers' and teenagers' responses to young English speakers in Wales. *Language in Society*, 28 (3): 321–54.

Gass, S. M. and Houck, N. (1999) *Interlanguage Refusals: A Cross-cultural Study of Japanese–English*. Berlin: Mouton.

Gass, S. M. and Mackey, A. (2000) *Stimulated Recall Methodology in Second Language Research*. Mahwah, NJ: Lawrence Erlbaum.

Geertz. C. (1960) *The Region of Java*. Chicago: Chicago University Press.

Gergen, K. J. (1994) *Realities and Relationships – Soundings in Social Construction*. Cambridge: Harvard University Press.

Gibbs, R. (1981) Your wish is my command: convention and context in interpreting indirect requests. *Journal of Verbal Learning and Verbal Behaviour*, 20: 431–44.

Gibbs, R. (1986) What makes some indirect speech acts conventional? *Journal of Memory and Language*, 25: 181–96.

Giddens, A. (1991) *Modernity and Self-Identity. Self and Society in the Late Modern Age*. Cambridge: Polity Press (in association with Blackwell Publishers).

Giles, H. (1973) Accent mobility: a model and some data. *Anthropological Linguistics*, 15: 87–105.

Giles, H. and Coupland, N. (1991) *Language: Contexts and Consequences*. Milton Keynes: Open University Press.

Giles, H., Coupland, J. and Coupland, N. (eds) (1991) *Contexts of Accommodation. Developments in Applied Sociolinguistics*. Cambridge: Cambridge University Press.

Giles, H. and Johnson, P. (1987) Ethnolinguistic identity theory: a social psychological approach to language maintenance. *International Journal of the Sociology of Language*, 68: 69–99.

Giles, H. and Ogay, T. (2006) Communication accommodation theory. In B. B. Whaley and W. Samter (eds) *Explaining Communication: Contemporary Theories and Exemplars*. Mahwah, NJ: Lawrence Erlbaum, 293–310.

Giles, H., Taylor, D. M. and Bourhis, R. (1973) Towards a theory of interpersonal accommodation through language: some Canadian data. *Language in Society*, 2: 177–92.

Giles, H., Willemyns, M., Gallois, C. and Chernikoff Anderson, M. (2007) Accommodating a new frontier: the context of law enforcement. In K. Fiedler (ed.) *Social Communication*. New York: Psychology Press, 129–62.

Gilroy, P. (1993) *The Black Atlantic: Modernity and Double Consciousness*. London: Verso.

Glanz, L., Williams, R. and Hoeksema, L. (2001) Sensemaking in expatriation – a theoretical basis. *Thunderbird International Business Review*, 43(1): 101–19.

Godard, D. (1977) Same setting, different norms: phone call beginnings in France and the United States. *Language in Society*, 6: 209–19.

Goffman, E. (1956) Embarrassment and social organization. *American Journal of Sociology*, 62: 264–71.

Goffman, E. (1963) *Behavior in Public Places*. New York: Free Press.

Goffman, E. (1967) *Interaction Ritual: Essays on Face-to-Face Behavior*. New York: Pantheon Books.

Goffman, E. (1986) *Frame Analysis: An Essay on the Organization of Experience*. Boston: Northeastern University Press.

Golato, A. (2003) Studying compliment responses: a comparison of DCTs and recordings of naturally occurring talk. *Applied Linguistics*, 24: 90–121.

Golato, A. (2005) *Compliments and Compliment Responses: Grammatical Structure and Sequential Organization*. Amsterdam: John Benjamins.

Golato, A. and Taleghani-Nikazm, C. (2006) Negotiation of face in web chats. *Multilingua*, 25: 293–322.

Gonzales-Lloret, M. (in press) CA for computer-mediated interaction in the Spanish L2 classroom. In G. Kasper and H.T. Nguyen (eds) *Talk-in-Interaction across Languages*. Honolulu, HI: National Foreign Language Resource Center.

Goodwin, C. and Goodwin, M. (1987) Concurrent operations on talk: notes on the interactive organization of assessments. *Papers in Pragmatics*, 1(1): 1–54.

Goodwin, M. H. (1980) 'He-said-she-said': formal cultural procedures for the construction of a gossip dispute activity. *American Ethnologist*, 7(4): 674–95.

Goodwin, M. H. (1983) Aggravated correction and disagreement in children's conversations. *Journal of Pragmatics*, 7: 657–77.

Goodwin, M. H. and Goodwin, C. (1987) Children's arguing. In S. U. Phillips, S. Steele and C. Tanz (eds) *Language, Gender and Sex in Comparative Perspective*, Cambridge: Cambridge University Press, 200–48.

Graumann, C. F. (1989) Perspective setting and taking in verbal interaction. In R. Dietrich and C. Graumann (eds) *Language Processing in Social Context: An Interdisciplinary Account.* Amsterdam: Elsevier Science Publishers, 95–122.

Gregory, M. and Carroll, S. (1978) *Language and Situation. Language Varieties and their Social Contexts.* London: Routledge and Kegan Paul.

Grice, H. P. (1989) Logic and conversation. William James Lectures, 1967. Reprinted in H. P. Grice, *Studies in the Way of Words*, Cambridge, MA: Harvard University Press, 22–40.

Grieshaber, W. (1987) *Authentisches und zitierendes Handeln. Bd. II: Rollenspiele im Sprachunterricht.* [Authentic and Citing Action. Vol. II: Roleplay in Language Teaching]. Tübingen: Narr.

Gu, Y. (1990) Politeness phenomena in modern Chinese. *Journal of Pragmatics*, 14: 237–57.

Gu, Y. (1998) Politeness and Chinese Face. Lecture given in the Department of Linguistics, University of Luton, Summer 1998.

Guba, E. G. and Lincoln, Y. S. (2005) Paradigmatic controversies, contradictions, and emerging confluences. In N. K. Denzin and Y. S. Lincoln (eds) *The Sage Handbook of Qualitative Research.* 3rd edition. Thousand Oaks, CA: Sage, 191–215.

Gubrium, J. F. and Holstein, J. A. (eds) (2002) *Handbook of Interview Research: Contexts and Methods.* Thousand Oaks, CA: Sage.

Gudykunst, W. B. (1998) *Bridging Differences: Effective Intergroup Communication.* London: Sage.

Gudykunst, W. B. and Kim, Young Y. (1997) *Communicating with Strangers: An Approach to Intercultural Communication.* Boston: McGraw Hill.

Gudykunst, W. B. and Nishida, T. (1999) The influence of culture and strength of cultural identity on individual values in Japan and the United States. *Intercultural Communication Studies* 9 (1): 1–18.

Gumperz, J. J. (1970) Verbal strategies in multilingual communication. In J. E. Alatis (ed.) *Bilingualism and Language Contact*, Washington, DC: Georgetown University Press, 129–47.

Gumperz, J. J. (1982) *Discourse strategies.* Cambridge: Cambridge University Press.

Gumperz, J. J. (1992a) Contextualization and understanding. In A. Duranti and C. Goodwin (eds) *Rethinking Context. Language as an Interactive Phenomenon.* Cambridge: Cambridge University Press, 229–52.

Gumperz, J. J. (1992b) Interviewing in intercultural situations. In J. Heritage and P. Drew (eds) *Talk at Work.* Cambridge: Cambridge University Press, 302–30.

Gumperz, J. J. (1996) The linguistic and cultural relativity of conversational inference. In J. J. Gumperz and S. L. Levinson (eds) *Rethinking Linguistic Relativity.* Cambridge: Cambridge University Press, 1–21.

Gumperz, J. J. and Cook-Gumperz, J. (1982) Introduction: language and the communication of social identity. In J. J. Gumperz (ed.) *Language and Social Identity.* Cambridge: Cambridge University Press, 1–21.

Gumperz, J. J. and Levinson, S. C. (1996) *Rethinking Linguistic Relativity.* Cambridge: Cambridge University Press.

Gumperz, J. J., Jupp, T. C. and Roberts, C. (1979) *Crosstalk: A Study of Cross-Cultural Communication.* Southall: National Center for Industrial Language Training.

Günthner, S. (1993) *Diskursstrategien in der interkulturellen Kommunikation. Analysen deutsch– chinesischer Gespräche.* Tübingen: Niemeyer.

Günthner, S. (1994) 'Also moment SO seh ich das NICHT' – Informelle Diskussionen im interkulturellen Kontext. *LiLi* [Zeitschrift für Literaturwissenschaft und Linguistik], 24: 97–122.

Günthner, S. (2007) Intercultural communication and the relevance of cultural specific repertoires of communicative genres. In H. Kotthoff and H. Spencer-Oatey (eds) *Handbook of Intercultural Communication*, Berlin: Mouton de Gruyter, 127–51.

Gupta, A. and Ferguson, J. (2002) Beyond 'culture': space, identity and the politics of difference. In J. X. Inda and R. Rosaldo (eds) *The Anthropology of Globalization – A Reader*. Oxford: Blackwell, 65–80.

Gutt, E. A. (1989) Translation and relevance. UCL Working Papers in Linguistics. Vol. 1: 75–94.

Haberland, H. (1996) Communion or communication? A historical note on one of the 'founding fathers' of pragmatics. In R. Sackman (ed.) *Theoretical Linguistics and Grammatical Description. Papers in Honour of Hans-Heinrich Lieb*. Amsterdam: Benjamins, 163–166.

Hagiwara, A. (2005) Comprehending utterances in Japanese as a first and a second language: literality and conventionality. Ph.D. dissertation, University of Hawai'i at Manoa.

Haiman, J. (1998) *Talk is Cheap: Sarcasm, Alienation, and the Evolution of Language*. Oxford: OUP.

Hall, E. T. (1976) *Beyond Culture*. New York: Doubleday.

Hall, S. (1994) Cultural identity and diaspora. In P. Williams and L. Chrisman (eds) *Colonial Discourse and Post-colonial Theory: A Reader,* New York: Columbia University Press, 392–403.

Hall, S. (1995) New cultures for old. In D. Massey and P. Jess (eds) *A Place in the World?* Oxford: Oxford University Press, 175–213.

Hall, S. and du Gay, P. (eds) (1996) *Questions of Cultural Identity*. London: Sage.

Halliday, M. A. K. (1973) *Explorations in the Functions of Language*. London: Edward Arnold.

Hammond, S. A. (1996) *The Thin Book of Appreciative Inquiry*. Plano, TX: Thin Book Publishing Co.

Hartford, B. S. and Bardovi-Harlig, K. (1992) Experimental and observational data in the study of interlanguage pragmatics. In L. F. Bouton and Y. Kachru (eds) *Pragmatics and Language Learning Monograph Series, Vol. 3*. Urbana, IL: Division of English as an International Language, University of Illinois at Urbana-Champaign, 33–52.

Hassall, T. J. (2001) Modifying requests in a second language. *International Review of Applied Linguistics*, 39: 259–83.

Hassall, T. J. (2006) Learning to take leave in social conversations: a diary study. In M. A. DuFon and E. Churchill (eds) *Language Learners in Study Abroad Contexts*. Clevedon, UK: Multilingual Matters, 31–58.

Heath, C. C. (2004) Analysing face-to-face interaction: video, the visual and material. In D. Silverman (ed.) (2004) *Qualitative Research*. 2nd edition. London: Sage, 266–82.

Henne, H. and Rehbock, H. (1979) *Einführung in die Gesprächsanalyse*. Berlin: de Gruyter.

Herbert, R. K. (1989) The ethnography of English compliments and compliment responses: a contrastive sketch. In W. Olesky (ed.) *Contrastive Pragmatics*, Amsterdam: Benjamins, 3–35.

Herbert, R. K. (1991) The sociology of compliment work: an ethnographic study of Polish and English compliments. *Multilingua*, 10: 381–402.

Heritage, J. (1984) A change-of-state token and aspects of its sequential placement. In J. M. Atkinson and J. Heritage (eds) *Structures of Social Action*. Cambridge: Cambridge University Press, 299–395.

Higgins, C. (2007) Introduction: a closer look at cultural difference: 'interculturality' in talk-in-interaction. *Pragmatics* 17(1): 1–7.

Hinkel, E. (1996) When in Rome: evaluations of L2 pragmalinguistic behaviors. *Journal of Pragmatics*, 26: 51–70.

Hinkel, E. (1997) Appropriateness of advice: DCT and multiple choice data. *Applied Linguistics*, 18: 1–26.

Hinton, P. R. (2000) *Stereotypes, Cognition and Culture*. Hove: Psychology Press.

Hofstede, G. (1991) *Cultures and Organizations: Software of the Mind*. London: McGraw-Hill.

Hofstede, G. (2001) *Culture's Consequences. Comparing Values, Behaviors, Institutions, and Organizations across Nations*. 2nd edition. London: Sage.

Holmes, J. (1986) Compliments and compliment responses in New Zealand English. *Anthropological Linguistics*, 28(4): 485–508.

Holmes, J. (1990) Apologies in New Zealand English. *Language in Society*, 19: 155–99.

Holmes, J. (1995) *Women, Men and Politeness*. London: Longman.

Holmes, J. (1997) Maori and Pakeha English: some New Zealand social dialect data. *Language in Society*, 26(1): 65–101.

Holmes, J. (2005) Using Maori English in New Zealand. *International Journal of Sociology of Language*, 172: 91–115.

Holmes, J. (2007) Humour and the construction of Māori leadership at work. *Leadership*, 3 (1): 5–27.

Holmes, J., Joe, A. Marra, M., Newton, J., Riddiford, N. and Vine B. (In preparation) Applying linguistic research to real world problems: the case of the Wellington Language in the Workplace Project. To appear in C. N. Candlin and S. Sarangi (eds) *Handbook of Applied Linguistics Vol 3 Communication in the Professions*. Berlin: Mouton de Gruyter.

Holmes, J. and Meyerhoff, M. (1999) *Language in Society: Special Issue: Communities of Practice in Language and Gender Research*, 28 (2).

Holmes, J. and Stubbe, M. (2003) *Power and Politeness in the Workplace. A Sociolinguistic Analysis of Talk at Work*. London: Pearson Education.

Holtgraves, T., Srull, T. K. and Socall, D. (1989) Conversation memory: the effects of speaker status on memory for the assertiveness of conversation remarks. *Journal of Personality and Social Psychology*, 56(2): 149–60.

Holtgraves, T. and Yang, J.-N. (1990) Politeness as universal: cross-cultural perceptions of request strategies and inferences based on their use. *Journal of Personality and Social Psychology*, 59(4): 719–29.

Holtgraves, T. and Yang, J.-N. (1992) Interpersonal underpinnings of request strategies: general principles and differences due to culture and gender. *Journal of Personality and Social Psychology*, 62: 246–56.

Holyoak, K. J. and Thagard, P. (1995) *Mental Leaps: Analogy in Creative Thought*. Cambridge, MA: MIT Press.

Hopper, R. (1992) *Telephone Conversation*. Bloomington: Indiana University Press.

House, J. (1996) Developing pragmatic fluency in English as a foreign language: routines and metapragmatic awareness. *Studies in Second Language Acquisition*, 18: 225–52.

House, J. (2003) Misunderstanding in intercultural university encounters. In J. House, G. Kasper and S. Ross (eds) *Misunderstanding in Social Life. Discourse Approaches to Problematic Talk*. London: Longman, 22–56.

House, J. and Kasper, G. (1981) Politeness markers in English and German. In F. Coulmas (ed.) *Conversational Routine: Explorations in Standardized Communication and Prepatterned Speech*. The Hague: Mouton, 289–304.

Hudson, R. A. (1980) *Sociolinguistics*. Cambridge: Cambridge University Press.

Hunter, A. (1994) *Etiquette*. Glasgow: HarperCollins.

Hutchby, I. and Barnett, S. (2005) Aspects of the sequential organization of mobile phone conversation. *Discourse Studies*, 7: 147–71.

Hymes, D. (1971) Competence and performance in linguistic theory. In R. Huxley and E. Ingram (eds) *Language Acquisition: Models and Methods*. London: Academic Press, 3–28.

Ide, R. (1998) 'Sorry for your kindness': Japanese interactional ritual in public discourse. *Journal of Pragmatics*, 29: 509–29.

Ide, S. (1989) Formal forms and discernment: two neglected aspects of universals of linguistic politeness. *Multilingua*, 8(2/3): 223–48.

Iino, M. (1996) Excellent foreigner: Gaijinization of Japanese language and culture in contact situations. Ph.D. dissertation, University of Pennsylvania, Philadelphia.

Ikoma, T. and Shimura, A. (1994) Pragmatic transfer in the speech act of refusal in Japanese as a second language. *Journal of Asian Pacific Communication*, 5(1 and 2): 105–29.

Imai, M. (1981) *Sixteen Ways to Avoid Saying No in Japan*. Tokyo: Nihon Keizai Shimbunsha.

Irvine, J. T. (1974) Strategies of status manipulation in Wolof greeting. In R. Bauman and J. Sherzer (eds) *Explorations in the Ethnography of Speaking*. Cambridge: Cambridge University Press, 167–91.

Itani, R. (1996) *Semantics and Pragmatics of Hedges in English and Japanese*. Tokyo: Hituzi Syobo.

Jaworski, A., Thurlow, C., Lawson, S. and Ylänne, V. (2008) *Language, Tourism, Globalisation*. London: Routledge.

Johnston, B., Kasper, G., and Ross, S. (1998) The effect of rejoinders in production questionnaires. *Applied Linguistics*, 19: 157–82.

Jones, E., Gallois, C., Callan, V. and Barker, M. (1999) Strategies of accommodation: development of a coding system for conversational interaction. *Journal of Language and Social Psychology*, 18: 123–52.

Karim, H. K. (1997) The historical resilience of primary stereotypes: core images of the Muslim other. In S. H. Riggins (ed.) *The Language and Politics of Exclusion. Others in Discourse*. Thousand Oaks, London and New Delhi: Sage, 153–82.

Kasper, G. (1992) Pragmatic transfer. *Second Language Research*, 8(3): 203–31.

Kasper, G. (2000) Data collection in pragmatics. In H. Spencer-Oatey (ed.) *Culturally Speaking*. 1st edition. London and New York: Continuum, 316–41.

Kasper, G. (ed.) (2006a) *Politeness in Interaction*. Special Issue, *Multilingua* 25(3).

Kasper, G. (2006b) When once is not enough: politeness in multiple requests. *Multilingua*, 25: 323–49.

Kasper, G. and Dahl, M. (1991) Research methods in interlanguage pragmatics. *Studies in Second Language Acquisition*, 13: 215–47.

Kasper, G. and Rose, K. R. (2002) *Pragmatic Development in a Second Language*. Oxford: Blackwell.

Keith, M. and Pile, S. (eds) (1993) *Place and the Politics of Identity*. London: Routledge.

Kennedy, G. and Yamazaki, S. (1999) The influence of Māori on the New Zealand English lexicon. In J. Kirk (ed.) *Corpora Galore: Analyses and Techniques in Describing English*. Amsterdam: Rodopi, 33–44.

Kerekes, J. (1992) *Development in Nonnative Speakers' Use and Perception of Assertiveness and Supportiveness in Mixed-Sex Conversations*. (Occasional Paper No. 21). Honolulu, HI: University of Hawai'i at Manoa, Department of English as a Second Language.

Kerekes, J. (2007) Gatekeeping encounters. Special Issue, *Journal of Pragmatics*, 39 (11).

Kern, F. (2000) *Kulturen der Selbstdarstellung. Ost- und Westdeutsche in Bewerbungsgesprächen*. Wiesbaden: Deutscher Universitäts-Verlag.

Kern, J. M. (1991) An evaluation of a novel role-play methodology: the standardized idiographic approach. *Behavior Therapy*, 22: 13–29.

Kim, Y. Y. (2001) *Becoming Intercultural: An Integrative Theory of Communication and Cross-Cultural Adaptation*. London: Sage.

King, A. Y. and Bond, M. H. (1985) The Confucian paradigm of man: a sociological view. In W. S. Tseng and D. H. Wu (eds) *Chinese Culture and Mental Health*. Orlando, FL: Academic Press, 29–45.

King, A. Y. and Myers, J. T. (1977) *Shame as an incomplete conception of Chinese culture*. Occasional Paper. Social Research Center, The Chinese University of Hong Kong.

Kinjo, H. (1987) Oral refusals of invitations and requests in English and Japanese. *Journal of Asian Culture*, 11: 83–106.

Kipper, D. A. (1988) The differential effect of role-playing conditions on the accuracy of self- evaluation. *Journal of Group Therapy, Psychodrama, and Sociometry*, 41: 30–5.

Kluckhohn, F. R. and Strodtbeck, F. L. (1961) *Variations in Value Orientations*. New York: Harper & Row.

Knapp, M., Hopper, R. and Bell, R. (1984) Compliments: a descriptive taxonomy. *Journal of Communication*, 34: 19–31.

Koike, D. A. (1989) Pragmatic competence and adult L2 acquisition: speech acts in interlanguage. *Modern Language Journal*, 73: 279–89.

Kotani, M. (1997) Accounting practices of the Japanese in the United States: explorations of their meanings of apology. Paper presented at the 47th Annual Meeting of the International Communication Association, Montreal.

Kottak, C. P. (1999) *Mirror for Humanity*. 2nd edition. Boston: McGraw Hill College.

Kotthoff, H. (1993) Disagreement and concessions in disputes: on the context sensitivity of preference structures. *Language in Society*, 22: 193–216.

Kristeva, J. (1988) *Etrangers à nous-mêmes*. Paris: Gallimard.

Kroeber, A. L. and Kluckhohn, C. (1952) *Culture: A Critical Review of Concepts and Definitions* (Vol. 47, No.1). Cambridge, MA: Peabody Museum.

Kuha, M. (1997) The computer-assisted interactive DCT: a study in pragmatics research methodology. In L. Bouton (ed.) *Pragmatics and Language Learning, Monograph Series, Vol. 8*. Urbana- Champaign: Division of English as an International Language, University of Illinois, 99–127.

Labov, W. (1966) *The Social Stratification of English in New York City*. Washington, DC: Center for Applied Linguistics.

Labov, W. (1984) Field methods of the project on linguistic change and variation. In J. Baugh and J. Sherzer (eds) *Language in Use*. Englewood Cliffs, NJ: Prentice-Hall, 28–53.

Lado, R. (1957) *Linguistics across Cultures*. Ann Arbor: University of Michigan Press.

Lambert, H. (2001) Not talking about sex in India: Indirection and the communication of bodily intention. In J. Hendry and C.W. Watson (eds) *An Anthropology of Indirect Communication*. London and New York: Routledge, 51–67.

Lave, J. and Wenger, E. (1991) *Situated Learning: Legitimate Peripheral Participation*. Cambridge: Cambridge University Press.

Laver, J. (1975) Communicative functions of phatic communion. In A. Kendon, R. M. Harris and M. R. Key (eds) *The Organization of Behavior in Face-to-Face Interaction*. The Hague: Mouton, 215–38.

Laver, J. (1981) Linguistic routines and politeness in greeting and parting. In F. Coulmas (ed.) *Conversational Routine: Explorations in Standardized Communication and Prepatterned Speech*. The Hague: Mouton, 289–304.

Leech, G. N. (1983) *Principles of Pragmatics*. London: Longman.

Leech, G. N. (2005) Politeness: is there an east-west divide? 外国语2005 年第6期 [*Journal of Foreign Languages* 6]. Available at http://www.ling.lancs.ac.uk/staff/geoff/leech2006politeness.pdf/ [Accessed 16 June 2007].

Leech, G.N. (2007) Politeness: is there an East-West divide. *Journal of Politeness Research: Language, Behaviour, Culture*, 3(2): 167–206.

Lerner, G.H. (1996) Finding 'face' in the preference structures of talk-in-interaction. *Social Psychology Quarterly*, 59: 303–21.

Levine, D. R., Baxter, J. and McNulty, P. (1987) *The Culture Puzzle. Cross-Cultural Communication for English as a Second Language*. Englewood Cliffs: Prentice-Hall.

Levinson, S. C. (1979) Activity types and language. *Linguistics*, 17 (5/6): 365–99.

Levinson, S. C. (1983) *Pragmatics*. Cambridge: Cambridge University Press.

Lewandowska-Tomaszczyk, B. (1989) Praising and complimenting. In W. Oleksy (ed.) *Contrastive Pragmatics*, Amsterdam: John Benjamins, 73–100.

Liao, C.-C. (1994) *A Study on the Strategies, Maximes, and Development of Refusals in Mandarin Chinese*. Taipeh: Crane Publishing.

Liao, C.-C. (1997) *Comparing Directives: American English, Mandarin and Taiwanese English.* Taipeh: Crane Publishing.

Liebscher, G. (2006) Perspectives in conflict. An analysis of German–German conversation. In K. Bührig and J. ten Thije (eds) *Beyond Misunderstanding: The Linguistic Reconstruction of Intercultural Communication.* Amsterdam and Philadelphia: Benjamins, 155–74.

Liefländer-Koistinen, L. and Neuendorff, D. (1991) Telefongespräche im Deutschen und Finnischen: Unterschiede in ihrer interaktionalen Struktur. Paper presented at the Akten des VIII Internationalen Germanisten-Kongresses, Tokyo 1990, München.

Lim, T.-S. (1994) Facework and interpersonal relationships. In S. Ting-Toomey (ed.) *The Challenge of Facework. Cross-Cultural and Interpersonal Issues.* New York: State University of New York Press, 209–29.

Lim, T.-S. and Bowers, J. W. (1991) Facework: solidarity, approbation, and tact. *Human Communication Research,* 17(3): 415–50.

Linell, P. and Jönsson, L. (1991) Suspect stories: perspective setting in an asymmetrical situation. In I. Marková and K. Foppa (eds) *Asymmetries in Dialogue.* Hemel Hempstead: Harvester Wheatsheaf, 75–100.

LoCastro, V. (1986) 'Yes, I agree with you, but . . .': Agreement and disagreement in Japanese and American English. Paper presented at the Japan Association of Language Teachers' International Conference on Language Teaching and Learning, Seiri Gakuen, Hamamatsu, Japan.

Locher, M. A. (2006) Polite behavior within relational work: The discursive approach to politeness. *Multilingua,* 25: 249–67.

Loh, W. C. T. (1993) *Responses to Compliments across Languages and Cultures: a Comparative Study of British and Hong Kong Chinese.* Department of English, Research Report Series No. 30, City Polytechnic of Hong Kong, pp. 1–89.

Low, S. M. and Lawrence-Zúñiga, D. (eds) (2003) *The Anthropology of Space and Place – Locating Culture.* Oxford: Blackwell.

Luke, K. K. and Pavlidou, T.-S. (eds) (2002a) *Telephone Calls: Unity and Diversity in Conversational Structure across Languages and Cultures.* Amsterdam: Benjamins.

Luke, K. K. and Pavlidou, T.-S. (2002b) Studying telephone calls: beginnings, developments, and perspectives. In K. K. Luke and T.-S. Pavlidou (eds) *Telephone Calls: Unity and Diversity in Conversational Structure across Languages and Cultures.* Amsterdam: Benjamins, 3–21.

Luke, K. K. and Pavlidou, T.-S. (eds) (2002) *Telephone Calls.* Amsterdam: Benjamins.

Macalister, J. (2003) 'The presence of Māori words in New Zealand English'. (Unpublished Ph.D. thesis, Victoria University of Wellington, Wellington, New Zealand).

Malinowski, B. (1966 [1923]) The problem of meaning in primitive languages. Supplement to C. K. Ogden and I. A. Richards *The Meaning of Meaning,* London: Routledge and Kegan Paul, 296–336.

Manes, J. and Wolfson, N. (1981) The compliment formula. In F. Coulmas (ed.) *Conversational Routine.* The Hague: Mouton, 115–132.

Mao, L. R. (1994) Beyond politeness theory: 'face' revisited and renewed. *Journal of Pragmatics,* 21: 451–86.

Markham, A. N. (2004) Internet communication as a tool for qualitative research. In D. Silverman (ed.) *Qualitative Research.* 2nd edition. London: Sage, 95–124.

Markus, H. R. and Kitayama, S. (1991) Culture and the self: implications for cognition, emotion, and motivation. *Psychological Review,* 98: 224–53.

Márquez Reiter, R., Rainey, I. and Fulcher, G. (2005) A comparative study of certainty and conventional indirectness: evidence from British English and Peninsular Spanish. *Applied Linguistics,* 26: 1–31.

Marra, M. (1998) "Okay we'll start now I think': the boundaries of meetings. Opening and closing sequences, and framing devices'. (Unpublished MA paper. Victoria University of Wellington, New Zealand).

Marra, M. (2006) Talking up, talking down: ethnicised communities of practice at work. Paper presented at the New Zealand Language and Society Conference, Christchurch Arts Centre, 19–20 August 2006.

Massey, D. and Jess, P. (eds) (1995) *A Place in the World*? Oxford: Oxford University Press.

Matsumoto, D. (1996) *Culture and Psychology*. Pacific Grove, CA: Brooks/Cole.

Matsumoto, Y. (1985) A sort of speech act qualification in Japanese: chotto. *Journal of Asian Culture*, 9: 143–59.

Matsumoto, Y. (1988) Reexamination of the universality of face: politeness phenomena in Japanese. *Journal of Pragmatics*, 12: 403–26.

Matsumoto, Y. (1989) Politeness and conversational universals – observations from Japanese. *Multilingua*, 8(2/3): 207–21.

McCann, R. and Giles, H. (2006) Communication with people of different ages in the workplace: Thai and American data. *Human Communication Research*, 32(1), 74–108.

McEntegart, D. and Le Page R B. (1982) An appraisal of the statistical techniques used in the sociolinguistic survey of mulitilingual communities. In S. Romaine (ed.) *Sociolinguistic Variation in Speech Communities*. London: Edward Arnold, 105–24.

McNeill, D. (2000) *Language and Gesture*. Cambridge: Cambridge University Press.

Merritt, M. (1994) Repetition in situated discourse: exploring its forms and functions. In B. Johnstone (ed.) *Repetition in Discourse. Interdisciplinary Perspectives. Volume One*. Norwood, NJ: Ablex, 23–36.

Metge, J. (2001) *Korero Tahi Talking Together*. Auckland: Auckland University Press.

Metge, J. and Kinloch, P. (1978) *Talking Past Each Other: Problems of Cross-Cultural Communication*. Wellington: Victoria University Press.

Miles, P. (1994) Compliments and gender. University of Hawai'i Occasional Papers Series, No. 26, 85–137.

Miller, D.C., and Salkind, N. J. (2002) *Handbook of Research Design and Social Measurement*. 6th edition. Newbury Park, CA: Sage.

Miller, L. (1991) Verbal listening behavior in conversations between Japanese and Americans. In J. Blommaert and J. Verschueren (eds) *The Pragmatics of Intercultural and International Communication*. Amsterdam: John Benjamins, 110–30.

Miller, L. (1994a) Japanese and American indirectness. *Journal of Asian and Pacific Communication*, 5(1 and 2): 37–55.

Miller, L. (1994b) Japanese and American meetings and what goes on before them. *Pragmatics*, 4(2): 221–38.

Miller, L. (1995) Two aspects of Japanese and American co-worker interaction: giving instruction and creating rapport. *Journal of Applied Behavioral Sciences*, 3(2): 141–61.

Miller, L. (1997) Wasei eigo: English 'loanwords' coined in Japan. In J. Hill, P. J. Mistry and L. Campbell (eds) *The Life of Language: Papers in Linguistics in Honor of William Bright*. The Hague: Mouton/de Gruyter, 123–39.

Miller, L. (1998) Stereotype legacy: culture and person in Japanese/American business interactions. In Y. T. Lee, C. McCauley and J. Draguns (eds) *Through the Looking Glass: Personality in Culture*. Mahwah, NJ: Lawrence Erlbaum, 213–232

Mizutani, O. and Mizutani, N. (1977) *Nihongo Notes 1*. Tokyo: The Japan Times.

Mizutani, O. and Mizutani, N. (1979) *Nihongo Notes 2*. Tokyo: The Japan Times.

Moeran, B. (1996) *A Japanese Advertising Agency: An Anthropology of Media and Markets*. Honolulu: University of Hawaii Press.

Morgan, J. (1978) Two types of convention in indirect speech acts. In P. Cole (ed.) *Syntax and Semantics 9: Pragmatics.* New York: Academic Press, 261–280

Mori, J. (2003) The construction of interculturality: a study of initial encounters between Japanese and American students. *Research on Language and Social Interaction*, 36: 143–84.

Mulac, A., Wiemann, J. M., Widenmann, S. and Gibson, T. W. (1988) Male/female language differences and effects in same-sex and mixed-sex dyads: the gender-linked language effect. *Communication Monographs*, 55: 315–35.

Naotsuka, R. (1980) *Oobeejin ga chinmoku suru toki: ibunka kan no comyunikeeshon.* Tokyo: Taishuukan-shoten.

Naotsuka, R., Sakamoto, N. Hirose, T., Hagihara, H., Ohta, J., Maeda, S., Hara, T. and Iwasaki, K. (1981) *Mutual Understanding of Different Cultures.* Osaka: Taishukan.

Neustupný, J. V. (1987) *Communicating with the Japanese.* Tokyo: The Japan Times.

Niedzielski, N. and Giles, H. (1996) Linguistic accommodation. In H. Goebl, P. H. Nelde, Z. Star and W. Wölk (eds) *Contact Linguistics.* Berlin and New York: Walter de Gruyter, 332–42.

Nunan, D. (1992) *Research Methods in Language Learning.* Cambridge: Cambridge University Press.

Odlin, T. (1989) *Language Transfer.* Cambridge: Cambridge University Press.

Oka, N. (2006). 'Nihonjin shuwa washa no gengo koodoo – shazai o megutte' ['Linguistic Behaviour of Japanese Sign Language Users: Responses to Unfounded Accusations'] (Unpublished MA thesis submitted to Hitotsubashi University).

Oliver, R. T. (1971) *Communication and Culture in Ancient India and China.* Syracuse: Syracuse University Press.

Olshtain, E. (1989) Apologies across languages. In S. Blum-Kulka, J. House and G. Kasper (eds) *Cross-Cultural Pragmatics: Requests and Apologies.* Norwood, NJ: Ablex, 155–73.

Olshtain, E. and Cohen, A. D. (1983) Apology: a speech-act set. In N. Wolfson and E. Judd (eds) *Sociolinguistics and Language Acquisition.* Rowley: Newbury House, 18–35.

Olshtain, E., and Weinbach, L. (1993) Interlanguage features of the speech act of complaining. In G. Kasper and S. Blum-Kulka (eds) *Interlanguage Pragmatics.* New York: Oxford University Press, 108–22.

Owen, M. (1983) *Apologies and Remedial Interchanges.* Berlin: Mouton de Gruyter.

Pavlenko, A. (2007) Autobiographic narratives as data in applied linguistics. *Applied Linguistics*, 28: 163–88.

Pavlidou, T.-S. (1991) [in Greek]. *Politeness on the telephone: contrastive analysis of Greek and German conversations.* Proceedings of the 11th Annual Meeting of the Department of Linguistics, Faculty of Philosophy, Aristotle University of Thessaloniki, 26–28 April 1990. Thessaloniki: Kyriakidis.

Pavlidou, T.-S. (1994) Contrasting German–Greek politeness and the consequences. *Journal of Pragmatics*, 21: 487–511.

Pavlidou, T.-S. (1995) [in Greek]. *Phatic communi(cat)ion and phatic elements.* Proceedings of the 15th Annual Meeting of the Department of Linguistics, Faculty of Philosophy, Aristotle University of Thessaloniki, 11–14 May 1994. Thessaloniki, 710–21.

Pavlidou, T.-S. (1997) The last five turns: preliminary remarks on closings in Greek and German telephone calls. *International Journal of the Sociology of Language*, 126: 196–220.

Pavlidou, T.-S. (1998a) Greek and German telephone closings: patterns of confirmation and agreement. *Pragmatics*, 8(1): 79–94.

Pavlidou, T.-S. (1998b) Zum Stellenwert der phatischen Kommunion in einer Theorie der Kommunikation, Perspektiven einer Komunikations wissenschaft. Akten des Internationalen Gerold Ungeheuer-Symposiums, Essen 6.7.–8.7.1995, Münster.

Pavlidou T.-S. (2005) Telephone talk. In K. Brown (editor-in-chief) *Encyclopedia of Language and Linguistics, Vol.12*. 2nd edition. Oxford: Elsevier, 546–48.

Peirce, B.N. (1994) Using diaries in second language research and teaching. *English Quarterly*, 26: 22–9.

Penman, R. (1990) Facework and politeness: multiple goals in courtroom discourse. *Journal of Language and Social Psychology*, 9(1–2): 15–38.

Pennington, M. (1999) Equivalence classification in language transfer. Paper presented at the Transfer Colloquium, TESOL Annual Convention and Exposition, New York City, March 1999.

Pieke, F. N. (1992) The ordinary and the extraordinary. Dissertation, University of California at Berkeley.

Piirainen-Marsh, A. (1995) *Face in Second Language Conversation*. Jyväskylä, Finland: University of Jyväskylä.

Piirainen-Marsh, A. (2006) Managing adversarial questioning in broadcast interviews. *Journal of Politeness Research*, 1: 193–217.

Pile, S. and Thrift, N. (eds) (1995) *Mapping the Subject: Geographies of Cultural Transformation*. London: Routledge.

Pomerantz, A. (1975) *Second Assessments: A Study of Some Features of Agreements/Disagreements.* Unpublished PhD dissertation, University of California at Irvine.

Pomerantz, A. (1978) Compliment responses: notes on the co-operation of multiple constraints. In J. Schenkein (ed.) *Studies in the Organization of Conversational Interaction*. New York: Academic Press, 79–112.

Pomerantz, A. (1984a) Agreeing and disagreeing with assessments: some features of preferred/ dispreferred turn shapes. In J. M. Atkinson and J. Heritage (eds) *Structures of Social Action: Studies in Conversation Analysis*. Cambridge: Cambridge University Press, 57–101.

Pomerantz, A. (1984b) Pursuing a response. In J.M. Atkinson and J. Heritage (eds) *Structures of Social Action: Studies in Conversation Analysis*. Cambridge: Cambridge University Press, 152–163.

Pratt, M. L. (1992) *Imperial Eyes: Travel Writing and Transculturation*. London: Routledge.

Pringle, J. K. (2005) Reflections on amplifying 'others' voices: dilemmas that face 'white' researchers who aim to make research and scholarship more inclusive by 'writing in' the experiences of the 'others' – those that are members of historically disadvantaged groups. Paper presented in the Advanced Research Methodologies Seminar Series 2005, Faculty of Commerce and Administration, Victoria University of Wellington, 11 November 2006.

Rampton, B. (1995) *Crossing: Language and Ethnicity Among Adolescents*. London and New York: Longman.

Rampton, B. (1998) Language crossing and the redefinition of reality. In P. Auer (ed.) *Codeswitching in Conversation*. London: Routledge, 290–317.

Relph, E. (1976) *Place and Placelessness*. London: Pion.

Richards, J. C. and Sukwiwat, M. (1983) Language transfer and conversational competence. *Applied Linguistics*, 4(2): 113–25.

Riggins, S. H. (ed.) (1997) *The Language and Politics of Exclusion. Others in Discourse*. Thousand Oaks, London and New Delhi: Sage.

Ringland, G. A. and Duce, D. A. (1988) *Approaches to Knowledge Representation*. Taunton: Research Studies Press.

Rintell, E. (1981) Sociolinguistic variation and pragmatic ability: a look at learners. *International Journal of the Sociology of Language*, 27: 11–34.

Rintell, E. and Mitchell, C. J. (1989) Studying requests and apologies: an inquiry into method. In S. Blum-Kulka, J. House, and G. Kasper (eds) *Cross-cultural Pragmatics*. Norwood, NJ: Ablex, 248–72.

Ritchie, J. E. (1992) *Becoming Bicultural*. Wellington: Huia Publishers.

Roberts, C. (1985) *The Interview Game and How It's Played*. London: British Broadcasting Corporation.

Roberts, C. (2003) Applied linguistics applied. In S. Sarangi and T. van Leeuwen (eds) *Applied Linguistics and Communities of Practice*. London: Continuum, 132–49.

Roberts, C., Davies, E. and Jupp, T. (1992) *Language and Discrimination. A Study of Communication in Multi-ethnic Workplaces*. London and New York: Longman.

Roberts, C. and Sayers, P. (1987) Keeping the gate: how judgements are made in intercultural interviews. In K. Knapp, W. Enninger and A. Knapp-Potthoff (eds) *Analyzing Intercultural Communication*. Berlin: Mouton de Gruyter, 111–35.

Roberts, M. (1999) 'Immigrant language maintenance and shift in the Gujurati, Dutch and Samoan communities of Wellington'. (Unpublished Ph.D. thesis. Victoria University of Wellington, Wellington, New Zealand).

Robinson, M. (1992) Introspective methodology in interlanguage pragmatics research. In G. Kasper (ed.) *Pragmatics of Japanese as Native and Target Language. Technical Report #3*: Second Language Teaching and Curriculum Center, University of Hawai'i at Manoa, HI, 27–82.

Robinson, W. P. (ed.) (1996) *Social Groups and Identities.Developing the Legacy of Henri Tajfel*. Oxford: Butterworth Heinemann.

Rose, G. (1995) Place and identity: a sense of place. In D. Massey and P. Jess (eds) *A Place in the World?* Oxford: Oxford University Press, 87–132.

Rose, K. R. (1992) Speech acts and questionnaires: the effect of hearer response. *Journal of Pragmatics*, 17: 49–62.

Rose, K. R. (1994) On the validity of discourse completion tests in non-Western contexts. *Applied Linguistics*, 15: 1–14.

Rose, K. R. (1999) Teachers and students learning about requests in Hong Kong. In E. Hinkel (ed.) *Culture in Second Language Teaching and Learning*. Cambridge: Cambridge University Press, 167–80.

Rose, K. R. and Ono, R. (1995) Eliciting speech act data in Japanese: the effect of questionnaire type. *Language Learning*, 45: 191–223.

Rosenwald, G. C. and Ochberg, R. L. (1992) Introduction: life stories, cultural politics, and self- understanding. In: G. C. Rosenwald, and R. L. Ochberg (eds) *Storied Lives: The Cultural Politics of Self-Understanding*. New Haven, CT: Yale University Press, 1–18.

Roth, M. (2005) *Stereotype in gesprochener Sprache. Narrative Interviews mit Ost- und Westberliner Sprechern 1993–1996*. Tübingen: Stauffenburg.

Röver, C. (2005) *Testing ESL Pragmatics*. Frankfurt am Main: Lang.

Rubin, J. (1983) How to tell when someone is saying 'no' revisited. In N. Wolfson and E. Judd (eds) *Sociolinguistics and Language Acquisition*. Rowley: Newbury House, 10–17.

Ruhi, Ş. (2006) Politeness in compliment responses: a perspective from naturally occurring exchanges in Turkish. *Pragmatics*, 16 (1): 43–101.

Ruwhiu, D. and Wolfgramm, R. (2006) Kaupapa Maori research: a contribution to critical management studies in New Zealand. In C. Pritchard, D. Jones and R. Jacques (eds) *Organization, Identity and Locality (OIL)* II Conference Proceedings. Palmerston North: Department of Management, Massey University, 51–8. Available at http://www.massey.ac.nz/~cprichar/Oil%20Conference%20Proceedings_revised.pdf [Accessed 21 June 2007].

Sack, R. D. (1997) *Homo Geographicus – A Framework for Action, Awareness, and Moral Concern*. Baltimore: The Johns Hopkins University Press.

Sacks, H. (1987) On the preference for agreement and contiguity in sequences in conversation. In G. Button and J. R. E. Lee (eds) *Talk and Social Organisation*. Clevedon: Multilingual Matters, 54–69.

Sacks, H. (1992) *Lectures on Conversation*. Edited by G. Jefferson, introduction by E. A. Schegloff. Cambridge: Blackwell.

Saeki, M. and O'Keefe, B. (1994) Refusals and rejections: designing messages to serve multiple goals. *Human Communication Research*, 2(2): 67–102.

Said, E. W. (1978) *Orientalism*. New York: Pantheon.

Said, E. W. (1999) *Out of Place: A Memoir*. New York: Viking.

Salmond, A. (1974) Rituals of encounter among the Māori: sociolinguistic study of a scene. In R. Bauman and J. Shearer (eds) *Explorations in the Ethnography of Speaking*. Cambridge: Cambridge University Press, 192–212.

Salmond, A. (1975) *Hui: A Study of Maori Ceremonial Gatherings*. Wellington: Reed.

Sanjek, R. (ed.) (1990) *Fieldnotes. The Makings of Anthropology*. Ithaca and London: Cornell University Press.

Sarangi, S. (1994) Accounting for mismatches in intercultural selection interviews. *Multilingua (Cross Cultural Communication in the Professions, Special Issue*, edited by Anne Pauwels) 13(1/2): 163–94.

Sarangi, S. (2006) The conditions and consequences of professional discourse studies. In R. Kiely, P. Rea-Dickens, H. Woodfield and G. Clibbon (eds) *Language, Culture and Identity in Applied Linguistics (British Studies in Applied Linguistics* 21). London: Equinox, 199–220.

Sarangi, S. and Candlin, C. N. (2003) Trading between reflexivity and relevance: new challenges for applied linguistics. *Applied Linguistics*, 24 (3): 271–85.

Sasaki, M. (1998) Investigating EFL students' production of speech acts: a comparison of production questionnaires and role plays. *Journal of Pragmatics*, 30: 457–84.

Sasaki, T. (2003) Recipient orientation in verbal protocols: methodological issues in concurrent think-aloud. *Second Language Studies*, 22(1): 1–54.

Sawyer, M. (1992) The development of pragmatics in Japanese as a second language: The sentence-final particle ne. In G. Kasper (ed.) *Pragmatics of Japanese as a Native and Foreign Language*. Technical Report # 3, Second Language Teaching and Curriculum Center, University of Hawaii at Manoa, 83–125.

Scarcella, R. (1983) Discourse accent in second language performance. In S. Gass and L. Selinker (eds) *Language Transfer in Language Learning*. Rowley, MA: Newbury House, 306–26.

Schegloff, E. (1972) Sequencing in conversational openings. In J. Gumperz and D. Hymes (eds) *Directions in Sociolinguistics*. New York: Holt, Rinehart and Winston, 346–80.

Schegloff, E. (1992) On talk and its institutional occasions. In P. Drew and J. Heritage (eds) *Talk at Work*. Cambridge: Cambridge University Press, 101–34.

Schegloff, E. (1994) Telephone conversation. In R. E. Asher (ed.) *The Encyclopedia of Language and Linguistics*, Oxford: Pergamon, 4547–49.

Schegloff, E. (2002) Reflections on research on telephone conversations: issues of cross-cultural scope and scholarly exchange, interactional import and consequences. In K. K. Luke and T.-S. Pavlidou (eds) *Telephone Calls: Unity and Diversity in Conversational Structure across Languages and Cultures*. Amsterdam: Benjamins, 249–81.

Schegloff, E. and Sacks, H. (1973) Opening up closings. *Semiotica*, 8: 289–327.

Schiffrin, D. (1987) *Discourse Markers*. Cambridge: Cambridge University Press.

Schiffrin, D. (1994) *Approaches to Discourse*. Oxford: Blackwell.

Schnurr, S., Marra, M. and Holmes, J. (2007) Being (im)polite in New Zealand workplaces: Māori and Pākehā leaders. *Journal of Pragmatics*, 39: 712–29.

Schönfeldt, J. and Golato, A. (2003) Repair in chats: a conversation analytic approach. *Research on Language and Social Interaction*, 36: 241–84.

Schumann, J. H. (1998) *The Neurobiology of Affect in Language*. Oxford: Blackwell.

Schwandt, T. A. (2003) Three epistemological stances for qualitative inquiry: Interpretivism, hermeneutics, and social, constructionism. In N. K. Denzin and Y. S. Lincoln (eds) *The Landscape of Qualitative Research*. 2nd edition. Thousand Oaks, CA: Sage, 292–331.

Schwartz, S. H., Melech, G., Lehmann, A., Burgess, S., Harris, M. and Owens, V. (2001) Extending the cross-cultural validity of the theory of basic human values with a different method of measurement. *Journal of Cross-Cultural Psychology*, 32(5): 519–42.

Schwitalla, J. (2001) Language issues: communication between East and West Germans. In D. Lewis (ed.) *Contemporary Germany. A Handbook*. London: Arnold, 238–47.

Scollon, R. and Scollon, S. W. (1991) Topic confusion in English–Asian discourse. *World Englishes*, 10(2): 113–25.

Scollon, R. and Scollon, S. W. (1995) *Intercultural Communication: A Discourse Approach*. Oxford, UK: Blackwell.

Seamon, D. (1984) A phenomenology of lifeworld and place. *Phenomenology + Pedagogy*, 2(2), 130–5. Available at: http://www.phenomenologyonline.com/articles/seamon.html [Accessed 21 June 2007].

Searle, J. R. (1996) *The Construction of Social Reality*. London: Penguin Books.

Shea, D. P. (1994) Perspective and production: structuring conversational participation across cultural borders. *Pragmatics*, 4(3): 357–89. (Special Issue: M. Meeuwis (ed.) Critical perspectives on intercultural communication.)

Shepard, C. A., Giles, H. and Le Poire, B. A. (2001) Communication accommodation theory. In W. P. Robinson and H. Giles (eds) *The New Handbook of Language and Social Psychology*. Chichester: John Wiley and Sons, 33–56.

Shimanoff, S. (1987) Types of emotional disclosure and request compliance between spouses. *Communication Monographs*, 54: 85–100.

Shing-Lung, C. (2003) *Kulturelle Kontraste bei deutschen und chinesischen Bewerbungsgesprächen. Am Beispiel des Berufsbereiches der Informationstechnologie*. Frankfurt am Main: P. Lang.

Sifianou, M. (1989) On the telephone again! Differences in telephone behaviour: England vs. Greece. *Language in Society*, 18: 524–44.

Sifianou, M. (1992a) *Politeness Phenomena in England and Greece: A Cross-Cultural Perspective*. Oxford: Clarendon.

Sifianou, M. (1992b) The use of diminutives in expressing politeness: modern Greek versus English. *Journal of Pragmatics*, 17: 155–73.

Silverman, D. (2006) *Interpreting Qualitative Data*. 3rd edition. London: Sage.

Silverman, D. (ed.) (2004) *Qualitative Research*. 2nd edition. London: Sage.

Simon, B. (2004) *Identity in Modern Society: A Social Psychological Perspective*. Oxford: Blackwell.

Skoutarides, A. (1986) *Foreigner Talk in Japanese*. Monash University, Melbourne.

Slugoski, B. R. and Turnbull, W. (1988) Cruel to be kind and kind to be cruel: sarcasm, banter, and social relations. *Journal of Language and Social Psychology*, 7: 101–21.

Smagorinsky, P. (1998) Thinking and speech and protocol analysis. *Mind, Culture, and Activity*, 5: 157–77.

Smagorinsky, P. (2001) Rethinking protocol analysis from a cultural perspective. *Annual Review of Applied Linguistics*, 21: 233–45.

Smith, L. T. (1999) *Decolonizing Methodologies: Research and Indigenous Peoples*. Dunedin: University of Otago Press.

Smith, N. V. (ed.) (1982) *Mutual Knowledge*. London: Academic Press.

Soja, E. (1989) *Postmodern Geographies – The Reassertion of Space in Critical Social Theory*. London: Verso.

Spencer-Oatey, H. (1993) Conceptions of social relations and pragmatics research. *Journal of Pragmatics*, 20: 27–47.

Spencer-Oatey, H. (1996) Reconsidering power and distance. *Journal of Pragmatics*, 26: 1–24.

Spencer-Oatey, H. (1997) Unequal relationships in high and low power distance societies. A comparative study of tutor–student role relations in Britain and China. *Journal of Cross-Cultural Psychology*, 28(3): 284–302.

Spencer-Oatey, H. (2005) Rapport management theory and culture. *Intercultural Pragmatics*, 2–3: 335–346.

Spencer-Oatey, H. (2007) Theories of identity and the analysis of face. *Journal of Pragmatics*, 39: 639–56.

Spencer-Oatey, H. (2009) Face, identity and interactional goals. In F. Bargiela and M. Haugh (eds) *Face, Communication and Social Interaction.* London: Equinox Publishing.

Spencer-Oatey, H. and Franklin, P. (2009) *Intercultural Interaction: A Multidisciplinary Approach to Intercultural Communication.* Basingstoke: Palgrave Macmillan.

Spencer-Oatey, H. and Jiang, W. (2003) Explaining cross-cultural pragmatic findings: moving from politeness maxims to sociopragmatic interactional principles (SIPs). *Journal of Pragmatics*, 35(10–11): 1633–50.

Spencer-Oatey, H. and Xing, J. (1998) Relational management in Chinese–British business meetings. In S. Hunston (ed.) *Language at Work.* Clevedon: British Association for Applied Linguistics in association with Multilingual Matters Ltd., 31–46.

Spencer-Oatey, H. and Xing, J. (2004) Rapport management problems in Chinese–British business interactions: a case study. In J. House and J. Rehbein (eds) *Multilingual Communication.* Amsterdam: Benjamins, 197–221.

Sperber, D. (1996) *Explaining Culture.* Oxford: Blackwell.

Sperber, D. (2000) (ed.) *Metarepresentation: A Multidisciplinary Perspective.* Oxford: Oxford University Press.

Sperber, D. and Wilson, D. (1986/2nd edition with postface1995) *Relevance: Communication and Cognition.* Oxford: Blackwell.

Sperber, D., Premack, D. and Premack, A. J. (1995) *Causal Cognition: A Multidisciplinary Debate.* Oxford: Oxford University Press.

Spradley, J. P. (1979) *The Ethnographic Interview.* New York: Holt, Rinehart and Winston.

Starbuck, W. H. and Milliken, F. J. (1988) Executives' perceptual filters: what they notice and how they make sense. In D. C. Hambrick (ed.) *The Executive Effect: Concepts and Methods for Studying Top Managers.* Greenwich, CT: JAI, 35–65.

Steinberg Du, J. (1995) The performance of face-threatening acts in Chinese. In G. Kasper (ed.) *Pragmatics of Chinese as Native and Target Language.* Technical Report #5. Honolulu, HI: University of Hawai'i, Second Language Teaching and Curriculum Center, 165–206.

Stemmer, B. (1981) Kohäsion im gesprochenen Diskurs deutscher Lerner des Englischen. Paper presented at the Manuskripte zur Sprachlehrforschung, 18, Bochum, Germany.

Sternberg, R. J. (1995) *In Search of the Human Mind.* Fort Worth: Harcourt Brace College Publishers.

Stevenson, P. (2002) *Language and German Disunity: A Sociolinguistic History of East and West Germany, 1945–2000.* Oxford: Oxford University Press.

Stevenson, P. and Theobald, J. (2000) (eds) *Relocating Germanness: Discursive Disunity in Unified Germany,* Basingstoke: Palgrave Macmillan.

Street, R. L. J. (1982) Evaluation of noncontent speech accommodation. *Language and Communication*, 2: 13–31.

Stubbe, M. (1998) Researching language in the workplace: a participatory model. *Proceedings of the Australian Linguistics Society Conference.* Brisbane University of Queensland. July 1998. http://emsah.uq.edu.au/linguistics/als/als98/ [Accessed 21 June 2007].

Stubbe, M. (2001) From office to production line: collecting data for the Wellington Language in the Workplace Project. *Language in the Workplace Occasional Papers* 2 . http://www.victoria.ac.nz/lals/lwp/resources/occasional-papers.aspx [Accessed 1 December 2007]

Stubbe, M. and Brown, P. (2002) *Talk That Works. Communication in Successful Factory Teams: A Training Resource Kit*. Wellington: School of Linguistics and Applied Language Studies, Victoria University of Wellington.

Sugimoto, N. (1998) Norms of apology depicted in U.S. American and Japanese literature on manners and etiquette. *International Journal of Intercultural Relations*, 22(3): 251–76.

Svennevig, J. (1999) *Getting Acquainted in Conversation*. Amsterdam: Benjamins.

Tajfel, H. (1974) Social identity and intergroup behaviour. *Social Science Information*, 13: 65–93.

Tajfel, H. (ed.) (1978) *Differentiation between Social Groups*. London: Academic Press.

Takahashi, S. (1995) 'Pragmatic transferability of L1 indirect request strategies perceived by Japanese learners of English' (Unpublished Ph.D. dissertation, University of Hawai'i at Manoa).

Takahashi, S. (1996) Pragmatic transferability. *Studies in Second Language Acquisition*, 18: 189–223.

Takahashi, T. and Beebe, L. M. (1993) Cross-linguistic influence in the speech act of correction. In G. Kasper and S. Blum-Kulka (eds) *Interlanguage Pragmatics*. New York: Oxford University Press, 138–57.

Takahashi, Y. (2005) Toward a balancing approach: the use of apology in Japanese society. *International Review of Victimology*, 12(1): 23–45.

Tanaka, N. (1991) An investigation of apology: Japanese in comparison with Australian. *Meikai Journal*, 4: 35–53.

Tanaka, N. (1999) 'Apology' re-visited: some cultural differences between English and Japanese. *Meikai Journal*, 11: 23–44.

Tao, H. and Thompson, S. A. (1991) English backchannels in Mandarin conversation: a case study of superstratum pragmatic 'interference'. *Journal of Pragmatics*, 16: 209–23.

Tateyama, Y., Kasper, G., Mui, L., Tay, H.-M., and Thananart, O. (1997) Explicit and implicit teaching of pragmatic routines. In L. Bouton (ed.) *Pragmatics and Language Learning*, vol. 8. Urbana: University of Illinois at Urbana-Champaign, 163–77.

ten Have, P. (2002) Comparing telephone call openings: theoretical and methodological considerations. In K. K. Luke and T.-S. Pavlidou (eds) *Telephone Calls: Unity and Diversity in Conversational Structure across Languages and Cultures*. Amsterdam: Benjamins, 233–48.

ten Have, P. (2003) *Understanding Qualitative Research and Ethnomethodology*. Thousand Oaks: Sage.

ten Have, P. (2007) *Doing Conversation Analysis*. 2nd edition. Thousand Oaks: Sage.

ten Thije, J. (2006) Beyond misunderstanding: Introduction. In K. Bührig, and J. ten Thije (eds) *Beyond Misunderstanding: The Linguistic Reconstruction of Intercultural Communication*. Amsterdam and Philadelphia: Benjamins, 1–8.

Thakerar, J. N., Giles, H. and Cheshire, J. (1982) Psychological and linguistic parameters of speech accommodation theory. In C. Fraser and K. R. Scherer (eds) *Advances in the Social Psychology of Language*. Cambridge: Cambridge University Press, 205–55.

Thomas, J. (1981) 'Pragmatic failure'. (Unpublished MA dissertation, Lancaster University).

Thomas, J. (1983) Cross-cultural pragmatic failure. *Applied Linguistics*, 4(2): 91–112.

Thomas, J. (1995) *Meaning in Interaction. An Introduction to Pragmatics*. London: Longman.

Thompson, R. B. and Tenenbaum, H. (2002) Review of 'Culturally Speaking: Managing Rapport through Talk across Cultures'. *Journal of Language and Social Psychology* 21(2): 183–87.

Thüne, E. M. and Leonardi, S. (eds) (2003) *Telefonare in diverse lingue. Organizzazione sequenziale, routine e rituali in telefonate di servizio, di emergenza e fàtiche* [Telephone calls in different languages. Sequence organization, routine and ritual in service calls, emergency calls, and business calls]. Milano: FrancoAngeli.

Ting-Toomey, S. (1999) *Communicating across Cultures*. New York: The Guilford Press.

Ting-Toomey, S. and Cocroft, B.-A. (1994) Face and facework: theoretical and research issues. In S. Ting-Toomey (ed.) *The Challenge of Facework*. New York: State University of New York Press, 307–40.

Ting-Toomey, S. and Kurogi, A. (1998) Facework competence in intercultural conflict: an updated face-negotiation theory. *International Journal of Intercultural Relations*, 22(2): 187–225.

Tokuda, M. (2001) L2 learners' perceptions of politeness in Japanese: The evaluations on non-native speaker in L2 Japanese. Ph.D. dissertation, University of Hawai'i at Manoa.

Tracy, K. (1990) The many faces of facework. In H. Giles and W. P. Robinson (eds) *Handbook of Language and Social Psychology*. Chichester: John Wiley and Sons, 209–26.

Tracy, K. and Baratz, S. (1994) The case for case studies of facework. In S. Ting-Toomey (ed.) *The Challenge of Facework*. Albany: State University of New York Press, 287–305.

Trosborg, A. (1995) *Interlanguage Pragmatics*. Berlin: Mouton de Gruyter.

TSG (1975) *Texte Gesprochener Sprache, Band III*. Erarbeitet im Institut für Deutsche Sprache. Forschungsstelle Freiburg. München: Hueber.

Tsuruta, Y. (1998) 'Politeness, the Japanese Style: an investigation into the use of honorific forms and people's attitudes towards such use'. (Unpublished Ph.D. Thesis, University of Luton).

Tuan, Y.-F. (1976) Humanistic Geography. *Annals of the Association of American Geographers*, 66(2): 266–76.

Tuan, Y.-F. (1977) *Space and Place – The Perspective of Experience*. London: Edward Arnold.

Tuan, Y.-F. (1996) *Cosmos and Hearth – A Cosmopolite's Viewpoint*. Minneapolis: University of Minnesota Press.

Turnbull, W. (2001) An appraisal of pragmatic elicitation techniques for the social psychological study of talk: The case of request refusals. *Pragmatics*, 11(1): 31–61.

Turner, K. (1996) The principal principles of pragmatic inference: politeness. *Language Teaching*, 29: 1–13.

Tyler, A. (1995) The coconstruction of cross-cultural miscommunication: conflicts in perception, negotiation, and enactment of participant role and status. *Studies in Second Language Acquisition*, 17: 129–52.

Ueda, K. (1974) Sixteen ways to avoid saying 'no' in Japan. In J. Condon and M. Saito (eds) *In Intercultural Encounters with Japan: Communication-Contact and Conflict*. Tokyo: Simul Press, 185–92.

Victor, D. A. (1992) *International Business Communication*. London: HarperCollins.

Vollmer, H. J. and Olshtain, E. (1989) The language of apologies in German. In S. Blum-Kulka, J. House and G. Kasper (eds) *Cross-Cultural Pragmatics: Requests and Apologies*. Norwood, NJ: Ablex, 197–218.

Vuchinich, S. (1990) The sequential organization of closing in verbal family conflict. In A. D. Grimshaw (ed.) *Conflict Talk*. Cambridge: Cambridge University Press, 118–38.

Watts, R. (2003) *Politeness*. Cambridge: Cambridge University Press.

Watzlawick, P., Beavin, J. B. and Jackson, D. (1967) *Pragmatics of Human Communication. A Study of Interactional Patterns, Pathologies, and Paradoxes*. London: Norton.

Weick, K. E. (1995) *Sensemaking in Organizations*. London: Sage.

Wenger, E. (1998) *Communities of Practice: Learning Meaning and Identity*. New York: Cambridge University Press.

Werlen, I. (1984) *Ritual und Sprache. Zum Verhältnis von Sprechen und Handeln in Ritualen*. Tübingen: Günter Narr.

Wetherell, M. (1996) Constructing social identities: the individual/social binary in Henri Tajfel's social psychology. In W. P. Robinson (ed.) *Social Groups and Identities. Developing the Legacy of Henri Tajfel*. Oxford: Butterworth Heinemann, 269–83.

White, R. (1997) Going round in circles: English as an international language, and cross-cultural capability. Paper prepared for the Cross-Cultural Capability Conference 1997, Leeds Metropolitan University, 15–16 December 1997. Available at http://www.rdg.ac.uk/app_ling/circles.htm [Accessed 16 June 2007].

White, S. (1989) Backchannels across cultures: a study of Americans and Japanese. *Language in Society*, 18: 59–76.

Widjaja, C.S. (1997) A study of data refusal: Taiwanese vs. American females. *University of Hawai'i Working Papers in ESL*, 15(2): 1–43.

Wieland, M. (1991) Turn-taking structure as a source of misunderstanding in French–American cross-cultural conversation. In L. F. Bouton and Y. Kachru (eds) *Pragmatics and Language Learning. Vol.2*, Urbana: Division of English as an International Language, University of Illinois at Urbana-Champaign, 101–18.

Wierzbicka, A. (2003) *Cross-Cultural Pragmatics. The Semantics of Human Interaction*. Berlin: Mouton de Gruyter.

Wilden, A. (1987) *The Rules are No Game: The Strategy of Communication*. London: Routledge and Kegan Paul.

Wildner-Bassett, M. (1984) *Improving Pragmatic Aspects of Learners' Interlanguage*. Tübingen: Narr.

Wildner-Bassett, M. (1994) Intercultural pragmatics and proficiency: 'polite' noises for cultural appropriateness. *International Review of Applied Linguistics*, 32: 3–17.

Williams, C. H. (1987) Location and context in Welsh language reproduction: a geographic interpretation. *International Journal of the Sociology of Language*, 66: 61–83.

Wilson, D., and Sperber, D. (1986) Outline of relevance theory. In *Encontro de Liguistas Actas*. Braga, Portugal: University of Minho, 21–41. Also published in 1987 in *Notes on Linguistics*, 1987, 39: 5–24.

Witte, S. P., and Cherry, R. D. (1994) Think-aloud protocols, protocol analysis, and research design: An exploration of the influence of writing tasks on writing processes. In P. Smagorinsky (ed.) *Speaking about Writing*. Thousand Oaks, CA: Sage, 3–19.

Wolfson, N. (1981) Compliments in cross-cultural perspective. *TESOL Quarterly*, 15(2): 117–24.

Wolfson, N. (1983) An empirically based analysis of complimenting in American English. In N. Wolfson and E. Judd (eds) *Sociolinguistics and Language Acquisition*. Rowley, MA: Newbury House, 82–95.

Wolfson, N. (1989) *Perspectives. Sociolinguistics and TESOL*. Rowley, MA: Newbury House.

Wolfson, N., d'Amico-Reisner, L., and Huber, L. (1983) How to arrange for social commitments in American English: the invitation. In N. Wolfson and E. Judd (eds) *Sociolinguistics and Second Language Aacquisition*. Rowley, MA: Newbury House, 116–28.

Wood, L. A. and Kroger, R. O. (1991) Politeness and forms of address. *Journal of Language and Social Psychology*, 10(3): 145–68.

Yamashita, S. O. (1996) *Six measures of JSL pragmatics* (Technical Report #14) Honolulu: University of Hawaii, Second Language Teaching and Curriculum Center.

Ye, L. (1995) Complimenting in Mandarin Chinese. In G. Kasper (ed.) *Pragmatics of Chinese as Native and Target Language*. Honolulu: University of Hawaii Press, 207–95.

Ylänne-McEwen, V. (1993) Complimenting behaviour. *Journal of Multilingual and Multicultural Development*, 14(6): 499–508.

Yoon, K. K. (1991) Bilingual pragmatic transfer in speech acts: bi-directional responses to a compliment. In L. F. Bouton and Y. Kachru (eds) *Pragmatics and Language Learning. Vol. 2*. Urbana: Division of English as a Second Language, University of Illinois at Urbana-Champaign, 75–100.

Yoshimi, D. (1999) L1 socialization as a variable in the use of *ne* by L2 learners of Japanese. *Journal of Pragmatics*, 31: 1513–25.

Young, L. W. L. (1994) *Crosstalk and Culture in Sino–American Communication*. Cambridge: Cambridge University Press.

Young, R. (1988) Variation and the interlanguage hypothesis. *Studies in Second Language Acquisition*, 10: 281–302.

Yu, M-c (2003) On the universality of face: evidence from Chinese compliment response behaviour. *Journal of Pragmatics* 35: 1679–1710.

Yuan, Y. (1996) Responding to compliments: a contrastive study on the English pragmatics of advanced speakers of English. *BUILD 20 Proceedings*, 861–72.

Yuan, Y. (2001) An inquiry into empirical pragmatics data-gathering methods: Written DCTs, oral DCTs, field notes, and natural conversations. *Journal of Pragmatics*, 33: 271–92.

Zhan, K. (1992) *The Strategies of Politeness in the Chinese Language.* Berkeley: Institute of East Asian Studies.

Žegarac, V. (2004) Relevance theory and 'the' in second language acquisition. *Second Language Research*, 20 (3): 193–211.

Žegarac, V. (2007) A cognitive pragmatic perspective on communication and culture. In H. Kotthoff and H. Spencer-Oatey (eds) *Handbook of Intercultural Communication.* Berlin: Mouton de Gruyter, 31–53.

Index

Page numbers in **bold** indicate a glossary entry. Those with a letter after the page number refer to an entry in a figure (*f*), in a note (n) or in a table (*t*).

Abe, K. 85
accent mobility 165–6
accommodation *see* Communication Accommodation Theory (CAT)
activity types 38–9, **326**
Adachi, T. 235
Adelswärd, V. 243, 245
affect 36
affective involvement–detachment 16
agreement 40, 110–11, 229; *see also* disagreement
Akinnaso, F. N. 244
American English speakers
  African Americans 176–8
  compliment responses 99*t*, 146, 153, 296–7
  miscommunication 147–8, 149, 151, 152, 153, 156*t*, 157
  self-enhancement–self-effacement 31
  turn-taking 27–8
  see also negative assessments in Japanese–American workplace interaction
apologies 19–20, 24*t*, 25–7, 26*t*
  see also apologies in Japanese and English
apologies in Japanese and English 73–94
  contextual assessments 80–1, 80*t*
  discussion 85–7
  linguistic studies 76–7
  production responses 81–4, 84*t*
  questionnaire 77–8, 79*t*, 89–93
  rating scales 91, 93–4
  research procedure 77–80, 87
  respondents 79–80, 86
  situation effect 86
  stereotypical conceptions 74–6
  'sumimasen' *vs.* 'I'm sorry' 85
approbation 40
approximation strategies 171, 173
Apte, M. 3
argumentative discourse *see* negotiating rapport: German–Chinese conversation
Arminen, I. 283
Ashcroft, B. et al. 178
assessments 228, 229; *see also* negative assessments in Japanese–American workplace interaction
association–dissociation 16, 41
associative expressiveness–restraint 28, 29*t*
audio recording 285–6
Austin, J. L. 336
autonomy–imposition 16

backchannelling 168
backtranslation **326**
Bailey, B. 176–8
Ball, P. et al. 18n 3
Baratz, S. 264, 270
Bardovi-Harlig, K. 283, 293
Barnett, S. 283
Barnlund, D. C. 76–7
Beebe, L. 168
Beebe, L. M. et al. 24–5*t*, 78, 231
Beekman, J. 66
behaviour
  appropriacy 1, 2
  and culture 6
  negatively eventful 42–3
  rapport-threatening 17–21
  sociality rights and obligations 15–17, 15*t*
belonging, sense of 191–5
  centre and periphery dynamics 194–5

belonging, sense of (*Cont'd*)
centre and periphery dynamics 194–5
competence and role fulfilment 193–4
insideness and outsideness 191–3
Berardo, K. 67
Bhabha, H. K. 178, 337
Billmyer, K. 293
Birkner, K. 249
Blum-Kulka, S. et al. 23, 24*t*, 25*t*, 26*t*, 34, 36, 286, 292
bluntness 30
Bodman, J. W. 24*t*, 290
boosters *see* upgraders/downgraders
borderlands 198
Bourhis, R. Y. et al. 175
Bowring, R. 75
Bremer, K. et al. 300
Brislin, R. 78, 328
British English speakers 31, 39, 154–5; *see also* apologies in Japanese and English; Chinese business visit to Britain; compliment responses: British and Chinese reactions
Brons-Albert, R. 126, 13n 5
Brown, G. 2
Brown, P. 12–13, 17, 19, 20, 21, 28, 30, 31–2, 34, 39, 111, 124, 18n 2, 264, 270, 289, 312, 318, 329, 330, 332, 334, 335
Brown, R. 34, 35
Bruner, J. 189, 190, 196
Buttimer, A. 192, 196, 197
Button, G. 126, 128
Byrne, D. 166

CA *see* conversation analysis
Caley, J. 60
Callow, J. 66
Cameron, D. et al. 305, 32n 4
Casey, E. S. 196
CAT *see* Communication Accommodation Theory
centre and periphery dynamics 194–5
Chen, R. 99, 99*t*
Chinese business visit to Britain 258–73
anticipating preferences 266–7
aspects of face 264–5
attempts at meeting 263–4
business background 259
cultural conventions 269
face, identity and attributes 270
group/individual face 265–6, 271
hotel arrangements 260
independent–interdependent face 271–2
judging importance of visitors 267–8, 267*t*
practical constraints 268–9
programme of activities 263
research procedure 259
welcome meeting: discourse issues 262–3
welcome meeting: seating 260–1, 261*f*
Chinese speakers
business discourse 28
directness–indirectness 31
face 11–12, 13
modesty 109–10
politeness 1, 109
speech act strategies 23
see also Chinese business visit to Britain; compliment responses: British and Chinese reactions; negotiating rapport: German–Chinese conversation
Cocroft, B.-A. 32, 46n3
code-switching 231, 236–8
cognitive anthropology 149
cognitive pragmatics 142, 149, **335**
Cognitive Principle of Relevance 57
Cohen, A. D. 22, 298
collectivism 5*t*
communication 1–2, 52–70
content component 2
context 53, 56, 64
contextual knowledge 59–60, 64, 65, **327**
Co-operative Principle 55, 56, **332–3**
and culture 64–8
directness–indirectness 23, 25*t*, 28, 30–1, 53, 62–4, **328–9**
explicitness-implicitness 30, 64
frames 53, 61–2, **330**
interpretation 53
Maxims of Conversation 55–6, 58
meaning 56
mutual knowledge 59–60
relationship component 2, 132–3
Relevance Theory 53–4, 56–8, **335–6**
schemata 53, 60–2, 65–7, **336**
scripts 53, 61–2, **336**
as social interaction 53
see also Communication Accommodation Theory; communication styles
Communication Accommodation Theory (CAT) 153, 164–86, **326**
approximation strategies 171, 173
central concepts 165–74
convergence 33, 166, 175–6, 180, 271–2, **328**
cultural difference 178–81

discourse analysis 169
discourse attuning 171–4, 172*f*
discourse management strategies 173
divergence 33, 166–7, 174, 175–6, 180, **329**
field 173
intergroup communication 174–5
intergroup orientation 33, 271
interpersonal control strategies 173
interpersonal orientation 33
interpretability strategies 173
maintenance 166–7
mode 173
over-accommodation/under-accommodation 168–9, 173, **333**
processes model 170*f*, 171
psychological convergence/divergence 167
research in multicultural settings 174–8
strategic use of codes and styles 166, 171
subjective/objective accommodation 167–8
symmetrical/asymmetrical accommodation 168
tenor 173
upward/downward speech modifications 168
communication styles **326**
associative expressiveness–restraint 28, 29*t*
definition 28
directness–indirectness 25*t*, 28, 30–1
explicitness-implicitness 30
and interactional ethos 28–31, **332**
self-enhancement–self-effacement 31, 38–9, 41
social goals and motivations 166
communicative competence 158, 295, 296
communicative efficiency *see* Communicative Principle of Relevance
communicative genres 38, **326–7**
Communicative Principle of Relevance 57–8, 150–2, **335–6**
communicative strength 30, 63–4
communities of practice 317, **327**
Community of Practice framework 317
competence and role fulfilment 193–4
compliment responses: British and Chinese reactions 95–117
acceptance responses 101–3, 102*t*
agreement and face 110–11
Chinese responses 99, 99*t*
compliment response strategies 96, 97–8*t*
English responses 96, 99*t*
evaluating compliment responses 99–100
modesty 109–10
questionnaire 100–1, 114–17
rejection responses 104–9, 104*t*
respondents 101
self-presentation 111
compliments 20, 25, 95
data collection 284, 293–4, 296–7
responses to 144, 146, 293–4, 296–7
see also compliment responses: British and Chinese reactions
comprehension strategy 151
compromises 221–2
computer-mediated communication 283–4
concessions 220–1
constraints 41
constructionism **327**; *see also* social constructionism
context 30, 31, 53, 56, 64, 148, 167, **327**
context selection 151–2, 155
contextual knowledge 59–60, 64, 65, **327**
conventionalization 30, 63, **327–8**
convergence 33, 166, 175–6, 180, 271–2, **328**
conversation 55–6, 58, 282
conversation analysis (CA) 242, 285–6, **328**
conversation tasks 287
Cook, H. M. 286
Cook-Gumperz, J. 290, 300
Co-operative Principle 55, 56, **332–3**
cost–benefit considerations 16, 37, 41
Coupland, J. et al. 122–3
Coupland, N. et al. 170*f*, 171–3, 172*f*
Crookall, D. 288
cross-cultural pragmatics
definition 6–7
ideas for projects 322–3
see also apologies in Japanese and English; compliment responses: British and Chinese reactions; telephone conversations: Greek and German
crossing 179
Culpeper, J. 3, 32
cultural geographies 188
cultural representations 50–1, 52
culture 49–52
basic values/orientations 4, 5*t*, 6
and behaviour 6
and communication 64–8
and contextual knowledge 65
definitions 3–4, 49, **328**
discourse 179, 180
epidemiological perspective 51
and identity 3–4, 178–81

culture (*Cont'd*)
  individual variation 4, 6
  and language use 4
  moral values 51–2
  and schemata 65–7
  Cummings, M. C. 78

data collection 279–303
  audio recording 285–6
  authentic discourse 282–6
  conversation tasks 287
  diaries 297–8
  discourse completion tasks (DCT) 231, 292–4
  discourse type 282–3
  elicited conversation 287–8
  field notes 284–5, 290
  interaction 281–91
  interviews 296–7
  medium 283–4
  multiple choice (MC) 294–5
  questionnaires 290, 291–6
  rating scales 295–6
  recording authentic talk 284–6
  role plays 288–91
  sociolinguistic interviews 287
  verbal report (VR) 298–300
  video recording 286
Davidson, J. 285–6
DCT *see* discourse completion tasks
De Certeau, M. 199, 200
decentring 78, 101, 312, **328**
delays 229
development and change 197–200
  dwelling in-between 199–200
  heterotopias and the third space 197–9
diary studies 297–8
directness–indirectness 23, 25*t*, 28, 30–1, 53, 62–4, **328–9**
disagreements 23, 24–5*t*, 110–11, 236, 249–55; *see also* agreement; negotiating rapport: German–Chinese conversation
discourse 179, 180
discourse analysis 169
discourse attuning 171–4, 172*f*
discourse completion tasks (DCT) 231, 292–4
discourse domain 21, 27
discourse management strategies 173
dispreferred responses 228
dissent-formats 209–11
dissent-tying 211–13, 253
distance 34, 35–6, 176–8
divergence 33, 166–7, 174, 175–6, 180, **329**
DuFon, M. A. 286, 298

ecological fallacy 6
Eisenstein, M. 24*t*, 290
English-Canadian speakers 175; *see also* apologies in Japanese and English
epistemology **329**
equity 16, 41
Ericsson, K.A. 298, 299
Ervin-Tripp, S. 13n 10
essentialism **329**
ethnography **329**
Ethnolinguistic Identity Theory 174
ethos 28
explicatures 62
explicitness-implicitness 30, 64

face 3, **329**
  Chinese speakers 11–12, 13
  definition 13, 14
  and dis/agreement 110–11, 236
  and identity 14–15, 270
  independent–interdependent self-construals 271–2
  losing face 17, 18–20
  negative face 12–13
  number of participants 36
  positive face 13
  social perspective 13
  terminology 12
  see also Chinese business visit to Britain; rapport management
face threatening acts (FTAs) 17, 18–20, 236, **329–30**
Falk, J. 211, 226n5
Fant, L. 289
Ferguson, C. 169, 173, 239n5
field 173
field notes 284–5, 290
Fiksdal, S. 300
Fiske, A. P. 310
Flemish speakers 175
focus groups **330**
foreigner talk 169, 173, 238, 239n5
Foucault, M. 198, 330
frame breaks 222
frames 53, 61–2, **330**
framing devices **330**
Fraser, B. 2, 334
Fraser, H. 311

Freiburger Korpus 126
French, J. R. P. 34–5
French speakers 27–8, 190–200
French-Canadian speakers 175
FTAs *see* face threatening acts

Gal, S. 175–6
Gallois, C. et al. 168, 171, 174
Gao, G. 265–6, 269
Garner, M. et al. 310, 311, 318, 32n 4
Gass, S. 289, 291
gatekeeping **330**
gender roles 5*t*
generosity 40, 41
Gergen, K. J. 189
German speakers 175–6, 293–4; *see also* impression management in 'intercultural' German job interviews; negotiating rapport: German–Chinese conversation; telephone conversations: Greek and German
Giddens, A. 179
Giles, H. et al. 165, 174, 175
Gilman, A. 34, 35
Glanz, L. et al. 188
Goffman, E. 13, 42–3, 222, 329, 330, 331
Golato, A. 293–4
Goodwin, C. 228
Goodwin, M. 228
Goodwin, M. H. 252, 253
Grand Strategy of Politeness (GSP) 41
gratitude 22–3, 24*t*, 25, 27, 154–5, 290
Greek speakers 23, 154–5; *see also* telephone conversations: Greek and German
Grice, H. P. 55–6, 332–3
Grieshaber, W. 291
Gu, Y. 13, 109
Gudykunst, W. B. 6, 86
Gumperz, J. J. et al. 231, 244, 290, 300, 332
Günthner, S. 38, 255
Gutt, E. A. 66

Haberland, H. 122–3
Haiman, J. 235
Hall, E. T. 7
Hall, S. 179, 199–200
Hammond, S. A. 307
Hartford, B. S. 283
Hassall, T. J. 298
hedges *see* upgraders/downgraders
Herbert, R. K. 99*t*, 284
hesitation 229
heterotopias 197–9, **330**
hidden agendas 243–4
Hofstede, G. 5*t*, 6
Hollings, M. 311
Holmes, J. 95, 96, 97–8*t*, 99*t*, 284
Holtgraves, T. 39
Hong Kong Chinese speakers *see* compliment responses: British and Chinese reactions
Houck, N. 289, 291
House, J. 31
Hudson, R. A. 158
human activity, mode of 5*t*
human nature, beliefs about 5*t*
Hungarian speakers 175–6
Hutchby, I. 283
hybridity **331**; *see also* third space

Ide, R. 85
Ide, S. 13
identity 187–203, **331**
  and culture 3–4, 178–81
  development and change 197–200
  and face 14–15, 270
  psycholinguistic distinctiveness 174
  research: French *coopérants* 190–200
  self-narrative 189–90
  sense of belonging 191–5
  sensemaking 188–9, 197
  space and place 195–7, 198
  spatial metaphors 191–200
Iino, M. 239n5, 286
Ikoma, T. 231
illocutionary acts **336**
illocutionary domain 21; *see also* speech act strategies
illocutionary force indicating devices (IFID) 24*t*, **331**; *see also* speech acts
implicatures 62
impression management 111, **331**
  see also impression management in 'intercultural' German job interviews
impression management in 'intercultural' German job interviews 241–57
  assertiveness 253–5
  conversation analysis (CA) 242
  critical questions 249–53
  data 243
  disagreement 249–55
  hidden agendas 243–4
  job interviews: genre 243–4

impression management in 'intercultural' German job interviews (*Cont'd*)
  linguistic differences: East and West Germans 244–53
  self- and other perspectives 245–9
independent–interdependent self-construals 271–2, **331–2**
individualism 5*t*, 86
in-groups/out-groups **332**
insideness and outsideness 191–3
institutional interaction 282–3
interactional ethos 28–31, **332**
interactional goals 14, 14*f*, 17
interactional involvement–detachment 16
interactional language 2
interactional sociolinguistics 285–6, **332**
interactional surplus 131–2, 133
intercultural interaction
  definition 6–7
  ideas for projects 323–4
  see also Communication Accommodation Theory (CAT); French speakers; negotiating rapport: German–Chinese conversation; pragmatic transfer
intercultural personhood **332**
intergroup communication 174–5
intergroup orientation 33, 271
interpersonal control strategies 173
interpersonal orientation 33
interpretability strategies 173
interviews 39, 287, 296–7
  see also impression management in 'intercultural' German job interviews

Jakobson, R. 334
Japanese speakers 13, 20, 31, 109; *see also* apologies in Japanese and English; negative assessments in Japanese–American workplace interaction
Johnston, B. et al. 293

Kasper, G. 155, 157
Kim, Y. Y. 200, 332
King, A. Y. 265–6
Kinjo, H. 24*t*
Kinloch, P. 312, 316
Kitayama, S. 331–2
Kluckhohn, C. 3, 49
Kluckhohn, F. R. 5*t*
Knapp, M. et al. 296–7
Korean speakers 146–7, 148–9, 151–3, 156*t*, 157, 176–8
Kotani, M. 77
Kottak, C. P. 232
Kristeva, J. 200
Kroeber, A. L. 3, 49
Kroger, R. O. 34
Kurogi, A. 271

Labov, W. 165, 231, 287, 334
Lado, R. 157–8
Language in the Workplace (LWP) project 304–6, 317, 32n 1
language transfer 157–8, 159–60
Lave, J. 327
Laver, J. 120, 132
Le Page, R. B. 317
Leech, G. 40–1, 109–10, 111, 155, 332–3, 334, 336
Leinonen, M. 283
Levinson, S. C. 12–13, 17, 19, 20, 21, 28, 30, 31–2, 34, 38, 39, 111, 124, 18n 2, 264, 270, 289, 312, 326, 329, 330, 332, 334, 335
Lim, T.-S. 14
LoCastro, V. 231
locutionary acts **336**
Loh, W. C. T. 99*t*
LWP *see* Language in the Workplace (LWP) project

McEntegart, D. 317
maintenance 166–7
Malinowski, B. 122–3, 334
Manes, J. 284
Mao, L. R. 13
Maori English speakers *see* recording and analysing talk: New Zealand
Markus, H. R. 331–2
Matsumoto, Y. 13, 20, 230
maxims 41, **332–3**
Maxims of Conversation 55–6, 58
mental sets 142
Merritt, M. 128
message content 37
metapragmatic **333**
metarepresentations 50
Metge, J. 312, 316
methodology 7; *see also* data collection; recording and analysing talk: New Zealand
Miles, P. 296–7

Miller, L. 229, 239n4
Milliken, F. J. 188
Mizutani, N. 230
Mizutani, O. 230
mode 173
modesty 31, 38–9, 40, 41
  Chinese–British interactions 109–10
  Korean speakers 147, 149, 151, 152, 153, 156*t*, 157
  Maori speakers 314–15
Moeran, B. 239n3
Mulac, A. et al. 168
multiple choice (MC) 294–5
mutual knowledge 59–60
mutual support 31
mutual T 35, 46n4
Myers, J. T. 265–6

Naotsuka, R. 75
negative assessments in Japanese–American workplace interaction 227–40
  code-switching 236–8
  empirical study 232–8
  foreigner talk 238
  negative assessments 228–30
  research intercultural interaction 230–2
  sarcasm 235–6
  second assessments 235
negative transfer 144–5, 151, **337**
negotiating rapport: German–Chinese conversation 154, 207–26
  background to conversation 208–9
  change of activity 222–3
  closing strategies 220–3
  compromises 221–2
  concessions 220–1
  dissent organization: Chinese 215–20
  dissent organization: Germans 209–15
  dissent-formats 209–11
  dissent-tying 211–13
  reported speech as confrontation strategy 213–15
Neustupný, J. V. 230
New Zealand English speakers 99*t*; *see also* recording and analysing talk: New Zealand
Nishida, T. 86
Nolan, W. 2
non-verbal domain 21
Nunan, D. 317

objective accommodation 167
observer's paradox *see* participant observers
Ohama, R. 85
Oka, Norie 85
Oliver, R. T. 226n6
Olshtain, E. 22, 34
ontology **333**
orders and requests 19
Orientalism 179–80, 195, **333**
originary identity **331**
out-groups **333**
over-accommodation/under-accommodation 168–9, 173, **333**

participant observers 286, 312, **334**
participant relations
  distance 34, 35–6, 176–8
  number of participants 36
  power 34–5, 36
participation domain 21–2, 27
Pavlenko, A. 298
Pavlidou, T.-S. 27, 128
Penman, R. 3
perlocutionary acts **336**
perspective/perspectivization 245–9, **334**
phatic talk/phatic utterances/phatic communion **334**; *see also* telephone conversations: Greek and German
Pilkington, E. 75
Politeness Principle 40–1, 99, 109–11, **332–3**
politeness/impoliteness 1, 2–3, 20, 40–1, 124, **334**; *see also* face; rapport management
politics of polarity **337**
Pomerantz, A. 96, 97–8*t*, 111, 229, 233, 235
positive transfer 145, **337**
power 5*t*, 34–5, 36, 179–80, 195
pragmalinguistic assessment 295
pragmalinguistic conventions 42, 43
pragmalinguistic transfer 157
pragmalinguistics 40, 155, **334**; *see also* sociopragmatics
pragmatic competence 149–55
pragmatic transfer 141–63, **337**
  concept 142–4
  definition 143
  explanations 148–55
  identification of 144–5
  negative transfer 144–5, 151, **337**
  positive transfer 145, **337**
  pragmalinguistic transfer 157

pragmatic transfer (*Cont'd*)
  pragmatic analysis 148–9
  and pragmatic competence 149–55
  qualitative studies 145, 146–8
  quantitative studies 145, 146–7
  relevance 150–1, **335–6**
  and second language acquisition 157–8
  sociopragmatic transfer 157
  terminology 157, 158–61
pragmatics 142, **335**
prefaces 229
production strategy 150
projects: ideas
  cross-cultural pragmatics 322–3
  intercultural interaction 323–4
  issues to consider 324
pronouns 34
psychological convergence/divergence 167

questionnaires 290, 291–6
  discourse completion tasks (DCT) 231, 292–4
  multiple choice 294–5
  rating scales 295–6

Rampton, B. 179
rapport **335**
rapport management 12–47, **335**
  across cultures 43–4
  activity types 38–9
  bases of rapport 13, 14*f*
  concept 1–2, 3, 12
  contextual variables 33–40, 42, 43
  domains 20–1, **335**
  face 13, 14–15, 14*f*, 18–20
  interactional goals 14, 14*f*, 17
  message content 37
  outcomes 42–3
  participant relations 34–6
  pragmalinguistic conventions 42, 43
  social/interactional roles 37–8
  sociality rights and obligations 13–14, 14*f*, 15–17, 15*t*, 18–20, **336**
  sociopragmatic principles 40–2, 43
  and speech acts 19–20
  strategies 21–31, 44
  see also negotiating rapport: German–Chinese conversation
rapport orientation 31–3, **335**
rapport-threatening behaviour 17–21
rating scales 295–6

Raven, B. 34–5
recording and analysing talk: New Zealand 304–21
  analysis 315–17
  basic methodological principles 306–7
  data collection procedures 307–9
  in-depth analysis 313–14
  initial feedback 313
  Language in the Workplace (LWP) project 304–6, 317, 32n 1
  making contact 312–13
  Maori Kaupapa philosophies 311–15, 318
  researching in Maori workplaces 309–11, 317–19
  social relations approach 310–11
  volunteers' record 313, 314
refusals of invitations 24*t*, 290, 291
Relevance Theory 53–4, 56–8, **335–6**
  Cognitive Principle of Relevance 57
  Communicative Principle of Relevance 57–8, 150–2, **335–6**
Relph, E. 192, 196
repairs 229
reported speech as confrontation strategy 213–15
requests 19, 22, 23, 24*t*, 25–7, 26*t*, 46n1, 285
Riggins, R. H. 179
Ritchie, J. E. 310
Roberts, C. 243, 244, 305
Roberts, M. 317
Robinson, M. 299
role plays 288–91
  closed role plays 288–9
  definition 288
  idiographic role play 288, 291
  open role plays 289–90
  validity 290–1
Rose, K. R. 285, 293, 294
Röver, C. 295
Rubin, J. 228
Ruhi, S. 41–2, 111
Ruwhiu, D. 309

Sack, R. D. 197
Sacks, H. 220
Said, E. W. 179–80, 333
Salmond, A. 315
Sarangi, S. 244
sarcasm 235–6
Sasaki, T. 299–300

Saunders, D. 288
Sayers, P. 244
Schegloff, E. 120, 220, 287
schemata 53, 60–2, 65–7, **336**
Schiffrin, D. 288
Schnurr, S. et al. 317
Schwartz, S. H. et al. 6
Scollon, R. 29*t*
Scollon, S. W. 29*t*
scripts 53, 61–2, **336**
Seabrook Ajirotutu, C. 244
Seamon, D. 192
second language acquisition 157–8
Self-Aspect Model of Identity 270
self-concept 14, 270
self-enhancement–self-effacement 31, 38–9, 41
self-narrative 189–90
self-politeness 41
self-presentation 111, **331**; *see also* impression management
sensemaking 188–9, 197
Shea, D. P. 255
Shimanoff, S. 46n3
Shimura, A. 231
Shing-Lung, C. 255
Sifianou, M. 37
Silverman, D. 296
similarity attraction 166
Simon, B. 270
Simon, H.A. 298, 299
SIPs *see* sociopragmatic interactional principles
Skoutarides, A. 239n5
Smagorinsky, P. 299
Smith, L. T. 309, 310, 311, 312
social constructionism 179, 181, 18n 4, **327**
social pragmatics 142, 149, **335**
social relations approach to research 310–11
social/interactional roles 37–8
sociality rights and obligations 13–14, 14*f*, 15–17, 15*t*, 18–20, **336**
sociocultural conventions 152–5
sociolinguistic interviews 287
sociopragmatic assessments 295
sociopragmatic interactional principles (SIPs) 16, 41–2, **333**
sociopragmatic principles 40–2, 43
sociopragmatic transfer 157
sociopragmatics 40, 155, 157, **336**
Soja, E. 198
solidarity *see* distance
South African English speakers 99*t*
space and place 195–7, 198
Speech Accommodation Theory 165
speech act sets 22–3, 24–5*t*
speech act strategies 22–7
  apologies 19–20, 24*t*, 25–7, 26*t*
  compliments 20, 25, 95
  directness–indirectness 23, 25*t*, 28, 30–1, 53, 62–4, **328–9**
  disagreements 23, 24–5*t*, 110–11, 236, 249–55
  gratitude 22–3, 24*t*, 25, 27, 154–5, 290
  orders 19
  refusals of invitations 24*t*, 290, 291
  requests 19, 22, 23, 24*t*, 25–7, 26*t*, 46n1, 285
  upgraders/downgraders 23, 25–7, 26*t*, 30, 147
  see also apologies in Japanese and English
speech acts 19–21, **336**
Spencer-Oatey, H. 17, 20, 21, 28, 36, 111, 18n 2, 264, 335
Sperber, D. 56–8, 60, 148, 150
Starbuck, W. H. 188
stereotypes 67, 74–6, 180, **336**
Strodtbeck, F. L. 5*t*
Stubbe, M. 305, 317, 318
stylistic domain 21–2
subjective accommodation 167–8
Sugimoto, N. 75–6
Svennevig, J. 287–8
symmetrical/asymmetrical accommodation 168
sympathy 40

tact 40, 41
Tajfel, H. 174
Takahashi, T. 24–5*t*
Takahashi, Yoshiko 76
Tanaka, N. 77, 86
telephone communication 283–4; *see also* telephone conversations: Greek and German
telephone conversations: Greek and German 27, 118–35
  data samples 120, 126
  interactional surplus 131–2, 133
  phatic communion 122–5, 123*t*, 124*t*, 125*t*, 131–3
  reasons for calling 123–4, 124*t*
  relationship aspect of communication 132–3
  repetition/redundancy 128–31

telephone conversations: Greek and German (*Cont'd*)
  telephone closings 126–31
  telephone openings 118–19, 120–5
Tenenbaum, H. 7
tenor 173
terminology 3, 6–7, 12, 28, 41, 157, 158–61
Thai–Chinese bilinguals 168
think-aloud protocols 299
third spaces 198–9, **337**
Thomas, J. 36, 38, 42, 334, 336
Thompson, R. B. 7
time orientation 5*t*
Times, The 75
Ting-Toomey, S. 31, 32, 46n3, 269, 271
token agreements 229
Tracy, K. 3, 264, 270
transactional language 2
transcription conventions xi–xii
transfer **337**; *see also* language transfer; pragmatic transfer
Tsuruta, Y. 20
Tuan, Y.-F. 196
Turnbull, W. 290
Turner, K. 3, 32
turn-taking 27–8, 39, 283–4
Tyler, A. 146–8, 151, 152, 156*t*, 157

uncertainty avoidance 5*t*
under-accommodation *see* over-accommodation/under-accommodation
upgraders/downgraders 23, 25–7, 26*t*, 30, 147

Varghese, M. 293
verbal report (VR) 298–300
video recording 286
Vuchinich, S. 221

Watzlawick, P. et al. 1–2
Weick, K. E. 188
Welsh speakers 180–1
Wenger, E. 317, 327
Werlen, I. 128
Wetherell, M. 18n 4
White, R. 42
White, S. 168
white lies 58
Wieland, M. 27
Wilson, D. 56–8, 60, 148, 150
Wolfgramm, R. 309
Wolfson, N. 284
Wood, L. A. 34
workplace interaction *see* negative assessments in Japanese–American workplace interaction; recording and analysing talk: New Zealand

Xing, J. 20, 21, 28

Yang, J.-N. 39
Ye, L. 96, 97–8*t*, 99, 99*t*
Ylänne-McEwen, V. 99*t*
Yoon, K. K. 146, 153
Yoshioka, M. 76–7
Young, R. 168
Yu, M.-C. 99, 109
Yuan, Y. 99*t*
Yule, G. 2

Žegarac, V. 4, 46n2, 150